Statistics for Criminology and Criminal Justice

Second Edition

SAGE was founded in 1965 by Sara Miller McCune to support the dissemination of usable knowledge by publishing innovative and high-quality research and teaching content. Today, we publish more than 750 journals, including those of more than 300 learned societies, more than 800 new books per year, and a growing range of library products including archives, data, case studies, reports, conference highlights, and video. SAGE remains majority-owned by our founder, and after Sara's lifetime will become owned by a charitable trust that secures our continued independence.

Los Angeles | London | Washington DC | New Delhi | Singapore | Boston

Statistics for Criminology and Criminal Justice

Second Edition

Jacinta M. Gau

University of Central Florida

Los Angeles | London | New Delhi
Singapore | Washington DC | Boston

Los Angeles | London | New Delhi
Singapore | Washington DC | Boston

FOR INFORMATION:

SAGE Publications, Inc.
2455 Teller Road
Thousand Oaks, California 91320
E-mail: order@sagepub.com

SAGE Publications Ltd.
1 Oliver's Yard
55 City Road
London EC1Y 1SP
United Kingdom

SAGE Publications India Pvt. Ltd.
B 1/I 1 Mohan Cooperative Industrial Area
Mathura Road, New Delhi 110 044
India

SAGE Publications Asia-Pacific Pte. Ltd.
3 Church Street
#10-04 Samsung Hub
Singapore 049483

Printed in the United States of America.

A catalog record of this book is available from the Library of Congress.

ISBN 978-1-4833-7845-9

Executive Editor: Jerry Westby
Digital Content Editor: Nick Pachelli
Editorial Assistant: Laura Kirkhuff
Production Editor: Bennie Clark Allen
Copy Editor: Colleen Brennan
Typesetter: C&M Digitals (P) Ltd.
Proofreader: Wendy Jo Dymond
Indexer: Maria Sosnowski
Cover Designer: Leonardo March
Marketing Manager: Terra Schultz

This book is printed on acid-free paper.

SFI Certified Sourcing
www.sfiprogram.org
SFI-00453

SFI label applies to text stock

15 16 17 18 19 10 9 8 7 6 5 4 3 2 1

Brief Contents

Detailed Contents

Preface to the Second Edition

Statistics, like any other challenging subject, can create a self-fulfilling prophecy among the students who find it intimidating. Students often arrive in statistics classrooms with preconceptions such as "I'm not a math person" and "I just don't *get* numbers." These mental blocks worsen the anxiety of learning new material, and when these students submit their final exams and leave the room at the end of the term knowing they did poorly in the course, they feel reaffirmed in the accuracy of their self-described innumeracy.

Statistics should be an enlightening and eye-opening course. Many of my students, coming to pick up their graded final exams, have remarked, "This class wasn't nearly as bad as I thought it would be." A quasi-compliment to professors of other subjects, perhaps, this is an important statement coming from statistics students, because it demonstrates that their preconceived notions about their academic inadequacies can be falsified. Key to successful falsification is the use of a good textbook.

A good statistics book is one that balances the quantity and the complexity of information presented in its pages. Skimping on the details for the sake of simplicity can create a superficial text that is too sparse. Insufficient information can be as confusing as an overload can be. Many of the details sacrificed may pertain to the underlying theory and logic that drive statistical analyses. Whereas some might argue that the logical underpinnings of statistics are too complicated for novice undergraduates, my pedagogical technique is guided by the belief that students have to know the logic in order to understand the math. Without the theory of probability, the logic of hypothesis testing, and the understanding of their practical application, statistics is mere form of numbers and students will resort to trying to memorize rather than truly understand.

Of course, an overly complex textbook can have an eye-glazing effect. An overdose of details is tantamount to throwing students into the deep end: Many sink immediately, a few float without trouble, and the remainder hover at near-drowning levels for the 10 or 15 weeks it takes for the term to end. The amount of information presented in such a textbook, moreover, may be unrealistic given the time constraints of semesters and quarters.

Statistics for Criminology and Criminal Justice (2nd edition) attempts to strike a balance among depth, breadth, and accessibility. The aim of this text is to limit jargon and present only that information necessary for the comprehension of the material being presented while still including coverage of the theoretical fundamentals such as probability and sampling distributions. The goal is to pare the information down enough such that students do not get lost in the details, yet to provide the information vital to the understanding of theory and logic.

That said, instructors who wish to do so can skip the sampling distribution chapter and portions of the probability chapter. The last chapter of the book, which introduces bivariate and multiple regression, can also be dropped pursuant to instructor discretion. This book is designed to be flexible so that a wide variety of instructors and students can be accommodated.

This book is set apart from similar texts designed for criminal justice and criminology by its use of real data and research. Chapters contain *Data Sources* boxes that describe some common, publicly available data sets such as the Uniform Crime Reports, National Crime Victimization Survey, General Social Survey, and others. Most in-text examples and end-of-chapter review problems utilize data drawn from the sources highlighted in the book. The goal is to lend a practical, tangible bent to the often-abstract topic of statistics. Students get to work with the data that their professors use. They get to see how elegant statistics can be at times and how messy they can be at others, how analyses can sometimes lead to clear conclusions and other times end in ambiguity.

The *Research Examples* boxes embedded throughout the chapters illustrate criminal justice and criminology research in action and are meant to stimulate students' interest. Statistics is a dry subject, so the *Research Examples* highlight that even though the math might be boring, the act of scientific inquiry is anything but. In the second edition, the examples have been expanded to include additional contemporary criminal justice and criminology studies. Most of the examples utilized in the first edition were retained; this enables students to see firsthand the rich variety of research that has been taking place over time. The full text of all articles is available on the Sage companion site.

The second edition also sees the debut of *Learning Check* boxes. These are scattered throughout the text and are mini-quizzes that test students' comprehension of certain concepts. They are short so that students can complete them without disrupting their learning process. Students can use these *Learning Checks* to make sure they are on the right track in their understanding of the material, and instructors can use them for in-class discussion. The answer key is in the back of the book, following the key for the odd-numbered chapter review problems.

Each chapter ends with a section on SPSS and comes with one or more pared-down versions of a major data set in SPSS format. These data sets all contain a small number of variables and fewer than 1,500 cases and are thus compatible with the student version of SPSS. Students can download these small data sets to answer the review questions presented at the end of the chapter. The full data sets are all available from the Inter-University Consortium for Political and Social Research at www.icpsr.umich.edu/icpsrweb/ICPSR/. If desired, instructors can download the data sets and provide supplementary examples and practice problems for hand calculations or SPSS analyses.

The book is presented in three parts. Part I covers descriptive statistics. It starts with the very basics of levels of measurement and moves on to frequency distributions, graphs and charts, proportions and percentages, central tendency, and dispersion. Part II focuses on probability theory and sampling distributions. As mentioned earlier, instructors can assign this entire section or can cut out chapters or portions of chapters as they prefer. Part II ends with confidence intervals, which provide students' first foray into inferential statistics.

Part III begins with an introduction to bivariate hypothesis testing, which is intended to ease students into inferential tests by explaining what these tests do and what they are for. The book then covers chi-square tests, *t* tests, ANOVA, correlation, and introductory ordinary least squares regression. The order of these chapters is not accidental; the sequence is designed such that some topics flow logically into others. Chi-square tests are presented first because they are the only nonparametric test type covered here. Two-population *t* tests are the subject of the following chapter, and they flow logically into ANOVA in the proceeding chapter. Correlation, likewise, segues into regression, although the latter is not required and the correlation chapter can stand alone.

This book goes into its second edition still dedicated to offering an attractive compromise between depth and straightforwardness with an emphasis on real-world applications. The use of articles, data sets, and SPSS provides a hands-on experience that makes statistics more tangible as well as more vivid, interesting, and alive. It is my hope that this book facilitates learning in a manner such that students leave the course with a solid comprehension of the basics of statistics, a large hole punched in their notions about their inadequacy at math, and the belief that although they feared the class, it turned out to not be nearly as bad as they thought it would be.

Acknowledgments

The second edition of this book came about with input and assistance from multiple people. With regard to the development and preparation of this manuscript, I wish to thank Jerry Westby and the staff at SAGE for their support and encouragement. You guys are the best! Geoffery McDole provided a meticulous list of technical and typographical edits on the first edition. Numerous reviewers supplied advice, recommendations, and critiques that helped shape this book. They are listed in alphabetical order here. Of course, any errors contained in this text are mine alone.

Jeb A. Booth, Salem State University

Ayana Conway, Virginia State University

Matthew D. Fetzer, Shippensburg University

Anthony W. Hoskin, University of Texas of the Permian Basin

Shelly A. McGrath, University of Alabama at Birmingham

Bonny Mhlanga, Western Illinois University

Carlos E. Posadas, New Mexico State University

Scott Senjo, Weber State University

Nicole L. Smolter, California State University, Los Angeles

Brian Stults, Florida State University

George Thomas, Albany State University

About the Author

Jacinta M. Gau received her PhD from Washington State University in 2008. She is currently Associate Professor in the Department of Criminal Justice at the University of Central Florida. Her work has appeared in journals such as *Justice Quarterly, Criminal Justice and Behavior, Crime & Delinquency, Criminology & Public Policy, Police Quarterly, Policing: An International Journal of Police Strategies & Management*, the *Journal of Criminal Justice*, and the *Journal of Criminal Justice Education*. She is coauthor of the book *Key Ideas in Criminology and Criminal Justice*, published by SAGE. Additionally, she coedits *Race and Justice: An International Journal*, published by SAGE.

Part

1

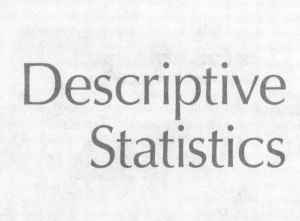

Descriptive
Statistics

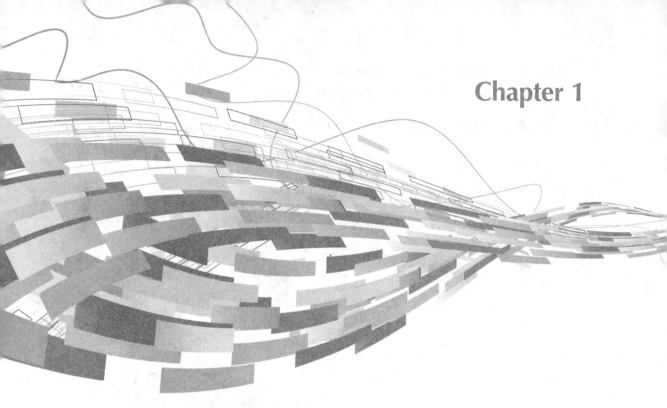

Introduction to the Use of Statistics in Criminal Justice and Criminology

Learning Objectives

- Explain how data collected using scientific methods are different from anecdotes and other nonscientific information.
- List and describe the types of research in criminal justice and criminology.
- Explain the difference between the research methods and statistical analysis.
- Define samples and populations.
- Describe probability sampling.
- List and describe the three major statistics software packages.

You might be thinking, "What do statistics have to do with criminal justice or criminology?" It is reasonable for you to question the requirement that you spend an entire term poring over a book about statistics instead of one about policing, courts, corrections, or criminological theory. Many criminology and criminal justice undergraduates wonder, "Why am I here?" In this context, the question is not so much existential as it is practical; luckily, the answer is equally practical.

You are "here" (in a statistics course) because the answer to the question of what statistics have to do with criminal justice and criminology is "Everything!" Statistical methods are the backbone of criminal justice and criminology as fields of scientific inquiry. Statistics enable the construction and expansion of knowledge about criminality and the criminal justice system. Research that tests theories or examines criminal justice phenomena and is published in academic journals and books is the basis for most of what we know about criminal offending and the system that has been designed to deal with it. The majority of this research would not be possible without statistics.

Statistics can be abstract, so this book uses two techniques to add a realistic, pragmatic dimension to the subject. The first technique is the use of examples of statistics in criminal justice and criminology research. These summaries are contained in the *Research Example* boxes embedded in each chapter. They are meant to give you a glimpse into the types of questions that are asked in this field of research and the ways in which specific statistical techniques are utilized to answer those questions. You will see firsthand how lively and diverse criminal justice and criminology research is. Research Example 1.1 summarizes five studies. Take a moment now to read through them.

RESEARCH EXAMPLE 1.1

What Do Criminal Justice and Criminology Researchers Study?

Researchers in the field of criminology and criminal justice examine a wide variety of issues pertaining to the criminal justice system and theories of offending. Included are things such as prosecutorial charging decisions, racial and gender disparities in sentencing, police use of force, drug and domestic violence courts, and recidivism. The following are examples of studies that have been conducted and published. You can find the full text of each of these articles and of all those presented in the following chapters at (**http://www.sagepub.com/gau**).

1. *Can an anticrime strategy that has been effective at reducing certain types of violence also be used to combat open-air drug markets?* The "pulling levers" approach involves deterring repeat offenders from crime by targeting them for enhanced prosecution while also encouraging them to change their behavior by offering them access to social services. This strategy has been shown to hold promise with gang members and others at risk for committing violence. The Rockford

(Continued)

(Continued)

(Illinois) Police Department (RPD) decided to find out if they could use a pulling levers approach to tackle open-air drug markets and the crime problems caused by these nuisance areas. After the RPD implemented the pulling levers intervention, Corsaro, Brunson, and McGarrell (2013) used official crime data from before and after the intervention to determine whether this approach had been effective. They found that although there was no reduction in violent crime, nonviolent crime (e.g., drug offenses, vandalism, and disorderly conduct) declined noticeably after the intervention. This indicated that the RPD's efforts had worked, because drug and disorder offenses were exactly what the police were trying to reduce.

2. *Are prisoners with low self-control at heightened risk of victimizing, or being victimized by, other inmates?* Research has consistently shown that low self-control is related to criminal offending. Some studies have also indicated that this trait is a risk factor for victimization, in that people with low self-control may place themselves in dangerous situations. One of the central tenets of this theory is that self-control is stable and acts in a uniform manner regardless of context. Kerley, Hochstetler, and Copes (2009) tested this theory by examining whether the link between self-control and both offending and victimization held true within the prison environment. Using data gathered from surveys of prison inmates, the researchers discovered that low self-control was only slightly related to in-prison offending and victimization. This result may call into question the assumption that low self-control operates uniformly in all contexts; to the contrary, something about prisoners themselves, the prison environment, or the interaction between the two may change the dynamics of low self-control.

3. *How prevalent is victim precipitation in intimate partner violence?* A substantial number of violent crimes are initiated by the person who ultimately becomes the victim in an incident. Muftić, Bouffard, and Bouffard (2007) explored the role of victim precipitation in instances of intimate partner violence (IPV). They gleaned data from IPV arrest reports and found that victim precipitation was present in cases of both male and female arrestees but that it was slightly more common in instances where the woman was the one arrested. This suggests that some women (and, indeed, some men) arrested for IPV might be responding

to violence initiated by their partners rather than themselves being the original aggressors. The researchers also discovered that victim precipitation was a large driving force behind dual arrests (cases in which both parties are arrested), as police could either see clearly that both parties were at fault or, alternatively, were unable to determine which party was the primary aggressor. Victim precipitation and the use of dual arrests, then, could be contributing factors behind the recent rise in the number of women arrested for IPV against male partners.

4. *Does having a close personal friend who is black influence whites' perceptions of crime as a problem?* The racialization of violent crime has been argued to have indelibly linked blacks with predatory violence and spawned a general antipathy toward blacks among white Americans. Mears, Mancini, and Stewart (2009) hypothesized that whites who had at least one close friend who was black would be less concerned about crime because their personal exposure to blacks would cause a breakdown in the stereotype about blacks as crime-prone. The researchers examined survey data from white respondents and found the opposite of what they had predicted—rather than lessening whites' concern about crime, having a black friend *heightened* that concern. The researchers suggested that having a black friend may increase whites' exposure to, and knowledge about, the dangerous urban environment that many blacks must navigate daily and thereby elevate whites' concern about local and national crime.

5. *How safe and effective are conducted energy devices as used by police officers?* Conducted energy devices (CEDs; e.g., Tasers) have proliferated in recent years. Their widespread use and occasional high-profile instances of misuse have generated controversy over whether these devices are safe for suspects and officers alike. Paoline, Terrill, and Ingram (2012) collected use-of-force data from six police agencies nationwide and attempted to determine whether officers who deployed CEDs against suspects were more or less likely to sustain injuries themselves. The authors' statistical analysis suggested a lower probability of officer injury when only CEDs were used. When CEDs were used in combination with other forms of force, however, the probability of officer injury increased. The results suggest that CEDs can enhance officer safety, but they are not a panacea that uniformly protects officers in all situations.

(Continued)

(Continued)

6. *What are the risk factors in a confrontational arrest that are most commonly associated with the death of the suspect?* There have been several high-profile instances of suspects dying during physical confrontations with police wherein the officers deployed CEDs against these suspects. White and colleagues (2013) collected data on arrest-related deaths (ARDs) that involved CEDs and gained media attention. The researchers triangulated the data using information from medical-examiner reports.

They found that in ARDs, suspects were often intoxicated and extremely physically combative with police; police, for their part, had used several other types of force before or after trying to solve the situation using CEDs. Medical examiners most frequently attributed these deaths to drugs, heart problems, and excited delirium. These results suggest that police departments should craft policies to guide officers' use of CEDs against suspects who are physically and mentally incapacitated.

The second technique to add a realistic, pragmatic dimension to the subject of this book is the use of real data from reputable and widely used sources such as the Bureau of Justice Statistics (BJS). BJS is housed within the U.S. Department of Justice and is responsible for gathering, maintaining, and analyzing data on various criminal justice topics at the county, state, and national levels. Visit http://bjs.ojp.usdoj.gov/ to familiarize yourself with BJS. The purpose behind the use of real data is to give you the type of hands-on experience that you cannot get from fictional numbers. You will come away from this book having worked with some of the same data that criminal justice and criminology researchers use. Two sources of data that will be used in upcoming chapters are the Uniform Crime Reports (UCR) and the National Crime Victimization Survey (NCVS). See Data Sources 1.1 and 1.2 for information about these commonly used measures of offending and victimization, respectively. All of the data sets used in this book are publicly available and were downloaded from the archive maintained by the Inter-University Consortium for Political and Social Research at www.icpsr.umich.edu.

In this book, emphasis is placed on both the production and consumption of statistics. Every statistical analysis has a "producer" (someone who runs the analysis) and a "consumer" (someone to whom an analysis is being presented). Regardless of which role you play in any given situation, it is vital that you are sufficiently versed in quantitative methods that you can identify the proper statistical technique and correctly interpret the results. When you are in the consumer role, you must also be ready to question the methods used by the producer so that you can determine for yourself how trustworthy the results are. Critical thinking skills are an enormous component of statistics. You are not a blank slate standing idly by, waiting to be written on—you are an active agent in your acquisition of knowledge about criminal justice, criminology, and the world in general. Be critical, be skeptical, and never hesitate to ask for more information.

DATA SOURCES 1.1

The Uniform Crime Reports (UCR)

The Federal Bureau of Investigation (FBI) collects annual data on crimes reported to police agencies nationwide and maintains the Uniform Crime Reports (UCR). Crimes are sorted into eight index offenses: homicide, rape, robbery, aggravated assault, burglary, larceny-theft, motor vehicle theft, and arson. An important aspect of this data set is that it includes only those crimes that come to the attention of police—crimes that are not reported or otherwise detected by police are not counted. The UCR also conforms to the hierarchy rule, which mandates that in multiple-crime incidents, only the most serious offense ends up in the UCR. If, for example, someone breaks into a residence with intent to commit a crime inside the dwelling and while there, he kills the homeowner and then sets fire to the structure to hide the crime, he has committed burglary, murder, and arson. Because of the hierarchy rule, though, only the murder would be reported to the FBI—it would be as if the burglary and arson had never occurred. Because of underreporting by victims and the hierarchy rule, the UCR undercounts the amount of crime in the United States. It nonetheless offers valuable information and is widely used. You can explore this data source at www.fbi.gov/about-us/cjis/ucr/ucr.

DATA SOURCES 1.2

The National Crime Victimization Survey (NCVS)

The Bureau of the Census conducts the periodic NCVS under the auspices of BJS to estimate the number of criminal incidents that transpire each year and to collect information about crime victims. Multistage cluster sampling is used to select a random sample of households, and each member of that household who is 12 years or older is asked to participate in an interview. Those who agree to be interviewed are asked over the phone or in person about any and all criminal victimizations that transpired in the 6 months prior to the interview. The survey employs a rotating panel design, so respondents are called at 6-month intervals for a total of 3 years, and then new respondents are selected (Bureau of Justice Statistics, 2006). The benefit of the NCVS over the UCR is that NCVS respondents might disclose victimizations to interviewers that they did not report to police, thus making the NCVS a better estimation of the total volume of crime in the United States. The NCVS, though, suffers from the weakness of being based entirely on victims' memory and honesty about the timing and circumstances surrounding criminal incidents. The NCVS also excludes children younger than 12 years, institutionalized populations (e.g., persons in prisons, nursing homes, and hospitals), and the homeless. Despite these problems, the NCVS is useful because it facilitates research into the characteristics of crime victims. The 2012 wave of the NCVS is the most recent version currently available.

Science: Basic Terms and Concepts

There are a few terms and concepts that you must know before you get into the substance of the book. Statistics are a tool in the larger enterprise of scientific inquiry. **Science** is the process of gathering information and developing knowledge using techniques and procedures that are accepted by other scientists in a discipline. Science is grounded in **methods**—research results are trustworthy only when the procedures used to reach them are considered correct by others in the scientific community. Nonscientific information is that which is collected informally or without regard for correct methods. Anecdotes are a form of nonscientific information. If you ask one person why he or she committed a crime, that person's response will be an anecdote; it cannot be assumed to be broadly true of other offenders. If you use scientific methods to gather multiple offenders and you ask all of them about their motivations, you will have data that you can analyze using statistics and that can be used to draw general conclusions.

In scientific research, **samples** are drawn from **populations** using scientific techniques designed to ensure that samples are representative of populations. For instance, if the population is 50% male, then the sample should also be approximately 50% male. A sample that is only 15% male is not representative of the population. Research-methods courses instruct students on the proper ways to gather representative samples. In a statistics course, the focus is on techniques used to analyze the data to look for patterns and test for relationships. Together, proper methods of gathering and analyzing data form the groundwork for scientific inquiry. If there is a flaw in either the gathering or the analyzing of data, then the results may not be trustworthy. "Garbage in, garbage out" (GIGO) is the mantra of statistics. Data gathered with the best of methods can be rendered worthless if the wrong statistical analysis is applied to them; likewise, the most sophisticated, cutting-edge statistical technique cannot salvage improperly collected data. When the data or the statistics are defective, the results are likewise deficient and cannot be trusted.

LEARNING CHECK

Identify whether each of the following is a sample or a population.

 a. A group of 100 police officers pulled from a department with 300 total officers

 b. Fifty prisons selected at random from all prisons nationwide

 c. All persons residing in the state of Wisconsin

 d. A selection of 10% of the defendants processed through a local criminal court in 1 year

---

Everybody who conducts a study bears an obligation to be clear and open about the methods they used. You should expect detailed reports on the procedures used so that you can evaluate whether they conformed to proper scientific methods. When the methods used to collect data are sound, it is not appropriate to question scientific results on the basis of a moral, emotional, or opinionated disagreement with them, but it is entirely correct to question results when the procedures used to arrive at them are shoddy or inadequate, since GIGO applies anytime the methods are poor.

Science: The process of gathering and analyzing data in a systematic and controlled way using procedures that are generally accepted by others in the discipline.

Methods: The procedures used to gather and analyze scientific data.

Sample: A subset pulled from a population with the goal of ultimately using the people, objects, or places in the sample as a way to generalize to the population.

Population: The universe of people, objects, or locations that researchers wish to study. These groups are often very large.

A key aspect of science is the importance of replication. No single study ever "proves" something definitively; quite to the contrary, much testing must be done before firm conclusions can be drawn. Replication is important because there are times when a study is flawed and needs to be redone, or when the original study is methodologically sound but an alteration of the statistical procedure produces different results. The scientific method's requirement that all researchers divulge the steps they took to gather and analyze data allows other researchers and members of the public to examine those steps and, if warranted, to undertake replications.

Replication: The repetition of a particular study that is conducted for purposes of determining whether the original study's results hold when new samples or measures are employed.

Types of Scientific Research in Criminal Justice and Criminology

Criminal justice and criminology research is diverse in nature and purpose. Much of it involves theory testing. Theories are proposed explanations for certain events. Hypotheses are small "pieces" of theories that must be true in order for the entire theory to hold up. You can think of a theory as a chain and hypotheses as the links forming that chain. Research Example 1.1 discusses a test of the general theory of crime conducted by Kerley et al. (2009). The general theory holds that low self-control is a static predictor of offending and victimization, regardless of context. From this proposition, the researchers deduced the hypothesis that the relationship between low self-control and both offending and victimization must hold true in the prison environment. Their results showed an overall lack of support for the hypothesis that low self-control operates uniformly in all contexts, thus calling that aspect of the general theory of crime into question. This is an example of a study designed to test a theory.

Theory: A set of proposed and testable explanations about reality that are bound together by logic and evidence.

Hypothesis: A single proposition, deduced from a theory, that must hold true in order for the theory itself to be considered valid.

Evaluation research is also common in criminal justice and criminology. In Research Example 1.1, the article by Corsaro et al. (2013) is an example of evaluation research. This type of study is undertaken when a new policy, program, or intervention is put into place and researchers want to know whether the intervention accomplished its intended purpose. In this study, the Rockford Police Department implemented a pulling levers approach to combat drug and nuisance offending. After the program had been put into place, the researchers analyzed crime data to find out whether or not the approach was effective.

Exploratory research occurs when there is limited knowledge about a certain phenomenon; researchers essentially embark into unfamiliar territory when they attempt to study this social event. The study by Muftic et al. (2007) in Research Example 1.1 was exploratory in nature because so little is known about victim precipitation, particularly in the realm of intimate partner violence. It is often dangerous to venture into new areas of study when the theoretical guidance is spotty; however, exploratory studies have the potential to open new areas of research that have been neglected but that provide rich information that expands the overall body of knowledge.

Finally, some research is **descriptive** in nature. The analysis of arrest-related deaths deployments by White et al. (2013) exemplifies a descriptive study. White and colleagues did not set out to test a theory or to explore a new area of research—they merely offered basic descriptive information about the suspects, officers, and situations involved in instances where CED use was associated with a suspect's death. In descriptive research, no generalizations are made to larger groups; the conclusions drawn from these studies are specific to the objects, events, or people being analyzed. This type of research can be very informative when knowledge about a particular phenomenon is scant.

Evaluation research: Studies intended to assess the results of programs or interventions for purposes of discovering whether those programs or interventions appear to be effective.

Exploratory research: Studies that address issues that have not been examined much or at all in prior research and that therefore may lack firm theoretical and empirical grounding.

Descriptive research: Studies done solely for the purpose of describing a particular phenomenon as it occurs in a sample.

For each of the following scenarios, identify the type of research being conducted.

a. A researcher wants to know more about female serial killers. He gathers news articles that report on female serial killers and records information about the killer's life history and the type of victim the killer preyed on.

b. A researcher wants to know whether a new in-prison treatment program is effective at reducing recidivism. She collects a sample of inmates that participated in the program and a sample that did not and gathers recidivism data for each group to see if those who participated had lower recidivism rates.

c. The theory of collective efficacy predicts that social ties between neighbors, coupled with neighbors' willingness to intervene when a disorderly or criminal event occurs in the area, protect the area from violent crime. A researcher gathers a sample of neighborhoods and records the level of collective efficacy and violent crime in each one to determine whether those with higher collective efficacy have lower crime rates.

d. A researcher notes that relatively little research has been conducted on the possible effects of military service on later crime commission. She collects a sample of people who served in the military and a sample that did not and compares them to find out whether the military group differs from the nonmilitary group in terms of the numbers or types of crimes they committed.

With the exception of purely descriptive research, the ultimate goal in most statistical analyses is to generalize from a sample to a population. A population is the entire set of people, places, or objects that a researcher wishes to study. Populations, though, are usually very large. Consider, for instance, a researcher trying to estimate attitudes about capital punishment in the general U.S. population. That is a population of more than 300 million! It would be impossible to measure everyone directly. Researchers thus draw samples from populations and study the samples instead. **Probability sampling** helps ensure that a sample mirrors the population from which it was drawn (e.g., a sample of people should contain a breakdown of race, gender, and age similar to that found in the population). Samples are smaller than populations, and researchers are therefore able to measure and analyze them. The results found in the sample are then generalized to the population.

Probability sampling: A sampling technique in which all people, objects, or areas in a population have a known chance of being selected into the sample.

Software Packages for Statistical Analysis

Hand computations are the foundation of this book because it is through seeing the numbers and working with the formulas that you gain an understanding of statistical analyses. In the real world, however, statistical analysis is generally conducted using a software program. Microsoft Excel contains some rudimentary statistical functions and is commonly used in situations where the only things sought are basic descriptive analyses; however, this program's usefulness is exhausted quickly because researchers usually want far more than descriptives. Many statistical packages are available. The most common in criminal justice and criminology research are SPSS, Stata, and SAS. Each of these packages has strengths and weaknesses. Simplicity and ease of use makes SPSS a good place to start for people new to statistical analysis. Stata is a powerful program excellent for regression modeling. The SAS package is the best one for extremely large data sets.

This book incorporates SPSS into each chapter. This allows you to get a sense for what data look like when displayed in their raw format and permits you to run particular analyses and read and interpret program output. Where relevant, the chapters offer SPSS practice problems and accompanying data sets that are available for download from http://www.sagepub.com/gau. This offers a practical, hands-on lesson about the way that criminal justice and criminology researchers use statistics.

Organization of the Book

This book is divided into three parts. Part I covers descriptive statistics. Chapter 2 provides a basic overview of types of variables and levels of measurement. Some of this material will be review for students who have taken a methods course. Chapter 3 delves into charts and graphs as means of graphically displaying data. Measures of central tendency are the topic of Chapter 4. These are descriptive statistics that let you get a feel for where the data are clustered. Chapter 5 discusses measures of dispersion. Measures of dispersion complement measures of central tendency by offering information about whether the data tend to cluster tightly around the center or whether they are very spread out.

Part II describes the theoretical basis for statistics in criminal justice and criminology: probability and probability distributions. Part I of the book can be thought of as the nuts-and-bolts of the mathematical concepts used in statistics, and Part II can be seen as the theory behind the math. Chapter 6 introduces probability theory. Binomial and continuous probability distributions are discussed. In Chapter 7, you will learn about population, sample, and sampling distributions. Chapter 8 provides the book's first introduction to inferential statistics with its coverage of point estimates and confidence intervals. The introduction of inferential statistics at this juncture is designed to help ease you into Part III.

Part III of the book merges the concepts learned in Parts I and II to form the discussion on inferential hypothesis testing. Chapter 9 offers a conceptual introduction to this framework, including a description of the five steps of hypothesis testing that will be used in every proceeding chapter. In Chapter 10, you will encounter your first bivariate statistical technique: chi-square. Chapter 11 describes two-population t tests and tests for differences between proportions. Chapter 12 covers analysis of variance, which is an extension of the two-population *t* test. In Chapter 13, you will learn about correlations. Finally, Chapter 14 wraps up the book with an introduction to bivariate and multiple regression.

The prerequisite that is indispensible to success in this course is a solid background in algebra. You absolutely must be comfortable with basic techniques such as adding, subtracting, multiplying, and dividing. You also need to understand the difference between positive and negative numbers. You will be required to plug numbers into equations and solve those equations. You should not have a problem with this as long as you remember the lessons you learned in your high school and college algebra courses. Appendix A offers an overview of the algebraic concepts you will need to know, so look those over and make sure that you are ready to take this course. If necessary, use them to brush up on your skills.

Statistics are cumulative in that many of the concepts you learn at the beginning form the building blocks for more complex techniques that you will learn about as the course progresses. Means, proportions, and standard deviations, for instance, are things you will learn about in Part I, but they will remain relevant throughout the remainder of the book. You must, therefore, learn these fundamental calculations well and you must remember them.

Repetition is the key to learning statistics. Practice, practice, practice! There is no substitute for doing and redoing the end-of-chapter review problems and any other problems your instructor may provide. You can also use the in-text examples as problems if you just copy down the numbers and do the calculations on your own without looking at the book. Remember, even the most advanced statisticians started off knowing nothing about statistics. The learning process is something everyone has to go through. You will complete this process successfully as long as you have basic algebra skills and are willing to put in the time and effort it takes to succeed.

CHAPTER 1 REVIEW PROBLEMS

1. Define science and explain the role of methods in the production of scientific knowledge.

2. What is a population? Why are researchers usually unable to study populations directly?

3. What is a sample? Why do researchers draw samples?

4. Explain the role of replication in science.

5. List and briefly describe the different types of research in criminal justice and criminology.

6. Name three theories that you have encountered in your criminal justice or criminology classes. For each one, write one hypothesis that you could gather data on and test.

7. Think of three types of programs or policies you have heard or read about in your criminal justice or criminology classes. For each one, suggest a possible way to evaluate that program or policy's effectiveness.

8. If a researcher were conducting a study on a topic about which very little is known and the researcher does not have theory or prior evidence to make predictions about what she will find in her study, what kind of research would she be doing? Explain your answer.

9. If a researcher were solely interested in finding out more about a particular phenomenon and focused entirely on a sample without trying to make inference to a population, what kind of research would he be doing? Explain your answer.

10. What does *GIGO* stand for? What does this cautionary concept mean in the context of statistical analyses?

KEY TERMS

Science	Replication	Exploratory research
Methods	Theory	Descriptive research
Sample	Hypothesis	Probability sampling
Population	Evaluation research	

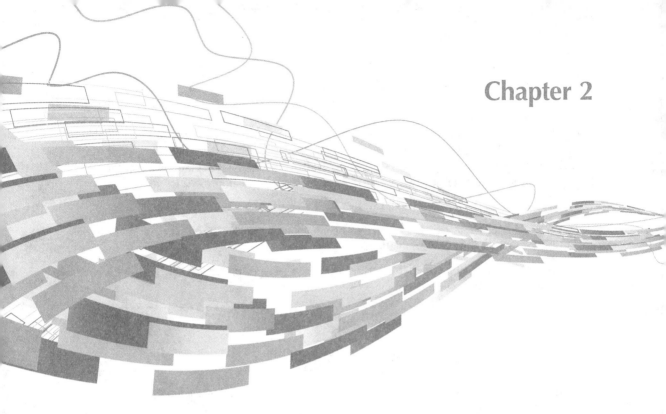

Chapter 2

Types of Variables and Levels of Measurement

Learning Objectives

- Define variables and constants.
- Define unit of analysis and be able to identify the unit of analysis in any given study.
- Define independent and dependent variables and be able to identify each in a study.
- Explain the difference between associations and causal relationships.
- List and describe the four levels of measurement, including similarities and differences between them, and be able to identify the level of measurement of different variables.

The first thing you must be familiar with in statistics is the concept of a **variable**. A variable is, quite simply, something that varies. It is a coding scheme used to measure a particular characteristic of interest. If, for instance, you asked all of your statistics classmates, "How many classes are you taking this term?" you would receive many different answers. This would be a variable. Variables sit in contrast to **constants**, which are characteristics that assume only one value in a sample. It would be pointless for you to ask all of your fellow classmates whether they are taking statistics this term because of course the answer they would all provide is "yes."

Variable: A characteristic that describes people, objects, or places and takes on multiple values in a sample or population.

Constant: A characteristic that describes people, objects, or places and takes on only one value in a sample or population.

RESEARCH EXAMPLE 2.1

Choosing Variables for a Study on Police Use of Conducted Energy Devices

Conducted energy devices (CEDs) such as the Taser have garnered national—indeed, international—attention in the past few years. Police practitioners contend that CEDs are invaluable tools that minimize injuries to both officers and suspects during contentious confrontations, whereas critics argue that police may use CEDs in situations where such a high level of force is not warranted. Do police seem to be using CEDs appropriately? Gau, Mosher, and Pratt (2010) set out to address this question. They sought to determine whether suspects' race or ethnicity influenced the likelihood that police officers would deploy or threaten to deploy CEDs against those suspects. In an analysis of this sort, it is important to account for other variables that might be related to police use of CEDs or other types of force; therefore, the researchers included suspects' age, sex, and resistance level. They also measured officers' age, sex, and race. Finally, they included a variable indicating whether it was light or dark outside at the time of the encounter. The researchers found that police use of CEDs was driven primarily by the type and intensity of suspect resistance but that even controlling for resistance, Hispanic suspects faced an elevated probability of having CEDs either drawn or deployed against them.

Units of Analysis

It seems rather self-evident, but nonetheless bears explicit mention, that every scientific study contains *something* that the researcher conducting the study gathers and examines. These "somethings" can be objects or entities such as rocks, people, molecules, or prisons. This is called the **unit of analysis,** and it is, essentially, whatever the sample under study consists of. In criminal justice and criminology research, individual people are often the units of analysis. These individuals might be probationers, police officers, criminal defendants, or judges. Prisons, police departments, criminal incidents, or court records can also be units of analysis. Larger units are also popular; for example, many studies focus on census tracks, block groups, cities, states, or even countries. Research Example 2.2 describes the methodological setup of a selection of criminal justice studies, each of which employed a different unit of analysis.

Unit of analysis: The object or target of a research study.

RESEARCH EXAMPLE 2.2

Units of Analysis

Each of the following studies used a different unit of analysis.

1. *Does self-defensive gun use help or hurt crime victims?* Hart and Miethe (2009) used the National Crime Victimization Survey to cull all criminal victimizations in which the victim attempted to thwart the attack by using a firearm in self-defense. The units of analysis were, therefore, criminal incidents. The researchers' goal was to find out whether self-defensive gun use by victims successfully warded off attack or, conversely, whether it made things worse. The statistical analyses revealed that although defensive gun use sometimes had adverse consequences for crime victims, this type of self-defense effort did prove advantageous for most victims under most circumstances.

2. *Is the individual choice to keep a firearm in the home affected by local levels of crime and police strength?* Kleck and Kovandzic (2009), using individual-level data from the General Social Survey (GSS) and city-level data from the FBI, set out to determine whether city-level homicide rates and the number of police per 100,000 city residents affected GSS respondents' likelihood of owning a firearm. There were two units of analysis in this study: individuals and cities. The statistical models indicated that high homicide rates and low police levels both modestly increased the likelihood that a given person would own a handgun; however, the relationship between city homicide rate and individual gun ownership decreased markedly when the authors controlled for whites' and other nonblacks' racist attitudes toward African Americans.

(Continued)

(Continued)

It thus appeared that the homicide–gun ownership relationship was explained in part by the fact that those who harbored racist sentiments against blacks were more likely to own firearms regardless of the local homicide rate.

3. *Do neighborhoods have unique "criminal careers," and if so, what factors drive those careers?* Stults (2010) mapped out the trajectory of concentrated disadvantage and homicide over time in Chicago. He used Chicago homicide data broken down by neighborhood to analyze homicide trends in these neighborhoods from 1965 to 1995. The units of analysis were, therefore, neighborhoods. He analyzed the neighborhoods to determine whether area levels of structural disadvantage and social disorganization affected homicide rates over time. He found that, overall, the intensity of disadvantage and disorganization present in each neighborhood over time did impact neighborhood homicide rates.

4. *Does gentrification reduce gang homicide?* Gentrification is the process by which distressed inner-city areas are transformed by an influx of new businesses or higher-income residents. Gentrification advocates argue that the economic boost will revitalize the area, provide new opportunities, and reduce crime. Is this assertion true? Smith (2014) collected data from 1994 to 2005 on all 342 neighborhoods in Chicago with the intention of determining whether gentrification over time reduces gang-motivated homicide. Smith measured gentrification in three ways: recent increases in neighborhood residents' socioeconomic statuses, increases in coffee shops, and demolition of public housing. The author predicted that the first two would suppress gang homicide and that the last one would increase it; even though public-housing demolition is supposed to reduce crime, it can also create turmoil, residential displacement, and conflict among former public-housing residents and residents of surrounding properties. Smith found support for all three hypotheses. Socioeconomic-status increases were strongly related to reductions in gang-motivated homicides, coffee-shop presence was weakly related to reductions, and public-housing demolition was robustly associated with increases. These results suggest that certain forms of gentrification might be beneficial to troubled inner-city neighborhoods but that demolishing public housing might cause more problems than it solves, at least in the short term.

Independent and Dependent Variables

Researchers in criminal justice and criminology typically seek to examine relationships between two or more variables. Observed or empirical phenomena give rise to questions about the underlying forces driving those phenomena. One empirical event is homicide and city homicide rates. It is worthy of note, for instance, that Washington, D.C., has a higher violent crime rate relative to Portland, Oregon. Researchers usually want to do more than merely note empirical findings, however—they want to know *why* things are the way they are. They might, then, attempt to identify the criminogenic (crime-producing) factors that are present in Washington, D.C., but that are absent in Portland or, conversely, the protective factors possessed by Portland and lacked by Washington, D.C.

Researchers undertaking quantitative studies must specify dependent variables (DVs) and independent variables (IVs). Dependent variables are the empirical events that a researcher is attempting to explain. Neighborhood or city crime rates, ex-prisoner recidivism, and judicial sentencing decisions are examples of dependent variables. Independent variables are those factors that a researcher believes might either enhance or suppress the dependent variable. It might be predicted, for instance, that compared to their male counterparts, female judges sentence defendants less harshly because they tend to endorse the rehabilitation philosophy of punishment and the importance of keeping families and communities intact. The opposite, though, might also be predicted: An investigator may expect female judges to sentence offenders more harshly than do male judges pursuant to the hypothesis that women take special affront to criminal behaviors that threaten the safety and solidarity of the community. It is important to note that certain variables—crime rates, for instance—can be used as both independent and dependent variables across different studies. The designation of a certain phenomenon as an IV or a DV depends on the nature of the research study.

Empirical: Having the qualities of being measurable, observable, or tangible. Empirical phenomena are detectable with senses such as sight, hearing, or touch.

Dependent variable: The phenomenon that a researcher wishes to study, explain, or predict.

Independent variable: A factor or characteristic that is used to try to explain or predict a dependent variable.

Relationships Between Variables: A Cautionary Note

It is vital to understand that *independent* and *dependent* are *not* synonymous with *cause* and *effect*, respectively. A particular independent variable might be related to a certain dependent variable, but this is far from definitive proof that the former is the cause of the latter. One problem is that there could be a third variable that explains the dependent variable as well as, or even better than, the independent variable does. The inadvertent exclusion of one or more important variables can result in erroneous conclusions because the researcher might mistakenly believe that the IV is strongly related to the DV when, in fact, the relationship is actually weak or is due to intervening factors. Research Example 2.3 offers an example of the problem of omitted variables with respect to so-called crack babies.

The Problem of Omitted Variables

Remember the "crack baby" panic? A media and political frenzy propelled this topic to the top of the national agenda for a time. The allegations were that "crack mothers" were abusing the drug while pregnant and were doing irreparable damage to their unborn children. Stories of low-birth-weight, neurologically impaired newborns abounded. What often got overlooked, though, was the fact that women who use crack cocaine while pregnant are also likely to use drugs such as tobacco and alcohol, which are known to cause problems to fetuses. These women are also more likely to have low incomes and little or no access to prenatal health care. Finally, if a woman abuses crack—or any other drug—while pregnant, she may also be at risk for mistreating her child after its birth (see Logan, 1999, for a review). Given the array of variables that can affect a baby's development both in utero and after birth, do you think it is wise for the public to focus solely on crack use? What public policy problems do you think could arise from such a focus?

Finally, independent variables cannot be viewed as the final determinants of dependent variables, because statistical analyses are examinations of aggregate trends. Uncovering an association between an IV and a DV means only that the presence of the IV has the tendency to be related to either an increase or a reduction in the DV in the sample as a whole—it is not an indication that the IV–DV link holds true for every single person or object in the sample. For example, victims of early childhood trauma are more likely than non-victims to develop substance abuse disorders later in life (see Dass-Brailsford & Myrick, 2010). Does this mean that every person who was victimized as a child has substance abuse problems as an adult? Certainly not! Many people who suffer childhood abuse do not become addicted to alcohol or other drugs. Early trauma is a risk factor that may elevate the risk of substance abuse, but it is not a guarantee of this outcome. Associations present in a larger group cannot be assumed to be uniformly true of all members of that group.

In sum, you should always be cautious when interpreting IV–DV relationships. It is better to think of IVs as *predictors* and DVs as *outcomes* rather than to view them as causes and effects. As the adage goes, correlation does not mean causation. Variables of all kinds may be related to each other, but it is important not to leap carelessly to causal conclusions on the basis of statistical associations.

Levels of Measurement

Every variable possesses a **level of measurement**. Levels of measurement are ways of classifying or describing variable type. There are two overarching classes of variables: **categorical** (also sometimes called *qualitative*) and **continuous** (also sometimes referred to as *quantitative*). Categorical variables are composed of groups or classifications that are represented with labels, whereas continuous variables are made up of numbers that measure how much of a particular characteristic a person or object possesses. Each of these variable types contains two subtypes. They are discussed in turn in the following sections.

Level of measurement: A variable's specific type or classification. There are four types: *nominal, ordinal, interval,* and *ratio.*

Categorical variable: A variable that classifies people or objects into groups. There are two types: *nominal* and *ordinal.*

Continuous variable: A variable that numerically measures the presence of a particular characteristic. There are two types: *interval* and *ratio.*

The Categorical Level of Measurement: Nominal and Ordinal Variables

Categorical variables are made up of categories. They represent ways of divvying up people and objects according to some characteristic. Categorical variables are subdivided into two types: *nominal* and *ordinal.* The **nominal** level of measurement is the most rudimentary of all the levels. It is the least descriptive and sometimes the least informative. Race is an example of a nominal-level variable. See Table 2.1 for an example of a nominal variable (see also Data Sources 2.1 for a description of the data set used in Table 2.1). The variable *race of stopped drivers* is nominal because races are groups into which people are placed. The group labels offer descriptive information about the people or objects within each group.

These classifications, however, only represent *differences*; there is no way to arrange the categories in any meaningful rank or order. Nobody in one racial group can be said to have "more race" or "less race" than someone in another category—they are merely of different races. The same applies to gender. Most people identify as being either female or male, but members of one gender group do not have more or less gender relative to members of the other group.

Figure 2.1   Levels of Measurement

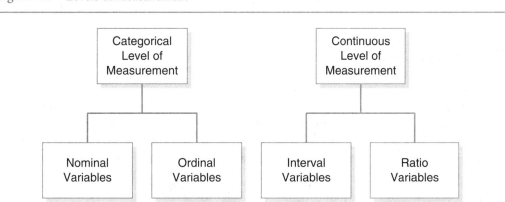

Table 2.1 Race of Stopped Drivers (Police–Public Contact Survey)

Driver Race	Frequency
White	416
Black	63
Asian	14
Other, including multiracial	26
	Total = 519

DATA SOURCES 2.1

The Police-Public Contact Survey

The Bureau of Justice Statistics (BJS; see Data Sources 2.3) conducts the Police-Public Contact Survey (PPCS) periodically as a supplement to the National Crime Victimization Survey (NCVS; see Data Sources 1.2). Interviews are conducted in English only. NCVS respondents aged 16 and older are asked about recent experiences they may have had with police. Variables include respondent demographics, the reason for respondents' most recent contact with police, whether the police used or threatened force against the respondents, the number of officers present at the scene, whether the police asked to search respondents' vehicles, and so on (BJS, 2011). This data set is used by BJS statisticians to estimate the total number of police–citizen contacts that take place each year, and it is used by researchers to study suspect, officer, and situational characteristics of police–public contacts. The 2011 wave of the PPCS is the most current one available at this time.

Nominal variable: A classification that places people or objects into different groups according to a particular characteristic that cannot be ranked in terms of quantity.

Ordinal variable: A classification that places people or objects into different groups according to a particular characteristic that can be ranked in terms of quantity.

Ordinal variables are one step up from nominal ones terms of descriptiveness because they can be ranked according to the quantity of a characteristic possessed by each person or object in a sample. University students' class level is an ordinal variable because freshmen, sophomores, juniors, and seniors can be rank-ordered according to how many credits they have earned. Numbers can also be represented as ordinal classifications when the numbers have been grouped into ranges like those in Table 2.2, where the income categories of respondents to the General Social Survey (GSS; see Data Sources 2.2) are shown.

Ordinal variables are useful because they allow people or objects to be ranked in a meaningful order. Ordinal variables are limited, though, by the fact that no algebraic techniques can be applied to them. This includes ordinal variables made from numbers such as those in Table 2.2. It is impossible, for instance, to subtract < *$1,000* from *$15,000 to $19,999*. It is likewise impossible to determine exactly how far apart two respondents are in their income levels. The difference between someone in the *$20,000 to $24,999* group and the ≥ *$25,000* group might only be one dollar if the former makes $24,999 and the latter makes $25,000. The difference could be enormous, however, if the person in the ≥ *$25,000* group has an annual family income of $500,000 per year. There is no way to figure this out from an assortment of categories like those in Table 2.2. The same limitation applies to the *year in college* variable—there is no way to find out how many more units a given senior has relative to any given junior.

LEARNING CHECK

In a study of people incarcerated in prison, the variable "offense type" captures the crime that each person was convicted of and imprisoned for. This variable could be coded as either a nominal or an ordinal variable. Explain why this is. Give an example of each type of measurement approach.

Table 2.2   GSS Respondents' Reported Annual Family Income

Family Income	*Frequency*
<$1,000	25
$1,000–$2,999	26
$3,000–$3,999	18
$4,000–$4,999	10
$5,000–$5,999	8
$6,000–$6,999	24
$7,000–$7,999	24
$8,000–$9,999	38
$10,000–$14,999	140
$15,000–$19,999	106
$20,000–$24,999	125
≥ $25,000	1,214
	Total = 1,758

The General Social Survey

The National Opinion Research Center has conducted the General Social Survey (GSS) annually or every 2 years since 1972. Respondents are selected using a multistage clustering sample design. First, cities and counties are randomly selected. Second, block groups or districts are selected from those cities and counties. Trained researchers then canvass each block group or district on foot and interview people in person. Interviews are offered in both English and Spanish. The GSS contains a large number of variables. Some of these variables are asked in every wave of the survey, whereas others are only asked once. The variables include respondents' attitudes about religion, politics, abortion, the death penalty, gays and lesbians, persons of racial groups other than respondents' own, free speech, marijuana legalization, and a host of other topics (Davis & Smith, 2009). The most current wave of the GSS available at this time is the one conducted in 2012.

The Continuous Level of Measurement: Interval and Ratio Variables

Continuous variables differ from categorical ones in that the former are represented not by categories but, rather, by numbers. **Interval variables** are numerical scales in which there are equal distances between all adjacent points on those scales. Ambient temperature is a classic example of an interval variable. This scale is measured using numbers representing degrees, and every point on the scale is exactly one degree away from the nearest points on each side. Twenty degrees Fahrenheit, for instance, is exactly 1 degree cooler than 21 degrees and exactly 4 degrees warmer than 16 degrees. *Age* is also interval level. Figure 2.2 shows the age of PPCS respondents who reported that they had called the police for help within the past 24 months.

Ratio variables are the other subtype within the continuous level of measurement. The ratio level resembles the interval level in that ratio, too, is numerical and has equal and known distance between adjacent points. The difference is that ratio-level scales have meaningful zero points that represent the absence of a given characteristic. Temperature, for instance, is not ratio level because the zeros in the various temperature scales are just placeholders. Zero does not signify an *absence* of temperature.

Table 2.3 is a frequency distribution displaying the number of state prisoners who were executed in 2012. These data come from the Bureau of Justice Statistics (BJS; Snell, 2014; see Data Sources 2.3). The left-hand column of the table displays the number of people executed per state, and the right-hand column shows the frequency with which each of those state-level numbers occurred (note that the frequency column sums to 50 to represent all of the states in the country). Can you explain why *number of persons executed* is a ratio-level variable?

Zip codes are five-digit sequences that numerically identify certain locations. What is the level of measurement of zip codes? Explain your answer.

Interval variable: A quantitative variable that numerically measures the extent to which a particular characteristic is present or absent and does not have a true zero point.

Ratio variable: A quantitative variable that numerically measures the extent to which a particular characteristic is present or absent and has a true zero point.

Figure 2.2   Age of PPCS Respondents Who Called the Police for Help in the Past 24 Months

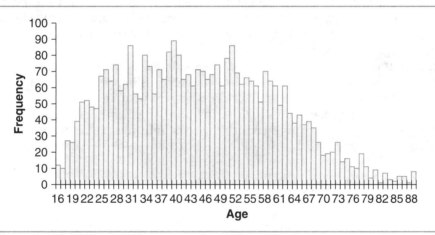

Table 2.3   Number of Persons Executed, 2012

Number Executed	Frequency
0	41
1	2
2	1
3	2
6	3
15	1
	Total = 50

In the "real world" of statistical analysis, interval and ratio variables are often used interchangeably. It is the overarching categorical-versus-continuous distinction that usually matters most when it comes to statistical analyses. Continuous variables can be added, subtracted, multiplied, and divided, but categorical variables cannot be. When a researcher is collecting data and has a choice about level of measurement, the best strategy is to always use the highest level possible. A continuous variable can always be made categorical later, but a categorical variable can never be made continuous.

Level of measurement is a very important concept. It may be difficult to grasp if this is the first time you have been exposed to this idea; however, it is imperative that you gain a firm understanding because level of measurement determines what analyses can and cannot be conducted. This fundamental point will form an underlying theme of this entire book, so be sure you understand it. Do not proceed with the book until you can readily identify a given variable's level of measurement.

Table 2.4   Characteristics of Each Level of Measurement

Level of Measurement	Variable Characteristic		
	Rank-orderable	Equal intervals	True zero
Nominal			
Ordinal	✓		
Interval	✓	✓	
Ratio	✓	✓	✓

CHAPTER SUMMARY

This chapter discussed the concept of a variable. You also read about units of analysis, independent variables, dependent variables, and about the importance of not drawing strict causal conclusions about statistical relationships. It is important to consider whether important variables have been left out and to keep in mind that relationships present at a group level do not apply uniformly to every single person or object within that group.

This chapter also described the two overarching levels of measurement: categorical and continuous. Categorical variables are qualitative groupings or classifications into which people or objects are placed on the basis of some characteristic. The two subtypes of categorical variables are nominal and ordinal. These two kinds of variables are quite similar in appearance, with the distinguishing feature being that nominal variables cannot be rank-ordered, whereas ordinal variables can be. Continuous variables are quantitative measurements of the presence or absence of a certain characteristic in a group of people or objects. Interval and ratio variables are both continuous. The difference between them is that ratio-level variables possess true zero points and interval-level variables do not.

You must understand this concept and be able to identify the level of measurement of any given variable because in statistics, the level at which a variable is measured is one of the biggest determinants of the graphing and analytic techniques that can be employed. In other words, each type of graph or statistical analysis can be used with some levels of measurement and cannot be used with others. Using the wrong statistical procedure can produce wildly inaccurate results and conclusions. You must therefore possess an understanding of level of measurement before leaving this chapter.

CHAPTER 2 REVIEW PROBLEMS

1. A researcher wishes to test the hypothesis that low education affects crime. She gathers a sample of people aged 25 and older.

    a. What is the independent variable?
    b. What is the dependent variable?
    c. What is the unit of analysis?

2. A researcher wishes to test the hypothesis that arrest deters recidivism. She gathers a sample of people who have been arrested.

    a. What is the independent variable?
    b. What is the dependent variable?
    c. What is the unit of analysis?

3. A researcher wishes to test the hypothesis that poverty affects violent crime. He gathers a sample of neighborhoods.

    a. What is the independent variable?
    b. What is the dependent variable?
    c. What is the unit of analysis?

4. A researcher wishes to test the hypothesis that prison architectural design affects the number of inmate-on-inmate assaults that take place inside a facility. He gathers a sample of prisons.

    a. What is the independent variable?
    b. What is the dependent variable?
    c. What is the unit of analysis?

5. A researcher wishes to test the hypothesis that the amount of money a country spends on education, health, and welfare affects the level of violent crime in that country. She gathers a sample of countries.

    a. What is the independent variable?
    b. What is the dependent variable?
    c. What is the unit of analysis?

6. A researcher wishes to test the hypothesis that police officers' job satisfaction affects the length of time they stay in their jobs. He gathers a sample of police officers.

    a. What is the independent variable?
    b. What is the dependent variable?
    c. What is the unit of analysis?

7. A researcher wishes to test the hypothesis that the location of a police department in either a rural or an urban area affects starting pay for entry-level police officers. She gathers a sample of police departments.

    a. What is the independent variable?
    b. What is the dependent variable?
    c. What is the unit of analysis?

8. A researcher wishes to test the hypothesis that the level of urbanization in a city or town affects residents' social cohesion. She gathers a sample of municipal jurisdictions (cities and towns).

    a. What is the independent variable?
    b. What is the dependent variable?
    c. What is the unit of analysis?

9. Suppose that a researcher found a statistical relationship between ice cream sales and crime—during months when a lot of ice cream is purchased, crime rates are higher. The researcher concludes that ice cream causes crime. What has the researcher done wrong?

10. Suppose that in a random sample of adults, a researcher found a statistical relationship between parental incarceration and a person's own involvement in crime. Does this mean that every person who had a parent in prison committed crime? Explain your answer.

11. Identify the level of measurement of each of the following variables:

    a. Suspects' race measured as *white*, *black*, *Latino*, and *other*
    b. The age at which an offender was arrested for the first time
    c. The sentences received by convicted defendants, measured as *jail*, *prison*, *probation*, *fine*, and *other*
    d. The total number of status offenses that adult offenders reported having committed as juveniles.
    e. The amount of money, in dollars, that a police department collects annually from drug asset forfeitures

    f. Prison security level, measured as *minimum, medium,* and *maximum*

    g. Trial judges' gender

12.   Identify the level of measurement of each of the following variables:

    a. The amount of resistance a suspect displays toward the police, measured as *not resistant, somewhat resistant,* or *very resistant*

    b. The number of times someone has shoplifted in her or his life

    c. The number of times someone has shoplifted, measured as *0 – 2, 3 – 5,* or *6 or more*

    d. The type of attorney a criminal defendant has at trial, measured as *privately retained* or *publicly funded*

    e. In a sample of juvenile delinquents, whether or not those juveniles have substance abuse disorders

    f. Prosecutors' charging decisions, measured as *filed charges* and *did not file charges*

    g. In a sample of offenders sentenced to prison, the number of days in their sentences

13.   If a researcher is conducting a survey and wants to ask respondents about their self-reported involvement in shoplifting, there are a few different ways he could phrase this question.

    a. Identify the level of measurement that each type of phrasing shown below would produce.

    b. Explain which of the three possible phrasings would be the best one to choose and why this is.

        Possible phrasing 1: How many times have you taken small items from stores without paying for those items?

        Please write in: _____

        Possible phrasing 2: How many times have you taken small items from stores without paying for those items? Please circle one of the following:

        Never   1–2 times   3–4 times   5+ times

        Possible phrasing 3: Have you ever taken small items from stores without paying for those items? Please circle one of the following:

        Yes   No

14.   If a researcher is conducting a survey and wants to ask respondents about the number of times each of them has been arrested, there are a few different ways she could phrase this question. Write down the three possible phrasing methods.

15.   The following table contains BJS data on the number of prisoners under sentence of death, by region. Use the table to do the following

Number of Prisoners Under Sentence of Death at Year-End 2012 (Snell, 2014)

Region	Prisoners
Northeast	211
Midwest	221
South	1,556
West	989
	Total = 2,977

a. Identify the level of measurement of the variable *region*.
b. Identify the level of measurement of *number of prisoners under sentence of death*.

16. The following table contains data from the 2012 National Crime Victimization Survey showing the number of victimization incidents and whether or not those crimes were reported to the police. The data are broken down by victims' household income level. Use the table to do the following:

Number of NCVS Victimizations Reported to Police, by Household Income (U.S. Department of Justice, 2012)

	Victimization Reported		
Income	Yes	No	Total
$12,499 or less	399	697	1,096
$12,500–$24,999	393	840	1,233
$25,000–$49,999	680	1,206	1,886
$50,000 or more	1,048	1,840	2,888
Total	2,520	4,583	$N = 7,103$

a. Identify the level of measurement of the *variable income*.
b. Identify the level of measurement of the variable *victimization reported*.

17. Haynes (2011) conducted an analysis to determine whether victim advocacy affects offender sentencing. She gathered a sample of courts and measured victim advocacy as a yes/no variable indicating whether or not there was a victim witness office located inside each courthouse. She measured sentencing as the number of months of incarceration imposed on convicted offenders in the courts.

a. Identify the independent variable in this study.
b. Identify the level of measurement of the independent variable.
c. Identify the dependent variable in this study.
d. Identify the level of measurement of the dependent variable.
e. Identify the unit of analysis.

18. Bouffard and Piquero (2010) wanted to know whether arrested suspects' perceptions of the way police treated them during the encounter affected the likelihood that those suspects would commit more crimes in the future. Their sample consisted of males who had been arrested at least once during their lives. They measured suspects' perceptions of police behavior as *fair* or *unfair*. They measured recidivism as the number of times suspects came into contact with police after that initial arrest.

   a. Identify the independent variable in this study.
   b. Identify the level of measurement of the independent variable.
   c. Identify the dependent variable in this study.
   d. Identify the level of measurement of the dependent variable.
   e. Identify the unit of analysis.

19. Kleck and Kovandzic (2009; see Research Example 2.2) examined whether the level of homicide in a particular city affected the likelihood that people in that city would own firearms. They measured homicide as the number of homicides that took place in the city in 1 year divided by the total city population. They measured handgun ownership as whether survey respondents said they did or did not own a gun.

   a. Identify the independent variable used in this study.
   b. Identify the level of measurement of the independent variable.
   c. Identify the dependent variable in this study.
   d. Identify the level of measurement of the dependent variable.
   e. Identify the unit of analysis. (Hint: This study has two!)

20. Gau, Mosher, and Pratt (2010; see Research Example 2.1) examined whether suspects' race or ethnicity influenced the likelihood that police would brandish or deploy Tasers against them. They measured race as *white*, *Hispanic*, *black*, or *other*. They measured Taser usage as *Taser used* or *some other type of force used*.

   a. Identify the independent variable used in this study.
   b. Identify the level of measurement of the independent variable.
   c. Identify the dependent variable in this study.
   d. Identify the level of measurement of the dependent variable.
   e. Identify the unit of analysis.

KEY TERMS

Variable	Independent variable	Ordinal variable
Constant	Level of measurement	Interval variable
Unit of analysis	Categorical variable	Ratio variable
Empirical	Continuous variable	
Dependent variable	Nominal variable	

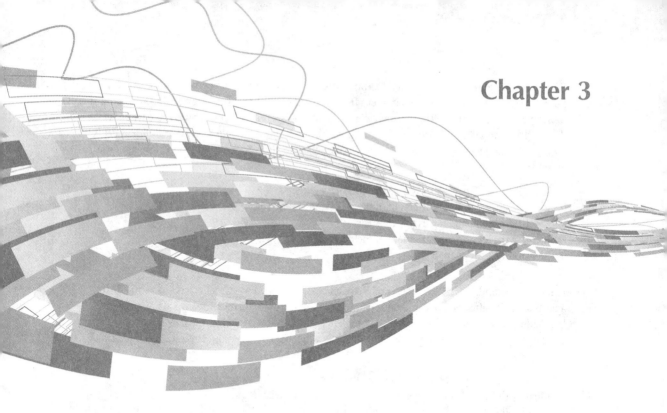

Chapter 3

Organizing, Displaying, and Presenting Data

Data are usually stored in electronic files for use with software programs designed to conduct statistical analyses. The program SPSS is one of the most common data software programs in criminal justice and criminology. The SPSS layout is a data spreadsheet. You might be familiar with Microsoft Excel; if so, then the SPSS data window should look familiar. Figure 3.1 depicts what a typical SPSS file may look like.

The data in Figure 3.1 are from the Bureau of Justice Statistics' 2011 Police-Public Contact Survey (PPCS; see Data Sources 2.1). Each row (horizontal line) in the grid represents one respondent, and each column (vertical line) represents one variable. Where any given row and column meet is a **cell** containing a given person's response to a particular question.

Your thoughts as you gaze on the data screen in Figure 3.1 can probably be aptly summarized as "Huh?" That is a very appropriate response, because there is no way to make sense of the data when they are in this raw format. This brings us to the topic of this chapter: methods for organizing, displaying, and presenting data. You can see from the figure that something has to be done to the data set to get it into a useful format. This chapter will teach you how to do just that.

Cell: The place in a table or spreadsheet where a row and column meet.

Chapter 2 introduced levels of measurement (nominal, ordinal, interval, and ratio). A variable's level of measurement determines which graphs or charts are and are not appropriate for that variable. Various data displays exist, and many of them can only be used with variables of particular types. As you read this chapter, take notes on two main concepts: (1) the proper construction of each type of data display and (2) the level of measurement for which each display type is applicable.

Data Distributions

Univariate Displays: Frequencies, Proportions, and Percentages

Perhaps the most straightforward type of pictorial display is the **univariate** (one variable) **frequency** distribution. A frequency is simply a raw count; it is the number of times a particular

Figure 3.1   SPSS Data File

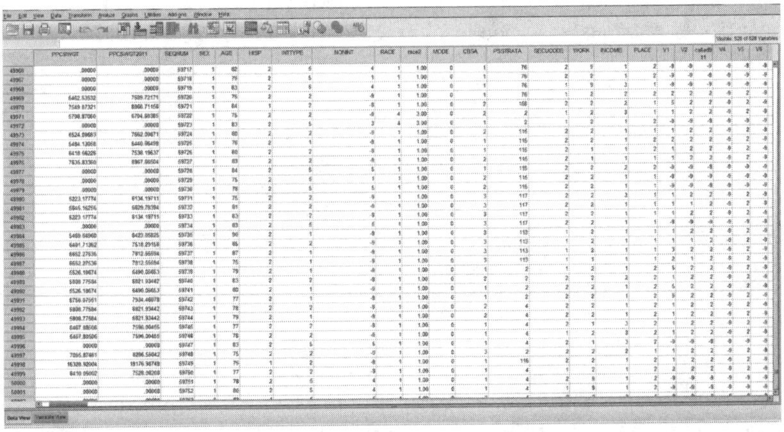

characteristic appears in a data set. A frequency distribution is a tabular display of frequencies. Table 3.1 shows the frequency distribution for the variable *respondent gender* in the 2011 PPCS. Let us pause and consider two new symbols. The first is the *f* that sits atop the right-hand column in Table 3.1. This stands for *frequency*. You can see that there are 25,078 males in this sample. An alternative way of phrasing this is that the characteristic *male* occurs 25,078 times. A more formal way to write this would be $f_{male} = 25{,}078$; for females, $f_{female} = 27{,}451$. The second new symbol is the *N* found in the bottom right-hand cell. This represents the total sample size; here, $f_{male} + f_{female} = N$. Numerically, $25{,}078 + 27{,}451 = 52{,}529$.

Table 3.1   Gender of PPCS Respondents

Gender	f
Male	25,078
Female	27,451
	N = 52,529

Univariate: Involving one variable.

Frequency: A raw count of the number of times a particular characteristic appears in a data set.

Proportion: A standardized form of a frequency that ranges from 0.00 to 1.00.

Percentage: A standardized form of a frequency that ranges from 0.00 to 100.00.

Raw frequencies are of limited use in graphical displays because they are often difficult to interpret and do not offer much information about the variable being examined. What is needed is a way to standardize the numbers to enhance interpretability. **Proportions** do this. Proportions are defined as the number of times a particular characteristic appears in a sample relative to the total sample size. Formulaically,

$$p = \frac{f}{N}$$

Formula 3(1)

p = proportion

f = raw frequency

N = total sample size.

Proportions range from 0.00 to 1.00. A proportion of exactly 0.00 indicates a complete absence of a given characteristic. If there were no males in the PPCS, their proportion would be

$$p_{male} = \frac{0}{52,529} = 0.00$$

Conversely, a trait with a proportion of 1.00 would be the only characteristic present in the sample. If the PPCS contained only men, then the proportion of the sample that was male would be

$$p_{male} = \frac{52,529}{52,529} = 1.00$$

Another useful technique is to convert frequencies into **percentages** (abbreviated *pct*). Percentages are a variation on proportions and convey the same information, but percentages offer the advantage of being more readily interpretable by the public. Percentages are computed similarly to proportions, with the added step of multiplying by 100:

$$pct = \left(\frac{f}{N}\right)100 \qquad\qquad \textit{Formula 3(2)}$$

Proportions and percentages can be used in conjunction with frequencies to form a fuller, more informative display like that in Table 3.2. Note that the two proportions (p_{males} and $p_{females}$) sum to 1.00 because the two categories contain all respondents in the sample; the percentage column sums to 100.00 for the same reason. The "Σ" symbol in the table is the Greek letter *sigma* and is a summation sign. It instructs you to add up everything that is to the right of the symbol. When all cases in a sample have been counted once and only once, proportions will sum to 1.00 and percentages to 100.00 or within rounding error of these totals.

Table 3.2   Gender of PPCS Respondents

Sex	f	p	pct
Male	25,078	.48	47.74
Female	27,451	.52	52.26
	N = 52,529	Σ = 1.00	Σ = 100.00

LEARNING CHECK

If you were summing proportions or percentages across the different levels of a categorical variable and you arrived at a result that was greater than the maximum of 1.00 or 100.00, respectively, what error might have occurred in the calculations? What about if the result were lower than 1.00 or 100.00?

Another useful technique for frequency distributions is the computation of cumulative measures. Cumulative frequencies, cumulative proportions, and cumulative percentages can facilitate meaningful interpretation of distributions, especially when data are continuous. Consider Table 3.3, which contains the ratio-level variable measuring the number of criminal attacks or threats experienced by male, Hispanic respondents to the 2012 National Crime Victimization Survey (NCVS; see Data Sources 1.2) in the 6 months leading up to the interview. The number of incidents reported and the frequency of each response are located in the two leftmost columns. To their right is a column labeled *cf*, which stands for *cumulative frequency*. The *cp* and *cpct* columns contain cumulative proportions and percentages, respectively.

Table 3.3   Number of Attacks or Threats Involving Male, Hispanic Victims

Victimizations	*f*	*cf*	*p*	*cp*	*pct*	*cpct*
0	639	639	.88	.88	88.14	88.14
1	78	717	.11	.99	10.76	98.90
2	8	725	.01	1.00	1.10	100.00
	$N = 725$		$\Sigma = 1.00$		$\Sigma = 100.00$	

Cumulative columns are constructed by summing the *f*, *p*, and *pct* columns successively from row to row. In the second row of Table 3.3's *cf* column, for instance, 717 is the sum of 639 and 78. In the *cp* column, likewise, .99 = .88 + .11. Cumulatives allow for assessments of whether the data are clustered at one end of the scale or spread fairly equally throughout. In Table 3.3, it can be readily concluded that the data cluster at the low end of the scale, as .88 (or 88.14%) of Hispanic, male respondents reported no violent attacks, and .99 (or 98.90%) reported one or none. The NCVS data indicate that this type of victimization is relatively rare among this group.

LEARNING CHECK

What is the level of measurement of the variable *Hispanic male*? What is the level of measurement of the variable *number of violent victimizations*? Refer back to Chapter 2 if needed.

Cumulative: A frequency, proportion, or percentage obtained by adding a given number to all numbers below it.

Univariate Displays: Rates

Suppose someone informed you that 2,199,125 burglaries were reported to the police in 2014. What would you make of this number? Nothing, probably, because raw numbers of this sort are simply not very useful. They lack a vital component—a denominator. The question that would leap to your mind immediately is "2,199,125 *out of what*?" You would want to know if this number was derived from a single city, from a single state, or from the United States as a whole. This is where rates come in. A *rate* is a method of standardization that involves dividing the number of events of interest (e.g., burglaries) by the total population:

$$rate = \frac{f}{population} \qquad\qquad \text{Formula 3(3)}$$

Table 3.4 contains data from the 2012 Uniform Crime Report (UCR; see Data Sources 1.1) for the property crime index offense categories. The column titled *Rate* displays the rate per capita that is obtained by employing Formula 3(3).

Table 3.4   UCR Index Offenses and Offense Rates, 2012

Crime	f	Rate	Rate per 10,000
Burglary	2,103,787	.01	67.02
Larceny	6,150,598	.02	195.93
Motor vehicle theft	721,053	.002	22.97

2012 U.S. Population = 313,914,040

Note how tiny the numbers in the rate column are. Rates per capita do not make sense in the context of low-frequency events like crime because they end up being so small. It is, therefore, customary to multiply rates by a certain factor. This factor is usually 1,000, 10,000, or 100,000. You should select the multiplier that makes the most sense with the data. In Table 3.4, the 10,000 multiplier has been used to form the *Rate per 10,000* column. Multiplying in this fashion lends clarity to rates because now it is no longer the number of crimes *per person* but, rather, the number of crimes *per 10,000 people*. If you randomly selected a sample of 10,000 people from the general population, you would expect 67.02 of them to have been the victim of burglary in the past year and 195.93 of them to have experienced larceny. These numbers and their interpretation are more real and more tangible than those derived using Formula 3(3) without a multiplier.

Sometimes rates must be calculated using multiple denominators, in contrast to Table 3.4 where there was only one. Table 3.5 shows a sample of states and the number of property crimes they reported in 2012.

Each state has a different population, so rates have to be calculated for each one according to its unique denominator. Table 3.6 shows the property-crime rates per 10,000 for each state.

Table 3.5   UCR Property Crimes in Four States

State	f	Population
Alabama	168,878	4,822,023
Connecticut	76,834	3,590,347
Delaware	30,639	917,092
Michigan	250,101	9,883,360

Table 3.6   UCR Property-Crime Rates in Four States

State	f	Rate per 10,000
Alabama	168,878	350.22
Connecticut	76,834	214.00
Delaware	30,639	334.09
Michigan	250,101	253.05

LEARNING CHECK

Rates and percentages have similar computational steps but very different meanings. Explain the differences between them, including the additional information needed to calculate a rate that is not needed for a percentage; the reason rates do not sum to 100 the way percentages do; and the substantive meaning of each one (i.e., the information that is provided by each type of number).

Bivariate Displays: Contingency Tables

Researchers are often interested not just in the frequency distribution of a single variable (a univariate display) but, rather, in the overlap between two variables. The Census of State and Federal Adult Correctional Facilities (CSFACF; see Data Sources 3.1) collects data from all adult correctional facilities in the United States. Two of the variables in this data set capture the gender of the inmates a facility is authorized to house (male, female, or both) and whether the facility makes college courses available to inmates. The variables *gender* and *college courses* can be merged to form a contingency table (also sometimes called *crosstabs*). This is a bivariate display, meaning it contains two variables.

The Census of State and Federal Adult Correctional Facilities

Every 5 years, the Bureau of Justice Statistics (BJS) sends surveys to all correctional facilities operated by federal, state, and local governments, as well as by private corporations. The surveys capture institution-level data such as the total inmate population; the number of correctional staff; the number of inmate disciplinary actions, assaults, and escapes; whether or not the facility offers vocational, educational, or mental-health services; and so on. The 2005 wave of CSFACF is the most recent version available.

Contingency table: A table showing the overlap between two variables.

Bivariate: An analysis containing two variables. Usually, one is designated the independent variable and the other the dependent variable.

Researchers studying prisons might be interested in knowing whether male, female, and mixed facilities differ in terms of whether they provide inmates with the opportunity to take college courses. A contingency table offers this information. Raw frequencies such as those shown in Table 3.7, however, are not as informative as they could be. To organize the data into a more readily interpretable format, proportions or, more likely, percentages can be computed and entered into the contingency table in place of frequencies.

There are two types of proportions and percentages that can be computed in a bivariate contingency table: *row* and *column*. Row proportions and percentages are computed using the row marginals in the denominator, whereas column proportions and percentages employ the column marginals. If we want to discover the percentage of each facility type that offers college courses, we can calculate row percentages. Table 3.8 shows the percentage distribution.

Table 3.7   Gender of Inmates and College Courses Offered, per Facility (Frequencies)

Gender	College Courses Offered?		Row Total
	Yes	*No*	
Male	497	861	1,358
Female	76	111	187
Both	69	207	276
Column Total	642	1,179	N = 1,821

Interesting results emerge from the row percentages in Table 3.8. It appears that male-only prisons are the least likely of all correctional facilities to offer college courses; nearly two-thirds do not. More than half of female-only prisons and a full 75% of mixed-gender facilities do not provide this service. It appears that, overall, prisons are relatively unlikely to make college courses available to inmates.

Table 3.8   Gender of Inmates and College Courses Offered, per Facility (Row Percentages)

| | College Courses Offered? | | |
Gender	Yes	No	Row Total
Male	$\left(\dfrac{497}{1,358}\right)100 = 36.60$	$\left(\dfrac{861}{1,358}\right)100 = 63.40$	100.00
Female	$\left(\dfrac{76}{187}\right)100 = 40.64$	$\left(\dfrac{111}{187}\right)100 = 59.36$	100.00
Both	$\left(\dfrac{69}{276}\right)100 = 25.00$	$\left(\dfrac{207}{276}\right)100 = 75.00$	100.00
			$N = 1,821$

LEARNING CHECK

Table 3.8 displays row percentages (i.e., percentages computed on the basis of row marginal). This shows the percentage of each type of facility that offers college courses. How would column percentages be interpreted in this instance? As practice, calculate the column percentages for Table 3.8 and explain their meaning.

RESEARCH EXAMPLE 3.1

Jail Inmates' Sexual-Assault Victimization

Research has shown that criminal offenders have higher rates of victimization relative to the general population. This victimization might have predated the beginning of their criminal involvement, or it might have occurred because of the risky lifestyles that many offenders lead. Female offenders, in particular, experience high levels of sexual abuse and assault. Lane and Fox (2013) gathered data on a sample of jail inmates and asked them about their victimization histories and their fear of future victimization (the numbers in the table are averages, with higher scores indicating greater levels of fear). The following table displays the results, broken down by gender.

More than half of female inmates (51%) reported having been sexually assaulted; this number was 7% for men.

Women were also more worried about future victimization of all types, although their scores on the fear-of-victimization variables showed that their fear of sexual assault outweighed their fear of other crimes. It has been argued in the past that sexual assault takes a unique physical and psychological toll on women—even those who have never actually experienced it—because it is an ever-present threat. Lane and Fox's results confirm the poignant impact that sexual assault has on female offenders.

	Women	Men
Sexual-assault victimization	51%	7%
Fear of property crime	1.73	1.55
Fear of violent crime	1.87	1.69
Fear of sexual assault	2.12	1.59
Fear of gang crime	1.74	1.57

Graphs and Charts

Frequency, proportion, and percentage distributions are helpful ways of summarizing data; however, they are rather dull to look at. It is sometimes desirable to arrange data in a more attractive format. If you were giving a presentation to a local police department or district attorney's office, for instance, you would not want to throw numbers at your audience for 20 or 30 minutes. The monotony is boring. Presentations can be diversified by the introduction of charts and graphs, of which there are many different types. This chapter concentrates on five of the most common: *pie charts*, *bar graphs*, *histograms*, *frequency polygons*, and *line graphs*.

Categorical Variables: Pie Charts

Pie charts can only be used with categorical data, and they are most appropriate for variables that have relatively few classes (i.e., categories or groups) because pie charts get messy fast. A good general rule is to use a pie chart only when a variable contains five or fewer classes. Pie charts are based on percentages; the entire circle represents 100%, and the "slices" are sized according to their level of contribution to that total.

The variable that will be used here to illustrate a pie chart is the race and ethnicity of stopped drivers from Table 2.1. The first step is to transform the raw frequencies into percentages using Formula 3(2).

Once percentages have been computed, the pie chart can be built by dividing 100% into its constituent parts. Figure 3.2 contains the pie chart. Flip back to Table 2.1 and compare this pie chart to the raw frequency distribution to note the dramatic difference between the two presentation methods.

Figure 3.2   Race of Stopped Drivers (Percentages)

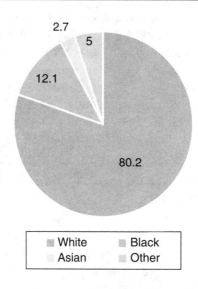

Figure 3.3   Physical Security Level of Prisons in the United States (Percentages)

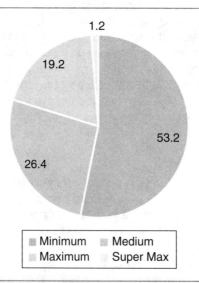

A pie chart can also be used to break down all of the prisons in the CSFACF by security level. The chart in Figure 3.3 shows the percentage of prisons at each level of physical security (minimum, medium, maximum, and super maximum). You can see that the majority (more than half) are minimum security, roughly one-quarter are medium security, about one-fifth are maximum security, and just over 1% are super-maximum facilities.

LEARNING CHECK

Pie charts like the one in Figures 3.2 and 3.3 are made of percentages. Rates cannot be used for pie charts. Why is this?

Classes: The categories or groups within a nominal or ordinal variable.

Categorical Variables: Bar Graphs

Like pie charts, bar graphs are meant to be used with categorical data; unlike pie charts, though, bar graphs can accommodate variables with many classes without damage to the charts' readability. Bar graphs are thus more flexible than pie charts are. For variables with five or fewer classes, pie charts and bar graphs may be equally appropriate; when there are six or more classes, bar graphs should be used.

In Chapter 1, you learned that one of the reasons for the discrepancy between crime prevalence as reported by the Uniform Crime Reports (UCR) and the National Crime Victimization Survey (NCVS) is that a substantial portion of crime victims do not report the incident to police. Truman, Langton, and Planty (2013) analyzed NCVS data and reported the percentage of people victimized by different crime types who reported their victimization to police. Figure 3.4 contains a bar graph illustrating the percentage of victims who contacted the police. Bar graphs provide ease of visualization and interpretation. It is simple to see from Figure 3.4 that substantial portions of all types of victimizations are not reported to the police and that motor vehicle theft is the most reliably reported crime.

Rates can also be presented as bar graphs. Figure 3.5 is a bar graph of the rates in Table 3.6.

A useful feature of bar graphs is that they can also be used to show the overlap between two variables. Recall that Table 3.7 displayed the number of prisons offering college courses, broken down by the gender of the inmates the facility was authorized to house. These variables can be entered into a bar graph with the horizontal axis representing inmate gender and the vertical axis representing the number of prisons that do and do not offer college courses.

The frequencies in Figure 3.6 can also be turned into percentages and graphed like Figure 3.7. Now the bars represent the percentage of prisons in each category that offer college classes.

Figure 3.4   Percentage of Victimizations Reported to Police

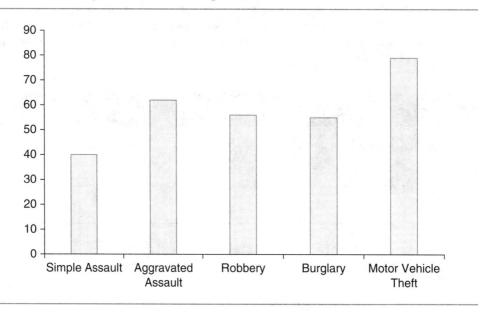

Figure 3.5   Bar Graph of UCR Property-Crime Rates (per 10,000) in Four States

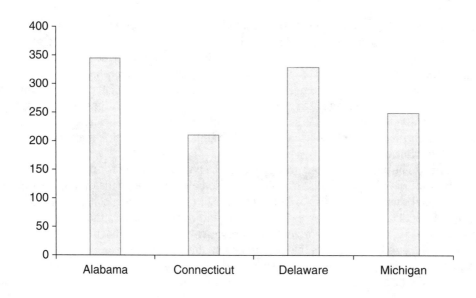

Figure 3.6 College Courses Offered in Prisons, by Inmate Gender

Figure 3.7 Percentage of Prisons Offering College Courses, by Inmate Gender

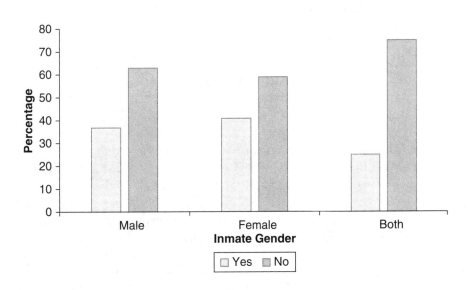

Continuous Variables: Histograms

Histograms are for use with continuous data. Histograms resemble bar charts, with the exception that in histograms, the bars touch one another. In bar charts, the separation of the bars signals that each category is distinct from the others; in histograms, the absence of space symbolizes the underlying continuous nature of the data. Figure 3.8 contains a histogram showing the ages of Hispanic respondents to the 2011 Police-Public Contact Survey (PPCS; see Data Sources 2.1) who reported that they had called the police for help within the past 24 months.

Figure 3.8   Age of Hispanic Respondents Who Called the Police in the Past 24 Months

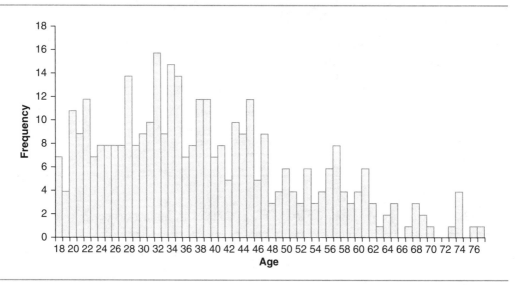

RESEARCH EXAMPLE 3.2

Are women's violent-crime commission rates rising?

Over the past few years, arrest rates for women have risen dramatically, even as crime itself has been declining or remaining stable. Women have historically experienced a very small arrest rate, much smaller than that among men. This rate has increased markedly. Critics argue, however, that the change in the arrest rate is not caused by actual changes in women's criminality; instead, they say, it is because tough-on-crime policies have resulted in a reduction in the leniency that women have typically enjoyed. Police are more likely to take crime by women seriously and are more likely to arrest women today than in the past. Who is right? Has women's violent-crime rate truly risen? Or are women just more likely to be arrested today? Steffensmeier and colleagues (2006) set out to answer these questions. The researchers used two data sources. First, they relied on the Uniform

Crime Reports (UCR) to track the arrest rates for women and men across different types of violent crime from the year 1980 through 2003. Second, they used the National Crime Victimization Survey (NCVS) to measure violent victimizations perpetrated by women and men during this same time. The authors knew that the UCR would show a rise in women's arrest rates, at least for certain kinds of offenses. The real question was whether the NCVS would also show a rise. The authors displayed their results in histograms.

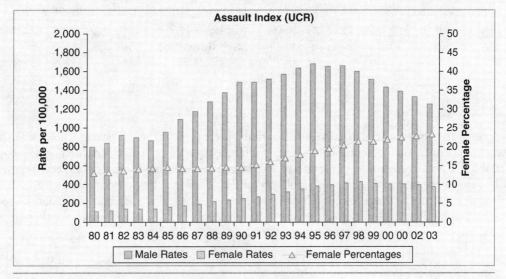

Assault Index (UCR)

Note: Includes aggravated and simple assaults.

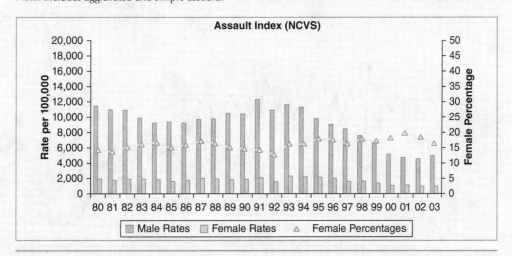

Assault Index (NCVS)

Note: Includes aggravated and simple assaults.

(Continued)

(Continued)

The top histogram displays UCR arrest data and the bottom one shows NCVS victimization data. The shorter bars in each one represent the percentage of arrestees and offenders, respectively, who were female. Together, these graphs show that even though female arrests for assault have risen, their participation in criminal assaults has not; assaults perpetrated by women have remained constant. The authors concluded that women are not committing violent crimes at higher rates now than in the past; their increasing arrest rates are caused by criminal-justice policies that lead police to arrest women in situations where, a few decades ago, they would have shown them leniency.

Continuous Variables: Frequency Polygons

Frequency polygons are an alternative to histograms. There is no "right" or "wrong" choice when it comes to deciding whether to use a histogram or a frequency polygon with a particular continuous variable; the best strategy is to mix it up a bit so that you are not using the same chart type repeatedly. Figure 3.9 contains the frequency polygon for data similar to that used in Figure 3.8 except this time containing the ages of non-Hispanic respondents instead of Hispanic respondents. Frequency polygons are created by placing a dot in the places where the tops of the bars would be in a histogram and then connecting those dots with a line.

Figure 3.9   Age of Non-Hispanic Respondents Who Called the Police in the Past 24 Months

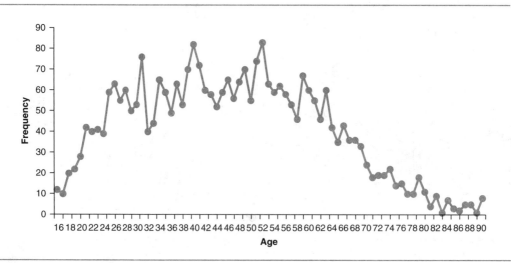

Longitudinal Variables: Line Charts

People who work with criminal justice and criminology data often encounter longitudinal variables. Longitudinal variables are measured repeatedly over time. Crime rates are often presented longitudinally as a means of determining trends. Line graphs can make discerning trends easy.

Longitudinal variables: Variables measured repeatedly over time.

Trends: Patterns that indicate whether something is increasing, decreasing, or staying the same over time.

Figure 3.10 shows a line graph of data from the Uniform Crime Reports measuring the annual number of hate-crime incidents per year from 1996 to 2012. Figure 3.11 shows the annual percentage of all hate crimes that are motivated by sexual-orientation bias. Together, these two line charts show two trends. First, total hate-crime incidents have declined slightly in recent years. Second, despite the downward trend in total incidents, the percentage of incidents that are based on the victims' sexual orientation has risen steadily, albeit with a small drop from 2011 to 2012.

Figure 3.10   Annual Number of Hate-Crime Incidents, 1996–2012

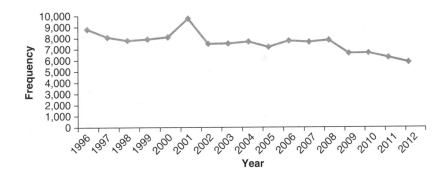

Grouped Data

The overarching purpose of a frequency distribution, chart, or graph is to display data in an accessible, readily understandable format. Sometimes, though, continuous variables do not lend themselves to tidy displays. Consider Table 3.9's frequency distribution for the amount of money, in dollars per person, that local governments in each state spent on criminal justice operations (Morgan, Morgan, & Boba, 2010; Data Sources 3.2). Figure 3.12 displays a histogram of the data. You can see that neither the frequency distribution nor the histogram is useful; there are too many values, and

Figure 3.11   Percentage of Hate-Crime Incidents Motivated by Victims' Sexual Orientation, 1996–2012

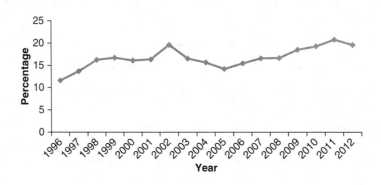

Table 3.9   Per Capita Local Government Expenditures on Criminal Justice, Ungrouped

Dollars per Capita	f	Dollars per Capita	f	Dollars per Capita	f
123	1	266	1	357	2
164	1	267	2	358	1
169	1	268	1	374	1
188	1	272	1	375	1
209	1	273	1	387	1
214	1	281	1	390	1
215	2	287	1	414	1
220	1	292	1	427	1
230	1	306	2	433	1
246	1	310	1	439	1
248	1	321	1	462	1
251	1	345	1	500	1
252	1	348	1	552	1
255	1	351	1	603	1
258	1	354	1	623	1
263	1			$N = 50$	

most of the values occur only once in the data set. There is no way to discern patterns or draw any meaningful conclusion from these data displays.

DATA SOURCES 3.2

CQ Press's State Factfinder Series

The Factfinder Series' Crime Rankings are compilations of various crime and crime-related statistics from the state and local levels. These volumes are comprehensive reports containing data derived from the FBI, Bureau of Justice Statistics, Census Bureau, and Drug Enforcement Administration. The data used here come from Morgan, Morgan, and Boba (2010).

Figure 3.12 Per Capita Local Government Expenditures on Criminal Justice, Ungrouped

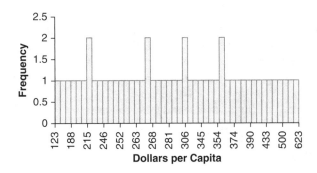

Grouping the data can provide a solution to this problem by transforming a continuous variable (either interval or ratio) into an ordinal one. There are several steps to grouping. First, find the range in the data by subtracting the smallest number from the highest. Second, select the number of intervals you want to use. This step is more art than science; it might take you a bit of trial and error to determine the number of intervals that is best for your data.

The ultimate goal is to find a middle ground between having too few and too many intervals—too few can leave your data display flat and uninformative, whereas too many will defeat the whole purpose of grouping.

Third, determine interval width by dividing the range by the number of intervals. This step is probably best illustrated in formulaic terms:

$$width = \frac{range}{intervals}$$

This will often produce a number with a decimal, so round either up or down depending on your reasoned judgment as to the optimum interval width for your data. Fourth, construct the stated class limits by starting with the smallest number in the data set and creating intervals of the width determined in Step 3 until you run out of numbers. Finally, make a new frequency (*f*) column by counting the number of people or objects within each stated class interval.

Let us group the legal expenditure data in Table 3.7. First, we need the range:

$$Range = 623 - 123 = 500$$

Now, we have to choose the number of intervals we want to use. With a large range like 500, it is advisable to select relatively few intervals so that each interval will encompass enough raw values to make it meaningful. We will start with 10 intervals. The next step is to compute the interval width. Using the formula from above,

$$width = \frac{500}{10} = 50$$

Each interval will contain 50 raw scores. Now the stated class limits can be constructed. See the left-hand column in Table 3.11. There are three main points to keep in mind when building stated class limits. The stated limits must be *inclusive*—in this example, the first interval contains the number 123, the number 172, and everything in between; *mutually exclusive*; and *exhaustive*. Once the stated class limits have been determined, the frequency for each interval is calculated by summing the number of raw data points that fall into each stated class interval. The sum of the frequency column in a grouped distribution should equal the sum of the frequencies in the ungrouped distribution.

You can see that Table 3.10 is much neater and more concise than Table 3.9. It is more condensed and easier to read. Where you will really see the difference, though, is in the histogram. Take a look at Figure 3.13 and compare it to Figure 3.12. Quite an improvement! It has a real shape now. This demonstrates the utility of data grouping.

Table 3.10   Per Capita Local Government Expenditures on Criminal Justice, Grouped

Stated Class Limits	f
123–172	3
173–222	6
223–272	13
273–322	8
323–372	7
373–422	5

(Continued)

(Continued)

Stated Class Limits	f
423–472	4
473–522	1
523–572	1
573–622	1
623–672	1
	N = 50

Figure 3.13 Per Capita Local Government Expenditures on Criminal Justice, Grouped

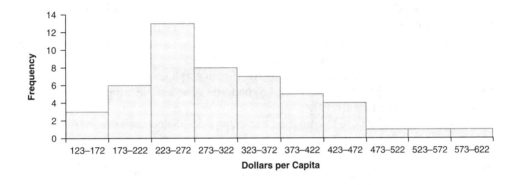

LEARNING CHECK

The data displayed in Figure 3.12 clearly need to be grouped, for the reasons described in the text. Refer back to the age variables shown in the histogram in Figure 3.8 and in the frequency polygon in Figure 3.9. Do you think these variables should be grouped for better ease of interpretation? Explain your answer.

SPSS

This is our first encounter with SPSS. There are a few preliminary things you should know before you start working with data. First, GIGO alert! Garbage in, garbage out. Using the wrong statistical technique will produce unreliable and potentially misleading results. Statistical software programs will generally not alert you to errors of this sort; they will give you output even if that output is garbage. It is your responsibility to ensure that you are using the program correctly. Second, pay attention to the SPSS file extension. The *.sav* extension signifies an SPSS data file; you should memorize this so that anytime you see this extension, you recognize it immediately. SPSS is the only program that will open a file with the *.sav* extension, so make sure you are working on a computer equipped with SPSS when you sit down to do homework or practice problems involving *.sav* files.

To obtain a frequency distribution, click on *Analyze* → *Descriptive* → *Statistics* → *Frequencies,* as shown in Figure 3.14. Select the variable you want from the list on the left side and either drag it to the right or click the arrow to move it over. For this illustration, we will use the Census of State and Federal Adult Correctional Facilities data. First, we will do a simple frequency analysis of the variable *securitylevel,* which measures whether a facility is minimum, medium, maximum, or super maximum. In SPSS, select *securitylevel* and move it to the right-hand window. Selecting *OK* will produce the output shown in Figure 3.15.

The SPSS Chart Builder (accessible from the *Graphs* drop-down menu) allows you to select a chart type and choose the variable you want to use. The SPSS Chart Builder requires that the level of measurement for each variable be set properly. SPSS will not permit certain charts to be used with some levels of measurement. Before constructing graphs or charts, visit the *Measure* column in the Variable View and make sure that continuous variables are marked as *Scale* and that nominal and ordinal variables are designated as such.

We will use *securitylevel* again. In Figure 3.16, the chosen graph is a pie chart, which means that the *Count* in the *Element Properties* box must be changed to *Percent.* Clicking *Apply* and *OK* produces the chart, as shown in Figure 3.17.

The Chart Builder can be used to construct bar graphs, too. Selecting a graph from the "Bar" menu on the left (refer back to Figure 3.16) and dragging it to the preview area will tell SPSS which type of graph you want. We will once again use the *securitylevel* variable, and this time we will ask for counts (i.e., frequencies), which is the Chart Builder's default. Figure 3.18 shows the results.

Figure 3.14 Running Frequencies in SPSS

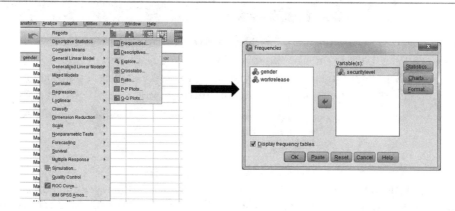

Figure 3.15   SPSS Frequency Output

Physical Security of Facility

		Frequency	Percentage	Valid Percentage	Cumulative Percentage
Valid	Super maximum	19	1.5	1.5	1.5
	Maximum	328	25.3	25.3	26.8
	Medium	395	30.5	30.5	57.3
	Minimum	553	42.7	42.7	100.0
	Total	1295	100.0	100.0	

Figure 3.16   Using the SPSS Chart Builder to Create a Pie Chart

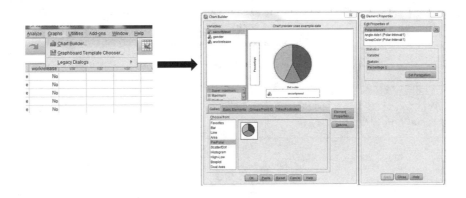

Bivariate contingency tables are available in SPSS, too. Locate this option through *Analyze* → *Descriptive Statistics* → *Crosstabs*, as shown in Figure 3.19. Select the variable that you would like to put in the rows of the table and the one you would like to place in the column. (Note that mathematically, you will get identical results no matter which of the two variables you put in the rows and which in the column. The table's appearance will change depending on which approach you take, but the numbers themselves will not.) We can replicate the crosstabs displayed in Tables 3.7 and 3.8 using SPSS. The variable *inmates* indicates whether a facility houses men, women, or both, and *college* measures whether a facility offers college courses for inmates. Placing *inmates* into the rows and *college* into the columns will yield the contingency table shown in Table 3.7. We can obtain percentages by clicking the *Cells* button and selecting row or column percentages. For present purposes, we will opt for row percentages. Figure 3.20 shows the output.

SPSS can also be used to transform raw numbers into rates. To demonstrate this, the Law Enforcement Management and Administrative Statistics (LEMAS; see Data Sources 3.2) data set will be used. We will compute the number of municipal police officers per 1,000 residents for each

Figure 3.17   SPSS Pie Chart

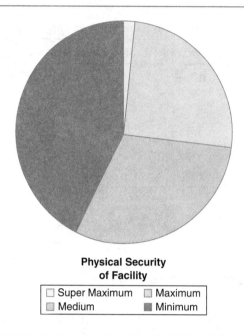

**Physical Security
of Facility**

☐ Super Maximum   ▨ Maximum
▨ Medium   ■ Minimum

Figure 3.18   SPSS Bar Graph

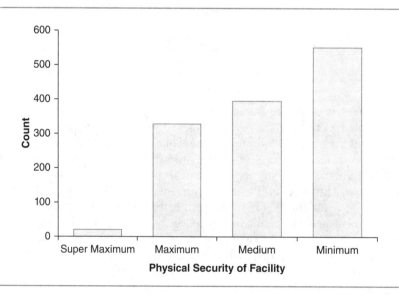

Figure 3.19   SPSS Contingency Table (Crosstabs) Analysis

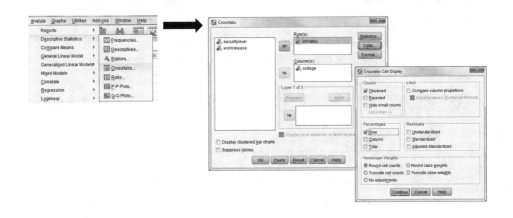

Figure 3.20   SPSS Contingency Table Output (With Row Percentages)

Inmates facility is authorized to house * COLLEGE COURSES Crosstabulation

			COLLEGE COURSES		Total
			No	Yes	
Inmates facility is authorized to house	Male	Count	861	497	1358
		% within inmates facility is authorized to house	63.4%	36.6%	100.0%
	Female	Count	111	76	187
		% within inmates facility is authorized to house	59.4%	40.6%	100.0%
	Both	Count	207	69	276
		% within inmates facility is authorized to house	75.0%	25.0%	100.0%
Total		Count	1179	642	1821
		% within inmates facility is authorized to house	64.7%	35.3%	100.0%

of the city police departments in the sample. Clicking on the *Transform* button at the very top of the SPSS data screen and then clicking *Compute* will produce the *Compute Variable* box pictured in Figure 3.21.

There is a good reason for using rates (such as the number of officers per 1,000 residents) to determine the size of an agency rather than simply using the number of officers employed by that police organization. Can you explain why rates are better than raw counts in this instance?

Figure 3.21 Creating Rates in SPSS

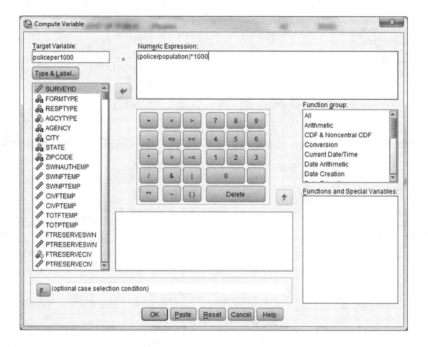

In the *Target Variable* box, type the name that you want to give your new variable; in the present example, the variable will be called *policeper1000*, as the rate of officers per 1,000 residents is what the new variable will be. In the *Numeric Expression* area, type the equation you wish SPSS to follow to create the new variable. Here, the portion of the equation reading *(police/population)* tells the program to divide the total number of police in a jurisdiction by that jurisdiction's population size, and the **1000* instructs SPSS to then multiply the results by 1,000. Click *OK*, and a new variable will appear at the very end of the data set. This is your rate variable.

The chapter review questions contain directions for accessing data sets that you can use to practice constructing charts and transforming variables into rates in SPSS. Play around with the data! Familiarize yourself with SPSS; we will be visiting it regularly throughout the book, so the more comfortable you are with it, the better prepared you will be. You do not have to worry about ruining the data set—if you change it in any way or make a mistake, just click *Don't save* when you exit the program and the file will be as good as new when you reopen it.

DATA SOURCES 3.2

The Law Enforcement Management and Administrative Statistics Survey

The Bureau of Justice Statistics conducts the Law Enforcement Management and Administrative Statistics (LEMAS) survey every 3 to 4 years. The sampling design involves two stages. First, all police agencies with 100 or more sworn personnel are included. Second, BJS pulls a random sample of agencies with fewer than 100 officers. The agencies in the sample are sent surveys to fill out. The surveys capture agency-level data such as the number of sworn law-enforcement personnel an organization employs, the number of civilian personnel, whether the agency participates in community policing, whether the agency has specialized units, and so on. At this time, the 2007 LEMAS is the most recent wave available.

CHAPTER SUMMARY

This chapter discussed some of the most common types of graphs and charts. Frequency distributions offer basic information about the number of times certain characteristics appear in a data set. Frequencies are informative and can convey valuable information; however, numbers are often difficult to interpret when they are in a raw format. Proportions and percentages offer a way to standardize frequencies and make it easy to determine which characteristics occur more often and which less often. Rates are another option for enhancing the interpretability of frequencies. Rates are generally multiplied by a number such as 1,000, 10,000, or 100,000.

Graphs and charts portray this same information—frequencies, proportions, percentages, and rates—using pictures rather than numbers. Pictorial representations are more engaging than their numerical counterparts and can capture audiences' interest more effectively. Pie charts may be used with categorical variables that have five or fewer classes and have been converted to percentages. Bar graphs are useful for categorical variables with any number of classes. They can be made from frequencies, proportions, percentages, or rates. For continuous data, histograms and frequency polygons can be used to graph frequencies, proportions, or percentages. Line graphs are useful for longitudinal data. Finally, some continuous variables that do not have a clear shape and are difficult to interpret in their raw form can be grouped. Grouping transforms continuous variables into ordinal ones. Histograms can be used to display data that have been grouped.

It is good to diversify a presentation by using a mix of pie charts, bar graphs, histograms, frequency polygons, and line charts. Simplicity and variety are the keys to a good presentation. Simplicity ensures that your audience can make sense of your data display quickly and easily. Variety helps keep your audience engaged and interested. Good data displays are key to summarizing data so that you and others can get a sense for what is going on in a data set.

1. The following table contains data from BJS's State Court Processing Statistics, which includes data on felony defendants in large urban counties in 2009 (Reaves, 2013). The variable is *most serious arrest charge*, which captures the most severe of the offenses for which defendants were arrested.

Most Serious Arrest Charge	f
Violent Offense	13,938
Property Offense	16,241
Drug Offense	18,220
Public-Order Offense	7,504
	N = 55,903

a. Construct columns for proportion, percentage, cumulative frequencies, cumulative proportions, and cumulative percentages.
b. Identify the types of charts or graphs that could be used to display this variable.
c. Based on your answer to (b), construct a graph or chart for this variable using percentages.

2. The following table contains data from the State Court Processing Statistics showing the number of urban felony defendants sentenced to prison time after conviction for different types of property offenses (Reaves, 2013).

Offense	f
Burglary	1,191
Larceny/Theft	901
Motor Vehicle Theft	329
Forgery	194
Fraud	256
Other Property Offense	365
	N = 3,236

a. Construct columns for proportion, percentage, cumulative frequencies, cumulative proportions, and cumulative percentages.
b. Identify the types of charts or graphs that could be used to display this variable.
c. Based on your answer to (b), construct a graph or chart for this variable using percentages.

3. The following table contains UCR data on the number of juveniles arrested for embezzlement for each state in 2012.

   a. Choose the appropriate graph type for this variable and construct that graph using frequencies.
   b. Group this variable using 10 intervals.
   c. Choose an appropriate graph type for the grouped variable and construct that graph using frequencies.

Juvenile Arrests	f	Juvenile Arrests	f	Juvenile Arrests	f
0	7	11	1	22	0
1	7	12	3	23	1
2	4	13	1	24	0
3	7	14	1	25	0
4	4	15	0	26	0
5	1	16	0	27	1
6	1	17	0	28	0
7	0	18	0	29	1
8	3	19	1	30	1
9	2	20	1		N = 50
10	2	21	0		

4. The following table contains Police-Public Contact Survey data on the ages of respondents who said that the police had requested consent to search their car during their most recent traffic stop.

Age	f	Age	f	Age	f
16	1	29	1	46	2
17	7	30	3	47	3
18	4	31	4	49	2
19	9	32	2	50	3
20	8	34	2	51	1
21	7	35	1	52	1
22	6	37	1	53	1
23	3	38	2	54	1
24	5	39	3	55	1
25	7	41	1	57	1

Age	f	Age	f	Age	f
26	5	42	4	58	1
27	6	44	3	59	1
28	5	45	4		N = 122

a. Choose the appropriate graph type for this variable and construct that graph using frequencies.
b. Group this variable using six intervals.
c. Choose an appropriate graph type for the grouped variable and construct that graph using frequencies.

5. The General Social Survey (GSS) asks respondents whether they think that marijuana should be legalized. The following table contains the percentage of respondents who supported legalization in each wave of the GSS from 1990 to 2012. Construct a line graph of these data, and then interpret the longitudinal trend. Does support for marijuana legalization appear to be increasing, decreasing, or staying the same over time?

Year	pct	Year	pct
1990	17	2002	36
1991	19	2004	36
1993	23	2006	37
1994	24	2008	40
1996	27	2010	48
1998	29	2012	48
2000	34		

6. The following table displays data from the official website of the U.S. courts (www.uscourts.gov) on the number of wiretap authorizations issued by state and federal judges per year from 1997 to 2012. Construct a line graph of the data and then interpret the longitudinal trend. Have wiretap authorizations been increasing, decreasing, or staying the same over time?

Year	f	Year	f
1997	1,186	2005	1,773
1998	1,329	2006	1,839
1999	1,350	2007	2,208
2000	1,190	2008	1,891
2001	1,491	2009	2,376
2002	1,358	2010	3,194

Year	f	Year	f
2003	1,442	2011	2,732
2004	1,710	2012	3,395

7. The following table contains data on the number of violent crimes that occurred in six cities during 2012. The table also displays each city's population.

City	Violent Crimes	Population
Birmingham, AL	3,237	213,266
Portland, ME	173	66,143
San Francisco, CA	5,777	820,363
Tampa, FL	2,162	350,758
Ann Arbor, MI	227	115,008
Washington, D.C.	7,448	632,323

a. Compute the rate of violent crime per 1,000 city residents in each city.
b. Select the appropriate graph type for this variable and construct that graph using rates.

8. The following table contains data on the number of property crimes that occurred in six cities during 2012. The table also displays each city's population.

City	Property Crimes	Population
Phoenix, AZ	60,777	1,485,509
Hartford, CT	5,319	125,203
Bellingham, WA	3,975	82,665
Cleveland, OH	24,309	393,781
Pinehurst, NC	120	15,008
East St. Louis, IL	1,827	27,040

a. Compute the rate of property crime per 1,000 city residents in each city.
b. Select the appropriate graph type for this variable and construct that graph using rates.

9. The website for this chapter (http://www.sagepub.com/gau) contains a data set called *Juvenile Embezzlement Arrests for Chapter 3.sav*. These are the data from Review Problem 3. Use the SPSS Chart Builder to construct a frequency histogram for the variable *embezzle*.

10. The file *City Police for Chapter 3.sav* contains data from the 2007 LEMAS. This is a subset of municipal agencies and contains the variable *footpatrol*, which indicates whether each agency uses foot patrol on a regular basis. Use SPSS to find the percentage of agencies that do and do not use foot patrol.

11. In the *City Police for Chapter 3.sav*, there is a variable called *sworn* that displays each police department's number of full-time sworn officers and a variable called *population* that records the city population served by each department. Use these two variables and the compute function to calculate the number of officers per 1,000 population for each department.

12. The website (http://www.sagepub.com/gau) also features a data file called *Hate Crimes for Chapter 3.sav*. This is the same data set used in the in-text demonstration of line graphs. Use the SPSS Chart Builder to construct a line graph mirroring the one in the text.

13. The website (http://www.sagepub.com/gau) contains a data set called *CSFACF for Chapter 3.sav*. This data file is a subset of the Census of State and Federal Adult Correctional Facilities described earlier in the chapter. The file has been narrowed to include only state-operated institutions. One of the variables in this file is *securitylevel*, which measures the physical security of each facility. Select an appropriate graph or chart type for this variable and use the SPSS Chart Builder to construct that graph or chart using percentages.

14. The *CSFACF for Chapter 3.sav* file also contains the variables *gender* and *workrelease*. Use SPSS to construct a contingency table with *gender* in the rows and *workrelease* in the columns. Include row percentages in your table.

KEY TERMS

Cell	Percentage	Classes
Univariate	Cumulative	Longitudinal variables
Frequency	Contingency table	Trends
Proportion	Bivariate	

GLOSSARY OF SYMBOLS AND ABBREVIATIONS INTRODUCED IN THIS CHAPTER

f	Frequency
p	Proportion
N	Sample size
pct	Percentage
cf	Cumulative frequency
cp	Cumulative proportion
$cpct$	Cumulative percentage

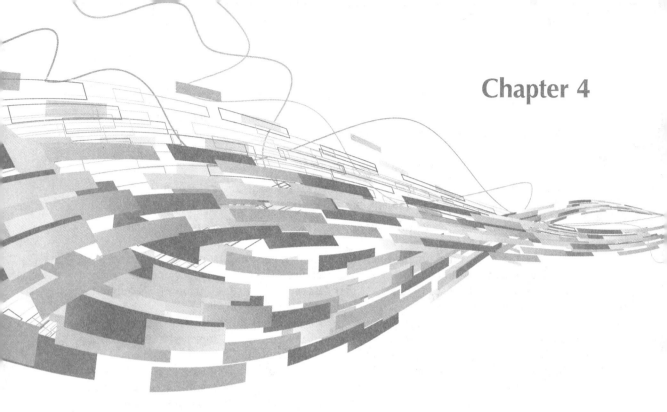

Chapter 4

Measures of Central Tendency

P eople in criminal justice and criminology are often interested in averages. Averages offer information about the centers or middles of distribution. They indicate where data points tend to cluster. This is an important thing to know. Consider the following questions that might be of interest to a researcher or practitioner in criminal justice:

1. What is the most common level of education among police officers?

2. How does the median income for people living in a structurally disadvantaged area of a certain city compare to that for all people in the city?

3. What is the average violent crime rate across all cities and towns in a particular state?

All of these questions make some reference to an average, a middle point, or, to use a more technical term, a measure of central tendency. Measures of central tendency offer information about where the bulk of the scores in a particular data set are located. A person who is computing a measure of central tendency is, in essence, asking, "Where is the middle?"

Averages offer information about the normal or typical person, object, or place in a sample. A group of people with an average age of 22, for instance, probably looks a lot different than a group averaging 70 years of age. Group averages help us predict the score for any individual within that group. Suppose in two samples of people, the only information you have is that one group has an average weight of 145 pounds and the other averages 200 pounds. If someone asked you, "How much does an individual person in the first group weigh?" your response would be, "About 145 pounds." If you were asked, "Who weighs more, a person randomly selected from the first group or from the second group?" you would respond that the person from the second group is probably the heavier of the two. You do not know, of course, if you are right; there might be people in the first group who are heavier than some people in the second group. The average, nonetheless, gives you predictive capability. It allows you to draw general conclusions and to form a basic level of understanding about a set of objects, places, or people.

Measures of central tendency: Descriptive statistics that offer information about where the scores in a particular data set tend to cluster. Examples include the mode, the median, and the mean.

Measures of central tendency speak to the matter of distribution shape. Data distributions come in many different shapes and sizes. Figure 4.1 contains data from the Police-Public Contact Survey (see Data Sources 2.1) showing the ages of non-Hispanic respondents who reported having called the police for help within the past 24 months. This is the same variable used in Figure 3.9 in the previous chapter. The shape this variable assumes is called a normal distribution. The normal curve represents an even distribution of scores. The most frequently occurring values are in the middle of the curve, and frequencies drop off as one traces the number line to the left and right. Normal distributions are ideal because the average is truly the best predictor of the scores for each case in the sample.

Normal distribution: A set of scores that clusters in the center and tapers off to the left (negative) and right (positive) sides of the number line.

Figure 4.1   Ages of Non-Hispanic Respondents Who Called the Police in the Past 24 Months

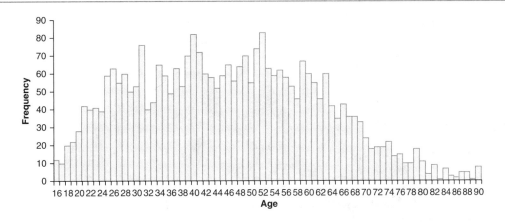

Positive skew: A clustering of scores in the left-hand side of a distribution with some relatively large scores that pull the tail toward the positive side of the number line.

Negative skew: A clustering of scores in the right-hand side of a distribution with some relatively small scores that pull the tail toward the negative side of the number line.

Standing in contrast to normal curves are skewed distributions. Skew can be either positive or negative. The distribution in Figure 4.2—the number of female administrators employed by male-only, privately owned correctional facilities (Census of State and Federal Adult Correctional Facilities; see Data Sources 3.1)—manifests what is called a positive skew. Positively skewed data cluster on the left-hand side of the distribution, with extreme values in the right-hand portion that pull the tail out toward the positive side of the number line. Positively skewed data are common in criminal justice and criminology research.

LEARNING CHECK

Skew type (positive versus negative) is determined by the location of the elongated tail of a skewed distribution. Positively skewed distributions are those in which the tail extends toward the positive side of the number line; likewise, negative skew is signaled by a tail extending toward negative infinity. Set aside your book and draw one of each type of distribution from memory.

Figure 4.3 shows 2012 General Social Survey (GSS; see Data Sources 2.2) respondents' annual individual incomes. This distribution has a negative skew: Scores are sparse on the left-hand side, and they increase in frequency on the right side of the distribution.

Figure 4.2 Female Administrators in Privately Operated, Male-Only Correctional Facilities

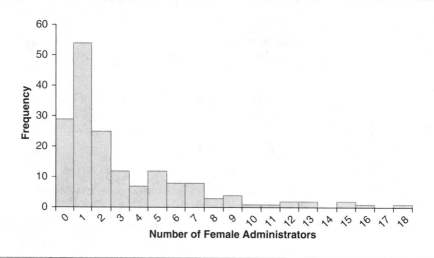

Figure 4.3 GSS Respondents' Annual Personal Incomes

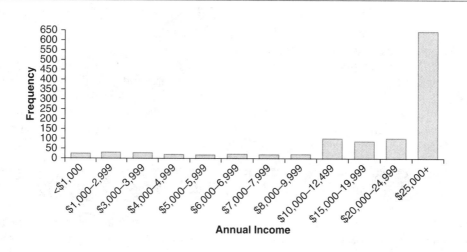

Knowing whether a given distribution of data points is normal or skewed is vital in criminal justice and criminology research. The average is an excellent predictor of individual scores when the curve is normal. When a distribution departs from normality, however, the average becomes a less useful bit of information and, in extreme cases, can be misleading. Distribution shape plays a key role in the more complicated statistical analyses we will get to in Parts II and III. Averages, moreover, factor in to some of the calculations for statistical tests. You must always know where the middle of your data set is located; measures of central tendency give you that information.

The Mode

The mode is the simplest of the three measures of central tendency covered in this chapter. It requires no mathematical computations and can be employed with any level of measurement. It is the only measure of central tendency available for use with nominal data. The mode is simply the most frequently occurring category or value. Table 4.1 contains data from the 2011 Police-Public Contact Survey (PPCS; Data Sources 2.1). Interviewers asked PPCS respondents whether they had been stopped by police while driving a vehicle. The people who answered yes were then asked to report the reason for that stop. This is a nominal-level variable. Table 4.1 presents the distribution of responses that participants gave for their stop. The mode is *speeding* because that is the stop reason that occurs most frequently (i.e., 2,040 people said that this is the violation for which they were pulled over by police).

A frequency bar graph of the same data is shown in Figure 4.4. The mode is easily identifiable as the category accompanied by the highest bar.

Mode: The most frequently occurring category or value in a set of scores.

The mode can also be used with continuous variables. Instead of identifying the most frequently occurring category as with nominal or ordinal data, you will identify the most common value. Figure 4.5 shows a frequency histogram for the variable from the PPCS that asks respondents how many face-to-face contacts they had with the police in the past 12 months. The sample has been narrowed to include only female respondents who were 21 or younger at the time of the survey. Can you identify the modal number of contacts? If you answered "1," you are correct!

Table 4.1   Among Stopped Drivers, Reason for the Stop

Stop Reason	Frequency
Speeding	2,040
Vehicle Defect	599
Record Check	381
Roadside Check	66
Seatbelt Violation	202
Illegal Turn or Lane Change	257
Stop Sign or Light Violation	275
Cellphone Usage	76
Other	283
Total	$N = 4,179$

Figure 4.4   Among Stopped Drivers, Reason for the Stop

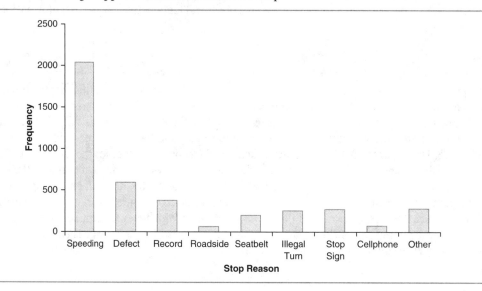

Figure 4.5   Number of Police Contacts in Past 12 Months Among Females Age 21 and Younger

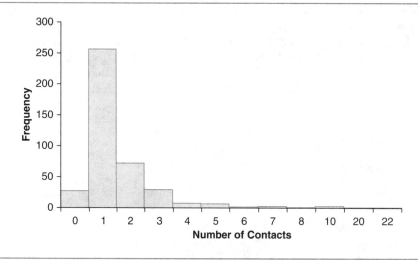

Instant Offense and Prison Violence

Are people convicted of homicide more violent in prison than people convicted of other types of offenses? Sorensen and Cunningham (2010) analyzed the institutional conduct records of all inmates incarcerated in Florida state correctional facilities in 2003, along with the records of inmates who entered prison that same year. They divided inmates into three groups. The stock population consisted of all inmates incarcerated in Florida prisons during the year 2003, regardless of the year they were admitted into prison. The new persons admitted into prison during 2002 and serving all of 2003 comprised the admissions cohort. The close custody group was a subset of the admissions cohort and was made of the inmates who were considered to be especially high threats to institutional security. The table below contains descriptive information about the three samples. For each group, can you identify the modal custody level and conviction offense type? Visit (http://www.sagepub.com/gau) to view the article and see the results of this study.

Demographics	Stock Population (N = 51,527)	Admissions Cohort (N = 14,088)	Close Custody Sample (N = 4,113)
Custody level			
Community	6.0%	10.4%	0.0%
Minimum	17.2%	23.7%	0.0%
Medium	27.2%	33.8%	0.0%
Close	48.9%	32.0%	100.0%
Death row	0.6%	0.1%	0.0%
Conviction offense type			
Homicide	18.6%	5.9%	10.9%
Other violent	39.6%	33.8%	46.2%
Property	21.4%	26.7%	21.0%
Drugs	14.7%	24.0%	14.7%
Public order/ weapons	5.7%	9.6%	7.2%

Source: Adapted from Table 1 in Sorensen and Cunningham (2010).

LEARNING CHECK

Remember that the mode is the category or value that occurs the most frequently—it is *not* the frequency itself.

The previous two examples highlight the relative usefulness of the mode for categorical data as opposed to continuous data. This measure of central tendency can be informative for the former but is usually not all that interesting or useful for the latter. This is because there are other, more sophisticated measures that can be calculated with continuous data.

The strengths of the mode include the fact that this measure is simple to identify and understand. It also, as mentioned previously, is the only measure of central tendency that can be used with nominal variables. The mode's major weakness is actually the flipside of its primary strength: Its simplicity means that it is usually too superficial to be of much use. It accounts for only one category or value in the data set and ignores the rest. It also cannot be used in more complex computations, which greatly limits its usefulness in statistics. The mode, then, can be an informative measure for nominal, and possibly ordinal, variables and is useful for audiences who are not schooled in statistics, but its utility is restricted, especially with continuous variables.

The Median

The median is another measure of central tendency. The median (*Md*) can be used with continuous and ordinal data; however, it cannot be used with nominal data because it requires that the variable under examination be rank orderable, which nominal variables are not.

Median: The score that cuts a distribution in half such that 50% of the scores are above that value and 50% are below it.

The median is the value that splits a data set exactly in half such that 50% of the data points are below it and 50% are above it. For this reason, the median is also sometimes called the *50th percentile*. The median is a positional measure, which means that it is not so much calculated as it is located. Locating the median is a three-step process. First, the categories or scores need to be rank ordered. Second, the median position (*MP*) can be computed using the formula

$$MP = \frac{(N+1)}{2},$$ *Formula 4(1)*

where *N* = total sample size.

The median position tells you where the median is located within the ranked data set. The third step is to use the median position to identify the median. When *N* is odd, the median will be a value in the data set. When *N* is even, the median will have to be computed by averaging two values.

Let us figure out the median violent crime rate among the five Colorado cities listed in Table 4.2. These numbers are derived from the 2012 Uniform Crime Reports (UCR; see Data Sources 1.1).

The first step is to rank the rates in either ascending or descending order. Ranked in ascending order, they look like this:

5.51[1]   13.70[2]   17.82[3]   42.34[4]   45.53[5]

Table 4.2   Violent Crime Rates in Colorado Cities

City	Violent Crimes per 10,000 Residents
Aspen	17.82
Colorado Springs	45.53
Grand Junction	42.34
Hayden	5.51
Woodland Park	13.70
$N = 5$	

Superscripts have been inserted to help emphasize the median's nature as a positional measure that is dependent on the *location* of data points rather than these points' actual values. The superscripts represent each number's position in the data set now that the values have been rank-ordered.

Second, the formula for the median position (*MP*) will tell you where to look to find the median. Here, $MP = \dfrac{(5+1)}{2} = \dfrac{6}{2} = 3$. This means that the median is in position 3. It is important to note that the MP is *not* the median; rather, it is a "map" that tells you where to look to find the median.

Finally, use the *MP* to identify the median. Since the median is in position 3, we can determine that *Md* = 17.82. This group of five Colorado cities has a median violent crime rate of 17.82 per 10,000.

In this example, the sample had five cases. When there is an even number of cases, finding the median is slightly more complex and requires averaging two numbers together. To demonstrate this, we will use 2012 property crime rates in North Dakota cities (Table 4.3).

Table 4.3   Property Crime Rates in North Dakota Cities

City	Property Crimes per 1,000 Residents
Bismarck	30.34
Fargo	25.82
Burlington	7.99
Minot	17.56
Valley City	18.87
Lisbon	20.16
$N = 6$	

First, rank the values: 7.99^1 17.56^2 18.87^3 20.16^4 25.82^5 30.34^6.

Second, find the median position: $MP = \dfrac{(6+1)}{2} = \dfrac{7}{2} = 3.5$. Notice that the MP has a decimal this time—this is what happens when the number of cases is even rather than odd. What this means is that the median is halfway between positions 3 and 4, so finding Md will require averaging these two numbers to find the middle. So the median is

$$Md = \frac{(18.87 + 20.16)}{2} = \frac{39.03}{2} = 19.52.$$

This sample of six North Dakota cities has a median property crime rate of 19.52 per 1,000 residents. Fifty percent of these cities have rates lower than this, and 50% have rates that are higher.

Medians can also be found in ordinal-level variables, too, though the median of an ordinal variable is less precise than that of a continuous variable because the former is a category rather than a particular number. To demonstrate, we will use an item from the Police-Public Contact Survey that measures the driving frequency among respondents who said that they had been pulled over by police for a traffic stop within the past 6 months, either as a driver or as a passenger in the stopped vehicle. Table 4.4 displays the data.

The first two steps to finding the Md of ordinal data mirror those for continuous data. First, the categories must be rank-ordered in either ascending or descending order according to their frequencies. For Table 4.4, this order is: 37, 82, 217, 457, 751. This is basically like lining up all the PPCS respondents in ascending order based on their answers to this question. Second, the median position must be calculated using Formula 4(1). Note that for ordinal data, the total sample size (N) is found by summing the frequencies; this is in contrast to continuous data where N is the number of categories in the variable (see Tables 4.2 and 4.3). For Table 4.4, $MP = \dfrac{(1,544+1)}{2} = \dfrac{1,545}{2} = 772.5$.

The median position in this case is a person—the person who is in position 772.5 is the median. The third step involves identifying the category in which the MP is located. Instead of ranking the categories according to frequencies, we are now going to arrange them in either ascending or descending order according to the categories themselves. In other words, the internal ranking system of the categories themselves is used to structure the sequence of the list. In Table 4.4, the categories are arranged from the most-frequent driving habits (*Every day or almost every day*) to the least-frequent ones (*Never*). As such, the categories are already in descending order and do not need to be rearranged. Next, sum the frequencies of the rank-ordered categories until the cumulative sum meets or exceeds the MP. Here, $751 + 217 = 968$, so the median is located in the *A few days a week* category. This means that half of the people in this sample drive a few days a week or more, and half drive a few days a week or less. Note how much less informative the median is for ordinal variables as compared to continuous ones. For the crime rates in Tables 4.2 and 4.3 we were able to identify the specific, numerical median; for the driving-frequency variable in Table 4.4, we are only able to say that the median case is contained within the *A few days a week* category. This is a rough estimate that paints only a limited picture.

Table 4.4   Driving Frequency of PPCS Respondents Who Experienced Traffic Stops

How often do you drive?	f
Every Day or Almost Every Day	751
A Few Days a Week	217
A Few Days a Month	82
A Few Times a Year	37
Never	457
	$N = 1,544$

LEARNING CHECK

Rearrange the frequencies from Table 4.4 so that they are in descending order, rather than in ascending order as was the case in the demonstration. Complete the cumulative-frequencies exercise to locate the median. What is your conclusion?

The median has advantages and disadvantages. Its advantages are that it uses more information than the mode does, so it offers a more descriptive, informative picture of the data. It can be used with ordinal variables, which is advantageous because, as we will see, the mean cannot be.

A key advantage of the median is that it is not sensitive to extreme values or outliers. To understand this concept, revisit Table 4.3 and replace Bismarck's rate of 30.34 with 60.00, then relocate the median. It did not change despite a near doubling of this city's crime rate! That is because the median does not get pushed and pulled in various directions when there are extraordinarily high or low values in the data set. As we will see, this feature of the median gives it an edge over the mean, the latter of which *is* sensitive to extremely high or extremely low values and does shift accordingly.

The median has the disadvantage of not fully utilizing all available data points. The median offers more information than the mode does, but it still does not account for the entire array of data. This shortfall of the median can be seen by going back to the previous example regarding Bismarck's property crime rate. The fact that the median did not change when the endpoint of the distribution was noticeably altered demonstrates how the median fails to offer a comprehensive picture of the entire data set. Another disadvantage of the median is that it usually cannot be employed in further statistical computations. There are limited exceptions to this rule, but generally speaking, the median cannot be plugged into statistical formulas for purposes of performing more complex analyses.

The Mean

This brings us to the third measure of central tendency that we will cover: the **mean**. The mean is the arithmetic average of a data set. Unlike that of the median, the calculation of the mean requires the use of every raw score in a data set. Each individual point exerts a separate and independent effect on the value of the mean. The mean can be calculated only with continuous (interval or ratio) data; it cannot be used to describe categorical variables.

Mean: The arithmetic average of a set of data.

There are two formulas for the computation of the mean, each of which is for use with a particular type of data distribution. The first formula is one with which you are likely familiar from college or high school math classes. The formula is

$$\bar{x} = \frac{\Sigma x}{N},$$

where $\bar{x}$ (x bar) = the sample mean,

Σ (*sigma*) = a summation sign directing you to sum all numbers or terms to the right of it,

x = values in a given data set, and

N = the sample size.

This formula tells you that to compute the mean, you must first add all the values in the data set together and then divide that sum by the total number of values. Division is required because all else being equal, larger data sets will produce larger sums, so it is vital to account for sample size when attempting to construct a composite measure such as the mean.

For the example concerning computation of the mean, we can reuse the Colorado violent crime rate data from Table 4.2:

$$\bar{x} = \frac{17.82 + 45.53 + 42.34 + 5.51 + 13.70}{5} = \frac{124.90}{5} = 24.98$$

These five cities have a mean violent crime rate of 24.98 per 10,000 residents.

The second formula for the mean is used for large data sets that are organized in tabular format using both an x column that contains the raw scores and a frequency (f) column that conveys information about how many times each x value occurs in the data set. Table 4.5 shows data from the Bureau of Justice Statistics on the number of death-sentenced prisoners received per state in 2012 (Snell, 2014). Note that the f column sums to 36 rather than 50 because 14 states do not authorize the death penalty and are thus excluded from this analysis.

To calculate the mean using frequencies, first add a new column to the table. This column—titled fx—is the product of the x and f columns. See Table 4.6.

The fx column saves time by using multiplication as a shortcut and thereby avoiding cumbersome addition. Using the conventional mean formula would require extensive addition because you would have to sum 36 numbers (i.e., 17 zeroes plus eight ones plus four twos, and so on). This process is unwieldy and impractical, particularly with very large data sets. Instead, merely multiply

76   Part 1 Descriptive Statistics

Table 4.5   Number of Death-Sentenced Prisoners Received by States, 2012

Number Received (x)	f
0	17
1	8
2	4
4	1
5	2
6	1
9	1
13	1
20	1
	N = 36

Table 4.6   Number of Death-Sentenced Prisoners Received by States, 2012

Number Received (x)	f	fx
0	17	0
1	8	8
2	4	8
4	1	4
5	2	10
6	1	6
9	1	9
13	1	13
20	1	20
	N = 36	Σ = 78

each value by its frequency and then sum these products to find the total sum of all x values. You can see from Table 4.6 that in 2012, states received a total of 78 new death-sentenced inmates.

Once the fx column is complete and has been summed, the mean can be calculated using a formula slightly different from the one presented in Formula 4(2). The mean formula for large data sets is

$$\bar{x} = \frac{\Sigma fx}{N},$$

Formula 4(3)

where f = the frequency associated with each raw score x and

    fx = the product of x and f.

The process of computing this mean can be broken down into three steps: (1) Multiply each x by its f, (2) sum the resulting fx products, and (3) divide by the sample size N. Plugging the numbers from Table 4.5 into the formula, it can be seen that the mean is

$$\bar{x} = \frac{78}{36} = 2.17.$$

In 2012, the 36 states that authorize use of the death penalty each received a mean of 2.17 new death-sentenced prisoners.

LEARNING CHECK

Anytime you need to compute a mean, you will have to choose between Formulas 4(2) and 4(3). This is a simple enough choice if you just consider that in order to use the formula with an f in it, there must be an "f" column in the table. If there is no f column, use the formula that does not have an f. Refer back to Table 2.3 in Chapter 2. Which formula would be used to calculate the mean? Explain your answer. As practice, use the formula and compute the mean number of prisoners executed per state in 2012.

Note that Table 2.3 contains all 50 states, including those states that do not authorize the capital punishment, whereas Table 4.6 contains only those 36 states that allow the death penalty. What would happen to the mean calculated on Table 4.6 if the 14 states that do not use this form of punishment were added to the table? What would happen to the mean number of executions per state if the non-authorizing states were removed from Table 2.3?

RESEARCH EXAMPLE 4.2

Do Short-Term, High-Rate Offenders Differ From Long-Term, Low-Rate Offenders?

It is well known that some offenders commit a multitude of crimes over their life and others commit only a few, but the intersection of offense volume (offending rate) and time (the length of a criminal career) has received little attention from criminal justice/criminology researchers. Piquero, Sullivan, and Farrington (2010) used a longitudinal data set of males in South London who demonstrated delinquent behavior early in life and were thereafter tracked by a research team who interviewed them and looked up their official conviction records. The researchers were interested in finding out whether males who committed a lot of crimes in a short amount of time (the short-term, high-rate offenders [STHR]) differed significantly from those who committed crimes at a lower rate over a longer period of time (the long-term, low-rate offenders [LTLR]) on criminal justice outcomes. The researchers gathered the following descriptive statistics. The numbers not in parentheses are means. The numbers in parentheses are standard deviations, which we will learn about in the next chapter.

You can see from the table that the long-term, low-rate offenders differed from the short-term, high-rate offenders on a number of dimensions. They were, overall, older at the time of their first arrest and had a longer mean career length. They committed many fewer crimes per year and were much less likely to have been sentenced to prison.

Piquero et al.'s analysis reveals a dilemma about what should be done about these groups of offenders with respect to sentencing; namely, it shows how complicated the question of imprisonment is. The short-term, high-rate offenders might seem to be the best candidates for incarceration based on their volume of criminal activity, but these offenders' criminal careers are quite short. It makes no sense from a policy and budgetary perspective to imprison a bunch of people who would not be committing crimes if they were free in society. The STHR offenders also tended to commit property offenses rather than violent ones. The long-term, low-rate offenders, by contrast, committed a disproportionate number of violent offenses despite the fact that their overall number of lifetime offenses was lower than that for the STHR group. Again, though, the question of the utility of imprisonment arises: Is it worth incarcerating someone who, though he may still have many years left in his criminal career, will commit very few crimes during that career? The dilemma of sentencing involves the balance between public safety and the need to be very careful in the allotting of scarce correctional resources.

| | Offender Type | |
Variable	LTLR (N = 44)	STHR (N = 21)
Overall career length	14.5 (6.50)	10.8 (4.40)
Offenses committed per year	.42 (.31)	1.25 (.72)
Age at first conviction	17.8 (4.70)	13.5 (2.30)
Total convictions	4.9 (2.40)	11.5 (4.10)
Percentage ever incarcerated	9.1%	61.9%
Number of times incarcerated	1.46 (.50)	1.23 (.66)
Years incarcerated	1.23 (.76)	1.05 (.56)

Source: Adapted from Table 1 in Piquero, Sullivan, and Farrington (2010).

The mean is sensitive to extreme values and outliers, which gives it both an advantage and a disadvantage relative to the median. The advantage is that the mean uses the entire data set and accounts even for the "weird" values that may appear at the high or low ends of the distribution. The median, by contrast, ignores these values. The disadvantage is that the mean's sensitivity to extreme values makes this measure somewhat unstable; it is vulnerable to the disproportionate impact that a small number of extreme values can exert on the data set.

To illustrate this property of the mean, consider Table 4.7, which contains the 2012 homicide rates for six cities in California. Trace the changes in the mean homicide rates from left to right. Do you notice how the rate increases with the successive introductions of San Bernardino and Oakland? San Bernardino pulls the mean up from 4.35 to 7.85. A more dramatic increase occurs when Oakland is added; the mean shoots up to 11.84, a nearly threefold increase in the mean rate as compared to the initial value of 4.35.

This demonstrates how the inclusion of extreme values can cause the mean to move in the direction of those values. A score that is noticeably greater than the others in the sample can draw the mean upward, while a value that is markedly lower than the rest can drive the mean downward. There is a good reason why, for example, average income in the United States is reported as a median rather than a mean—a mean would lump extremely poor people who are barely scraping by in with multibillionaires. That would not be accurate at all! The apparent "average" income in the United States would be huge. Finding the point at which 50% of households sit below that particular annual income and 50% above it is much more useful and accurate. The mean is, therefore, most informative when a distribution is normally distributed; the accuracy of the mean as a true measure of central tendency is reduced in distributions that are positively or negatively skewed. Another implication of the mean's sensitivity to extreme values is that the mean and the median can be compared to determine the shape of a distribution, as described in the following section.

Table 4.7   Homicide Rates in California Cities

Urban Area	Homicides per 100,000	Homicides per 100,000	Homicides per 100,000
San Diego	3.51	3.51	3.51
Redlands	2.84	2.84	2.84
Paso Robles	3.30	3.30	3.30
Los Angeles	7.76	7.76	7.76
San Bernardino		21.86	21.86
Oakland			31.79
	$N = 4$	$N = 5$	$N = 6$
	$\bar{x} = \dfrac{17.41}{4} \ 4.35$	$\bar{x} = \dfrac{39.27}{5} \ 7.85$	$\bar{x} = \dfrac{71.06}{6} = 11.84$

Table 4.8   Summary of the Measures of Central Tendency Available for Each Level of Measurement

	Mode	Median	Mean
Nominal	✓	✓	✓
Ordinal	✓	✓	✓
Grouped	✓	✓	✓
Interval	✓	✓	✓
Ratio	✓	✓	✓

Using the Mean and the Median to Determine Distribution Shape

Given that the median is invulnerable to extreme values but the mean is not, the best strategy is to report both of these measures when describing data shape. The mean and the median can, in fact, be compared to form a judgment about whether the data are normally distributed, positively skewed, or negatively skewed. In normal distributions, the mean and median will be approximately equal. Positively skewed distributions will have means markedly greater than their medians. This is because extremely high values in positively skewed distributions pull the mean up but do not affect the location of the median. Negatively skewed distributions, on the other hand, will have medians that are noticeably larger than their means because extremely low numbers tug the mean downward but do not alter the median's value. Figure 4.6 illustrates this conceptually.

To give a full picture of a data distribution, then, it is best to make a habit of reporting both the mean and the median.

The mean—unlike the mode or the median—forms the basis for further computations; in fact, the mean is an analytical staple of many inferential hypothesis tests. The reason that the mean can

Figure 4.6   The Mean and Median as Indicators of Distribution Shape

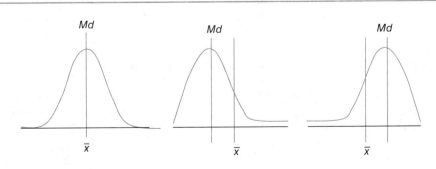

be used in this manner is that the mean is the midpoint of the magnitudes. This point merits its own section.

Midpoint of the magnitudes: The property of the mean that causes all deviation scores based on the mean to sum to zero.

Deviation Scores and the Mean as the Midpoint of the Magnitudes

The mean possesses a vital property that enables its use in complex statistical formulas. To understand this, we must first discuss deviation scores. A deviation score is a given data point's distance from its group mean. The formula for a deviation score is based on simple subtraction:

$$d_i = x_i - \overline{x},$$
Formula 4(4)

where x_i = a given data point,

d_i = the deviation score for a given data point x_i,

$\overline{x}$ = the sample mean.

Suppose, for instance, that a group's mean is $\overline{x} = 24$. If a certain raw score x_i is 22, then $d_{x=22} = 22 - 24 = -2$. A raw score of 25, by contrast, would have a deviation score of $d_{x=25} = 25 - 24 = 1$.

Deviation score: The distance between the mean of a data set and any given raw score in that set.

A deviation score embodies two pieces of information. The first is the absolute value of the score or, in other words, how far from the mean a particular raw score is. Data points that are exactly equal to the mean will have deviation scores of 0; therefore, deviation scores with larger absolute values are farther away from the mean, while deviation scores with smaller absolute values are closer to it.

The second piece of information that a deviation score conveys is whether the raw score associated with that deviation score is greater than or less than the mean. Positive deviation scores represent raw scores that are greater than the mean and negative deviation scores signify raw numbers that are less than the mean. You can thus discern two things about the raw score x_i that a given deviation score d_i represents: (1) the distance between x_i and $\overline{x}$ and (2) whether x_i is above $\overline{x}$ or below it. Notice that you would not even need to know the actual value of x_i or $\overline{x}$ in order to effectively interpret a deviation score. Deviation scores convey information about the position of a given data point with respect to its group mean; that is, deviation scores offer information about raw scores' *relative*, rather than absolute, positions within their group. Figure 4.7 illustrates this.

Figure 4.7   Deviation Scores in a Set of Data With a Mean of 24

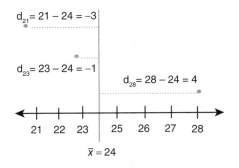

What lends the mean its title as the midpoint of the magnitudes is the fact that deviation scores computed using the mean (as opposed to the mode or median) always sum to zero. As Salkind (2011) put it, "[t]he mean is like the fulcrum on a seesaw. It's the centermost point where all the values on one side of the mean are equal in weight to all the values on the other side of the mean" (p. 22). The seesaw analogy is apt—the mean is the value in the data set at which all values below it balance out with all values above it. For an example of this, try summing the deviation scores in Figure 4.7. What is the result?

To demonstrate this concept more concretely, the raw homicide counts that were used as rates in Table 4.8 are listed in Table 4.9. These cities had a mean of 87.25 homicides in 2012. The d column contains the deviation score for each of the homicide counts.

Illustrative of the mean as the fulcrum of the data set, the positive and negative deviation scores ultimately cancel each other out, as can be seen by the sum of zero at the bottom of the deviation-score column. This represents the mean's property of being the midpoint of the magnitudes—it is the value that perfectly balances all of the raw scores. This characteristic is what makes the mean a central component in more complex statistical analyses. You will see in later chapters that the mean features prominently in many calculations.

Table 4.9   Homicides in California Cities

City	Homicides	d
San Diego	47	$47 - 87.25 = -40.25$
Redlands	2	$2 - 87.25 = -85.25$
Paso Robles	1	$1 - 87.25 = -86.25$
Los Angeles	299	$299 - 87.25 = 211.75$
$\bar{x} = \dfrac{349}{4} = 87.25$		$\Sigma = 0.00$

To test your comprehension of the concept of the mean as the midpoint of the magnitudes, go back to Table 4.2. Among these cities, the mean violent crime rate is 24.98. Compute each city's deviation score and then sum the scores.

SPSS

Criminal justice and criminology researchers generally work with large data sets, so computing measures of central tendency by hand is not feasible; luckily, it is not necessary, either, because statistical programs such as SPSS can be used instead. There are two different ways to obtain central tendency output. Under the *Analyze → Descriptive Statistics* menu, SPSS offers the options *Descriptives* and *Frequencies*. Both of these functions will produce central tendency analyses, but the *Frequencies* option offers a broader array of descriptive statistics and even some charts and graphs. For this reason, we will use *Frequencies* rather than *Descriptives*. Once you have opened the *Frequencies* box, click on the *Statistics* button to open a menu of options for measures of central tendency. Select *Mean, Median,* and *Mode,* as shown in Figure 4.8. Then click *OK* and the output displayed in Figure 4.9 will appear. The variable measuring the number of prisoners received under sentence of death in 2012 (see Table 4.6) is being used in this example.

Figure 4.8 Running Measures of Central Tendency in SPSS

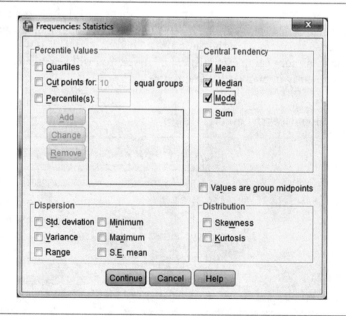

Figure 4.9   SPSS Output

Statistics

Number of death-sentenced prisoners received

N	Valid	36
	Missing	0
Mean		2.1667
Median		1.0000
Mode		.00

You can see from Figure 4.9 that the mean is identical to the result we arrived at by hand earlier. The mode is 0, which you can verify by looking at Table 4.6. The median is 1.00, meaning that half the states received less than one person in 2012, and half received more than one. We can also compare the mean and median to determine the shape of the distribution. With a mean of 2.17 and a median of 1.00, do you think that this distribution is normally distributed, positively skewed, or negatively skewed? If you said positively skewed, you are correct!

There is a GIGO alert relevant here. It is your responsibility to ensure that you use the correct measure(s) of central tendency given the level of measurement of the variable with which you are working. The SPSS program will not produce an error message if you make a mistake by, for instance, telling it to give you the mean of a nominal or ordinal variable. You will get a mean, just the same as you get when you correctly ask for the mean of a continuous variable. This statistical program is not a substitute for knowing which techniques are appropriate for which data types.

CHAPTER SUMMARY

This chapter introduced you to three measures of central tendency: the mode, median, and mean. These statistics offer summary information about the middle or average score in a data set. The mode is the most frequently occurring category or value in a data set. The mode can be used with variables of any measurement type (nominal, ordinal, interval, or ratio) and is the only measure that can be used with nominal variables. Its main weakness is in its simplicity and superficiality—it is generally not all that useful.

The median is a better measure than the mode for data measured at the ordinal or continuous level. The median is the value that splits a data set exactly in half. Since it is a positional measure, the median's value is not affected by the presence of extreme values—this makes the median a better reflection of the center of a distribution the mean is when a distribution is highly skewed. The median, though, does not utilize all data points in a distribution, which makes it less informative than the mean.

The mean is the arithmetic average of the data and is for use with continuous variables only. The mean accounts for all values in a data set, which is good because no data are omitted; however, the flipside is that the mean is susceptible to being pushed and pulled by extreme values.

It is good to report both the mean and the median because they can be compared to determine the shape of a distribution. In a normal distribution, these two statistics will be approximately equal. In a positively skewed distribution, the mean will be markedly greater than the median, and in a negatively skewed distribution, the mean will be noticeably smaller than the median. Reporting both of them provides your audience with much more information than they would have if you just reported one or the other.

The mode, the median, and the mean can all be obtained in SPSS using the *Analyze* → *Descriptive Statistics* → *Frequencies* sequence. As always, GIGO! When you order SPSS to produce a measure of central tendency, it is your responsibility to ensure that the measure you choose is appropriate to the variable's level of measurement. If you err, SPSS will probably not alert you to the mistake—you will get output that looks fine but is actually garbage. Be careful!

CHAPTER 4 REVIEW PROBLEMS

1. A survey item asks respondents "How many times have you shoplifted?" and allows them to fill in the appropriate number.

   a. What level of measurement is this variable?
   b. What measure or measures of central tendency can be computed on this variable?

2. A survey item asks respondents "How many times have you shoplifted?" and gives them the answer options: *0, 1–3, 4–6, 7 or more*.

   a. What level of measurement is this variable?
   b. What measure or measures of central tendency can be computed on this variable?

3. A survey item asks respondents "Have you ever shoplifted?" and tells them to circle *yes* or *no*.

   a. What level of measurement is this variable?
   b. What measure or measures of central tendency can be computed on this variable?

4. Explain what an extreme value is. Include in your answer (1) the effect extreme values have on the median, if any and (2) the effect extreme values have on the mean, if any.

5. Explain why the mean is the midpoint of the magnitudes. Include in your answer (1) what deviation scores are and how they are calculated and (2) what deviation scores always sum to.

6. In a negatively skewed distribution . . .

   a. the mean is less than the median.
   b. the mean is greater than the median.
   c. the mean and median are approximately equal.

7. In a normal distribution . . .

   a. the mean is less than the median.
   b. the mean is greater than the median.
   c. the mean and median are approximately equal.

8. In a positively skewed distribution . . .

   a. the mean is less than the median.
   b. the mean is greater than the median.
   c. the mean and median are approximately equal.

9. In a positively skewed distribution, the tail extends toward _____ of the number line.

   a. the positive side
   b. both sides
   c. the negative side

10. In a negatively skewed distribution, the tail extends toward _____ of the number line.

    a. the positive side
    b. both sides
    c. the negative side

11. The following table contains 2012 UCR data on the relationship between murder victims and their killers, among those crimes for which the relationship status is known.

Victim–Offender Relationships Among Murder Victims

Offender's Relationship to Victim	*f*
Family Member	1,005
Intimate Partner	1,256
Friend	343
Acquaintance	2,714
Other Nonstranger	133
Stranger	1,557
	$N = 7{,}008$

   a. Identify this variable's level of measurement and, based on that, state the appropriate measure or measures of central tendency.
   b. Determine or calculate the measure or measures of central tendency that you identified in part (a).

12. The frequency distribution in the following table shows rates of violent victimization, per victim racial group, in 2012 as per the National Crime Victim Survey (NCVS; Truman, Langton, & Planty, 2013). Use this table to do the following.

Violent Victimization Rate per 1,000 Persons

Race	Victimization Rate
Black/African American	34.2
White	25.2
Hispanic/Latino	24.5
American Indian/Alaska Native	46.9
Asian/Pacific Islander	16.4
$N = 5$	

a. Identify the median victimization rate using all three steps.
b. Compute the mean victimization rate across all racial groups.

13. Morgan, Morgan, and Boba (2010) report state and local government expenditures, by state, for police protection in the year 2007. The data in the following table contain a random sample of states and the dollars spent per capita in each state for police services.

Dollars Spent per Capita on Police Protection, 2007

State	Dollars
Illinois	317
Arkansas	170
Alabama	211
Ohio	258
Washington	219
Florida	345
Maine	176
Texas	220
$N = 8$	

a. Identify the median dollar amount using all three steps.
b. Calculate the mean dollar amount.

14. The following frequency distribution shows Law Enforcement Management and Administrative Statistics (LEMAS) data on the number of American Indian officers employed by local police agencies that have fewer than 75 total sworn employees.

American Indian Officers in the LEMAS Survey

Number	f	Number	f
0	1,167	14	1
1	62	15	1
2	8	23	1
3	3	24	1
4	3	32	1
9	2	37	1
12	1	59	1
			N = 1,253

a. Identify the modal number of American Indian officers in this sample of agencies.
b. Compute the mean number of American Indian officers in this sample.
c. The median number of American Indian officers is 0.00. Based on this median and the mean you calculated, would you say that this distribution is normally distributed, positively skewed, or negatively skewed? Explain your answer.

15. The following frequency distribution shows the number of juveniles arrested for embezzlement across all 50 states in 2012, according to the UCR.

Number of Juvenile Arrests for Embezzlement

Number	f	Number	f
0	7	11	1
1	7	12	3
2	4	13	1
3	7	14	1
4	4	19	1
5	1	20	1
6	1	23	1
8	3	27	1
9	2	29	1
10	2	30	1
			N = 50

a. Compute the mean number of juveniles arrested per state.

b. The median number of arrests was 3.50. Based on this median and the mean you calculated above, would you say that this distribution is normally distributed, positively skewed, or negatively skewed? Explain your answer.

16. The following table shows UCR data on the number of aggravated assaults that occurred in five Wyoming cities and towns in 2012.

Aggravated Assaults in Wyoming Jurisdictions

Urban Area	Assaults
Newcastle	3
Jackson	35
Laramie	17
Afton	0
Green River	72
$N = 5$	

a. Identify the median number of assaults in this sample.
b. Calculate the mean number of assaults.
c. Calculate each city's deviation score, and sum the scores.

17. The following table displays the number of juveniles arrested for arson in select states in 2012, according to the UCR.

Juveniles Arrested for Arson

State	Arrests
Alaska	13
Arkansas	9
Connecticut	32
Kansas	23
Montana	17
South Dakota	15
Vermont	8
$N = 7$	

    a. Identify the median number of arson arrests per state.

    b. Calculate the mean number of arrests in this sample.

    c. Calculate each state's deviation score and sum the scores.

18. The data set *NCVS for Chapter 4.sav* (**http://www.sagepub.com/gau**) contains the ages of respondents to the 2012 National Crime Victimization Survey. Run an SPSS analysis to determine the mode, the median, and the mean of this variable.

Helpful Hint: When running measures of central tendency on large data sets in SPSS, deselect the "Display frequency tables" option in the "Frequencies" dialog box. This will not alter the analyses you are running but will make your output cleaner and simpler to examine.

---

19. The data set *Weapons on School Property for Chapter 4.sav* (**http://www.sagepub.com/gau**) contains high school students' reports about whether they carried a weapon on school grounds in 2007 (Morgan et al., 2010). Run an SPSS analysis to determine the mode, the median, and the mean of this variable.

20. The data file *CSFACF for Chapter 4.sav* (**http://www.sagepub.com/gau**) contains a variable from the 2005 Census of State and Federal Adult Correctional Facilities showing the ratio of inmates to security staff per federally operated institution. Run an SPSS analysis to determine the mode, the median, and the mean of this variable.

KEY TERMS

Measures of central tendency	Negative skew	Mean
Normal distribution	Mode	Midpoint of the magnitudes
Positive skew	Median	Deviation score

GLOSSARY OF SYMBOLS AND ABBREVIATIONS INTRODUCED IN THIS CHAPTER

MP	Median position
Md	Median
$\bar{x}$	Mean
d_i	Deviation score for a raw score x_i

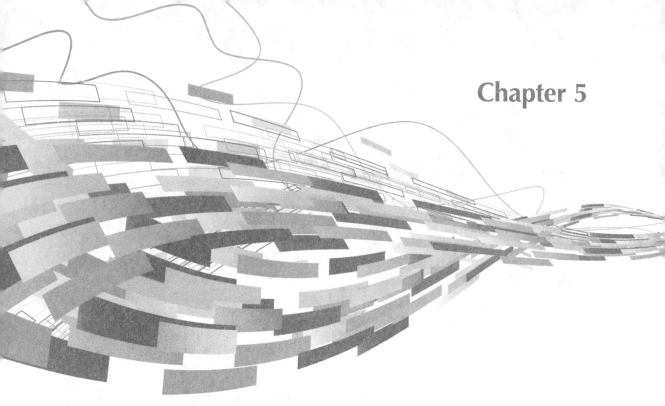

Measures of Dispersion

onsider this question: Do you think that there is more variability in the physical size of house cats or in that of dogs? In other words, if I gathered a random sample of house cats and a random sample of dogs, would I find a greater diversity of sizes and weights in the cat sample or in the dog sample? In the dog sample, of course! Dogs range from puny things you might lose in your sofa cushions all the way up to behemoths that look like they could eat your sofa. Cats, on the other hand, are . . . well, cat-sized. If I were to draw separate size distributions for dogs and house cats, they might look something like Figure 5.1.

The dog distribution would be wider and flatter than the cat distribution, while the cat distribution would appear somewhat tall and narrow as compared to the dog distribution. This is because dogs have greater variation in their size relative to cats.

Now, let us consider a situation in which two distributions have the same mean. (The dog and cat distributions would, of course, have different means.) Consider the hypothetical raw data for variables X_1 and X_2 in Table 5.1.

These distributions have the same mean, so if this was the only piece of information you had about them, you might be tempted to conclude that they are similar to one another. This conclusion would be quite wrong, though. Look at Figure 5.2, which displays a line chart for these two variables. Which series do you think represents Sample 1? Sample 2? If you said that the stars are Sample 1 and diamonds are Sample 2, you are correct. You can see that the raw scores of Sample 1 cluster quite tightly around the mean, while Sample 2's scores are scattered about in a much less cohesive manner.

The previous examples highlight the importance of the subject of this chapter: measures of dispersion. Dispersion (sometimes also called variability) is the amount of "spread" present in a set of raw scores. Dogs have more dispersion in physical size than house cats have, just as Sample 2 has more dispersion than Sample 1 has. Measures of dispersion are vital from an informational standpoint for the reason exemplified by the thought experiment just presented—measures of central tendency convey only so much information about a distribution and can actually be misleading,

---

Dispersion: The amount of spread or variability among the scores in a distribution.

Figure 5.1 Hypothetical Distributions of Dog and House Cat Sizes

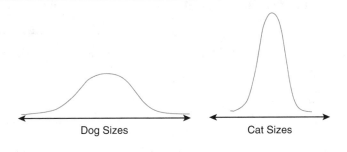

Dog Sizes   Cat Sizes

Table 5.1   Hypothetical Data in Two Samples

Sample 1	Sample 2
10	0
11	15
9	20
10	5
10	10
$\bar{x}_1 = 10$	$\bar{x}_2 = 10$

Figure 5.2   Line Chart for Variables X_1 and X_2

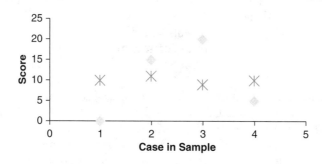

because it is possible for two very discrepant distributions to have similar means. It is also necessary to know the shape of a data distribution so that you can assess whether it appears fairly normal or whether it deviates from normality. We talked about skew in Chapter 3—skew occurs when values tend to cluster at one end of the distribution or the other. The dispersion analog of skew is kurtosis. There are two types of kurtosis: Leptokurtosis happens when values cluster together very tightly, and platykurtosis is evident when values are markedly spread out. In Figure 5.1, the dog-size distribution is platykurtic (representing a spread-out smattering of values) and the cat-size curve is leptokurtic (indicating that values are highly clustered and have minimal variability).

Kurtosis: A measure of how much a distribution curve's width departs from normality.

Leptokurtosis: A measure of how peaked or clustered a distribution is.

Platykurtosis: A measure of how flat or spread out a distribution is.

For all these reasons, measures of dispersion are necessary pieces of information about any distribution. They go hand in hand with measures of central tendency, and the two types of descriptive statistics are usually presented alongside one another. This chapter discusses four of the most common types of measures of dispersion: variation ratio, range, variance, and standard deviation. Like measures of central tendency, each measure of dispersion is suitable only for variables of certain levels of measurement. The chapter ends with an overview of SPSS.

The Variation Ratio

The **variation ratio** (*VR*) is the only measure of dispersion discussed in this chapter that can be used with categorical (nominal and ordinal) data; the remainder of the measures that will be covered can only be employed when a variable is continuous (interval or ratio). The *VR* is based on the mode (see Chapter 4) and measures the proportion of cases that are *not* in the modal category.

Recall from the discussion of proportions in Chapter 3 that the proportion of cases that are in a certain category can be found using Formula 3(1): $p = \dfrac{f}{N}$. It is easy to take this formula a step further in order to calculate the proportion that is not in a particular category.

Variation ratio: A measure of dispersion for variables of any level of measurement that is calculated as the proportion of cases located outside the modal category. Symbolized as *VR*.

Bounding rule: The rule stating that all proportions range from 0.00 to 1.00.

Rule of the complement: Based on the bounding rule, the rule stating that the proportion of cases that are not in a certain category can be found by subtracting the proportion that are in that category from 1.00.

For this inquiry, we rely on the **bounding rule**, which states that proportions always range from 0.00 to 1.00. The bounding rule leads to the **rule of the complement**. This rule states that the proportion of cases in a certain category (call this category *A*) and the proportion located in other categories (call this *Not A*) always sum to 1.00. Formally,

$$p(A) + p(Not\ A) = 1.00$$

If $p(A)$ is known, the formula can be reconfigured thusly in order to calculate $p(Not\ A)$:

$$p(Not\ A) = 1.00 - p(A) \hspace{3cm} \text{Formula 5(1)}$$

The variation ratio is a spinoff of the rule of the complement:

$$VR = 1.00 - \frac{f_{mode}}{N}, \hspace{3cm} \text{Formula 5(2)}$$

where f_{mode} = the number of cases in the modal category and

N = the sample size.

To illustrate use of the *VR*, consider Table 5.2, which contains data from the National Census of State Prosecutors (NCSCP; see Data Sources 5.1) on the size of the population served by full-time prosecutorial offices (Perry & Banks, 2011).

Table 5.2   Population Served by Full-Time Prosecutors' Offices

Population Served	*f*
1,000,000 or more	43
250,000 to 999,999	211
100,000 to 249,999	341
99,999 or fewer	1,389
	$N = 1,984$

To compute the *VR*, first identify the mode and its associated frequency. Here, the mode is *99,999 or fewer* and its frequency is 1,389. Now, plug the numbers into Formula 5(2):

$$VR = 1.00 - \frac{1,389}{1,984} = 1.00 - .70 = .30$$

The variation ratio is .30, which means that .30 (30%) of the cases fall outside the modal category. This is a fairly limited amount of variation—70% of offices serve relatively small populations, and just 30% serve midsized or large jurisdictions.

DATA SOURCES 5.1

National Census of State Court Prosecutors

Every 4 to 5 years, the Bureau of Justice Statistics (BJS) sends surveys to chief prosecutors in state courts. Some of the waves utilize random samples of all offices nationwide, and some waves employ censuses (i.e., contain the total population of offices). The most recent available wave is that for 2007, which was a census. The survey is delivered by phone, Internet, or mail to chief prosecutors, who are asked to report on various aspects of their offices' organization and operation. The data set contains information such as the number of attorneys on staff, the number of felony cases closed in the prior year, and whether the office regularly makes use of DNA analysis.

Table 5.3 displays another variable from the NCSCP. This survey item asked prosecutors whether, in the past year, their offices had pursued criminal actions against defendants suspected of elder abuse.

Table 5.3   Prosecution of Elder-Abuse Cases

Prosecuted Elder-Abuse Case in Past Year?	f
Yes	1,092
No	887
	$N = 1,979$

The mode is *Yes,* and the variation ratio is

$$VR = 1.00 - \frac{1,092}{1,979} = 1.00 - .55 = .45.$$

This *VR* of .45 is quite close to .50, indicating that the offices were split nearly in half with respect to whether or not they had prosecuted cases of elder abuse.

In sum, the variation ratio offers information about whether the data tend to cluster inside the modal category or a fair number of the cases are in other categories. This statistic can be used with nominal and ordinal variables, which makes it unique relative to the range, variance, and standard deviation. The problem with the *VR* is that it uses only a small portion of the data available in a distribution. It indicates the proportion of cases not in the modal category, but it does not actually show where those cases are located. It would be nice to know where the data are rather than merely where they are not.

LEARNING CHECK

The bounding rule and the rule of the complement are going to resurface in later chapters, so it is a good idea to make sure that you fully understand them before moving on to the next section of this chapter. To check your comprehension of this idea, quickly fill in the following blanks.

- 55% of a sample is female, and ____% is male.
- 96% of defendants in a sample were convicted, and ____% were not.
- A judge choosing from three sentencing options gave 70% of defendants jail time, 20% probation, and the remaining ____% fines.

The Range

The **range** (R) is the simplest measure of dispersion for continuous-level variables. It measures the span of the data or, in other words, the distance between the smallest and largest values. The range is very easy to compute:

$$R = x_{maximum} - x_{minimum}$$

Formula 5(3)

The first step in computing the range is identification of the maximum and minimum values in the data set. The minimum is then subtracted from the maximum, as shown in Formula 5(3). That is all there is to it!

For an example, we can use data from the Uniform Crime Reports (UCR; Data Sources 1.1) on the number of juveniles arrested on suspicion of homicide in 2012 in eight states. Table 5.4 shows the data.

Range: A measure of dispersion for continuous variables that is calculated by subtracting the smallest score from the largest. Symbolized as R.

To calculate the range, first identify the maximum and minimum values. The maximum is 20 and the minimum is 0. The range, then, is

$$R = 20 - 0 = 20.$$

Another example of the calculation of the range can be found using a different variable from the NCSCP. This variable collects information about the salary of the chief prosecutor in each office. Table 5.5 shows these data for the eight districts in Maine.

Table 5.4   Number of Juveniles Arrested for Homicide by State, 2012

State	Arrests
Maine	1
New Hampshire	0
Vermont	0
Massachusetts	2
Rhode Island	0
Connecticut	4
New York	15
New Jersey	20
$N = 8$	

Table 5.5 Chief Prosecutor's Salary in Maine Districts

District	Salary
District 1	87,573.00
District 2	91,628.60
District 3	66,511.06
District 4	97,500.00
District 5	98,000.00
District 6	96,860.33
District 7	97,572.00
District 8	97,000.00
$N = 8$	

The largest value in Table 5.5 is 98,000, and the smallest is 66,511.06, so the range is

$$R = 98,000 - 66,511.06 = 31,488.94.$$

There is a difference of nearly $32,000 between the lowest-paid and the highest-paid chief prosecutors in Maine.

The range has advantages and disadvantages. First, it is a nice measure because it is simple and straightforward. It offers useful information and is easy to calculate and understand. This same feature, however, makes this measure of dispersion too simplistic to be of much use. The range is a very superficial measure of dispersion and offers minimal information about a variable. It is silent as to the distribution of the data, such as whether they are normally distributed or whether there is kurtosis present. The range can be misleading, too: Table 5.5 shows clearly that salaries cluster at the upper end of the distribution (i.e., around the $90,000 mark) and that the salary of $66,511.06 is an outlier. The range of $31,488.94 is mathematically correct but, in a practical sense, overstates the amount of variation in salaries. Finally, because the range does not use all of the available data, it has no place in further computations.

LEARNING CHECK

If most prosecutors' salaries nationwide were between $90,000 and $100,000, with very few values that are higher or lower, would this distribution be normally distributed, leptokurtic, or platykurtic? Explain your answer.

The Variance

Like the range, the variance can only be used with continuous data; unlike the range, the variance utilizes every number in a data set. The variance and its offshoot, the standard deviation (discussed next), are the quintessential measures of dispersion. You will see them repeatedly throughout the remainder of the book. For this reason, it is crucial that you develop a comprehensive understanding of them both formulaically and conceptually.

Variance: A measure of dispersion calculated as the mean of the squared deviation scores. Notated as s^2.

The formula for the variance can appear rather intimidating, so let us work our way up to it piece by piece and gradually construct it. We will use the *Number of Juveniles Arrested for Homicide* data from Table 5.4 to illustrate the computation as we go. First, you should recall the concept of deviation scores that was discussed in the last chapter. Go back and review if necessary. A deviation score (symbolized d_i) is the difference between a raw score in a distribution and that distribution's mean. Recall Formula 4(4):

$$d_i = x_i - \overline{x},$$

where x_i = a given data point and

$\overline{x}$ = the sample mean.

The variance is constructed from mean-based deviation scores. The first step in computing the variance is to compute the mean, and the second is to find the deviation score for each raw value in a data set. The first piece of the variance formula, therefore, is $x_i - \overline{x}$ or every raw score x_i in the data. Table 5.6a shows the original data from Table 5.4 along with a deviation score column to the right of the raw scores. The mean of the data set has been calculated. In the deviation score column, the mean has been subtracted from each raw score to produce a variety of positive and negative deviation scores. Recall that the sigma symbol (Σ) is a summation sign.

Deviation scores are a good first step, but what we end up with is an array of numbers. A table full of deviation scores is no more informative than a table full of raw scores. What we need is a summary statistic of some kind, a single number that represents all of the individual deviation scores. The most obvious measure is the sum—sums are good ways of packaging multiple numbers into a single numerical term. The problem with this approach, though, should be obvious: As discussed in Chapter 4, deviation scores sum to zero. The sum of the deviation-score column will always be zero (or within rounding error of it), which makes summing useless as a measure of variance.

Since the sum of the deviation scores should always be zero or within rounding error of it, you can check your math up to this stage of the variance computation procedure by ensuring that the sum of your calculated deviation scores is zero or within rounding error of it. As practice, use your calculator to sum the deviation scores in Table 5.6b.

Table 5.6a   Number of Juveniles Arrested for Homicide in Eight States, 2012

State	Arrests	$x_i - \bar{x}$
Maine	1	$1 - 5.25 = -4.25$
New Hampshire	0	$0 - 5.25 = -5.25$
Vermont	0	$0 - 5.25 = -5.25$
Massachusetts	2	$2 - 5.25 = -3.25$
Rhode Island	0	$0 - 5.25 = -5.25$
Connecticut	4	$4 - 5.25 = -1.25$
New York	15	$15 - 5.25 = 9.75$
New Jersey	20	$20 - 5.25 = 14.75$
$N = 8$	$\bar{x} = \dfrac{\Sigma x}{N} = \dfrac{42}{8} = 5.25$	$\Sigma(x_i - \bar{x})$

We need to find a way to get rid of those pesky negative signs. If all of the numbers were positive, it would be impossible for the sum to be zero. Squaring is used to accomplish this objective. Squaring each deviation score eliminates the negative signs (because negative numbers always become positive when squared), and, as long as the squaring is applied to all of the scores, it is not a problematic transformation of the numbers. Table 5.6b contains a new right-hand column showing the squared version of each deviation score.

Now the numbers can be summed. We can write the sum of the right-hand column in Table 5.6b as $\Sigma(x_i - \bar{x})^2$ and we can compute the answer as such:

$$\Sigma(x_i - \bar{x})^2 = 18.06 + 27.56 + 27.56 + 10.56 + 27.56 + 1.56 + 95.06 + 217.56 = 425.48$$

This sum represents the total squared deviations from the mean. We are not quite done yet, though, because sample size must be taken into consideration in order to control for the number of scores present in the variance computation. The sum of the squared deviation scores must be divided by the sample size.

Table 5.6b Variance Calculation Table for Number of Juveniles Arrested for Homicide in Eight States, 2012

State	Arrests	$x_i - \bar{x}$	$(x_i - \bar{x})^2$
Maine	1	$1 - 5.25 = -4.25$	$(-4.25)^2 = 18.06$
New Hampshire	0	$0 - 5.25 = -5.25$	$(-5.25)^2 = 27.56$
Vermont	0	$0 - 5.25 = -5.25$	$(-5.25)^2 = 27.56$
Massachusetts	2	$2 - 5.25 = -3.25$	$(-3.25)^2 = 10.56$
Rhode Island	0	$0 - 5.25 = -5.25$	$(-5.25)^2 = 27.56$
Connecticut	4	$4 - 5.25 = -1.25$	$(-1.25)^2 = 1.56$
New York	15	$15 - 5.25 = 9.75$	$(9.75)^2 = 95.06$
New Jersey	20	$20 - 5.25 = 14.75$	$(14.75)^2 = 217.56$
$N = 8$	$\bar{x} = \dfrac{\Sigma x}{N} = \dfrac{42}{8} = 5.25$	$\Sigma(x_i - \bar{x}) = 0.00$	$\Sigma(x_i - \bar{x})^2 = 425.48$

LEARNING CHECK

Standardizing sums by dividing them by the sample size is a standard practice in statistics, as later chapters will continue to demonstrate. To understand the need for this type of division, imagine one sample that has 10 cases that sum to 100 and another sample containing 50 cases that sum to 100. Calculate the mean for each of these samples, and explain why they are different.

There is a bit of a hiccup, however: The variance formula for samples tends to produce an estimate of the population variance that is downwardly biased (i.e., too small) because samples are littler than populations and therefore contain less variability. This problem is especially evident in very small samples, such as when $N < 50$.

The way to correct for this bias in sample-based estimates of population variances is to subtract 1.00 from the sample size in the formula for the variance. The sample variance is symbolized s^2, whereas the population variance is symbolized σ^2, which is a lowercase sigma. The reason for the exponent is that, as described earlier, the variance is composed of squared deviation scores. The symbol s^2 thus signifies the squared nature of this statistic.

We can now assemble the entire s^2 formula and compute the variance of the juvenile homicide arrest data. The formula for the sample variance is

$$s^2 = \frac{\Sigma\left(x_i - \bar{x}\right)^2}{N - 1}$$

Formula 5(4)

Plugging in the numbers and solving yields

$$s^2 = \frac{425.48}{8-1} = \frac{425.48}{7} = 60.78.$$

The variance of the juvenile homicide arrest data is 60.78. This is the average squared deviation from the mean in this data set.

Let's try a second example of the variance. The National Census of State Court Prosecutors captures the number of felony cases each office tried before a jury in the past year. The vast majority of criminal defendants nationwide plead guilty, with a small portion opting to exercise their right to trial by jury. Table 5.7a shows the number of felony jury trials handled in the past year by a random sample of offices serving populations of 50,000 or less. (The letters in the left column represent the offices.) Table 5.7b displays the deviation scores and squared deviation scores.

Table 5.7a   Number of Felony Jury Trials Handled by Prosecutors' Offices

Office	Trials
A	8
B	15
C	12
D	10
E	1
F	40
G	16
N = 7	

Table 5.7b   Variance Calculation Table for Number of Felony Jury Trials Handled by Prosecutors' Offices

Office	Trials	$x_i - \bar{x}$	$(x_i - \bar{x})^2$
A	8	−6.57	274.56
B	15	.43	.18
C	12	−2.57	6.60
D	10	−4.57	20.88
E	1	−13.57	184.14
F	40	25.43	646.68
G	16	1.43	2.04
N = 7	$\bar{x} = \frac{102}{7} = 14.57$	$\Sigma(x_i - \bar{x}) = .00$	$\Sigma(x_i - \bar{x})^2 = 1{,}135.08$

Applying Formula 5(4),

$$s^2 = \frac{1{,}135.08}{7-1} = \frac{1{,}135.08}{6} = 189.18.$$

These offices' jury-trial variance is 189.18.

The variance is preferable to the variation ratio and range because it uses all of the raw scores in a data set and is therefore a more informative measure of dispersion. It offers information about how far the scores are from the mean. Every case in the sample is used when the variance is calculated. When the data are continuous, the variance is better than either the *VR* or the range.

LEARNING CHECK

Variances and squared deviation scores are always positive; it is impossible to do the calculations correctly and arrive at a negative answer. Why is this?

The Standard Deviation

Despite its usefulness, the variance has an unfortunate hitch. When we squared the deviations (refer to Table 5.7b), by definition we also squared the *units* in which those deviations were measured. The variance of the juvenile homicide arrest data, then, is 234.25 *arrests squared*, and the variance for prosecutors' offices is 189.18 *trials squared*. This obviously makes no sense. The variance produces oddities such as *crimes squared* and *years squared*. The variance is also difficult to interpret—the concept of the "average squared deviation score" is not intuitive and does not provide a readily understandable description of the data. Something needs to be done to correct this. Luckily, a solution is at hand. Since the problem was created by squaring, it can be solved by doing the opposite of squaring—taking the square root. The square root of the variance (symbolized *s*, or sometimes *sd*) is the **standard deviation**:

$$s = \sqrt{\frac{\Sigma\left(x_i - \bar{x}\right)^2}{N-1}} = \sqrt{s^2} \qquad\qquad \textit{Formula 5(5)}$$

The standard deviation of the juvenile homicide arrest data is

$$s = \sqrt{60.78} = 7.80.$$

And *s* for the prosecutors' jury trials is

$$s = \sqrt{189.18} = 13.75.$$

The square root transformation restores the original units; we are back to *arrests* and *trials* now and have solved the problem of impossible and nonsensical squares. Note that the standard deviation—just like the squared deviation scores and the variance—can never be negative.

Standard deviation: Computed as the square root of the variance, a measure of dispersion that is the mean of the deviation scores. Notated as *s* or *sd*.

Substantively interpreted, the standard deviation is the mean of the deviation scores. In other words, it is the average distance between the individual raw scores and the distribution mean. It indicates the general spread of the data by conveying information as to whether the raw values cluster close to the mean (thereby producing a relatively small standard deviation) or are more dispersed (producing a relatively large standard deviation). The standard deviation is generally presented in conjunction with the mean in the description of a continuous variable. We can say, then, that in 2012, the eight states considered here had a mean of 5.25 juvenile arrests for homicides, with a standard deviation of 7.80. Similarly, this sample of prosecutors' offices handled a mean of 14.57 felony jury trials, with a standard deviation of 13.75.

The standard deviation is reported more often than the variance is, for the reasons explained earlier. It is a good idea to present the *sd* in conjunction with any mean that you report (and to expect others to do the same!). We will be using the standard deviation a lot in later chapters; it is a fundamental descriptive statistic. The standard deviation also has another useful property: It can be employed to determine the upper and lower boundaries of the "typical" range in a normal distribution. When you know the mean and standard deviation for a sample, you can find out some important things about that distribution, as discussed in the next section.

The Standard Deviation and the Normal Curve

Recall that the standard deviation is the mean of the deviation scores; in other words, it is the mean deviation between each raw score and the distribution mean. Larger standard deviations represent greater variability, whereas smaller ones suggest less dispersion. Figure 5.3 displays the relationship between the mean and the standard deviation pictorially for populations and samples.

Figure 5.3   Mean and Standard Deviation for a Normally Distributed, Continuous Variable

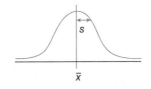

Like the mean, the standard deviation plays a key role in many statistical analyses. We will be using both the mean and the standard deviation a lot in the following chapters; therefore, be sure that you have a solid grasp on the calculation and the interpretation of the standard deviation. As practice, revisit Table 5.5 and try calculating the standard deviation of chief prosecutors' salaries.

RESEARCH EXAMPLE 5.1

Does the South Have a Culture of Honor That Increases Gun Violence?

Scholars have frequently noted that the South leads the nation in rates of violence and that gun violence is particularly prevalent in this region. This has led to the formation and proposal of multiple theories attempting to explain Southern states' disproportionate involvement in gun violence. One of these theories is the "culture of honor" thesis that predicts that white male Southerners are more likely than their counterparts in other regions of the country to react violently when they feel that they have been disrespected or that they, their family, or their property has been threatened. Copes, Kovandzic, Miller, and Williamson (2014) tested this theory using data from a large, nationally representative survey of adults' reported gun ownership and defensive gun use (the use of a gun to ward off a perceived attacker). A primary independent variable was whether respondents themselves currently lived in the South.

The main dependent variable was the number of times respondents had used a firearm (either fired or merely brandished) to defend themselves or their property against a perceived human threat within the past 5 years. The researchers reported the following descriptive statistics:

The authors ran a statistical analysis to determine if living in the South or in a state where the majority of the population was born in the South was related to defensive gun use. They found that it was not: Neither currently living in the South nor living in a state populated primarily with southerners increased the likelihood that respondents had used a gun defensively in the past 5 years. These findings refuted the Southern culture of honor thesis by suggesting that Southern white males are no more likely than white males in other areas of the country to resort to firearms to defend themselves.

Variable	Mean	Standard Deviation	Percentage
DV: Number of defensive gun uses in the past 5 years	1.04	.19	
Percentage of sample currently living in the South			34.0
Percentage of white state population born in the South	70.88	12.85	
White homicide rates in cities of respondents' residence	5.60	3.45	
Respondents' perceptions of crime in their neighborhoods (5-point scale)	2.50	1.12	

Source: Adapted from Table 1 in Copes, Kovandzic, Miller, and Williamson (2014).

A fundamental characteristic of any normal distribution, such as those displayed in Figure 5.4, is that approximately two-thirds of the scores in the distribution lie within one standard deviation below and one standard deviation above the mean. This distance between one standard deviation below and one standard deviation above the mean constitutes the "normal" or "typical" range in a distribution. Let us suppose that we have a sample of house cats with a mean weight of 11 pounds and a standard deviation of 2 pounds (see Figure 5.5). We can find the range of weights that fall within the "normal" zone using subtraction and addition. Two-thirds of the cats would be between 11 − 2 = 9 pounds (i.e., one standard deviation below the mean) and 11 + 2 = 13 pounds (one *sd* above the mean). The remaining one-third would weigh less than 9 pounds (i.e., they would be more than one *sd* below the mean) or more than 13 pounds (greater than one *sd* above the mean). These extreme values would indeed occur, but with relatively low frequency. People, objects, and places tend to cluster around their group means, with extreme values being infrequent and improbable. Remember this point; we will come back to it in later chapters.

Whenever you know the mean and standard deviation of a normally distributed, continuous variable, you can find the two values between which two-thirds of the cases lie (i.e., the outer boundaries of the "typical" area). In a distribution with a mean of 100 and a standard deviation of 15, two-thirds of cases will be between 85 and 115.

LEARNING CHECK

The concept regarding two-thirds of cases lying between −1*sd* and +1*sd* will form a fundamental aspect of later discussions. You will need to understand this concept both mathematically and conceptually. Practice computing the upper and lower limits using the means and the standard deviations listed in the table in Research Example 5.2.

Figure 5.4 In a Normal Distribution, Approximately Two-Thirds of the Scores Lie Within One Standard Deviation of the Mean

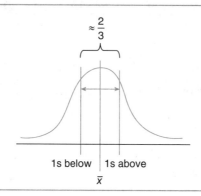

1s below | 1s above
$\bar{x}$

Figure 5.5 Hypothetical Distribution of House Cats' Weights

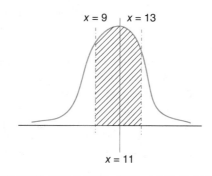

$x = 9$ $x = 13$

$x = 11$

RESEARCH EXAMPLE 5.2

Why Does Punishment Often Increase—Rather Than Reduce—Criminal Offending?

Deterrence is perhaps the most pervasive and ingrained punishment philosophy in the United States and, indeed, in much of the world. It is commonly assumed that punishing someone for a criminal transgression will lessen the likelihood of that person reoffending in the future. Several studies have noted, however, that offending actually *increases* after someone has been punished. Offenders who have been caught, moreover, tend to believe that their likelihood of being caught again are very low because they think that is improbable that the same event would happen to them twice. This flawed probabilistic reasoning is called the "gambler's bias."

Pogarsky and Piquero (2003) attempted to learn more about the way that the gambler's bias may distort people's perceptions of the likelihood of getting caught for criminal wrongdoing. They distributed a survey with a drunk driving scenario to a sample of university students and asked the respondents about two dependent variables: (a) on a scale of 0 to 100, how likely they would be to drive under the influence in this hypothetical situation, and (b) on a scale of 0 to 100, how likely it is that they would be caught by police if they did drive while intoxicated. The researchers also gathered data on several independent variables, such as respondents' criminal histories (which were used to create a risk index scale), levels of impulsivity in decision making, and ability to correctly identify the probability of a flipped coin landing on tails after having landed heads side up four times in a row. The coin-flip question tapped into respondents' ability to use probabilistic reasoning correctly; those who said that the coin is more likely to land tails up were coded as engaging in the type of logical fallacy embodied by the gambler's bias. The researchers obtained the following means and standard deviations.

Pogarsky and Piquero divided the sample into those at high risk of offending and those at low risk, and then analyzed the relationship between the gambler's fallacy and perceived certainty of punishment within each group. They found that the high-risk respondents' perceptions of certainty were not affected by the gambler's bias; even though 26% of people in this group did engage in flawed assessments of probabilities, this fallacious reasoning did not impact respondents' perceptions of the certainty of punishment.

Variable	Mean	Standard Deviation
DV: Offending likelihood	38.28	36.14
DV: Perceived certainty of punishment	28.48	36.13
Number times pulled over while driving drunk	.24	.63
Number of days in past month consumed 3+ drinks	4.69	5.00
Number of times shoplifted	3.69	11.74
Number of times vandalized property	3.78	4.46
Number of 10 closest friends who have driven drunk at least once	4.50	3.34
Total risk index score	4.84	2.67

Source: Adapted from appendix in Pogarsky and Piquero (2003).

(Continued)

(Continued)

Among low-risk respondents, however, there was a tendency for those who engaged in flawed probabilistic reasoning to believe that they stood a very low chance of detection relative to those low-risk respondents who accurately assessed the probability of a coin flip landing tails side up. The researchers concluded that people who are at high risk of offending may not even stop to ponder their likelihood of being caught and will proceed with a criminal act when they feel so inclined. Those at low risk, on the other hand, attempt to utilize probabilities to predict their chances of being apprehended and punished. The gambler's fallacy, therefore, may operate only among relatively naive offenders who attempt to use probabilistic reasoning when making a decision about whether or not to commit a criminal offense.

SPSS

SPSS offers ranges, variances, and standard deviations. It will not provide you with variation ratios, but those are easy to calculate by hand. The process for obtaining measures of dispersion in SPSS is very similar to that for measures of central tendency. The juvenile homicide data set from Table 5.4 will be used to illustrate SPSS. First, use the *Analyze* → *Descriptive Statistics* → *Frequencies* sequence to produce the main dialog box. Then click the *Statistics* button in the upper right to produce the box displayed in Figure 5.6. Select *Std. deviation*, *Variance*, and *Range* to obtain these three statistics. (SPSS does not offer the variation ratio.)

Figure 5.6   Using SPSS to Obtain Measures of Dispersion

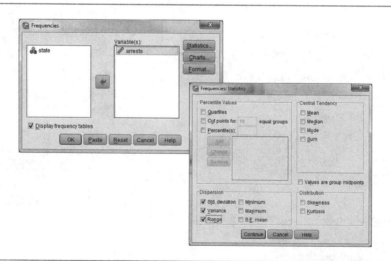

After you click *Continue* and *OK,* the output in Figure 5.7 will be produced.

You can see in Figure 5.6 that all of the numbers generated by SPSS match those that we obtained by hand. This data set is called *Juvenile Arrests for Chapter 5.sav* and is located on the companion website (http://www.sagepub.com/gau). Open this data file and run these measures of dispersion to replicate Figure 5.7.

Figure 5.7   SPSS Output for Measures of Dispersion

Statistics

Number of juveniles arrested for homicide, 2012

N	Valid	8
	Missing	0
Std. Deviation		7.797
Variance		60.786
Range		20

CHAPTER SUMMARY

This chapter introduced four measures of dispersion: variation ratio, range, variance, and standard deviation. *VR* tells you the proportion of cases not located in the modal category. *VR* can be computed on data of any level of measurement; however, it is the only measure of dispersion covered in this chapter that is available for use with categorical data. Range, variance, and standard deviation, conversely, can be used only with continuous variables.

The range is the distance between the lowest and highest value on a variable. The range provides useful information and so should be reported in order to give audiences comprehensive information about a variable; however, this measure's usefulness is severely limited by the fact that it only accounts for the two most extreme numbers in a distribution. It ignores everything that is going on between those two endpoints.

The variance improves on the range by utilizing all of the raw scores on a variable. The variance is based on deviation scores and is an informative measure of dispersion. This measure, though, has a conceptual problem: Because computation of the variance requires all of the deviation scores to be squared, the units in which the raw scores are measured also ends up getting squared. The variance thus suffers from a lack of interpretability.

The solution to the conceptual problem with the variance is to take the square root of the variance. The square root of the variance is the standard deviation. The standard deviation is the mean of the deviation scores. Raw scores have a mean, and so do deviation scores. The former is simply called the mean, and the latter is the standard deviation.

The mean and the standard deviation together are a staple set of descriptive statistics for continuous variables. The standard deviation will be key to many of the concepts that we will be discussing in the next few chapters. Approximately two-thirds of the cases in any normal distribution are located between one standard deviation below and one standard deviation above the mean. These scores are within the normal or typical range; scores that are more than one standard deviation below or above the mean are relatively uncommon.

CHAPTER 5 REVIEW PROBLEMS

1. Explain the reason why measures of dispersion are necessary in addition to measures of central tendency. That is, what information is given by measures of dispersion that is not provided by measures of central tendency?

2. A data distribution that was very narrow and peaked would be considered

    a. normal.
    b. platykurtic.
    c. leptokurtic.

3. In a normal curve, approximately _____ of values are between one standard deviation above and one standard deviation below the mean.

4. A data distribution that was very flat and spread out would be considered

    a. normal.
    b. platykurtic.
    c. leptokurtic.

5. The following table contains data from the Census of State and Federal Adult Correctional Facilities. Compute the variation ratio.

Security Level	f
Minimum	969
Medium	480
Maximum	350
Super maximum	22
	N = 1,821

6. The following table contains data from the Census of State and Federal Adult Correctional Facilities. Compute the variation ratio.

Gender of Inmates Housed in Facility	f
Male only	1,358
Female only	187
Both	276
	N = 1,821

7. The following table contains data from the Census of State and Federal Adult Correctional Facilities. Compute the variation ratio.

Race of Security Staff	f
White	3,131
Black	809
Hispanic	327
Other	97
	N = 4,364

8. The table below contains UCR data showing the rate of officer assaults (per 100 officers) in each of the four regions of the country. Use this table to do the following.

Region	Assaults per 100 Officers
Northeast	8.20
Midwest	9.90
South	10.20
West	11.60
N = 4	

a. Calculate the range.
b. Calculate the mean assault rate.
c. Calculate the variance.
d. Calculate the standard deviation.

9. The following table shows data from the Bureau of Justice Statistics on the number of death-row inmates housed by states in the Midwest. Use this table to do the following.

State	Inmates
Indiana	12
Kansas	9
Missouri	47
Nebraska	11
Ohio	139
South Dakota	3
N = 6	

a. Calculate the range.
b. Calculate the mean number of inmates per state.
c. Calculate the variance.
d. Calculate the standard deviation.

10. The following table contains UCR data on the number of murders in eight states that were committed with firearms in 2012. Use this table to do the following.

State	Murders
Alaska	11
Hawaii	3
Maine	14
Idaho	17
Nebraska	42
New Hampshire	9
Wisconsin	108
Utah	49
$N = 8$	

a. Calculate the range.
b. Calculate the mean number of firearm-perpetrated murders in these states.
c. Calculate the variance.
d. Calculate the standard deviation.

11. The following table shows UCR data on the percentage of burglaries cleared by arrest, as broken down by region. Use this table to do the following.

Region	Clearance Rate
New England	12.60
Middle Atlantic	16.60
East North Central	10.00
West North Central	12.20
South Atlantic	15.80
East South Central	13.20

Region	Clearance Rate
West South Central	10.40
Mountain	10.20
Pacific	11.80
$N = 9$	

    a. Calculate the range.

    b. Calculate the mean clearance rate per region.

    c. Calculate the variance.

    d. Calculate the standard deviation.

12. For each of the following means and standard deviations, calculate the upper and lower limits of the middle two-thirds of the distribution.

    a. $\bar{x} = 6.00$, $sd = 1.50$

    b. $\bar{x} = 14.00$, $sd = 3.40$

    c. $\bar{x} = 109.32$, $sd = 14.98$

13. For each of the following means and standard deviations, calculate the upper and lower limits of the middle two-thirds of the distribution.

    a. $\bar{x} = 63.10$, $sd = 18.97$

    b. $\bar{x} = 1.75$, $sd = .35$

    c. $\bar{x} = 450.62$, $sd = 36.48$

14. Explain the conceptual problem with the variance that is the reason why the standard deviation is generally used instead.

15. Explain the concept behind the standard deviation; that is, what does the standard deviation represent substantively?

16. The companion website (http://www.sagepub.com/gau) has an SPSS file called *Firearm Murders for Chapter 5.sav* that contains 2012 UCR data showing the percentage of murders, per state, that were committed with firearms. (Note that there are only 49 states in this file because Florida did not submit UCR data in 2012.) Use SPSS to obtain the range, the variance, and the standard deviation for the variable *pctfirearm*.

17. There is an SPSS file called *Census of State Prosecutors for Chapter 5.sav* on the website (http://www.sagepub.com/gau) that contains data from the 2007 National Census of State Court Prosecutors. This data set contains three variables. For the variable *yearsinoffice*, which measures the number of years chief prosecutors have held their positions, use SPSS to obtain the range, the standard deviation, and the variance.

18. Using *Census of State Prosecutors for Chapter 5.sav*, use SPSS to obtain the range, standard deviation, and variance of the variable *assistants*, which shows the number of full-time assistant prosecutors employed by each office.

19. Using *Census of State Prosecutors for Chapter 5.sav* and the variable *felclosed*, which captures the number of felony cases each office closed in 2007, use SPSS to obtain the range, the standard deviation, and the variance.

KEY TERMS

Dispersion
Kurtosis
Leptokurtosis
Platykurtosis

Variation ratio
Bounding rule
Rule of the complement
Range

Standard deviation
Variance

GLOSSARY OF SYMBOLS AND ABBREVIATIONS INTRODUCED IN THIS CHAPTER

VR	Variation ratio
R	Range
s^2	Variance
s	Standard deviation
sd	Alternative notation for the standard deviation

Part

2

Probability and
Distributions

Part 1 of this book introduced you to descriptive statistics. You learned the mathematical and conceptual underpinnings of proportions, means, standard deviations, and other statistics that describe various aspects of data distributions. Many times, though, researchers want to do more than merely describe a sample—they want to run a statistical test to analyze relationships between two or more variables. The problem is there is a gap between a sample and the population from which it was drawn. Sampling procedures produce a subset of the population, and it is not correct to assume that this subset's descriptive statistics (such as its mean) are equivalent to those of the population. Going back to our house cat example in the previous chapter, suppose you gather a sample of cats and find a mean weight of 9.50 pounds. Would it be safe to conclude that if you weighed all house cats in the world (i.e., the entire population), the mean would be exactly 9.50? Definitely not! In the process of pulling your sample, you might have picked up a few cats that are atypically small or large. We saw in the previous chapter how extreme values can pull the sample mean up or down; if you got an extremely large or extremely small cat in your sample, the mean would be thrown off as a result. There is always a possibility that any given sample contains certain values that cause the mean, proportion, or other descriptive statistic to be higher or lower than that for the entire population from which the sample was derived. For this reason, sample statistics cannot be automatically generalized to populations. We need a way of bridging the gap.

Inferential statistics (also called hypothesis testing, the subject of Part 3 of the book) provide this bridge between a descriptive statistic and the overarching population. The purpose of inferential statistics is to permit a descriptive statistic to be used in a manner such that the researcher can draw an inference about the larger population. This procedure is grounded in probability theory. Probability forms the theoretical foundation for statistical tests and is therefore the subject of Part 2 of this book. You can think of Part 1 as having established the foundational mathematical and formulaic concepts necessary for inferential tests and of Part 2 as laying out the theory behind the strategic use of those descriptive statistics. Part 3 is where these two areas of knowledge converge.

Inferential statistics: The field of statistics in which a descriptive statistic derived from a sample is employed probabilistically to make a generalization or inference about the population from which the sample was drawn.

Probability theory: Logical premises that form a set of predictions about the likelihood of certain events or the empirical results that one would expect to see in an infinite set of trials.

Part 2 is heavily grounded in theory. You will not see SPSS sections or much use of research examples. This is because probability is largely concealed from view in criminal justice and criminology research; probability is the "man behind the curtain" who is pulling the levers and making the machine run but who usually remains hidden. Although there will be formulas and calculations that you will need to understand, your primary task in Part 2 is to form conceptual comprehension of the topics presented. When you understand the logic behind inferential statistics, you will be ready for Part 3.

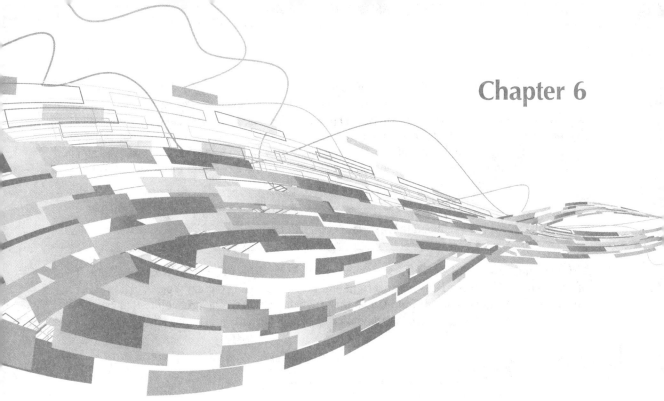

Chapter 6

Probability

A probability is the likelihood that a particular event will occur. We all use probabilistic reasoning every day. If I buy a lottery ticket, what are my chances of winning? What is the likelihood that I will get a promotion if I put in extra effort at work? What is the probability that I will get pulled over if I drive 5 miles per hour over the speed limit? These musings all involve predictions about the likelihood that a certain event will (or will not) occur. We use what we know (or what we presume, if our information is imperfect) about the world to inform our judgments about the chance of occurrence.

Probability: The likelihood that a certain event will occur.

Probabilities are linked intricately with proportions; in fact, the probability formula is a spinoff of Formula 3(1). Flip back to this formula right now for a refresher. Let us call a particular event of interest A. Events are phenomena of interest that are being studied. The probability that event A will occur can be symbolized as $p(A)$ (pronounced p of A) and written formulaically as

$$p(A) = \frac{The\ number\ of\ times\ event\ A\ can\ occur}{The\ total\ number\ of\ possible\ outcomes}. \qquad\qquad Formula\ 6(1)$$

Coin flips are the classic example of probabilities. Any two-sided, fair coin may land on either heads or tails when flipped, so the denominator in the probability formula is 2. There is only one tail side on a coin, so the numerator is 1. Probabilities, like proportions, are expressed as decimals, so the fraction must be divided out. The probability of the coin landing tails side up, then, is

$$p(tails) = \frac{1}{2} = .50.$$

Any time you flip a fair coin, there is a probability of .50 that the coin will land on tails. Of course, the probability that it will land heads side up is also .50. Note that the two probabilities together sum to 1.00; that is,

$$p(tails) + p(heads) = .50 + .50 = 1.00.$$

The probabilities sum to 1.00 because heads and tails are the only two possible results and thus constitute an exhaustive list of outcomes. The coin, moreover, must land (it will not hover in midair or fly around the room), so the probability sums to 1.00 because the landing of the coin is inevitable.

Think about rolling one fair die. A die has six sides, so any given side has $p = \frac{1}{6} = .17$ of being the one that lands face up. If you were asked, "What is the probability of obtaining a 3 on a single roll of a fair die?" your answer would be ".17." There are 52 cards in a standard deck and only one of

each number and suit, so if a card is randomly selected from that deck, each card has $p = \dfrac{1}{52} = .02$
probability of being the card that is selected. If someone asked you, "What is the probability of selecting the Two of Hearts from a full deck?" you would respond, ".02." Note, too, that in the instance of a die and a deck of cards—just as with the flipped coin—the sum of all events' individual probabilities is 1.00. This is a reflection of the bounding rule and the rule of the complement that we discussed in Chapter 5. A die has six sides, so there are six total possible events: the die can land on 1, 2, 3, 4, 5, or 6. The probability that it will land on a specific predicted value (say 5, for example) is .17, whereas the probability that it will land on *any* of its six sides is .17 + .17 + .17 + .17 + .17 + .17 = 1.02 (this sum is not precisely 1.00 because of rounding error). Likewise, the probability of pulling a predetermined playing card (the Four of Clubs, let's say) is .02, but the chance that you will, in fact, retrieve a card from the deck when you pull one out is .02 × 52 = 1.04 (again, rounding error).

LEARNING CHECK

Use probability to answer the following two questions.

   a. When you predict that a die will land on 2, what is the probability that it will actually land on 3 instead?

   b. When you predict that a card will be the Jack of Diamonds, what is the probability that you will actually pull the Ace of Hearts instead?

Based on what you know about the bounding rule and the rule of the complement, answer the following questions.

   a. When you predict that a die will land on 1, what is the probability that it will land on any other value *except* 1?

   b. When you predict that a card will be the Nine of Spades, what is the probability that the card you actually pull will be anything *except* the Nine of Spades?

Table 6.1   Gender of PPCS Respondents

Gender	f	p
Male	25,078	.48
Female	27,451	.52
	$N = 52,529$	$\Sigma = 1.00$

The major difference between proportions and probabilities is that proportions are purely descriptive, whereas probabilities represent predictions. Consider Table 6.1, which shows the proportion of the respondents to the Police-Public Contact Survey (PPCS; see Data Sources 2.1) that is male and the proportion that is female. If you threw all 52,529 people into a gigantic hat and randomly drew one, what is the probability that the person you selected would be female? It is .52! The probability that the person would be male? The answer is .48. This is the relationship between proportions and probabilities.

Let us try another example. Table 6.2 shows data from the Uniform Crime Reports (see Data Sources 1.1) showing the percentage of crimes cleared by arrest in 2012.

Table 6.2   Percentage of Crimes Cleared by Arrest

Crime Type	Percentage Cleared
Homicide	62.50
Rape	40.10
Robbery	28.10
Aggravated assault	55.80
Burglary	12.70
Larceny-theft	22.00
Motor vehicle theft	11.90

We can use the percentages in Table 6.2 just as if they were proportions (flip back to Formulas 3(1) and 3(2) if you need a refresher on this concept). What is the probability that a robbery reported to police will result in an arrest of the perpetrator? You can see that 28.10% of these crimes are cleared by arrest, which means that any given robbery has a .28 chance of resulting in an arrest. Try this exercise with the other crime types listed in the table.

LEARNING CHECK

In Table 6.2, the bounding rule and rule of the complement play out a little differently compared to the examples using coins, dice, and cards. In the clearance data, these two rules must be applied separately for each individual crime type. There are two possible outcomes anytime a crime occurs: that the police solve the crime or that they do not. As such, there is a 100.00% that *one* of these two outcomes will occur. We can use clearance rates and simple subtraction to find the chance that a particular crime will not be cleared by arrest. For example, if 12.70% of burglaries result in arrest of the suspect, then 100.00% − 12.70% = 87.30% of burglaries are not cleared (i.e., there is a .87 probability that any given burglary will not result in the arrest of a suspect). For each of the remaining crime types in Table 6.2, calculate the percentage of crimes not cleared, and state the probability that a crime will or will not be cleared.

Probability theory is grounded in assumptions about infinite trials; in other words, probabilities concern what is expected over the long run. Think back to the coin flip example. Since $p(tails)$ on any given flip is .50, then over the course of a long-term flipping session, exactly half of the flips will yield tails.

Theoretical prediction: A prediction, grounded in logic, about whether or not a certain event will occur.

Empirical outcome: A numerical result from a sample, such as a mean or frequency. Also called observed outcomes.

There is a distinct difference, though, between theoretical predictions and empirical outcomes (empirical outcomes can also be called *observed outcomes*; we will use the two terms interchangeably). Quite simply, and as you have undoubtedly already learned in life, you do not always get what you expect. You can see this in practice. First, imagine that you flipped a coin six times. How many of those flips would you expect to land tails side up? Three, of course, because every flip has $p(tails) = .50$ and so you would expect half of all flips to result in tails. Now, grab a real coin, flip it six times, and record each outcome. How many tails did you get? Try 20 flips. Now how many tails? Transfer the following chart to a piece of paper and fill it in with your numbers.

---

6 flips   proportion tails $= \dfrac{?}{6} =$

20 flips   proportion tails $= \dfrac{?}{20} =$

You might have found in your 6-flip exercise that the number of tails departed noticeably from three; you might have gotten one, five, or even six or zero tails. On the other hand, the number of tails yielded in the 20-flip exercise should be approximately 10 (with a little bit of error; it might have been 9 or 11). Why is this? It is because you increased the number of trials and thereby allowed the underlying probability to appear in the empirical outcomes. The knowledge that half of coin flips will produce tails over time is a theoretical prediction, whereas the flip experiment you just conducted is an empirical test and finding. Theory guides us in outlining what we expect to see (e.g., if you are asked how many times you would expect to see tails in a series of six flips, your best guess would be three), but sometimes empirical results do not match expectations (e.g., you may see one tail, or possibly all six of the flips will produce tails).

The relationship between theoretical predictions and empirical findings is at the heart of statistical analysis. Researchers constantly compare observations to expectations to determine if empirical outcomes conform to theory-based predictions about those outcomes. The extent of the match (or mismatch) between what we expect (theory) and what we see (reality) is what leads us to make certain conclusions about both theory and reality.

Now, let us add another layer to the discussion. We have thus far covered four examples of situations in which probability can be used to make predictions: coin tosses, die roles, card selections, and clearance rates. You might have noticed that clearance rates stand apart from the other three examples—unlike coins, dice, and cards, the probability of clearance is not equal across the different crime types. Whereas a rolled die offers equal probability of landing on 2 versus 6 (each one is .17), a crime will vary in its clearance probability based on the type of crime that it is. Motor vehicle theft has a .12 clearance probability, and there is a .63 chance of a homicide being cleared. Unlike each of the six sides of a die, any given crime does not have an equal probability of clearance.

This leads us to an important point: In most cases, the different possible outcomes have *unequal* probabilities of occurring. The existence of outcomes that have greater or lesser theoretical probabilities of being the one that actually occurs forms the basis for everything else we are going to discuss in this chapter. Some outcomes are much more likely than others.

A **probability distribution** is a table or graph showing the full array of theoretical probabilities for any given variable. These probabilities represent not what we *actually* see but, rather, the gamut of potential empirical outcomes and each outcome's probability of being the one that actually happens. Probability distributions are theoretical, not empirical. A probability distribution is constructed on the basis of an underlying parameter or statistic (such as a proportion or a mean) and represents the probability associated with each possible outcome. Two types of probability distributions are discussed in this chapter: binomial and continuous.

Probability distribution: A table or graph showing the entire set of probabilities associated with every possible empirical outcome.

Discrete Probability: The Binomial Probability Distribution

A trial is a particular act with multiple different possible outcomes (e.g., rolling a die, where the die will land on any one of its six sides). Binomials are trials that have exactly two possible outcomes (this type of trial is also called *dichotomous* or *binary*). Coin flips are binomials because coins have two sides. Research Example 6.1 describes two types of binomials that criminal justice and criminology researchers have examined. Binomials are used to construct binomial probability distributions. The binomial probability distribution is a list of expected probabilities; it contains all possible results over a set of trials and lists the probability of each result.

Trial: An act that has several different possible outcomes.

Binomial: A trial with two possible outcomes. Also called a dichotomous or binary variable empirical outcome.

RESEARCH EXAMPLE 6.1

Are Police Officers Less Likely to Arrest an Assault Suspect When the Suspect and the Alleged Victim Are Intimate Partners?

Critics of the police response to intimate partner violence have accused police of being "soft" on offenders who abuse intimates. Klinger (1995) used a variable measuring whether or not police made an arrest when responding to an assault of any type. The variable was coded as *arrest/no arrest*. He then examined whether the probability of arrest was lower when the perpetrator and victim were intimates as compared to assaults between strangers or nonintimate acquaintances. The results indicated that police were unlikely to make arrests in *all* types of assault, regardless of the victim-offender relationship and that they were not less likely to arrest offenders who victimized intimate partners relative to those who victimized strangers or acquaintances.

> **Binomial probability distribution:** A numerical or graphical display showing the probability associated with each possible outcome of a trial.
>
> **Binomial coefficient:** The formula used to calculate the probability for each possible outcome of a trial and to create the binomial probability distribution.

So, how do we go about building the binomial probability distribution? The distribution is constructed using the binomial coefficient. The formula for this coefficient is a bit intimidating, but each component of the coefficient will be discussed individually in the following pages so that when you are done reading, you will understand the coefficient and how to use it. The binomial coefficient is given by the formula:

$$p(r) = \binom{N}{r} p^r q^{N-r},$$
Formula 6(2)

where $p(r)$ = the probability of r,

   r = the number of successes,

   N = the number of trials/sample size,

   p = the probability that a given event will occur, and

   q = the probability that a given event will not occur.

The ultimate goal of binomials is to find the value of $p(r)$ for every possible value of r. The resulting list of $p(r)$ values is the binomial probability distribution.

Before we get into the math, let's first consider a conceptual example using the clearance data. Table 6.2 shows that 62.50% of homicides result in arrest, meaning that any given homicide has a .63 probability of clearance. Suppose you gathered a random sample of 10 homicide cases. Out of these 10, there are 11 separate possible (i.e., theoretical) outcomes: Anywhere from 0 to all 10 could have been cleared by arrest. Each of these individual outcomes has a certain probability of being the one that occurs in reality. You might have already guessed that the most likely outcome is that 6 or 7 of them would be cleared (since 62.50% of 10 is 6.25), but what are the other possible outcomes' probabilities of occurrence? This is what we use the binomial probability distribution for.

Successes and Sample Size: N and r

The binomial coefficient formula contains the variables N and r. The N represents sample size or the total number of trials. As an example, we will use a hypothetical study of jail inmates who have been booked on arrest and are awaiting word as to whether they will be released on bail or whether they will remain confined while they await criminal-court proceedings. The Bureau of Justice

Statistics reports that 62% of felony defendants are released from jail prior to the final disposition of their case (Reaves, 2013), so $p = .62$. Let's say we draw a random sample of five recently arrested jail inmates. This means that for the binomial coefficient formula, $N = 5$.

In the binomial coefficient, r represents the number of successes or, in other words, the number of times the outcome of interest happens over N trials. A researcher decides what "success" will mean in a given study. In the current example, we will define success as a defendant obtaining pre-trial release. There are multiple values that r takes on in any given study, since there are multiple possible successes. If we wanted to find the probability that three of the five defendants would be released, we would input $r = 3$ into the binomial coefficient formula; if we wanted the probability that all five would be released, then $r = 5$.

Success: The outcome of interest in a trial.

The Number of Ways r Can Occur, Given N: The Combination

In our sample of five defendants, there are a lot of possibilities for any given value of r. For instance, if one defendant was released (i.e., $r = 1$), then it could be that Defendant 1 was released and the remaining four were detained. Alternatively, Defendant 4 might have been the one who made bail. The point is, a given value of r can occur in multiple different ways. If a release is symbolized r, then for the purpose of an illustration, let us call a detention d (remember that release and detention are binary; each defendant receives one of these two possible outcomes). Consider the following sets of possible arrangements of outcomes:

$$\{r, d, d, d, d\} \{d, r, d, d, d\} \{d, d, r, d, d\} \{d, d, d, r, d\} \{d, d, d, d, r\}$$

What these sets tell you is that there are five different ways for $r = 1$ (i.e., one success) to occur over $N = 5$ trials. The same holds true for any number of successes—there are many different ways that $r = 2$, $r = 3$, and so on can occur in terms of which defendants are the successes and which are the failures.

The total number of ways that r can occur in a sample of size N is called a combination and is calculated as

$$\frac{N!}{r!(N-r)!},$$

Formula 6(3)

where N = the total number of trials or total sample size,

r = the number of successes, and

! = factorial.

In this chapter and subsequent ones, you will see various notations representing multiplication. The most popular symbol, x, will not be used; in statistics, x represents raw data values and so using this symbol to also represent multiplication would be confusing. Instead, we will rely on three other indicators of multiplication. First is the centered dot that connects the numbers being multiplied, such as $2 \cdot 3 = 6$. Second are parentheses; numbers separated by parentheses should be multiplied together. This could appear as $2(3) = 6$ or $(2)(3) = 6$. Third, sometimes no operand is used, and it is merely the placement of two numbers or symbols right next to each other that signals multiplication. An example of this is xy, where whatever numbers x and y symbolized, respectively, would be multiplied together. If $x = 2$ and $y = 3$, then $xy = 2 \cdot 3 = 6$.

The **factorial** symbol $!$ tells you to multiply together the series of descending whole numbers starting with the number to the left of the symbol all the way down to 1.00. If $r = 3$, then $r! = 3 \cdot 2 \cdot 1 = 6$. If $N = 5$, then $N! = 5 \cdot 4 \cdot 3 \cdot 2 \cdot 1 = 120$.

Combination: The total number of ways that a success r can occur over N trials.

Factorial: Symbolized $!$, the mathematical function whereby the first number in a sequence is multiplied successively by all numbers below it down to 1.00.

There is also shorthand notation for the combination formula that saves us from having to write the whole thing out. The shorthand notation is $\binom{N}{r}$, which is pronounced "N choose r." Be very careful! This is not a fraction. Do not mistake it for "N divided by r."

Most calculators meant for use in math classes (which excludes the calculator that came free with that new wallet you bought) will compute factorials and combinations for you. The factorial function is labeled $!$ The combination formula is usually represented by nCr or sometimes just C. Depending on the type of calculator you have, these functions are probably either located on the face of the calculator and accessed using a *2nd* or *alpha* key, or can be found in a menu accessed using the *math, stat,* or *prob* buttons, or a certain combination of these functions. Take a few minutes right now to find these functions on your calculator.

Also, note that 1 factorial and 0 factorial both equal 1. Try this out on your calculator to see for yourself. Since $0! = 1$, you do not need to worry if you end up with a zero in the denominator of your fractions.

$$1! = 1$$
$$0! = 1$$

The combination formula can be used to replicate the previously presented longhand demonstration wherein we were interested in the number of ways that one release and four detentions can occur. Plugging the numbers into the combination formula yields

$$\binom{5}{1} = \frac{5!}{1!(5-1)!} = \frac{120}{1(4)!} = \frac{120}{1(24)} = 5.$$

When we wrote out the possible ways for $r = 1$ to occur, we concluded that there were five options; we have now confirmed this mathematically using the combination formula. There are five different ways for one person to be released and the remaining four to be detained.

We will do one more example calculation before moving on. Suppose that three of the five defendants were released. How many combinations of three are there in a sample of five? Plug the numbers into the combination formula to find out:

$$\binom{5}{3} = \frac{5!}{3!(5-3)!} = \frac{120}{3!(2)!} = \frac{120}{6(2)} = \frac{120}{12} = 10$$

There are 10 combinations of three in a sample of five. In the context of the present example, there are 10 different ways for three defendants to be released and two to be detained. This has to be accounted for in the computation of the probability of each possible result, which is why you see the combination formula included in the binomial coefficient.

The Probability of Success and the Probability of Failure: *p* and *q*

The probability of success (symbolized p) is at the heart of the binomial probability distribution. This number is obtained on the basis of prior knowledge or theory. In the present example pertaining to pretrial release, we know that 62% of felony defendants obtain pretrial release. This means that each defendant's probability of release is $p = .62$.

We know that release is not the only possible outcome, though—defendants can be detained, too. The opposite of a success is a **failure**. Because we are dealing with events that have two potential outcomes, we need to know the probability of failure in addition to that of success. The probability of failure is represented by the letter q; to compute the value of q, the bound rule and the rule of the complement must be invoked. In Chapter 5, you learned that

$$p(A) + p(Not\ A) = 1.00;\ \text{therefore,}$$

$$p(Not\ A) = 1.00 - p(A).$$

What we are doing now is exactly the same thing, with the small change that $p(A)$ is being changed to simply p, and $p(Not\ A)$ will now be represented by the letter q. So,

$$q = 1.00 - p. \hspace{3cm} \textit{Formula 6(4)}$$

With $q = .62$, the probability that a felony defendant will be detained prior to trial (i.e., will *not* obtain pretrial release) is

$$q = 1.00 - .62 = .38.$$

Putting It All Together: Using the Binomial Coefficient to Construct the Binomial Probability Distribution

Using p and q, the probability of various combinations of successes and failures can be computed. When there are r successes over N trials, then there are $N - r$ failures over that same set of trials. There is a formula called the **restricted multiplication rule for independent events** that guarantees that the probability of r successes and $N - r$ failures is the product of p and q. In the present example, there are three successes (each with probability $p = .62$) and two failures (each with probability $q = .38$). You might also recall from prior math classes that exponents can be used as shorthand for multiplication when a particular number is multiplied by itself many times. Finally, we also have to account for the combination of N and r. The probability of three successes is thus

$$p(3) = \binom{5}{3} \cdot p(successs) \cdot p(successs) \cdot p(successs) \cdot p(failure) \cdot p(failure)$$

$$= \binom{5}{3} \cdot p \cdot p \cdot p \cdot q \cdot q$$

$$= \binom{5}{3} p^3 q^2$$

$$= \binom{5}{3} \left(.62^3\right)\left(.38^2\right)$$

$$= 10(.24)(.14)$$

$$= .34.$$

This result means that given a population probability of .62, there is a .34 probability that if we pulled a sample of five felony defendants, three would obtain pretrial release.

To create the binomial probability distribution, repeat this procedure for all possible values of r. The most straightforward way to do this is to construct a table like Table 6.3. Every row in the table uses a different r value, whereas the values of N, p, and q are fixed. The rightmost column, $p(r)$, is obtained by multiplying the $\binom{N}{r}$, p^r, and q^{N-r} terms.

Table 6.3   The Binomial Probability Distribution for Pretrial Release Among Five Felony Defendants

r	$\binom{N}{r}$	p^r	q^{N-r}	$p(r)$
0	$\binom{5}{0} = 1$	$62^0 = 1.00$	$.38^{5-0=5} = .01$	.01
1	$\binom{5}{1} = 5$	$62^1 = .62$	$.38^{5-1=4} = .02$	.06
2	$\binom{5}{2} = 10$	$62^2 = .38$	$.38^{5-2=3} = .05$	.19
3	$\binom{5}{3} = 10$	$62^3 = .24$	$.38^{5-3=2} = .14$	.34
4	$\binom{5}{4} = 5$	$62^4 = .15$	$.38^{5-4=1} = .38$	.29
5	$\binom{5}{5} = 1$	$62^5 = .09$	$.38^{5-5=0} = 1.00$	.09

The values in the $p(r)$ column tell you the probability of each possible outcome being the one that actually occurs in any given random sample of five defendants. The probability that two of the five defendants will be released pending trial is .19, and the probability that all five will be released is .09. Probabilities can also be added together. The probability of four *or more* defendants being released is $p(4) + p(5) = .29 + .09 = .38$. The chance that two *or fewer* would be released is $p(2) + p(1) + p(0) = .19 + .06 + .01 = .26$.

Our original question was, "With a population probability of .62, what is the probability that three of five defendants would be released?" You can see from the table that the answer is .34. This, as it happens, is the highest probability in the table, meaning that it is the outcome that we would most expect to see in any given random sample. Another way to think of it is to imagine that someone who was conducting this study asked you to predict—based on a population probability of .62 and $N = 5$ defendants—how many defendants would be released. Your "best guess" answer would be three, because this is the outcome with the highest likelihood of occurring.

Contrast this to the conclusion we would draw if none of the five defendants in the sample had been released. This is an extremely improbable event with only $p(0) = .01$ likelihood of occurring. It would be rather surprising to find this empirical result, and it might lead us to wonder if there was something unusual about our sample. We might investigate the possibility that the county we drew the sample from had particularly strict policies regulating pretrial release, or that we happened to draw a sample of defendants charged with especially serious crimes.

There are two neat and important things about the binomial probability distribution. The first is that it can be graphed using a bar chart (Figure 6.1) so as to form a visual display of the numbers in Table 6.3. The horizontal axis contains the r values and the bar height (vertical axis) is determined by $p(r)$. The bar chart makes it easy to determine at a glance which outcomes are most and least likely to occur.

Figure 6.1 The Binominal Probability Distribution for Pretrial Release in a Sample of Five Defendants, With $p = .62$

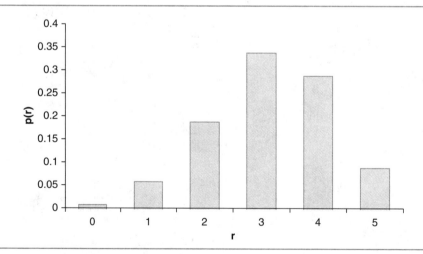

Part 2 Probability and Distributions

The second important thing about the binomial probability distribution is that the $p(r)$ column sums to 1.00. This is because the binomial distribution is exhaustive; that is, all possible values of r are included in it. Any time an exhaustive list of probabilities is summed, the result will be 1.00. In Table 6.3, we covered all of the values that r can assume (i.e., zero to five); therefore, all possible probabilities are included and the sum is 1.00. Memorize this point! It is applicable in the context of continuous probability distributions, too, and will be revisited shortly.

Continuous Probability: The Standard Normal Curve

The binomial probability distribution is applicable for trials with two potential outcomes; in other words, it is used for dichotomous categorical variables. Criminal justice and criminology researchers, however, often use continuous variables. The binomial probability distribution has no applicability in this context. Continuous variables are represented by a theoretical distribution called the **normal curve**. Figure 6.2 shows this curve's familiar bell shape.

Figure 6.2   The Normal Curve for Continuous Variables

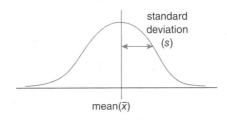

What Predicts Correctional Officers' Job Stress and Job Satisfaction?

Correctional officers work in a high-stress environment, and their job performance has implications for the quality and safety of the correctional institution. High stress levels can reduce these workers' performance levels and can increase their likelihood of physical injury; likewise, low job satisfaction can lead to constant staff turnover and to burnout, which also dampens the overall effectiveness of the correctional institution. It is important for corrections managers to understand the organizational factors that might increase or decrease stress and satisfaction among their staff so as to ensure the best work environment possible and thus keep the facility running smoothly.

Paoline, Lambert, and Hogan (2006) sought to uncover the predictors of correctional officers' attitudes toward their jobs. They gathered a sample of jail security staff and administered surveys that asked these respondents several questions about the levels of stress they experience at work and the amount of satisfaction they derive from their job. There were six stress variables and five satisfaction variables. Each set of variables was summed to form a single, overarching score on each index for each respondent. The indexes were continuous. Jail staff members with higher scores on the stress index experienced greater work anxiety and tension; likewise, those with lower scores on the satisfaction index felt relatively poorly about their job.

Paoline et al. found that the most consistent predictors of both stress and satisfaction were organizational factors specific to the jail itself; in particular, officers who felt that that the jail policies were clear and fair and who had positive views toward their coworkers experienced significantly less stress and greater satisfaction as compared to those officers who were not happy about the policies and their coworkers. These findings suggest that jail managers who seek to foster a positive work environment for their employees should ensure clear, fair policies and should promote harmony and teamwork among jail staff.

The normal curve is a *unimodal, symmetric* curve with an area of 1.00. It is unimodal because it peaks once and only once (i.e., it has one modal value; recall our discussion of the mode in Chapter 4). It is symmetric because the two halves (split by the mean) are identical to one another. It has an area of 1.00 because it encompasses all possible values of the variable in question. Just as the sum of the binomial probability distribution's $p(r)$ column always sums to 1.00 because all values that r could possibly take on are contained within the table, so the normal curve's tails stretch out to negative and positive infinity. This may sound impossible, but remember that this is a *theoretical* distribution. This curve is built on probabilities, not actual data.

The characteristics that determine a normal curve's location on the number line and its shape are its mean and standard deviation, respectively. When expressed in raw units, normal curves are scattered about the number line and take on a variety of shapes. This is a product of variation in metrics, means, and standard deviations. Figure 6.3 depicts this concept.

Figure 6.3   Variation in Normal Curves: Different Means and Standard Deviations

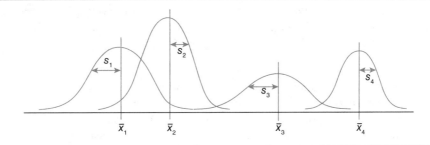

This inconsistency in locations and dimensions of normal curves can pose a problem in statistics. It is impossible to determine the probability of a certain empirical result when every curve differs from the rest. What is needed is a way to standardize the normal curve so that all variables can be represented by a single curve. This widely applicable single curve is constructed by converting all of a distribution's raw scores to *z* scores. The *z*-score transformation is straightforward:

$$z_x = \frac{x - \overline{x}}{s},$$

Formula 6(5)

where z_x = the *z* score for a given raw score *x*,

x = a given raw score,

$\overline{x}$ = the distribution mean, and

s = the distribution standard deviation.

A z score conveys two pieces of information about the raw score on which the z score is based. First, the absolute value of the z score reveals the location of the raw score in relation to the distribution mean. Z scores are expressed in standard deviation units. A z score of .25, for example, tells you that the underlying raw score is exactly one fourth of one standard deviation away from the mean. A z score of -1.50, likewise, signifies a raw score that is one and-one-half standard deviations away from the mean.

LEARNING CHECK

It is very important that you understand standard deviations; z scores will not make much sense if you did not fully grasp this earlier concept from Chapter 5. If necessary, go back and review these pages. What is a standard deviation, conceptually? What two pieces of complementary information are given by the mean and the standard deviation?

The second piece of information is given by the sign of the z score. Although standard deviations are always positive, z scores can be negative. A z score's sign indicates whether the raw score that the z score represents is greater than the mean (producing a positive z score) or is less than the mean (producing a negative z score). A z score of .25 is above the mean, while a score of -1.50 is below it. Figure 6.4 shows the relationship between raw scores and their z-score counterparts. You can see that every raw score has a corresponding z score. The z score tells you the distance between the mean and an individual raw score, as well as whether that raw score is greater than or less than the mean.

Figure 6.4   Raw Scores and z Scores

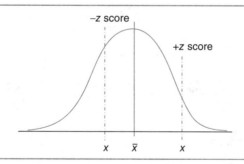

When all of the raw scores in a distribution have been transformed to z scores and plotted, the result is the **standard normal curve**. The z-score transformation dispenses with the original, raw values of a variable and replaces them with numbers representing their position *relative to* the distribution mean. A normal curve, then, is a curve constructed of raw scores, while the standard normal curve is composed of z scores.

Standard normal curve: A distribution of z scores. The curve is symmetric and unimodal and has a mean of zero, a standard deviation of 1.00, and an area of 1.00.

Like ordinary normal curves, the standard normal curve is symmetric, unimodal, and has an area of 1.00. Unlike regular normal curves, though, the standard normal curve's mean and standard deviation are fixed at 0 and 1, respectively. They remain fixed irrespective of the units in which the variable is measured or the original distribution's mean and standard deviation. This allows probabilities to be computed.

To understand the process of using the standard normal curve to find probabilities, it is necessary to comprehend that in this curve, area is the same as proportion and probability. A given area of the curve (such as the area between two raw scores) represents the proportion of scores that are between those two raw values. Figures 6.5 and 6.6 display the relationship between z scores and areas.

In Chapter 5, you learned that approximately two-thirds of the scores in any normal distribution lie between one standard deviation below and one standard deviation above the mean for that set of scores. (Refer back to Figure 5.4.) In Figure 6.5, you can see that .3413 (or 34.13%) of the scores are located between the mean and one standard deviation. If you add the proportion of cases—that is, area of the curve—that is one standard deviation below the mean to the proportion or area that is one standard deviation above, you get .3413 + .3413 = .6826, or 68.26%. This is just over two-thirds! The bulk of scores in a normal distribution cluster fairly closely to the center and those scores that are within one standard deviation of the mean (i.e., z scores that have absolute values of 1.00 or less) are considered the typical or *normal* scores. This affirms what we saw in Chapter 5 when we talked about the "normal" range being between 1 sd above and 1 sd below the mean.

Z scores that are greater than 1.00 or less than –1.00 are relatively rare, and they get increasingly rare as you trace the number line away from zero in either direction. These very large z scores do happen, but they are improbable, and some of them are incredibly unlikely. In Figure 6.6, you can see that a full 95% of scores (i.e., .9544) are within two standard deviations above and below the mean. In other words, only about 5% of scores in a normal distribution will be either greater than 2 sd above the mean (i.e., have a z value greater than 2.00) or more than 2 sd below the mean (a z value less than –2.00).

This is all getting very abstract, so let us get an example going. According to the 2005 Census of State and Federal Adult Correctional Facilities (CSFACF; see Data Sources 3.1), maximum-security state prisons with fewer than 750 inmates have a mean of 158 full-time correctional officers. The standard deviation is 97.

Suppose that a facility has 57 officers. To find this prison's z score, plug the numbers into Formula 6(5):

$$z_{57} = \frac{57 - 158}{97} = \frac{-101}{97} = -1.04$$

Figure 6.5   Standard Normal Curve: Area Between the Mean and One Standard Deviation

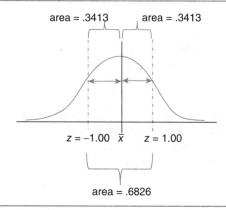

area = .3413   area = .3413

$z = -1.00$ $\bar{x}$ $z = 1.00$

area = .6826

Figure 6.6   Standard Normal Curve: Area Between the Mean and Two Standard Deviations

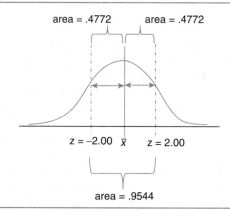

area = .4772   area = .4772

$z = -2.00$ $\bar{x}$ $z = 2.00$

area = .9544

This facility was just over one standard deviation below the group mean on staffing. Substantively speaking, this facility is right outside—but not by far—the typical zone of ± 1*sd*.

Now for another one. One institution employed 237 correctional officers, so its *z* score is

$$z_{237} = \frac{237 - 158}{97} = \frac{79}{97} = .81.$$

This institution is less than one standard deviation above the mean, so it is squarely within the typical zone. One more example. A third complex has 586 officers. Its *z* score is thus

$$z_{586} = \frac{586 - 158}{97} = \frac{428}{97} = 4.41.$$

Figure 6.7 Raw and z Scores in Relation to the Sample Mean

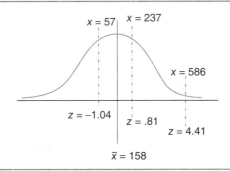

For this facility, $z = 4.41$; that is, this prison's raw score is nearly four and one-half standard deviations greater than the sample mean. Let's draw a hypothetical plot that offers a visualization of the three raw and z scores used in these examples and each one's relationship to the mean. You can see in Figure 6.7 each pair of xs and zs and how close to or far from the mean they are, as well as whether they are above or below it. The larger the z score is, the farther away from the mean that score is.

The z Table and Area Under the Standard Normal Curve

It is also possible to use z scores to find the area (i.e., proportion of values) between the mean and a particular score, or even the area that is *beyond* that score (in other words, the area that is in the tail of the distribution).

To do this, the z table is used. The z table is a chart containing the area of the curve that is between the mean and a given z score. Appendix B contains the z table. The area associated with a particular z score is found by decomposing the score into an *x.x* and *.0x* format such that the first half of the decomposed score contains the digit and the number in the 10ths position, and the second half contains a zero in the 10ths place and the number that is in the 100ths position. In the three previous examples, we calculated z scores of –1.04, .81, and 4.41. The first z score would be broken down as –1.0 + .04. Note that it does not matter that the z score is negative because the standard normal curve is symmetric and, therefore, the z table is used the same way irrespective of an individual score's sign. Go to the z table and locate the 1.0 row and .04 column; then trace them to their intersection. The area is .3508.

---

z table: A table containing a list of z scores and the area of the curve that is between the distribution mean and each individual z score.

The z score of .81 would decompose as .8 + .01, for an area of .2910. The z score of 4.41 is tricky because the table stops at 4.0; a z score that large encompasses the vast majority of values and leaves very few left. Figure 6.8 shows the areas between the mean and each of our three

Figure 6.8 Areas Between the Mean and *z*

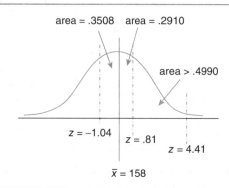

area = .3508   area = .2910

area > .4990

z = −1.04

z = .81

z = 4.41

$\bar{x}$ = 158

z scores. Approximately .35 or 35% of the scores lie between the mean and *z* = -1.04, about .29 or 29% are between the mean and *z* = .81, and more than .49 or 49% fall between the mean and *z* = 4.41.

Finding the area between the mean and a *z* score is informative, but what is generally of interest to criminology and criminal justice researchers is the area *beyond* that *z* score; that is, researchers usually want to know how big or small a *z* score would have to be in order to fall into the very tip of either the positive or negative tail of the distribution. To do this, we rely on a simple fact: Because the entire area of the standard normal curve is 1.00, the mean splits the curve exactly in half so that 50% of scores are below it and 50% are above. In other words, the area on each side of the mean is .50. As such, we have two pieces of information. First, we know that the total area on a particular side is .50. Second, we know, for any individual *z* score, the area between the mean and that score. We are looking for the third, unknown number, which is the area beyond that *z* score. How do you think we can find that number? If you said, "Subtraction," you are right! We subtract the known area from .50 to figure out what's left over.

Let us find the area beyond *z* for *z* = -1.04. The area between the mean and *z* is .3508 and the total area on the right-hand side is .50, so we use subtraction, as such:

$$.50 - .3508 = .1492$$

Thus, .1492 (or approximately 15%) of the scores in the standard normal distribution for correctional-facility staff size are less than 57 (*z* = −1.04). This is a relatively small proportion of scores, suggesting that it is rare for a correctional facility to have a staff this small. How about for a staff size of 237 officers (*z* = .81)? We found that the area between the mean and *z* is .2910, so

$$.50 - .2910 = .2090.$$

Approximately .21 (or 21%) of raw scores are greater than 237. Figure 6.9 depicts each of these calculated *z* scores' location on the standard normal curve.

Before moving on, double-check your understanding of areas between the mean and z and of areas beyond z by finding both of these numbers for each of the following z scores:

    a. $z = 1.38$

    b. $z = -.65$

    c. $z = 2.46$

    d. $z = -3.09$

Figure 6.9   Areas Between the Mean and z, Beyond z, and Total Area for Two z Scores

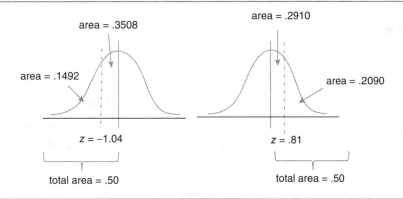

Another handy feature of the standard normal curve is that just as z scores can be used to find areas, areas can likewise be used to find z scores. Basically, you just use the z table backward. We might, for instance, want to know the z scores that lie in the upper 5% (.05) or 1% (.01) of the distribution. These are very unlikely values and are of interest because of their relative rarity. How large would a z score have to be such that only .05 or .01 of scores is above it?

The process of finding these z scores employs similar logic about the area of each side of the curve. First, we know that the z table provides the area between z and the mean; it does not tell you about the area beyond z, so it cannot be used yet. This problem is surmounted using subtraction, as we have already seen. Let us start with the area of .01. The area between the mean and z is

$$.50 - .01 = .49.$$

Thus, the area between the mean and the z score we are searching for is .49. Since we know this, we can now use the z table.

The second step is to scan the areas listed in the body of the *z* table to find the one that is *closest to .49*. The closest area is .4901. Third, find the *z* score associated with the identified area. Instead of tracing the two elements of a *z* score inward to locate the area, as you did before, now start at the area and trace outward along the row and column. The area of .4901 is in the *2.3* row and *.03* column, so the *z* score is

$$2.3 + .03 = 2.33.$$

And that is the answer! We now know that .01, or 1%, of scores in the standard normal distribution area have *z* scores greater than 2.33.

Now let us find the *z* score associated with an area of .05, but with a twist: We will place this area in the lower (left-hand) tail of the distribution. Recall that we were working in the upper (right-hand) tail when we did the previous example using an area of .01. The first and second steps of the process are the same no matter which side of the distribution is being analyzed. Subtraction shows that .50 – .05 = .45 of the scores is between the mean and *z*. Going to the table, you can see that there are actually two areas that are closest to .45. They are .4495 and .4505. The *z* score for the former is 1.64 and that for the latter is 1.65; *however*, since we are on the left (or negative) side of the curve, these *z* scores are actually −1.64 and −1.65. You must be aware of the sign of your *z* score! Scores on the left side of the standard normal curve are negative.

Finally, since there are two *z* scores in this instance, they must be averaged:

$$z = \frac{-1.64 + (-1.65)}{2} = \frac{-3.29}{2} = -1.645$$

That is the answer! *Z* scores less than −1.65 have a .05 *or less* probability of occurring. In other words, these extremely small scores happen only 5% of the time or less. That is unlikely indeed.

the left side of the standard normal z curve, scores will be negative but areas will not be. Second, areas/probabilities and z scores are two ways of expressing the same idea. Large z scores are associated with small probabilities, and small z scores represent large probabilities. The larger the absolute value of a z score is, the smaller the likelihood of observing that score will be. Z scores near zero (i.e., near the mean of the standard normal curve) are not unlikely or unusual, whereas scores that are very far away from zero are relatively rare (they are out in the far left or right tail). Take a moment now to graph the four z values listed in the previous Learning Check box.

CHAPTER SUMMARY

Probability is the basis of inferential statistics. This chapter introduced two of the major probability distributions: binomial and standard normal. The binomial distribution is for categorical variables that have two potential outcomes (dichotomous or binary variables), and the standard normal curve applies to continuous variables. The binomial probability distribution is constructed using an underlying probability derived from research or theory. This distribution shows the probability associated with each possible outcome, given an overarching probability of success and a predetermined number (N) of cases or trials.

The standard normal curve consists of z scores, which are scores associated with known areas or probabilities. Raw scores can be transformed to z scores using a simple conversion formula that employs the raw score, the mean, and the standard deviation. Because the area under the standard normal curve is a constant 1.00 (i.e., .50 on each side), areas can be added and subtracted, thus allowing probabilities to be determined on the basis of z scores and vice versa.

Both distributions are theoretical, which means that they are constructed on the basis of logic and mathematical theory. They can be contrasted to empirical distributions, which are distributions made from actual, observed raw scores in a sample or population. Empirical distributions are tangible; they can be manipulated and analyzed. Theoretical distributions exist only in the abstract.

CHAPTER 6 REVIEW PROBLEMS

1. Eight police officers are being randomly assigned to two-person teams.

    a. Identify the value of N.
    b. Identify the value of r.
    c. How many combinations of r are possible in this scenario? Do the combination by hand first, and then check your answer using the combination function on your calculator.

2. Nine jail inmates are being randomly assigned to three-person cells.

    a. Identify the value of N.
    b. Identify the value of r.

c. How many combinations of r are possible in this scenario? Do the combination by hand first, and then check your answer using the combination function on your calculator.

3. In a sample of seven parolees, three are rearrested within 2 years of release.

   a. Identify the value of N.
   b. Identify the value of r.
   c. How many combinations of r are possible in this scenario? Do the combination by hand first, and then check your answer using the combination function on your calculator.

4. Out of six persons recently convicted of felonies, five are sentenced to prison.

   a. Identify the value of N.
   b. Identify the value of r.
   c. How many combinations of r are possible in this scenario? Do the combination by hand first, and then check your answer using the combination function on your calculator.

5. Four judges in a sample of eight do not believe that the law provides them with sufficient sanction options when sentencing persons convicted of crimes.

   a. Identify the value of N.
   b. Identify the value of r.
   c. How many combinations of r are possible in this scenario? Do the combination by hand first, and then check your answer using the combination function on your calculator.

6. For each of the following variables, identify the distribution—either binomial or standard normal—that would be the appropriate theoretical probability distribution to represent that variable. Remember that this is based on the variable's level of measurement.

   a. Defendants' completion of a drug court program, measured as *success* or *failure*
   b. The total lifetime number of times someone has been arrested
   c. Crime victims' reporting of their victimization to police, measured as *reported* or *did not report*

7. For each of the following variables, identify the distribution—either binomial or standard normal—that would be the appropriate theoretical probability distribution to represent that variable. Remember that this is based on the variable's level of measurement.

   a. The number of months of probation received by juveniles adjudicated guilty on delinquency charges
   b. City crime rates
   c. Prosecutorial charging decisions, measured as *filed charges* or *did not file charges*

8. According to the Uniform Crime Reports (UCR), 56% of aggravated assaults reported to police in 2010 were cleared by arrest. Convert this percentage to a proportion and use it as your value of p to do the following:

   a. Compute the binomial probability distribution for a random sample of five aggravated assaults, with r defined as the number of assaults that are cleared.
   b. Based on the distribution, what is the outcome (i.e., number of successes) you would *most* expect to see?

c. Based on the distribution, what is the outcome (i.e., number of successes) you would *least* expect to see?

d. What is the probability that two or fewer aggravated assaults would be cleared?

e. What is the probability that three or more would be cleared?

9. According to the Bureau of Justice Statistics, of all criminal charges filed against defendants for domestic violence, 62% are for aggravated assault. Convert this percentage to a proportion and use it as your value of p to do the following:

a. Compute the binomial probability distribution for a random sample of six domestic-violence cases, with r defined as the number of cases charged as aggravated assault.

b. Based on the distribution, what is the outcome (i.e., number of successes) you would *most* expect to see?

c. Based on the distribution, what is the outcome (i.e., number of successes) you would *least* expect to see?

d. What is the probability that two or fewer of the charges would be for aggravated assault?

e. What is the probability that five or more of them would be for assault?

10. According to the UCR, 49% of the hate crimes that were reported to police in 2012 were racially motivated. Convert this percentage to a proportion and use it as your value of p to do the following:

a. Compute the binomial probability distribution for a random sample of six hate crimes, with r defined as the number that are racially motivated.

b. Based on the distribution, what is the outcome (i.e., number of successes) you would *most* expect to see?

c. Based on the distribution, what is the outcome (i.e., number of successes) you would *least* expect to see?

d. What is the probability that two or fewer of the hate crimes were motivated by race?

e. What is the probability that three or more were racially motivated?

11. According to the UCR, 61% of murders in 2009 were committed with firearms. Convert this percentage to a proportion and use it as your value of p to do the following:

a. Compute the binomial probability distribution for a random sample of five murders, with r defined as the number that are committed with firearms.

b. Based on the distribution, what is the outcome (i.e., number of successes) you would *most* expect to see?

c. Based on the distribution, what is the outcome (i.e., number of successes) you would *least* expect to see?

d. What is the probability that one or fewer murders were committed with firearms?

e. What is the probability that four or more murders were committed with firearms?

The 2007 Law Enforcement and Management Statistics (LEMAS) survey reported that the mean number of municipal police per 1,000 citizens in U.S. cities with populations of 100,000 or more was 1.99 ($s = .84$). Use this information to answer questions 12 through 15.

12. One department had 2.46 police per 1,000 citizens.

   a. Convert this raw score to a z score.
   b. Find the area between the mean and z.
   c. Find the area in the tail of the distribution beyond z.

$\frac{2.46 - 1.99}{.84} = .56$

13. One department had 4.28 police per 1,000 residents.

   a. Convert this raw score to a z score.
   b. Find the area between the mean and z.
   c. Find the area in the tail of the distribution beyond z.

$\frac{4.28 - 1.99}{.84} = 2.73$
$= .4928$
$.50 - .4928$
$= .0032$

14. One department had 1.51 police per 1,000.

   a. Convert this raw score to a z score.
   b. Find the area between the mean and z
   c. Find the area in the tail of the distribution beyond z.

15. One department had 1.29 officers per 1,000.

   a. Convert this raw score to a z score.
   b. Find the area between the mean and z.
   c. Find the area in the tail of the distribution beyond z.

$Z_{1.29} = \frac{1.29 - 1.99}{84}$
$= -.83$
$.50 - 2 = .2967$

16. What z scores fall into the upper .15 of the distribution?

17. What z scores fall into the upper .03 of the distribution?

18. What z scores fall into the lower .02 of the distribution?

19. What z scores fall into the lower .10 of the distribution?

20. What z scores fall into the lower .015 of the distribution?

KEY TERMS

Inferential statistics
Probability theory
Probability
Theoretical prediction
Empirical outcome
Probability distribution
Trial

Binomial
Binomial probability distribution
Binomial coefficient
Success
Combination
Factorial
Failure

Restricted multiplication rule for
   independent events
Normal curve
z score
Standard normal curve
z table

p	The probability of success
N	The total number of trials; the sample size
r	The number of successes over a set of N trials
$\binom{N}{r}$	The combination of "N choose r"; the number of ways for r successes to happen over N trials
q	The probability of failure
z	A score expressed in standard deviation units

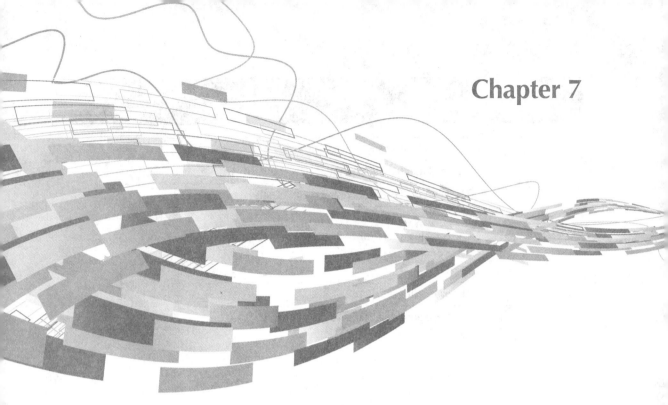

Chapter 7

Population, Sample, and Sampling Distributions

Learning Objectives

- Explain the difference between empirical and theoretical distributions.
- Define population, sample, and sampling distributions and identify each as either empirical or theoretical.
- Explain the difference between statistics and parameters.
- Define sampling error and explain how it affects efforts to generalize from a sample to a population.
- Define the central limit theorem.
- Describe the z and t distributions, including whether these are empirical or theoretical distributions and which one is appropriate depending on sample size.

A population is the entire universe of objects, people, places, or other units of analysis that a researcher wishes to study. Criminal justice and criminology researchers use all manner of populations. Bouffard (2010), for instance, examined the relationship between men's military service during the Vietnam era and their criminal offending later in life. Kane and Cronin (2010) attempted to determine whether there was a relationship between order maintenance policing and violent crime in communities. Morris and Worrall (2010) investigated whether prison architectural design influenced inmate misconduct. These are three examples of populations—male Vietnam veterans, communities, prison inmates—that can form the basis for study.

The problem is that populations are usually far too large for researchers to examine directly. There are millions of men in the United States, thousands of communities nationwide, and hundreds of thousands of inmates who engage in misconduct. Nobody can possibly study any of these populations in its entirety. Samples are thus drawn from populations of interest. Samples are subsets of populations. Morris and Worrall (2010), for example, drew a random sample of 2,500 inmates. This sample, unlike its overarching population, was of manageable size and could be analyzed directly.

Populations and samples give rise to three types of distributions: population, sample, and sampling. A **population distribution** contains all values in the entire population, while a **sample distribution** shows the shape and form of the values in a sample pulled from a population. Population and sample distributions are both empirical. They are made of raw scores derived from actual people or objects. **Sampling distributions**, by contrast, are theoretical arrays of sample statistics. Each of these is discussed in turn in this chapter.

Population distribution: An empirical distribution made of raw scores from a population.

Sample distribution: An empirical distribution made of raw scores from a sample.

Sampling distribution: A theoretical distribution made out of infinite sample statistics.

Empirical Distributions: Population and Sample Distributions

Population and sample distributions are both empirical because they exist in reality; every person or object in the population or sample has a value on a given variable that can be measured and plotted on a graph. To illustrate these two types of distributions, we can use the 2005 Census of State and Federal Adult Correctional Facilities (CSFACF; see Data Sources 3.1). This data set contains information on all adult correctional facilities that house prisoners convicted in state and federal courts ($N = 1,821$). No sampling was done; every adult correctional facility in the United States was asked to provide information. This makes the CSFACF a population data set.

Figure 7.1 displays the population distribution for the variable *total number of inmates*, which is a measure of the number of prisoners housed in each facility. Every facility's inmate count was plotted to form this histogram. You should be able to recognize immediately that this distribution has an extreme positive skew.

What might the distribution look like for a sample pulled from this population? The SPSS program can be commanded to select a random sample of cases from a data set, so this function will be used to simulate sampling. A random sample of 50 facilities was pulled from the CSFACF data file and the variable *total number of inmates* plotted to form Figure 7.2. The sample distribution looks somewhat similar to the population distribution in that they both evince a clear positive skew; however, you can see that there are clear differences between them. This is because there are only 50 cases in this sample, and 50 is a very small subset of 1,821.

Figure 7.1   Population Distribution for Total Inmates per Correctional Facility ($N = 1,821$)

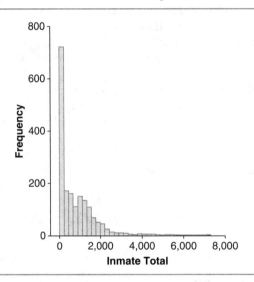

We can try the sampling exercise again and this time pull 300 cases randomly. Figure 7.3 shows the *total inmates* histogram for this second sample. This histogram is a close match to that for the entire population, which is a function of the larger sample size. We have thus demonstrated a fact that will be critical to the understanding of empirical distributions: All else being equal, larger samples are better reflections of the populations from which they are derived.

Some terms require definition before this discussion proceeds any further. First, although we have encountered the word *statistic* several times up to this point, it is relevant now to offer a formal definition of this concept. A **statistic** is a number that describes a sample. This might be a mean, proportion, or standard deviation. The second term is **parameter**. A parameter is just like a statistic except that it describes a population. Populations, like samples, have means, proportions, standard deviations, and so on. Statistics are estimates of parameters. Table 7.1 displays the symbols for some common statistics and their corresponding parameters. The statistic notations for the mean and standard deviation are familiar from previous chapters, but this is the first time we have considered the population symbols. They are Greek letters. The population mean is the lowercase version of the letter mu (μ; pronounced "mew"), and the standard deviation is a

Figure 7.2   Sample Distribution (*N* = 50)

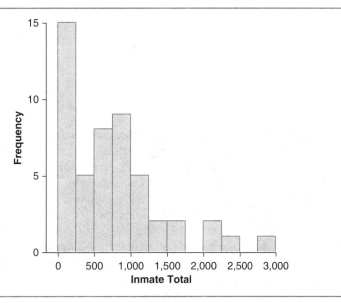

lowercase sigma (σ). The population proportion is a less exciting uppercase *P*. We have previously represented sample proportions with a lowercase *p*, but now that we are differentiating between samples and populations, we are going to change the letter to $\hat{p}$, which is pronounced "p hat."

Figure 7.3   Sample Distribution (*N* = 300)

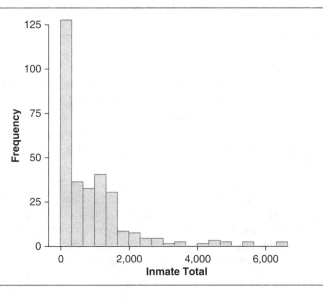

Table 7.1 Symbols for Common Statistics and Their Corresponding Parameters

	Sample Statistic	Population Parameter
Mean	$\bar{x}$	μ
Standard deviation	s	σ
Proportion	$\hat{p}$	P

Often, what criminal justice and criminology researchers want is to make a statement about a population, but what they actually have in front of them to work with is a sample. This creates a conundrum because sample statistics cannot simply be generalized to population parameters. Statistics are estimates of population parameters and, moreover, they are estimates that contain error (as demonstrated by Figures 7.1 through 7.3). Population parameters are fixed. This means that they have only one mean and standard deviation. Sample statistics, by contrast, vary from sample to sample because of sampling error. Sampling error arises from the fact that multiple (theoretically, infinite) random samples can be drawn from any population. Any given sample that a researcher *actually* draws is only one of a multitude that he or she *could* have drawn. Figure 7.4 depicts this. Every potential sample has its own distribution and set of descriptive statistics. In any given sample, these statistics might be exactly equal to, roughly equal to, or completely different from their corresponding parameters.

Statistic: A number that describes a sample that has been drawn from a larger population.

Parameter: A number that describes a population from which samples might be drawn.

Sampling error: The uncertainty introduced into a sample statistic by the fact that any given sample is one of many samples that could have been drawn from that population.

The CSFACF can be used to illustrate the effects of sampling error. As described earlier, this data set is a population; therefore, samples can be drawn from it. We will continue using the variable *total number of inmates housed*. The population means is $\mu = 785.53$, and the standard deviation is $\sigma = 935.20$. Drawing five random samples of 300 facilities each and computing the mean and standard deviation of each sample produces the data in Table 7.2.

Look how the means and standard deviations vary—this is sampling error! Sample 5's mean is 739.04, while Sample 2's is a very different 888.66. There is a substantial amount of variation among the samples, and each one differs from the true population mean by a smaller or larger amount. In this example, we have the benefit of knowing the true population mean and standard deviation, but that is usually not the case in criminal justice and criminology research. What researchers generally have is one sample and no direct information about the population as a whole. Imagine, for instance, that you drew Sample 3 in Table 7.2. This sample's mean and standard deviation are reasonable approximations of—though clearly not equivalent to—their corresponding population

Figure 7.4 Multiple Random Samples Can Be Drawn From a Population

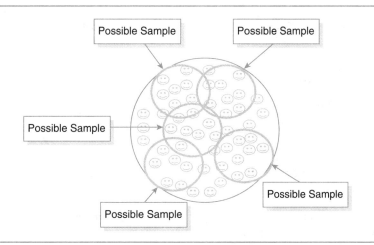

Table 7.2 Means and Standard Deviations for the Total Inmates in the Population (N = 1,821) and Five Random Samples of N = 300

	Population	*Sample 1*	*Sample 2*	*Sample 3*	*Sample 4*	*Sample 5*
Mean	μ = 785.53	806.66	888.66	772.98	751.16	739.04
Std. Dev.	σ = 935.20	919.68	1008.97	919.77	903.45	840.20

values, but you would not know that. Now picture Sample 2 being the sample you pulled for a particular study. This mean and standard deviation are markedly discrepant from the population parameters, but, again, you would be unaware of that.

There is, thus, a chasm between samples and populations that is created by sampling error and prevents inferences from being made directly. It would be a mistake to draw a sample, compute its mean, and automatically assume that the population mean must be equal or close to the sample mean. As displayed pictorially in Figure 7.5, sampling error prevents direct inference from a sample to the larger population from which it was drawn. What is needed is a bridge between samples and populations so that inferences can be reliably drawn. This bridge is the sampling distribution.

Theoretical Distributions: Sampling Distributions

Sampling distributions, unlike population and sample distributions, are theoretical; that is, they do not exist as empirical realities. We have already worked with theoretical distributions in the form of the binomial and standard normal distributions. Sampling distributions are theoretical

Figure 7.5   The Relationship Between Samples, Sampling Error, and Populations

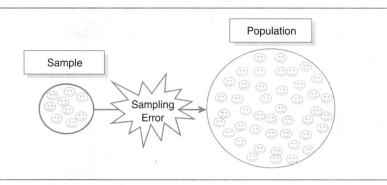

because they are based on the notion of multiple (even infinite) samples being drawn from a single population. What sets sampling distributions apart from empirical distributions is that sampling distributions are created not from raw scores but, rather, from sample statistics. These descriptors can be means, proportions, or any other statistic. Imagine plotting the means in Table 7.2 to form a histogram, like Figure 7.6.

Not terribly impressive, is it? Definitely leaves something to be desired. That is because there are only five samples. Sampling distributions start to take shape only when many samples have been drawn. If we continue the iterative process of drawing a sample, computing the mean, plotting that mean, throwing the sample back, and pulling a new sample, the distribution in Figure 7.6 gradually starts looking something like the curve in Figure 7.7.

Figure 7.6   Histogram of the Five Sample Means in Table 7.2

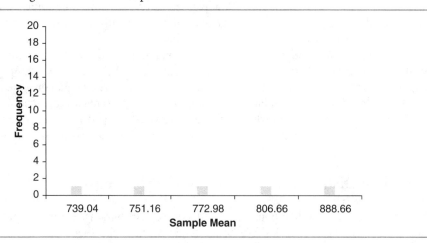

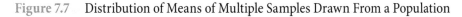

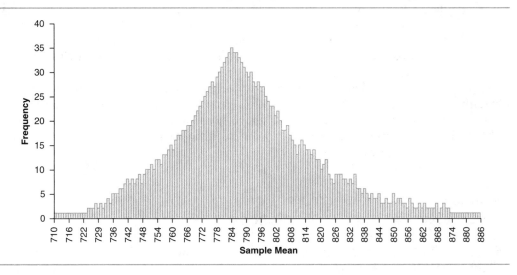

Now the distribution has some shape! It looks much better. It is, moreover, not just any old shape—it is a normal curve. What you have just seen is the **central limit theorem** (CLT) in action. The CLT states that any time descriptive statistics are computed from an infinite number of large samples, the resulting sampling distribution will be normally distributed. The sampling distribution clusters around the true population mean (here, 785.53) and if you were to compute the mean of the sampling distribution (i.e., the mean of means), the answer you obtained would match the true population mean. Its standard deviation (called the **standard error**) is smaller than the population standard deviation because there is less dispersion, or variability, in means than in raw scores. This produces a narrower distribution, particularly as the size of the samples increases. The mean of the sampling distribution is symbolized $\mu_{\bar{x}}$ and the standard error is represented as $\sigma_{\bar{x}}$.

Central limit theorem: The property of the sampling distribution that guarantees that this curve will be normally distributed when infinite samples of large size have been drawn.

Standard error: The standard deviation of the sampling distribution.

The CLT is integral to statistics because of its guarantee that the sampling distribution will be normal when a sample is large. Criminal justice and criminology researchers work with many variables that show signs of skew or kurtosis. The CLT saves the day by ensuring that even skewed or kurtotic variables will produce normal sampling distributions. The inmate count variable demonstrates this. Compare Figure 7.7 to Figure 7.3. Figure 7.3 is derived from a single sample ($N = 300$) and is highly skewed, yet the sampling distribution in Figure 7.7 is normal. That is because even when raw values produce skew, sample statistics will still hover around the population parameter and fall symmetrically on each side of it. Some statistics will be greater than the parameter and some will be smaller, but the majority will be close approximations of (or even precisely equal to) the true population value.

All descriptive statistics have sampling distributions to which the CLT applies. In Chapter 6, you learned that nationwide, .62 (or 62%) of felony defendants are granted pretrial release. Figure 7.8 sketches what the sampling distribution of proportions for the pretrial release variable might look like. You can see that this curve is roughly normal in shape, too, just like the sampling distributions of means in Figure 7.7.

Sample Size and the Sampling Distribution: The z and t Distributions

The key benefit of the sampling distribution being normally distributed is that the standard normal curve can be used. Everything we did in Chapter 6 with respect to using raw scores to find z scores, z scores to find areas, and areas to find z scores can be done with the sampling distribution. The applicability of z, though, is contingent on N being large. *Large* is a vague adjective in statistics because there is no formal rule specifying the dividing line between small and large samples. Generally speaking, large samples are those containing at least 100 cases. When $N \geq 100$, the sampling distribution can be assumed to be normally distributed, and the standard normal curve can be

Figure 7.8   Sampling Distribution of Proportions

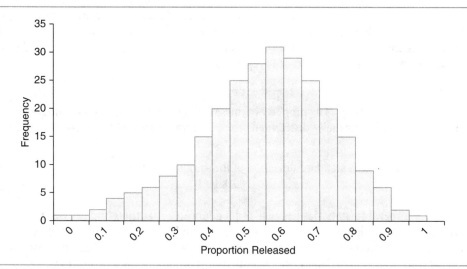

used. This requirement reduces the overall usefulness of the *z* distribution; it turns out that the standard normal curve makes somewhat rigid demands, and many real-world data sets fall short of these expectations.

Although it is generally not advisable to work with samples smaller than 100, there are times when it is unavoidable. In these situations, the *z* distribution cannot be employed and researchers turn to is the **t distribution** instead. The *t* distribution—like the *z* curve—is symmetric, unimodal, and has a constant area of 1.00. The key difference between the two is that *t* is a family of several different curves rather than one fixed, single curve like *z* is. The *t* distribution changes shape depending on the size of the sample. When the sample is small, the curve is wide and flattish; as the sample size increases, the *t* curve becomes more and more normal until it looks identical to the *z* curve. See Figure 7.9.

---

t distribution: A family of curves whose shapes are determined by the size of the sample. All *t* curves are unimodal, symmetric, and have an area of 1.00.

Figure 7.9   The Family of *t* Curves

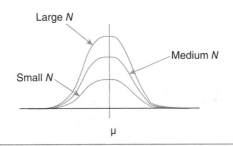

This phenomenon can also be demonstrated using hypothetical examples of random samples from the CSFACF data set. Figures 7.10 and 7.11 demonstrate how the *t* curve would change shape depending on the size of the samples being randomly selected from this population. The curve in Figure 7.10 is based on a sample size of 75, and that in Figure 7.11 is premised on *N* = 25. The top curve is taller and thinner; by contrast, the lower curve is wider and flatter. This is because there is more variability in smaller samples—it is difficult to get an accurate estimate of the true population parameter when there are only 25 cases. A sample of *N* = 75 is not ideal, by any means, but it is an improvement over 25.

The *t* distribution's flexibility allows it to accommodate samples of various sizes. It is an important theoretical probability distribution because it allows researchers to do much more than they would be able to if *z* were their only option. All else being equal, large samples are better than small ones, and it is always advisable to work with large samples when possible. When a small sample must be used, though, *t* is a trustworthy alternative. We will use both the *z* and *t* distributions in later chapters.

Figure 7.10   The *t* Distribution for Inmate Population at *N* = 75

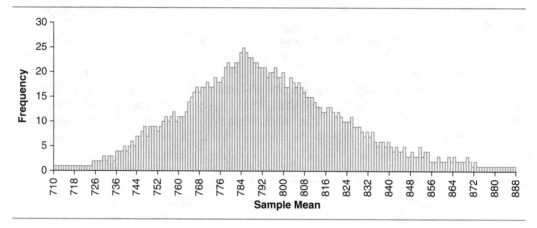

Figure 7.11   The *t* Distribution for Inmate Population at *N* = 25

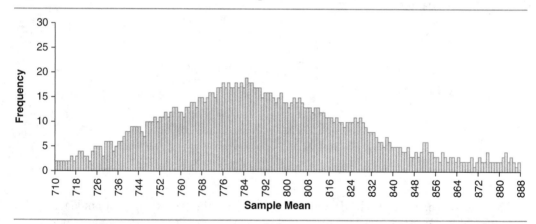

CHAPTER SUMMARY

Criminal justice and criminology researchers often seek information about populations. Populations, though, are usually too large to analyze directly. Samples are therefore pulled from them and statistical analyses are applied to these samples instead. Population and sample distributions are made of raw scores that have been plotted. These are empirical distributions.

Sampling error, though, introduces an element of uncertainty into sample statistics. Any given sample that is drawn is only one of a multitude of samples that could have been drawn. Because of sampling error, statistics are merely estimates of their corresponding population parameters and cannot be interpreted as matching them exactly. In this way, there is a gap between samples and populations.

The sampling distribution links samples to populations. Sampling distributions are theoretical curves made out of infinite sample statistics. All descriptive statistics have sampling distributions. The central limit theorem ensures that sampling distributions are normal when sample sizes are large (i.e., $N \geq 100$). When this is the case, the z distribution can be used. When samples are small, though, the sampling distribution cannot be assumed to be normal. The t distribution solves this problem because t is a family of curves that change shape depending on sample size. The t distribution is more flexible than z and must be used any time $N \leq 99$, though it can be used with large samples as well.

CHAPTER 7 REVIEW PROBLEMS

1. Population distributions are . . .

   a. empirical.
   b. theoretical.

2. Sample distributions are . . .

   a. empirical.
   b. theoretical.

3. Sampling distributions are . . .

   a. empirical.
   b. theoretical.

4. The _____ distribution is made from the raw scores in a sample.

5. The _____ distribution is made from statistics calculated on multiple or infinite samples.

6. The _____ distribution is made from the raw scores in a population.

7. The central limit theorem guarantees that as long as certain conditions are met, a sampling distribution will be . . .

   a. positively skewed.
   b. normally distributed.
   c. negatively skewed.

8. For the central limit theorem's promise of distribution shape to hold true, samples must be . . .

   a. large.
   b. small.

9. When a sample contains 100 or more cases, the correct probability distribution to use is the _____ distribution.

10. When a sample contains 99 or fewer cases, the correct probability distribution to use is the _____ distribution.

11. A researcher gathers a sample of 200 people, asks each one how many times he or she has been arrested, and then plots each person's response. From the list below, select the type of distribution that this researcher has created.

   a. A sample distribution with a large N
   b. A population distribution with a small N
   c. A sampling distribution with a large N
   d. A sample distribution with a large N

12. A researcher gathers a sample of 49 police departments, finds out how many officers were fired for misconduct in each department over a 2-year time span, and plots each department's score. From the list below, select the type of distribution that this researcher has created.

   a. A population distribution with a small N
   b. A population distribution with a large N
   c. A sampling distribution with a small N
   d. A sample distribution with a small N

13. A researcher gathers a sample of 20 cities, calculates each city's mean homicide rate, and plots that mean. Then the researcher puts that sample back into the population and draws a new sample of 20 cities and computes and plots the mean homicide rate. The researcher does this repeatedly. From the list below, select the type of distribution that this researcher has created.

   a. A sampling distribution with a large N
   b. A population distribution with a small N
   c. A sampling distribution with a small N
   d. A population distribution with a large N

14. A researcher has data on each of the nearly 2,000 adult correctional facilities in the United States and uses them to plot the number of inmate-on-inmate assaults that took place inside each prison in a 1-year span. From the list below, select the type of distribution that this researcher has created.

   a. A sample distribution with a large N
   b. A population distribution with a small N
   c. A sampling distribution with a large N
   d. A population distribution with a large N

15. A researcher gathers a sample of 132 people and computes the mean number of times the people in that sample have shoplifted. The researcher then puts this sample back into the population and draws a new sample of 132 people, for whom the researcher computes the mean number of times shoplifted. The researcher does this repeatedly. From the list below, select the type of distribution that this researcher has created.

   a. A sample distribution with a large N
   b. A sampling distribution with a large N
   c. A sample distribution with a small N
   d. A population distribution with a large N

Population distribution   Statistic   Central limit theorem

Sample distribution   Parameter   Standard error

Sampling distribution   Sampling error t distribution

μ	The population mean (mu)
σ	The population standard deviation (sigma)
P	The population proportion
$\hat{p}$	The sample proportion (p hat)
$\mu_{\bar{x}}$	The mean of the sampling distribution
$\sigma_{\bar{x}}$	The standard error
t	A distribution that is a family of curves that can accommodate both small and large sample sizes

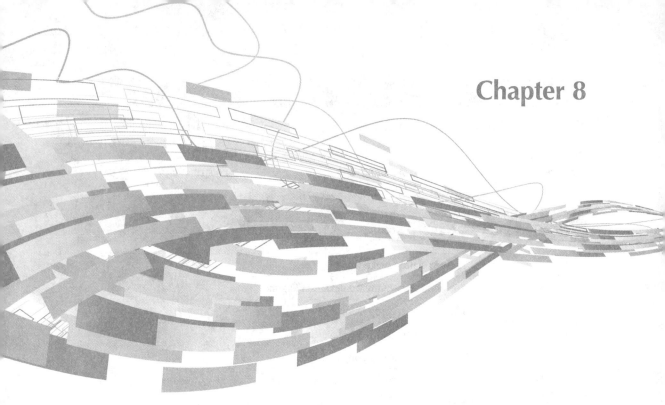

Chapter 8

Point Estimates and Confidence Intervals

Any given sample that is drawn from a population is only one of a multitude of samples that *could have* been drawn. Every sample that is drawn (and every sample that could potentially be drawn) has its own descriptive statistics, such as a mean or proportion. This phenomenon, as you learned in Chapter 7, is called sampling error. The variation in sample statistics such as means and proportions prevents direct inference from a sample to a population. It cannot be assumed that a mean or proportion in a sample is an exact match to the mean or proportion in the population because sometimes sample statistics are very similar to their corresponding population parameters and other times they are quite dissimilar. Flip back to Figure 7.5 for a pictorial illustration of this concept. What this means is that there is always an element of uncertainty in a sample statistic, or what can also be called a point estimate.

Point estimate: A sample statistic, such as a mean or proportion.

Confidence interval: A range of values spanning a point estimate that is calculated so as to have a certain probability of containing the population parameter.

Fortunately, though, a procedure exists for calculating a range of values within which the parameter of interest may lie. This range stretches out on each side of the point estimate and is called a confidence interval (*CI*). The confidence interval acts as a sort of "bubble" that introduces flexibility into the estimate. It is much more likely that an estimate of the value of a population parameter is accurate when the estimate is a range of values rather than one single value.

Try thinking about it this way: Suppose I guessed that you are originally from Chicago. This is a very precise prediction! Of all the cities and towns in the world, I narrowed my guess down to a single area. Given its precision, though, this prediction is very likely to be wrong; there are 7 billion people in the world and only about 2.8 million of them live in Chicago. My point estimate (Chicago) is probably incorrect.

But what if I instead guessed that you are from the state of Illinois? There are 12.9 million people in Illinois, so I have increased my chances of being correct because I have broadened the scope of my estimate. If I went up another step and predicted that you are from the Midwest—without specifying a city or state—I have further increased my probability of being right, since this is a much larger geographic region and contains more than 66 million residents. It is still possible that I am wrong, of course, but I am far more likely to guess your place of origin correctly when I guess a large geographical area, such as a region, than when I guess a much smaller one, such as a city.

This is, conceptually, what a confidence interval does. It offers a "buffer zone" that allows for greater confidence in the correctness of a prediction. It also allows us to determine the probability that the prediction we are making is accurate. Using distributions—specifically, the *z* and *t* probability curves—we can figure out how likely it is that our confidence interval truly does contain the true population parameter. The probability that the interval contains the parameter is called the level of confidence.

Level of confidence: The probability that a confidence interval contains the population parameter. Commonly set at 95% or 99%.

The Level of Confidence: The Probability of Being Correct

In the construction of confidence intervals, you get to choose your level of confidence (i.e., the probability that your confidence interval accurately estimates the population parameter). This may sound great at first blush—why not just choose 100% confidence and be done with it, right?—but confidence is actually the classic double-edged sword because there is a trade-off between it and precision. Think back to the Chicago/Illinois/Midwest example. The Chicago guess has a very low probability of being correct (we could say that there is a low level of confidence in this prediction), but it has the benefit of being a very precise estimate because it is just one city. The Illinois guess carries an improvement in confidence because it is a bigger geographical territory; however, because it is bigger, it is also less precise. If I guess that you are from Illinois and I am right, I am still left with many unknown pieces of information about you. I would not know which part of the state you are from, whether you hail from a rural farming community or a large urban center, what the socioeconomic characteristics of your place of origin are, and so on.

The problem gets worse if all I guess is that you are from the Midwest—now I would not even know which state you are from, much less which city! If I want to be 100% sure that I will guess your place of origin correctly, I have to put forth "planet Earth" as my prediction. That is a terrible estimate. If you want greater confidence in your estimate, then, you pay the price of reduced precision and, therefore, a diminished amount of useful information.

Confidence levels are expressed in percentages. Although there is no "right" or "wrong" level of confidence in a technical sense (i.e., there is nothing mathematically preventing you from opting for a 55% or 72% confidence level), 95% and 99% have become conventional in criminal justice and criminology research. Because of the trade-off between confidence and precision, a 99% *CI* has a greater chance than a 95% one of being correct, but the 99% one will be wider and less precise. A 95% *CI* will carry a slightly higher likelihood of error but will yield a more informative estimate. The 99% level would be akin to the Midwest guess in the previous example, whereas the 95% would be like the Chicago guess. You should select your level of confidence by deciding whether it is more important that your estimate be correct or that it be precise.

Confidence levels are set *a priori*, which means that you must decide whether you are going to use 95% or 99% before you begin constructing the interval. The reason for this is that the level of confidence affects the calculation of the interval. You will see this when we get to the *CI* formula.

Since we are dealing with probabilities, we have to face the unpleasant reality that our prediction may be incorrect. The flipside of the probability of being right (i.e., your confidence level) is the probability of being wrong. Consider

$$100\% - 95\% = 5\%$$

$$100\% - 99\% = 1\%$$

Each of these traditional levels of confidence carries a corresponding probability that a confidence interval does *not* contain the true population parameter. If the 95% level is selected, then there is a 5% chance that the *CI* will not contain the parameter; a 99% level of confidence generates a 1% chance of an inaccurate *CI*.

You will, unfortunately, likely never know whether the sample you have in front of you is one of the 95% or 99% that is correct, or whether it is one of the 5% or 1% that is not. There is no way to tell; you just have to compute the confidence interval and hope for the best. This is an intractable problem in statistics because of the reliance on probability.

Three types of confidence intervals will be discussed in this chapter: *CIs* for means with large samples ($N \geq 100$), for means with small samples ($N \leq 99$), and for proportions or percentages. All three types of *CIs* are meant to improve the accuracy of point estimates by providing a range of values that most likely contains the true population parameter.

Confidence Intervals for Means With Large Samples

When a sample is of large size ($N \geq 100$), the *z* distribution (the standard normal curve) can be used to construct a *CI* around a sample mean. Confidence intervals for means with large samples are computed as

$$CI = \bar{x} \pm z_{\alpha}\left(\frac{s}{\sqrt{N-1}}\right),$$ *Formula 8(1)*

where $\bar{x}$ = the sample mean,

z_{α} = the *z* score associated with a given alpha level (i.e., the critical value of *z*),

α = the probability of being wrong (the alpha level),

s = the sample standard deviation, and

N = the sample size.

This formula might appear intimidating, but we can read it left to right and break down the different elements. The starting point is the sample mean. A certain value will be added to and subtracted from the mean to form the interval. That value is the end result of the term on the right side of the ± operator. The *z* score's subscript α (this is the Greek letter *alpha*) represents the probability that the *CI* does not contain the true population parameter. Recall that every level of confidence carries a certain probability of inaccuracy; this probability of inaccuracy is α or, more formally, the **alpha level**. Alpha is computed as

$$\alpha = 1 - \text{confidence level}.$$ *Formula 8(2)*

Alpha level: The opposite of the confidence level; that is, the probability that a confidence interval does not contain the true population parameter. Symbolized α.

For 95% and 99% confidence, first convert the percentages to proportions. Then

$$\alpha_{95\%} = 1 - .95 = .05,$$

$$\alpha_{99\%} = 1 - .99 = .01.$$

Alpha, itself, is not inserted into the *CI* formula; rather, α is used to find the **critical value** of z, and you enter that critical value into the formula (this is the z_α term in Formula 8[1]). The critical value of z is the z score associated with a particular area on the curve. In other words, it is the score beyond which a certain area (this being alpha) is out in the tail. We will see later that the t curve has critical values, too.

There is another piece of information that you need to know about *CI*s: They are always **two-tailed**. This is because the normal curve has two halves that are split by the mean, with the result being—to put a rather pessimistic spin on it—that there are two ways to be wrong with a confidence interval. The first option is for the interval to be wholly above the mean and miss it by being too far out in the positive tail, and the second possibility is that it lands entirely below the mean and misses it by being too far out into the negative side. Since either error is possible—and since we have no control over which type of error we might end up with—we must utilize both sides of the curve. This is called a two-tailed test. In a two-tailed test, the alpha level is split in half and placed in each of the two tails of the distribution, as pictured in Figure 8.1. Two-tailed tests, then, actually have *two* critical values. The absolute value of these critical values is the same because the curve is symmetric, but one value is negative and the other is positive. Confidence intervals, by definition, utilize both of the critical values for any alpha level.

Figure 8.1   The Alpha Level and Critical Values of z

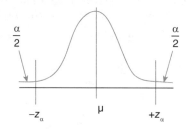

So, what are these critical values? For the standard normal curve, we can find them using the techniques we learned in Chapter 6. Recall that in the z-score exercises, we figured out how to find z scores using specified areas: essentially, the z table (see Appendix B) is used backward. Let us begin with the 95% confidence interval. First, we have to find α, which is 5%. Second, because this is a two-tailed test, we divide α in half, as shown in Figure 8.1. Doing this shows that the critical value of z is going to be the value that leaves 2.5% of cases in each tail of the distribution. Of course, we cannot work with percentages in the z table, so we have to convert this to .025. Third, the z table is used to find the critical value of z. We have done this before, in Chapter 6. What we are asking here is, "If the area in the tail is .025, what is z?" The tail must first be subtracted from .50:

$$.50 - .025 = .4750.$$

Next, go to the z table and locate the area that is equal to .4750 or, if there is no area that is exactly .4750, the area that is closest. In this instance, the value we are seeking is actually located in the table. Trace away from .4750 upward along the column and to the left along the row, and record each of the numbers you arrive at. Here,

$$z = 1.9 + .06 = 1.96.$$

We are not quite done! Remember that there are *two* critical values, not just one. Since the standard normal curve is symmetric and .025 is the area in each tail, these two z scores will take on the same absolute value but will have opposite signs. Thus, $z_{\alpha=.05} = \pm 1.96$. The critical value of z for the top .025 (the positive side of the curve) is 1.96, and the value for the bottom .025 (the negative side) is −1.96. Figure 8.2 displays the two critical values of z for a 95% confidence level.

Figure 8.2   Critical Values of z for a 95% Level of Confidence

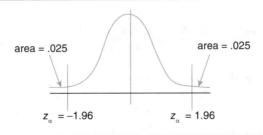

The same process is used to find z_α for a 99% confidence level. First, alpha is 100% – 99% = 1%. Second, 1% divided in half is .5% and converted to a proportion is .005. Third, .50 – .005 = .4950. This exact value does not appear in the z table, so the z scores associated with the two closest values (.4949 and .4951) must be averaged. These scores are 2.57 and 2.58. Therefore,

$$z = \frac{2.57 + 2.58}{2} = \frac{5.15}{2} = 2.575.$$

The critical value is 2.58. Again, remember that there are two values, so z is actually ±2.58. This is displayed graphically in Figure 8.3.

Figure 8.3   Critical Values of z for a 99% Level of Confidence

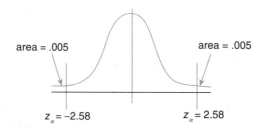

The standard normal curve is handy because it is fixed; therefore, the critical values of z for 95% and 99% confidence intervals will always be ±1.96 and ±2.58, respectively. Later on, you will see that this is not the case when the t distribution is employed; in that situation, the critical value of t will have to be located each time you calculate a confidence interval. For now, though, we can rely on these two critical values.

LEARNING CHECK

Now that you have seen the formula for calculating confidence intervals and you know that the critical value of z for 95% confidence is ±1.96 and that for 99% is ±2.58, which level of confidence do you think will produce a wider confidence interval (i.e., a less precise estimate)? Write down your prediction so that when we get to the calculations, you can see if you were correct.

The Census of Jail Inmates

The Bureau of Justice Statistics maintains the National Jail Census Series, which is a repository of data sets pertaining to jails across the nation. The Census of Jail Inmates (CJI) is one of the files in this series. The CJI contains inmate data for all local and federal jails, including those operated by private companies, that hold inmates who are awaiting trial or who have been convicted and are serving a short term of incarceration. Jail-level variables include the total confined population; the confined population broken down by race, gender, and conviction status; and admissions and discharges. The 2005 wave is the most recent version of the CJI. All 2,972 jails in operation in 2005 provided data for the CJI (Bureau of Justice Statistics, n.d.); therefore, this is a population rather than a sample.

Now let's consider an example. The Bureau of Justice Statistics maintains a data set called the Census of Jail Inmates (CJI; see Data Sources 8.1). This data set is ideal for present purposes because it contains population data (i.e., it is a census, not a sample, of jails), so we can compute the actual population mean and then pull a random sample, compute its mean and confidence interval, and see if the computed interval contains the true population value. Remember that ordinarily, researchers are not able to access information on the population parameters (and, obviously, if you knew the population mean, there would be no point in attempting to estimate that mean using a confidence interval); what we are doing here is for demonstration purposes only.

The variable that will be used is *unconvicted female inmates*, which is the mean number of women being held in pretrial detention across all facilities. The confidence level will be set at 95%.

In the population, the mean number of female inmates who have not been convicted is $\mu = 18.53$ ($\sigma = 60.51$). Let us use a sample size of $N = 150$, which is a modest sample size but is large enough to permit use of the z distribution. The SPSS random-sample generator produces a sample with a mean of $\overline{x} = 28.25$ and a standard deviation of $s = 76.24$. Since the confidence level is 95%, $z_\alpha = \pm 1.96$. Plugging values for N, $\overline{x}$, s, and z_α into Formula 8(1) yields

$$CI = \overline{x} \pm z_\alpha \left(\frac{s}{\sqrt{N-1}} \right)$$

$$= 28.25 \pm 1.96 \left(\frac{76.24}{\sqrt{150-1}} \right)$$

$$= 28.25 \pm 1.96 \left(\frac{76.24}{12.21} \right)$$

$$= 28.25 \pm 1.96\left(6.24\right)$$

$$= 28.25 \pm 12.23.$$

Let's pause for a moment and consider what we have calculated thus far. We have the mean (28.25) as the midpoint of the interval, and now we know that the "buffer" is going to extend 12.23 units above and 12.23 units below the mean. Picture these two extensions of the mean as forming the full width of the interval.

The next step is to compute the lower limit (*LL*) and the upper limit (*UL*) of the interval, which requires the ± operation to be carried out, as such:

$$LL = 28.25 - 12.23 = 16.02$$

$$UL = 28.25 + 12.23 = 40.48$$

Finally, the full interval can be written out:

$$95\% \ CI\text{: } 16.02 \leq \mu \leq 40.48$$

The interpretation of this interval is that there is a 95% chance that the true population mean is 16.02, 40.48, or some number in between those values (more formally, it can be stated, "There is a 95% chance that the interval 16.02 to 40.48, inclusive, contains the true value of μ"). Of course, this also means that there is a 5% chance that the true population mean is *not* in this range. In the present example, we know that $\mu = 18.53$, so we can see that here, the confidence interval does indeed contain the population mean. That is good! This sample was one of the 95% that produces accurate confidence intervals rather than one of the 5% that does not. Remember, though, that knowing the value of the true population mean is a luxury that researchers generally do not have; ordinarily, there is no way to check the accuracy of a sample-based confidence interval.

Let us repeat the previous example using a 99% confidence level. This set of calculations would proceed as such:

$$CI = \bar{x} \pm z_\alpha \left(\frac{s}{\sqrt{N-1}} \right)$$

$$= 28.25 \pm 2.58 \left(\frac{76.24}{\sqrt{150-1}} \right)$$

$$= 28.25 \pm 2.58 \left(\frac{76.24}{12.21} \right)$$

$$= 28.25 \pm 2.58\left(6.24\right)$$

$$= 28.25 \pm 16.10$$

$$LL = 28.25 - 16.10 = 12.15$$

$$UL = 28.25 + 16.10 = 44.35$$

$$99\% \ CI\!: 12.15 \leq \mu \leq 44.35$$

There is a 99% chance that the interval 12.15 to 44.35, inclusive, contains the population mean μ. Again, we know that $\mu = 18.53$, so this interval does, indeed, contain the parameter. Take a look at the difference in width between these two intervals. The 95% interval ranges from 16.02 to 40.48, and the 99% one spans 12.15 to 44.35; thus, the 99% interval is much wider than the 95% one. Can you explain the reason for this? If you said that it is because with a 99% confidence level we sacrifice precision in the estimate, you are correct! When we enhanced our confidence, we increased z from 1.96 to 2.58, thus causing an expansion of the interval. This demonstrates the trade-off between confidence and precision.

For a third example, we will use the Police-Public Contact Survey (PPCS; see Data Sources 2.1). This is not a population—the survey was administered to a random sample of U.S. residents. We must, therefore, use sample statistics to estimate the true population values. Let us consider the ages of respondents who reported having experienced multiple (i.e., more than one) contact with police officers during the past year and construct a 99% CI to estimate the mean age for the population. These multiple-contact respondents had $\bar{x} = 45.23$ and $s = 16.80$ ($N = 2{,}304$). The CI is

$$CI = 45.23 \pm 2.58 \left(\frac{16.80}{\sqrt{2304 - 1}} \right)$$

$$= 45.23 \pm 2.58 \left(\frac{16.80}{47.99} \right)$$

$$= 45.23 \pm 2.58 (.35)$$

$$= 45.23 \pm .90 \, .$$

Now calculate the lower and upper limits:

$$LL = 45.23 - .90 = 44.33$$

$$UL = 45.23 + .90 = 46.13$$

Finally, construct the interval:

$$99\% \ CI\!: 44.33 \leq \mu \leq 46.13$$

We can say with 99% confidence that the interval 44.33 and 46.13, inclusive, contains μ.

Something to note before we move on is the dramatic difference in width between the two 99% confidence intervals that we calculated using the z distribution. The reason is the sample size. In the first example, the sample size was 150. This is small by statistical standards; it is technically large enough to allow use of the z distribution, but it is not big enough to put a lot of faith in. There is a certain level of untrustworthiness present in a sample of 150—the statistic (in this case, the mean) is not a reliable estimate of the population parameter. This is why we ended up with such a wide confidence interval: There was a lot of uncertainty in the statistic, due to the sample size, so the interval had to be very wide in order to create a 99% probability of correctly encompassing the population mean. Contrast this to the second example, where the sample size was 2,304. This is a very large sample! Samples this big allow us to trust that their means are good estimates of the true population parameters; quite simply, the confidence interval can be more precise (narrower) because the data are of higher quality. All else being equal, larger samples will produce more accurate estimates and, thus, smaller confidence intervals.

RESEARCH EXAMPLE 8.1

Is There a Relationship Between Unintended Pregnancy and Intimate Partner Violence?

Intimate partner violence (IPV) perpetrated by a man against a female intimate is often associated with not just physical violence but a multifaceted web of control in which the woman becomes trapped and isolated. One of the possible consequences is that abused women may not have access to reliable birth control and may therefore be susceptible to unintended pregnancies. These pregnancies, moreover, might worsen the IPV situation because of the emotional and financial burden of pregnancy and childbearing. Martin and Garcia (2011) sought to explore the relationship between IPV and unintended pregnancy in a sample of Latina women in Los Angeles, California. Latinas may be especially vulnerable to both IPV and unintended pregnancy because of the social isolation faced by those who have not assimilated into mainstream U.S. culture. Staff at various prenatal clinics in Los Angeles distributed surveys to their Latina patients. The surveys asked women several questions pertaining to whether they intended to get pregnant, whether they experienced emotional or physical abuse by their partner before or during pregnancy, and their level of identification with Mexican versus with Anglo culture. They used a statistic called an *odds ratio*. An odds ratio measures the extent to which consideration of certain independent variables changes the likelihood that the dependent variable will occur. An odds ratio of 1.00 means that the independent variable (IV) does not change the likelihood of the dependent variable (DV). Odds ratios greater than 1.00 mean that an IV increases the probability that the DV will occur, and those less than 1.00 indicate that an IV reduces the chances of the DV happening.

In Martin and Garcia's study, the DVs in the first analysis were physical and emotional abuse and the DV in the second analysis was physical abuse during pregnancy. The researchers found the following odds ratios and confidence intervals.

	DV: Change in Odds of Unintended Pregnancy	95% CI
IV: Prepregnancy Physical Abuse	.92	.40 ≤ population odds ≤ 2.16
IV: Prepregnancy Emotional Abuse	.50	.26 ≤ population odds ≤ .97

Prepregnancy physical abuse was not related to the chances that a woman would become pregnant accidentally, as indicated by the odds ratio of .92, which is very close to 1.00. Emotional abuse, surprisingly, significantly reduced the odds of accidental pregnancy (odds ratio = .50).

This was an unexpected finding because the researchers predicted that abuse would increase the odds of pregnancy. They theorized that perhaps some emotionally abused women try to get pregnant out of a hope that having a child will improve the domestic situation.

	DV: Change in Odds of Physical Abuse
IV: Unintended Pregnancy	2.80
95% CI	1.01 ≤ population odds ≤ 7.73

Turning to the second analysis, it can be seen that unintended pregnancy substantially increased women's odds of experiencing physical abuse during pregnancy. Contrary to expectations, women's level of acculturation into either Mexican or Anglo culture did not alter the odds of abuse or pregnancy, once factors such as a woman's age and level of education were accounted for. The findings indicated that the relationship between IPV and unintended pregnancy is complex and deserving of further study in order to identify risk factors for both.

Confidence Intervals for Means With Small Samples

The z distribution can be used to construct confidence intervals when $N \geq 100$ because the sampling distribution of means can be safely assumed to be normal in shape. When $N \leq 99$, though, this assumption breaks down and a different distribution is needed. This alternative distribution is the t curve. The *CI* formula for means with small samples is nearly identical to that for large samples; the only difference is that the critical value of t is used instead of the critical value of z. The formula is

$$CI = \bar{x} + t_\alpha \left(\frac{s}{\sqrt{N-1}} \right),$$

Formula 8(3)

where t_α = the critical value of t at a given alpha level.

The critical value of t (i.e., t_α) is found using the t table (see Appendix C). We have not used this table yet, so take a few minutes now to familiarize yourself with it. There are three pieces of information you need in order to locate t_α. The first is the number of tails. As described previously, confidence intervals are always two-tailed, so this is the option that is always used with this type of test. The second determinant of the value of t_α is the alpha level, the computation of which was shown in Formula 8(2). Finally, finding t_α requires you to first compute the degrees of freedom (df). With the t distribution, degrees of freedom are related to sample size, as such:

$$df = N - 1$$

Formula 8(4)

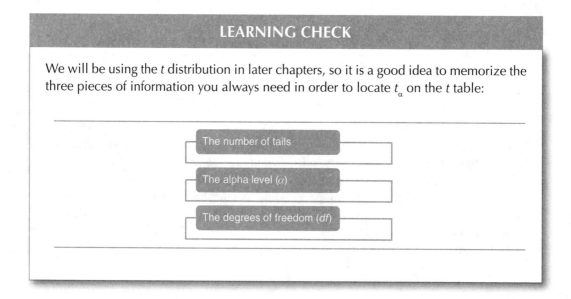

LEARNING CHECK

We will be using the t distribution in later chapters, so it is a good idea to memorize the three pieces of information you always need in order to locate t_α on the t table:

- The number of tails
- The alpha level (α)
- The degrees of freedom (df)

Take a moment now to practice using the *t* table. Find the critical value of *t* for each of the following:

  a. A two-tailed test with $\alpha = .05$ and $df = 10$

  b. A two-tailed test with $\alpha = .10$ and $df = 20$

  c. A two-tailed test with $\alpha = .01$ and $df = 60$

The *df* values are located in the rows of the *t* table. Note that not all of the possible values that *df* might assume are included on the table. When the number you are looking for is not there, it is customary to use the largest *df* that is less than the sample-derived *df*. If your sample size was 36, for instance, then your *df* would be 36 − 1 = 35; however, there is no *df* value of 35 on the table, so you would use the *df* = 30 row instead.

LEARNING CHECK

You have seen now that the value of *t* varies depending on the sample size. This is unlike *z*, which remains constant across samples of all sizes. Why is this? What is it about the *t* distribution that causes the critical value of *t* to change as the sample size changes? If you need a hint, flip back to Chapter 7 and, in particular, Figures 7.10 and 7.11.

For an example of *CIs* with means and small samples, the Firearm Injury Surveillance Study (FISS; see Data Sources 8.2) will be used. This data set contains information about a sample of patients treated in emergency departments for gunshot wounds between the years 1993 and 2010. For the current example, we will analyze the mean age of black female patients who were the victims of firearm assaults perpetrated by intimate partners (including ex-spouses). There were 68 such victims, and their mean age was 35.00 ($s = 13.31$). We will set a 95% confidence interval.

DATA SOURCES 8.2

The Firearm Injury Surveillance Study, 1993–2010

The Centers for Disease Control and Prevention maintain the National Electronic Injury Surveillance System, of which the Firearm Injury Surveillance Study (FISS) is a part. The

(Continued)

(Continued)

data are from a nationally representative sample of hospitals stratified by size. Detailed incident data include only those patients who did not die in the emergency department (ED) in which they were treated; those who died prior to arrival are assigned DOA status, and those who died after being transferred from the ED to some other hospital unit are coded as transfers (U.S. Department of Health and Human Services, n.d.). This is a limitation of the FISS that circumscribes its usefulness in criminal justice research, but this data set is nonetheless valuable as one of the few major studies that systematically tracks gun-related injuries. Data include patient age, sex, and race, as well as incident characteristics such as whether the shooting was intentional or unintentional and what the relationship was between the shooter and the victim. The most recent version of the FISS was collected in 2010.

The first thing that must be done to construct the *CI* is to find t_α. Going to the t table and using the three necessary pieces of information (this is a two-tailed test with $\alpha = 1 - .95 = .05$ and $df = 68 - 1 = 67$), you can see that $df = 67$ is not located on the table, so we must use the $df = 60$ row instead. The critical value of t is ± 2.000.

Next, plug all the numbers into Formula 8(2):

$$CI = \bar{x} + t_\alpha \left(\frac{s}{\sqrt{N-1}} \right),$$

$$= 35.00 \pm 2.000 \left(\frac{13.31}{\sqrt{68-1}} \right)$$

$$= 35.00 \pm 2.000 \left(\frac{13.31}{8.19} \right)$$

$$= 35.00 \pm 2.000 \left(1.63 \right)$$

$$= 35.00 \pm 3.26$$

Compute the lower and upper limits:

$$LL = 35.00 - 3.26 = 31.74$$

$$UL = 35.00 + 3.26 = 38.26$$

Finally, assemble the full confidence interval:

$$95\% \ CI: 31.74 \leq \mu \leq 38.26$$

There is a 95% chance that the interval 31.74 to 38.26, inclusive, contains the population mean.

Let's try one more example. We will again use the FISS and analyze the mean age of female victims of assault by an intimate partner, but this time we will focus on Hispanic women. In this sample, there were 19 Hispanic females with a mean age of 28.53 years and a standard deviation of 5.79. The confidence level will be 99%.

The three pieces of information needed for finding the critical value of t are that this is a two-tailed test, alpha is .01 (since $1 - .99 = .01$), and the degrees of freedom are $19 - 1 = 18$. With these criteria, $t_\alpha = 2.878$. Plugging all the numbers into Formula 8(2) yields

$$CI = 28.53 \pm 2.878 \left(\frac{5.79}{\sqrt{19-1}} \right)$$

$$= 28.53 \pm 2.878 \left(\frac{5.79}{4.24} \right)$$

$$= 28.53 \pm 2.878 (1.37)$$

$$= 28.53 \pm 3.94$$

The lower and upper limits are

$$LL = 28.53 - 3.94 = 24.59,$$

$$UL = 28.53 + 3.94 = 32.47.$$

The interval is

$$99\% \ CI: 24.59 \leq \mu \leq 32.47.$$

There is a 99% probability that the interval 24.59 to 32.47, inclusive, contains μ.

The interval calculated in the second example (24.59 to 32.47) is somewhat wide; it would be desirable to have a more precise estimate of μ. Use what you have learned thus far in the chapter to identify two actions that could be taken by a researcher who wished to shrink the interval and increase precision.

RESEARCH EXAMPLE 8.2

Why Do Suspects Confess to Police?

The U.S. Constitution's Fifth Amendment protection from compelled self-incrimination ensures that persons suspected of having committed criminal offenses do not have to speak to the police or answer any questions the police may ask. Despite this right, a good number of suspects do talk to police and do provide incriminating statements. As the wry saying goes, "Everyone has the *right* to remain silent, but not everyone has the *ability* to do so." So what makes suspects confess? Deslauriers-Varin, Beauregard, and Wong (2011) sought to identify some of the contextual factors that make suspects more likely to confess, even when those suspects initially indicated that they wished to remain silent. The researchers obtained a sample of 211 convicted male offenders from a Canadian prison and gathered extensive information about each participant. The researchers analyzed odds ratios, just as the study in Research Example 8.1 did. Recall that an odds ratio of 1.00 means

that the independent variable (IV) does not alter the odds that the dependent variable (DV) will occur. Odds ratios less than 1.00 mean the IV makes the DV less likely, whereas odds ratios greater than 1.00 indicate that the IV makes the DV more likely to happen. The researchers found the following odds ratios and confidence intervals.

The numbers in the following table that are flagged with asterisks are those that are statistically significant, meaning that the IV exerted a noteworthy impact on suspects' decision to remain silent rather than confessing. The initial decision to not confess was the strongest predictor of suspects' ultimate refusal to provide a confession; those who initially resisted confessing were likely to stick to that decision. Criminal history was also related—having only one or two priors was not related to nonconfession, but suspects with three or more prior convictions were substantially more likely to remain silent. This may be because these suspects were concerned about being sentenced harshly as habitual offenders. The presence of an accomplice also made nonconfession more likely, as did a lawyer's advice to not confess. Those accused of drug-related crimes were more likely to not confess, though crime type was not significant for suspects accused of other types of offenses. Finally, the strength of police evidence was a factor in suspects' decisions. Strong police evidence was related to a significant reduction in the odds of nonconfession (i.e., strong evidence resulted in a greater chance that the suspect would confess).

It appeared, then, that there are many factors that impact suspects' choice regarding confession. Most of these factors appear to be out of the control of police interrogators; however, the researchers did not include variables measuring police behavior during interrogation, so there may well be techniques police can use to elicit confessions even from those suspects who are disinclined to offer information. One policy implication from these results involves the importance of the initial decision in the final decision—79% of offenders stuck with their initial decision concerning whether to confess. Police might, therefore, benefit from focusing their efforts on influencing the initial decision rather than allowing a suspect to formulate a decision first and then applying interrogation tactics.

	DV: Suspect Did Not Confess	
Independent Variable	Change in Odds of No Confession	95% CI
Initial Decision: No Confession	25.33*	10.05, 63.82
Criminal History		
1 or 2 Prior Convictions	3.01	.79, 11.42
3+ Prior Convictions	13.29*	3.05, 57.91
Had an Accomplice	2.58*	1.02, 6.52
Police Evidence Is Strong	.23*	.10, .55
Lawyer Advised Nonconfession	3.29*	1.34, 8.07
Crime Was Drug-Related	3.55*	1.26, 10.02

Source: Adapted from Table 2 in Deslauriers-Varin, Beauregard, and Wong (2011).

*Statistically significant.

Confidence Intervals With Proportions and Percentages

The principles that guide the construction of confidence intervals around means also apply to confidence intervals around proportions and percentages. There is no difference in the procedure used for proportions versus that for percentages—percentages simply have to be converted to proportions before they are plugged into the *CI* formula. For this reason, we will speak in terms of proportions for the remainder of the discussion.

There are sampling distributions for proportions just as there are for means. Because of sampling error, a sample proportion (symbolized $\hat{p}$ pronounced "*p* hat") cannot be assumed to equal the population proportion (symbolized as an uppercase *P*), so confidence intervals must be created in order to estimate the population values with a certain level of probability.

Confidence intervals for proportions employ the *z* distribution. The normality of the sampling distribution of sample proportions is a bit iffy, but generally speaking, *z* is a safe bet as long as the sample is large (i.e., $N \geq 100$) and contains at least five successes and at least five failures. The formula for confidence intervals with proportions is

$$\hat{p} \pm z_\alpha \sqrt{\frac{\hat{p}(1-\hat{p})}{N}}, \qquad\qquad Formula\ 8(5)$$

where $\hat{p}$ = the sample proportion.

To illustrate *CIs* for proportions with large samples, we will again use the 2008 FISS. This time, we will examine the involvement of handguns in violent altercations. According to the FISS, handguns were the mechanism of injury in 49.50% of firearm injuries that resulted from fights, where the victim was a male between the ages of 13 and 18. The sample size is $N = 380$. Given this large sample size and the fact that the number of successes (defined here as the mechanism of injury being a handgun) and failures (the mechanism being any other type of firearm) both well exceed the minimum of five, the *z* distribution can be used and the analysis can proceed. Confidence will be set at 99%, which means $z_\alpha = \pm 2.58$.

First, the sample percentage needs to be converted to a proportion; dividing 49.50% by 100 and rounding to two decimal places yields .50.

Next, plug the numbers into Formula 8(5) and solve:

$$CI = \hat{p} \pm z_\alpha \sqrt{\frac{\hat{p}\left(1-\hat{p}\right)}{N}}$$

$$= .50 \pm 2.58 \sqrt{\frac{.50\left(1-.50\right)}{380}}$$

$$= .46 \pm 2.58 \sqrt{\frac{.50(.50)}{380}}$$

$$= .50 \pm 2.58 \sqrt{\frac{.25}{380}}$$

$$= .50 \pm 2.58 \left(\sqrt{.001} \right)$$

$$= .50 \pm 2.58 (.03)$$

$$= .50 \pm .08$$

The calculation of the lower and upper limits and the formal statement of the confidence interval proceeds along the same lines for proportions as for means. In the current example,

$$LL = .50 - .08 = .42$$

$$UL = .50 + .08 = .58$$

and

99% *CI*: $.42 \le P \le .58$.

We can say with 99% confidence that the interval .42 to .58, inclusive, contains the true population mean *P*.

LEARNING CHECK

Redo the confidence interval for the analysis of handgun usage in fights, this time using a 95% confidence level. What happened to the width of the interval? Why did this happen?

For a second example, we can again use the FISS and this time analyze gunshot wounds inflicted by law-enforcement officers. There were 403 people shot by police, and handguns were used in 88.3% of these cases (that is a proportion of .88). The confidence level will be set at 95%, making the critical value of $z \pm 1.96$. Using Formula 8(4),

$$CI = .88 \pm 1.96 \sqrt{\frac{.88(1-.88)}{403}}$$

$$= .88 \pm 1.96 \sqrt{\frac{.88(.12)}{403}}$$

$$= .88 \pm 1.96 \sqrt{\frac{.11}{403}}$$

$$= .88 \pm 1.96 \sqrt{.0003}$$

$$= .88 \pm 1.96(.02)$$

$$= .88 \pm .04,$$

the lower and upper limits are

$$LL = .88 - .04 = .84,$$

$$UL = .88 + .04 = .92.$$

Finally, the confidence interval is

$$95\% \ CI: .84 \leq P \leq .92.$$

There is a 95% chance that the interval .84 to .92, inclusive, contains the true population proportion P.

RESEARCH EXAMPLE 8.3

What Factors Influence Repeat Offenders' Completion of a DUI Court Program?

Specialized courts are an increasingly popular way for dealing with low-level offenders, especially those who have drug or mental-health problems. The rationale is that these people should not be incarcerated in jail or prison and should instead be allowed to remain in the community and complete one or more treatment programs to help them with their problems. Judges are responsible for supervising the defendants in these courts. Defendants typically appear before the judge every month or two, and the judge praises them when they have done well in their program and reprimands them when they have failed to follow through on an assignment. Usually, charges are dropped when defendants complete the program successfully, and those who drop out or are removed for noncompliance get sentenced to a previously agreed on penalty (such as a specified jail or probation term).

In recent years, courts dedicated to handling people convicted of driving under the influence (DUI) have appeared as a new incarnation of specialized courts. The success of these courts at reducing recidivism hinges on their ability to keep defendants in the program; defendants who drop out have to be sentenced to jail or probation (which is more expensive) and will not experience the benefits of the treatment regimen. Saum, Hiller, and Nolan (2013) sought to identify the factors associated with treatment completion versus dropout. They gathered records on 141 third-time DUI offenders who went through a DUI court program in Wisconsin. Most of the defendants (114) completed the program, but 27 did not. Overall, the researchers found very few differences between the groups. Having a mental-health problem did not affect the odds of completion, as shown by the wide confidence interval for this variable's predictive capability (.17 to 1.6). The only variable that emerged as significant was the number of days in the jail or work-release sentence; those who had been threatened with more severe sentences were more likely to drop out. This variable's confidence interval was very small (.95 to 1.00), suggesting that is was a good predictor of program completion versus program dropout. It would appear that more serious DUI offenders need enhanced supervision and greater incentives to stay in and successfully complete DUI court programs.

CHAPTER SUMMARY

Confidence intervals are a way for researchers to use sample statistics to form conclusions about the probable values of population parameters. Confidence intervals entail the construction of ranges of values predicted to contain the true population parameter. The researcher sets the level of confidence (probability of correctness) according to her or his judgment about the relative costs of a loss of confidence versus compromised precision. The conventional confidence levels in criminal justice and criminology research are 95% and 99%. The decision about level of confidence must be made with consideration to the trade-off between confidence and precision—as confidence increases, the quality of the estimate diminishes. All confidence intervals are two-tailed, which means that alpha is divided in half and placed in both tails of the distribution. This creates two critical values. The critical values have the same absolute value, but one is negative and one is positive.

There are two types of *CIs* for means: large sample and small sample. Confidence intervals for means with large samples employ the *z* distribution, while those for means with small samples use the *t* curve. When the *t* distribution is used, it is necessary to calculate degrees of freedom in order to locate the critical value on the *t* table.

Confidence intervals can be constructed on the basis of proportions, providing that two criteria are met. First, the sample must contain at least 100 cases. Second, there must be at least five successes and five failures in the sample. These two conditions help ensure the normality of the sampling distribution and, thus, the applicability of the *z* curve.

CHAPTER 8 REVIEW PROBLEMS

Answer the following questions with regard to confidence intervals.

1. How many cases must be in a sample for that sample to be considered "large"?

2. "Small" samples are those that have ＿＿＿ or fewer cases.

3. Which distribution is used with large samples?

4. Which distribution is used with small samples?

5. Why can the distribution that is used with large samples not also be used with small ones?

6. Explain the trade-off between confidence and precision.

7. The Law Enforcement Management and Administrative Statistics (LEMAS) survey asks agencies to report the number of sworn personnel who are designated school resource officers (SROs). In Florida municipal police departments serving populations of 1,000,000 or more, the agencies sampled in LEMAS ($N = 18$) reported a mean of 13.00 SROs ($s = 12.10$). Construct a 95% confidence interval around this sample mean, and interpret the interval in words.

8. The sheriff's offices sampled in LEMAS ($N = 827$) reported that their agencies require new recruits to complete a mean of 599 hours of academy training ($s = 226$). Construct a 99% confidence interval around this mean and interpret the interval in words.

9. The Police-Public Contact Survey (PPCS) asks respondents who have been stopped by the police while driving a vehicle how many officers were on the scene during the stop. Female stopped drivers ($N = 2,033$) reported a mean of 1.14 ($s = .36$) officers. Construct a 95% confidence interval around this sample mean, and interpret the interval in words.

10. In the PPCS, respondents who say that they have been stopped by police while driving vehicles are asked to report the reason why they were stopped and the total length of time that the stop took. Among female drivers stopped for illegal use of cellphones while driving ($N = 42$), stops lasted a mean of 9.00 minutes ($s = 5.48$). Construct a 95% confidence interval around this sample mean and interpret the interval in words.

11. The General Social Survey (GSS) contains an item asking respondents about their TV habits. In 2012, female respondents ($N = 707$) said they watched a mean of 3.06 ($s = 2.62$) hours of TV per day. Construct a 99% confidence interval around this sample value and interpret the interval in words.

12. In a random sample of prisons ($N = 49$) from the Census of State and Federal Adult Correctional Facilities (CSFACF), the mean number of inmates per security-staff member was 6.23 ($s = 3.20$). Construct a 95% confidence interval around this sample value and interpret the interval in words.

13. In a random sample of prisons ($N = 23$) from the CSFACF, the mean number of Asian inmates was 3.30 ($s = 2.24$). Construct a 99% confidence interval around this sample value and interpret the interval in words.

14. Respondents to the GSS ($N = 1,166$) worked a mean of 40.27 hours per week ($s = 15.54$). Construct a 99% confidence interval around this sample value, and interpret the interval in words.

15. The GSS asks respondents whether or not they keep a gun in their homes. In 2012, 34% of respondents ($N = 1,281$) said that they have at least one firearm in their home. Construct a 95% confidence interval around this sample value and interpret the interval in words.

16. In the LEMAS survey, 45% of sampled sheriff's offices ($N = 823$) reported that their agencies' formal mission statements do not include a community-policing component. Construct a 95% confidence interval around this sample value, and interpret the interval in words.

17. According to LEMAS, 31% of municipal law-enforcement agencies ($N = 1,967$) use computerized statistics to identify high-crime hot spots. Construct a 95% confidence interval around this sample value and interpret the interval in words.

18. The Firearm Injury Surveillance Survey (FISS) captures information on whether or not drugs were involved in the altercation that led up to the shooting. From 1993 to 2010, victims were male in 88% of the 1,655 cases that involved drugs. Construct a 99% confidence interval around this sample value and interpret the interval in words.

19. The FISS reports that in 2010, 29% of female shooting victims ($N = 295$) were shot by strangers. Construct a 95% confidence interval around this sample value and interpret the interval in words.

20. The 2012 GSS found that 74% of male respondents ($N = 573$) believe that people suffering from incurable diseases should be permitted to die if that is their choice. Construct a 99% confidence interval around this sample value and interpret the interval in words.

Point estimate	Level of confidence	Critical value
Confidence interval	Alpha level	Two-tailed test

α	The probability that a *CI* does not contain the population parameter
z_α	The z score associated with a given a level
t_α	The t score associated with a given a level

Part

3

Hypothesis
Testing

You have now learned about descriptive statistics (Part I) and the theories of probability and distributions that form the foundation of statistics (Part II). Part III brings all of this together to form what most criminal justice and criminology researchers consider to be the high point of statistics: **inferential analyses** or what is also called hypothesis testing. Hypothesis testing involves using a sample to arrive at a conclusion about a population. Samples are vehicles that allow you to make generalizations or predictions about what you believe is happening in the population as a whole. The problem, as we discussed in Chapter 7, is sampling error: It is erroneous to conclude that a sample statistic is an accurate reflection of the population parameter, because the sample is merely one of a multitude of samples that could have been drawn from the population and, therefore, there is an unknown amount of error. Refer back to Figure 7.5 for an illustration.

Inferential analysis: The process of generalizing from a sample to a population; the use of a sample statistic to estimate a population parameter. Also called hypothesis testing.

To accommodate sampling error, inferential statistics utilize sampling distributions to make probabilistic predictions about the sample statistic that is being analyzed. The basic strategy is a two-step process. First, a sample statistic is computed. Second, a probability distribution is used to find out whether this statistic has a low or high probability of occurrence. This process should sound very familiar—we already followed these steps when we worked with z scores and areas under the standard normal curve. Hypothesis testing is an expansion on this underlying idea. A sample statistic (such as a mean) can be used to find out whether this value is close to the center of the distribution (high probability of occurrence) or far out in the tail (low probability of occurrence). It is this probability assessment that guides researchers in making decisions and reaching conclusions.

Part III covers some of the bivariate (involving two variables) inferential tests commonly used in criminology and criminal justice research: chi-square tests of independence, two-population tests for differences between means and between proportions, analyses of variance, and correlations. Part III ends with an introduction to bivariate and multiple regression.

Levels of Measurement

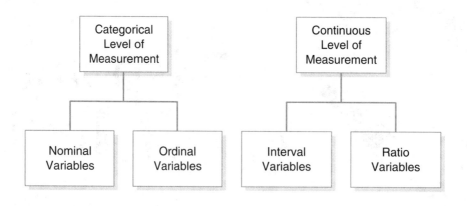

The proper test to use in a given hypothesis-testing situation is determined by the level of measurement of the variables with which you are working. If your memory of levels of measurement has become a bit fuzzy, go back to Chapter 2 now and review this important topic. You will not be able to select the correct analysis unless you can identify your variables' levels of measurement. The figure here is a reproduction of Figure 2.1 showing the levels of measurement. For purposes of hypothesis testing, the key distinction is that between categorical and continuous variables. Be sure you can accurately identify any given variable's level of measurement before you start Chapter 10.

There is no sense denying that you may find many of the concepts presented in the following chapters confusing at first. Take heart! The process of learning statistics hinges on repetition. Read and reread the chapters, study your lecture notes, and do the end-of-chapter review problems—things will start to sink in. Terms, formulas, and ideas that initially seemed incomprehensible will gradually take form in your mind and begin making sense. Remember that most criminology and criminal justice researchers started off in a position just like yours! There was a point when they knew nothing about statistics and had to study hard to construct a knowledge base. Commit the time and effort and there is a good chance that you will be pleasantly surprised by how well you do.

LEARNING CHECK

Take a moment now to test your memory of levels of measurement. Identify the level of measurement of each of the following variables:

a. The survey item that asks "How many times have you been arrested in your life?" and has respondents write in the answer
b. The survey item that asks "How many times have you been arrested in your life?" and has respondents circle never, 1–3 times, or 4 or more times
c. Whether a convicted defendant's sentence was jail, probation, or drug treatment
d. Defendants' annual household income, measured as $0–$9,999, $10,000–$19,999, or $20,000 or more
e. The method by which a defendant was convicted, measured as guilty plea, jury trial, or bench trial
f. In a sample of convicted offenders sent to prison, the number of months in each person's sentence

Now you try it! Create four variables, one representing each level of measurement.

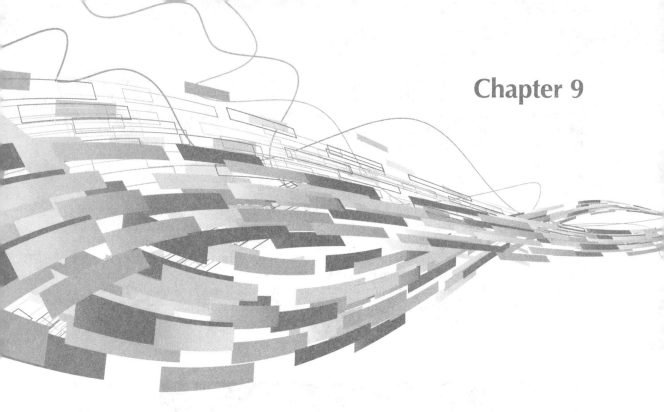

Hypothesis Testing

A Conceptual Introduction

- List the four types of bivariate inferential tests, and identify the correct one to use for any given independent variable and dependent variable combination depending on level of measurement.

The purpose of this chapter is to provide a clear conceptual foundation of the nature and purpose of hypothesis testing. It is worth developing a solid understanding of the substance of inferential statistics before approaching the specific types of hypothesis tests covered in the proceeding chapters. This chapter will help you grasp the overarching logic behind these sorts of tests so that you can approach the "trees" (specific tests) with a clear picture of what the "forest" (underlying conceptual framework) looks like.

By now, you should be very familiar with the idea that researchers are usually interested in populations but, because populations are so large, samples must suffice instead. Researchers draw random samples using a variety of methods. A researcher distributing surveys by mail might use an address database to electronically pull the home addresses of 10% of the residents of a particular city. Someone conducting phone surveys might use random-digit dialing to contact 200 respondents. The ultimate goal in statistical research is to generalize from the sample to the population. Hypothesis testing is the process of making this generalization. (Note that throughout the following discussion, we are going to assume that samples are simple and random. When either of these two criteria is not true in a given sample, adjustments sometimes have to be made to the statistics used to analyze them. For present purposes, we are going to assume the presence of simple, random samples.)

What we are really talking about in inferential statistics is the probability of empirical outcomes. There are many (even infinite) random samples that can be drawn from any given population and, therefore, there are numerous possible sample statistics. A population with a mean of 10, for instance, can produce samples with means of 9, 11, 10, 7, and so on. When we have a sample statistic that we wish to use inferentially, the question asked is, "Out of all the samples and sample statistics possible, what is the probability that I would draw *this* one?"

LEARNING CHECK

Remember the difference between expected and observed or empirical outcomes. Expected outcomes are the results you anticipate seeing on the basis of probability theory. In Chapter 6, you constructed a table of expected outcomes in the context of binomials. Observed outcomes, by contrast, are what you actually see. These results may or may not match expectations. A coin-flip exercise will help refresh your memory. Write down the probability of any given coin flip resulting in heads. Now flip a coin six times and record each outcome, and when you are done, tally up the total number of heads and tails. Did you see what you expected, on the basis of the underlying probability, or were you surprised at the outcome? Try again with 10 flips. Did the observed outcome match the one you expected?

Sample Statistics and Population Parameters: Sampling Error or True Difference?

Any time a sample statistic is not equal to a population parameter, there are two potential explanations for the difference. (Well, technically there are three, since a mismatch can result from mistakes in the sampling process. For our purposes, though, as mentioned earlier, we are assuming correct research methods and simple, random samples.) First, the inequality could be the product of the random fluctuations in sample statistics (i.e., sampling error). In other words, the disparity may simply be a meaningless fluke. If you flipped a fair coin six times, you would expect the coin to land tails side up three times. If, instead, you got four tails, you would not think that there was anything weird happening; the next set of six trials might result in two tails. This is sampling error—variation that is like white noise in the background. The second possible explanation for the difference is that there is a genuine discrepancy between the sample statistic and the population parameter. In other words, the disparity could represent a bona fide statistical effect. If you flipped a coin 20 times and got 19 tails, you would suspect there was something going on with the coin—this is an extremely unlikely outcome. Perhaps the coin is weighted on one side, which would mean that it is different from the ordinary quarter or dime you might have in your pocket. Large discrepancies between observed and expected outcomes are sufficiently improbable to lead us to conclude that there is something genuinely unique about the empirical outcome we have in front of us.

When researchers first approach an empirical finding, they do not know which of the two possible explanations accounts for the observed or empirical result. In the earlier coin-flip example, we knew the underlying population probability (.50), and we knew the number of trials that had been conducted (six in the first and 20 in the second). If either of those pieces of information is omitted, then it becomes difficult to make sense of the results. If your friend told you that he flipped a coin and it landed on tails seven times, but he did not tell you the total number of times he flipped it, then you would not know how to interpret his report about seven tails. Similarly, if you did not know that every flip has a .50 probability of tails (and that, by extension, roughly half of a string of flips will be tails), then your friend might say that he flipped a coin 14 times and got seven tails and you would not have a clue what to make of these results.

In the real world of criminal justice and criminology research, there are missing bits of information that prevent us from being able to immediately discriminate between sampling error and true difference. The overarching purpose of hypothesis testing is to determine which of them appears to be the more valid of the two. This is where probabilities come in. Researchers identify the probability of observing a particular empirical result and then use that probability to make a decision about which explanation seems to be correct.

This is pretty abstract, so an example is in order. We will use the Bureau of Justice Statistics (BJS) Census of State and Federal Adult Correctional Facilities (CSFACF; see Data Sources 3.1). This is a good data set for this example because we can draw simple, random samples from it to use for demonstration, but since it is a population data set, we can also calculate the population parameters so that they can be compared to the sample statistics. Remember that this second feature is a luxury that we are capitalizing on for the sake of demonstration—researchers usually do not know the true values of parameters.

The CSFACF contains information about the rate of inmate-on-inmate assaults at each facility. To account for facility size, we can standardize the raw counts to make them rates per 1,000 total inmates housed in a particular prison. Suppose we are investigating whether security level (minimum, medium, maximum, or super maximum) affects the rate of assaults within an institution. On one hand, we might presume that higher-security facilities house more dangerous inmates, so they should have higher assault rates. On the other hand, higher-security prisons more heavily restrict inmates' movement, which might limit their opportunities for violent confrontation. Using the SPSS program's random-sample generator, we get a sample of medium-security facilities with a mean of 20.68 assaults per 1,000 and a sample of maximum-security prisons with a mean of 33.29.

You can see that these means are unequal, the maximum-security mean being roughly 13 points greater than the medium-security mean; however, recall that there are *two potential reasons* for this disparity. Their inequality might be meaningless and the differences between the numbers purely the product of chance; in other words, the finding might be a fluke. We pulled random samples, so we cannot rule out the possibility that sampling error manufactured a seeming difference where there actually is none. On the other hand, the means might be unequal because security level truly does affect assault rates. In other words, there might be a significant difference between the means. These two competing potential explanations can be framed as hypotheses.

Null and Alternative Hypotheses

There are two hypotheses used to state predictions about whether or not a statistic is an accurate estimate of a parameter. The first is called the **null hypothesis**. The null (symbolized H_0) represents the prediction that the difference between the population and sample is purely the product of sampling error or, in other words, chance variation in the data. You can use the word *null* as its own mnemonic device because this word means "nothing." Something that is null is devoid of meaning. In the context of the present example, the null predicts that security level is not related to inmate-on-inmate assaults and that the observed difference between the means is just white noise.

The second possible explanation is that maximum-security prisons really do have a higher mean assault rate compared to medium-security ones. This prediction is spelled out in the **alternative hypothesis** (symbolized H_1). The alternative hypothesis is sometimes also called the research hypothesis. The alternative or research hypothesis is, essentially, the opposite of the null: The null predicts that there is no relationship between the two variables being examined, and the alternative predicts that they are related.

> **Null hypothesis:** In an inferential test, the hypothesis predicting that there is no relationship between the independent and dependent variables. Symbolized H_0.

> **Alternative hypothesis:** In an inferential test, the hypothesis predicting that there is a relationship between the independent and dependent variables. Symbolized H_1. Also referred to as a research hypothesis.

In the context of the present example, the null and alternative hypotheses can be written as

H_0: *Maximum- and medium-security prisons have the same mean assault rate; that is, the two means are equal, and there is no security-assault relationship.*

H_1: *Maximum-security prisons have a higher mean assault rate than do medium-security ones; that is, there is a relationship between security level and assaults, with maximum-security facilities experiencing significantly more assaults than do medium-security ones.*

More common than writing the hypotheses in words is to use symbols to represent the ideas embodied in the longhand versions. Transforming these concepts into such symbols turns the null and alternative hypotheses into:

$$H_0: \mu_1 = \mu_2$$

$$H_1: \mu_1 > \mu_2,$$

where μ_1 = the mean number of assaults in maximum-security prisons,

μ_2 = the mean number of assaults in medium-security prisons.

It might seem strange to write the hypotheses using the symbol for the population mean (μ) rather than the sample mean ($\bar{x}$), but remember that in inferential statistics, it is the population parameter that is of interest. We use the sample means to make a determination about the population mean(s). Basically, there are two options: There might be one population from which the samples derive (sampling error), or each sample might represent its own population (true difference). If the null is true and there is, in fact, no security-assault relationship, then we would conclude that all of the prisons come from the same population. If, instead, the alternative is true, then there are actually two populations at play here—one that is under court order for staffing and one that is not. Figure 9.1 shows this idea pictorially.

The assumption going into an inferential analysis is that the null is the true state of affairs. In other words, the default assumption is that there is no relationship between the two variables under examination. The goal in conducting the test is to decide whether to retain the null (concluding that there is no relationship) or to reject the null (concluding that there is, in fact, a relationship between the variables). The null can be rejected only if there is solid, compelling evidence that leads you to decide that this hypothesis is inaccurate.

Figure 9.1 One Population or Two?

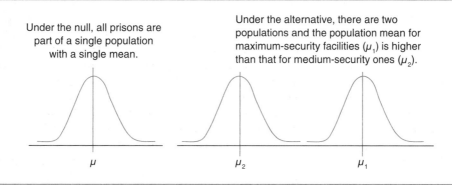

Under the null, all prisons are part of a single population with a single mean.

Under the alternative, there are two populations and the population mean for maximum-security facilities (μ_1) is higher than that for medium-security ones (μ_2).

μ μ_2 μ_1

A good analogy to the logic behind hypothesis testing is the presumption of innocence in a criminal trial. At the outset of a trial, the jury must consider the defendant to be legally innocent of the crime of which she or he is accused. The "null" here is innocence and the "alternative" is guilt. If the prosecutor fails to convincingly show guilt, then the innocence assumption stands and the defendant must be acquitted. If, however, the prosecutor presents sufficient incriminating evidence, then the jury rejects the assumption of innocence and renders a guilty verdict.

There are good reasons for the null being the default in scientific research. In clinical trials testing new pharmaceutical drugs, for example, it is of utmost importance that a drug be demonstrated to be effective before it is approved and put on the market. Medical researchers err on the side of caution—they look for convincing evidence of efficacy. If 80% of test subjects who take the drug see an improvement in their conditions or symptoms, then that might be enough to reject the null and conclude that the drug is good. If only 10% get better, though, then that is probably too low and the null should be retained and the drug should not be prescribed to patients just yet.

In criminal justice and criminology research, important questions about theory and policy hang in the balance. Like medical researchers, social scientists err on the side of caution. A criminologist testing a hypothesis about a theory of crime causation must tread carefully. Failing to reject the null hypothesis could lead to erroneous conclusions about the accuracy of the theory; however, the test can be repeated to determine whether there was a mistake in the research design that corrupted the results. Rejecting a null hypothesis that is true, however, could take this criminologist and others doing similar research down a completely wrong path in the study of crime causation. Criminal justice researchers, likewise, often deal with policy questions. They deal with matters such as whether or not a particular in-prison treatment program reduces recidivism, whether faster police response time to emergency calls for service increase the likelihood of offenders being apprehended, and whether black and Latino defendants are less likely than white defendants to be granted pretrial release. For each of these examples, you can see that neither of the two possible mistakes is entirely harmless but that retaining the null (and, possibly, conducting further research into the issue) is safer than leaping to a conclusion that might be false.

In inferential statistics, researchers construct a probability framework based on the assumption of a true null. The question they are trying to answer is, "What is the probability of observing the empirical result that I see in front of me *if the null hypothesis is correct?*" If the probability of the null being true is extremely low, then the null is rejected because it strains the imagination to think that something with such a low likelihood of being correct is the right explanation for an empirical phenomenon. The alternative would, thus, be taken as being the more likely version of reality. If the probability of the null being true is not low, then the null is considered to be a viable explanation for the results and it is retained. Think back to the study of prison security level and assault rates. Recall that the maximum-security facilities' mean was 33.29 and the medium-security mean was 20.68. Let us say, for the sake of example, that we determine that the probability of these two means being two parts of the same population is .70. That's a pretty high probability! We would conclude that the null is likely correct and there is only one population. What if we found that the probability was .20? This is a much smaller probability than .70, but it still means that there is a 20% chance that the null is true, so it would be retained. If, on the other hand, we found a probability of .01, meaning that there is only a 1% chance that the two samples are from the same population, then we would reject the null because it is extremely unlikely to be the true state of affairs (to be specific, there is a .99 or 99% chance that the null is false). With a probability of .01, it is highly likely that there are two populations, one of medium-security facilities and one of maximum-security ones, and that these populations have different means.

Of course, as you have probably already figured out, there is always a chance that a researcher's decision regarding whether to reject or retain the null is wrong. We saw when we worked with confidence intervals that the flipside of the probability of being right is the probability of being wrong—anytime you make a decision about the null, you are either right or wrong, so the two probabilities sum to 100% or 1.00. There are two types of errors that can be made in this regard. A Type I error occurs when a true null is erroneously rejected, while a Type II error happens when a false null is inaccurately retained. Type I errors are like false positives and Type II errors are like false negatives. Type I errors are often symbolized using α, which we have seen before. Recall from the confidence-interval lesson in Chapter 8 that alpha is the probability of being wrong about the interval containing the true population mean or proportion. The interpretation of alpha in inferential statistics is a little different from confidence intervals because of the involvement of null and alternative hypotheses; however, the underlying logic is the same. A Type I error corresponds to a wrongful conviction of an innocent defendant, a mistaken conclusion that a new drug works, or a decision that a prison treatment program is good when it is actually ineffective. A Type II error is analogous to a wrongful acquittal of a guilty defendant, a rejection of a drug that actually does work, or the conclusion that a truly effective treatment program is ineffectual. The symbol for a Type II error is the uppercase Greek letter beta (β). Researchers can often minimize the probability that they are wrong about a decision, but they can never eliminate it. For this reason, you should always be circumspect as both a producer and a consumer of statistical information. You should never rush haphazardly to conclusions. Any time you or anyone else runs a statistical analysis and makes a decision about the null hypothesis, there is a probability—however minute it may be—that that decision is wrong.

Type I error: The erroneous rejection of a true null hypothesis. Symbolized α.

Type II error: The erroneous retention of a false null hypothesis. Symbolized β.

Table 9.1   Type I and Type II Errors

	. . . *the null is actually false*	. . . *the null is actually true*
If you reject the null and . . .	Correct!	Type I Error (α)
If you retain the null and . . .	Type II Error (β)	Correct!

There is a trade-off between Type I and Type II error rates. The Type I error rate (α) is set *a priori* (in advance) of the start of the hypothesis test. A researcher who is worried about making a Type I error could help minimize the chance of this mistake occurring by setting alpha very low, which increases the difficulty of rejecting the null hypothesis. The flipside, however, is that when it is hard to reject a true null, it is also hard to reject a false one. By reducing the chance of a Type I error, then, the researcher has increased the risk of making a Type II error.

The following chapters will cover several different types of hypothesis testing procedures in the bivariate (i.e., two variables) context. The choice between the different tests is made on the basis of each variable's level of measurement. You must identify the levels of measurement of the independent and dependent variables and then select the proper test for those measurement types. This book covers four types of bivariate inferential tests. The first is chi-square, which is the statistical procedure used to test for an association between two categorical (i.e., nominal or ordinal) variables. If, for example, you had a sample of criminal defendants and wanted to find out whether there was a relationship between the type of crime a defendant was charged with (violent or property) and the disposition method that the defendant chose (guilty plea, jury trial, or bench trial), you would use a chi-square test.

The second type of analysis is a *t* test. The *t* test is used when the dependent variable of interest is continuous (interval or ratio) and the independent variable is categorical with two classes (e.g., gender as male or female). The *t* test is a test for differences between two means. In the prison-assault example used earlier, a *t* test would be the analysis we select to determine whether or not to reject the null hypothesis. The third type of test is the analysis of variance (ANOVA). The ANOVA is an extension of the *t* test and is used when the dependent variable is continuous and the independent variable is categorical with three or more classes (e.g., race as white, black, Latino, or other). The rationale behind this is that conducting multiple *t* tests is time consuming and cumbersome, and creates statistical problems. The ANOVA streamlines the process by using a single analysis across all classes of the independent variable. If we were to add minimum-security and super maximum-security prisons to our assault study, we would switch from a *t* test to an ANOVA.

The final bivariate inferential test we will discuss is correlation. This test is used when both the dependent and the independent variables are continuous. Correlations are tests for linear relationships between two variables. You might predict, for instance, that the level of correctional officer staffing in a prison (i.e., the inmate-to-staff ratio) affects the assault rate—it stands to reason that higher staffing results in better supervision and, thus, fewer assaults. You would test this prediction using a correlation analysis. Table 9.2 is a handy chart that you should study closely and refer to repeatedly throughout the next few chapters.

If you choose the wrong test, you will arrive at an incorrect answer. Period, no two ways around it; the result will be wrong. This is true in both hand calculations and SPSS programming. SPSS rarely gives error messages and will usually run analyses even when they are deeply flawed. Remember, GIGO! When garbage is entered into an analysis, the output is also garbage. You must be knowledgeable about the proper use of these statistical techniques, or you risk becoming either a purveyor or a consumer of erroneous results.

Before we leave this chapter and dive into inferential analyses, let's have an introduction to the steps of hypothesis testing. It is useful to outline a framework you can use consistently as you learn the different types of analyses. This lends structure to the learning process and allows you to see the similarities between various techniques. Hypothesis testing is broken down into five steps, as follows:

Step 1. **State the null (H_0) and alternative (H_1) hypotheses.**

- The two competing hypotheses that will be tested are laid out.

Step 2. **Identify the distribution and compute the degrees of freedom.**

- Each type of statistical analysis utilizes a certain probability distribution. You have already seen the z and t distributions, and more will be introduced in later chapters. You have encountered the concept of degrees of freedom (df) in the context of the t distribution. Other distributions also require the computation of df.

Step 3. **Identify the critical value of the test statistic and state the decision rule.**

- The critical value is based on probability. The critical value is the number that the obtained value (which will be derived in Step 4) must exceed in order for the null to be rejected. The decision rule is an a priori statement formally laying out the criteria that must be met for the null to be rejected. The decision rule is useful because it makes it very clear what must happen in order for the null to be rejected. You will return to the decision rule in Step 5 after computing the critical value in Step 4.

Step 4. **Compute the obtained value of the test statistic.**

- This is the analytical heart of the hypothesis test. You will select the appropriate formula, plug in the relevant numbers, and solve. The outcome is the obtained value of the test statistic.

Step 5. **Make a decision about the null and state the substantive conclusion.**

- You will revisit your decision rule from Step 3 and decide whether to reject or retain the null based on the comparison between the critical and obtained values of the test statistic. Then you will render a substantive conclusion. Researchers have the responsibility to interpret their statistical findings and draw substantive conclusions that make sense to other researchers and to the public.

Table 9.2 Choosing the Appropriate Bivariate Test Based on the Variables' Level of Measurement

	The Independent Variable is . . .	
The Dependent Variable is . . .	*Categorical*	*Continuous*
Categorical	Chi-square	*t* test
		ANOVA
Continuous	N/A	Correlation

CHAPTER SUMMARY

This chapter provided an overview of the nature, purpose, and logic of hypothesis testing. The goal of statistics in criminology and criminal justice is usually generalization from a sample to a population. This is accomplished by first finding a sample statistic and then determining the probability that that statistic would be observed by chance alone. If the probability of the result being attributable solely to chance is exceedingly low, then the researcher concludes that the finding is not due to chance and is, instead, a genuine effect.

When a researcher has identified two variables that might be related, there are two possible true or correct states of affairs. The first possibility is that the variables are actually not related. This possibility is embodied by the null hypothesis, symbolized H_0. The second possibility is that they are in fact related to one another. This is the alternative hypothesis, H_1, which is sometimes also called a research hypothesis. The null hypothesis is always assumed to be the one that is true, and formal hypothesis testing using probabilities and a sampling distribution is utilized to determine whether there is sufficient evidence to overrule the null and opt for the alternative instead. A hypothesis test using the five steps outlined in this chapter will ultimately result in the null being either rejected or retained and the researcher concluding that the variables are, or are not, related to each other.

CHAPTER 9 REVIEW PROBLEMS

1. Suppose a researcher was studying gender differences in sentencing. She found that males sentenced to jail received a mean of 6.45 months and females sentenced to jail received a mean of 5.82 months. Using what you learned in this chapter, describe the two possible reasons for the differences between these two means.

2. Write the symbol for the null hypothesis, and explain what this hypothesis predicts.

3. Write the symbol for the alternative hypothesis, and explain what this hypothesis predicts.

4. You learned in this chapter that the null is assumed to be true unless very compelling evidence suggests that the alternative hypothesis is actually the correct one. Why is this? That is, what is the rationale for the null being the default?

5. Explain what a Type I error is.

6. Explain what a Type II error is.

7. Explain the trade-off between Type I and Type II error rates.

8. Define the word *bivariate*.

9. List and describe each of the five steps for hypothesis tests.

10. If you computed an empirical result, identified the probability of observing that result, and found that the probability was high . . .

    a. would you conclude that this is the product of sampling error, or would you think that it is a true effect?
    b. would you reject or retain the null?

11. If you computed an empirical result, identified the probability of observing that result, and found that the probability was very low . . .

    a. would you conclude that this is the product of sampling error, or would you think that it is a true effect?
    b. would you reject or retain the null?

12. Which inferential statistical analysis would be used if the independent variable (IV) was criminal defendants' ages at sentencing (measured in years) and the dependent variable (DV) length of their terms of confinement (measured in months)?

    a. Chi-square
    b. *t* test
    c. ANOVA
    d. Correlation

13. Which inferential statistical analysis would be used if the IV was criminal defendants' gender (measured as male or female) and the DV was the length of their terms of confinement (measured in months)?

    a. Chi-square
    b. *t* test
    c. ANOVA
    d. Correlation

14. Which inferential statistical analysis would be used if the IV was criminal defendants' gender (measured as male or female) and the DV was whether or not they obtained pretrial release (measured as yes or no)?

    a. Chi-square
    b. *t* test
    c. ANOVA
    d. Correlation

15. Which inferential statistical analysis would be used if the IV was police force size (measured as the number of officers per 1,000 residents) and the DV was crime rates (measured as the number of crimes per 10,000 residents)?

    a. Chi-square
    b. *t* test

c. ANOVA

d. Correlation

16. Which inferential statistical analysis would be used if the IV was assault victims' race (measured as white, black, Latino, or other) and the DV was the length of prison terms given to their attackers (measured in months)?

   a. Chi-square
   b. *t* test
   c. ANOVA
   d. Correlation

17. Which inferential statistical analysis would be used if the IV was murder victims' race (measured as white, black, Latino, or other) and the DV was whether or not the killers were sentenced to death (measured as yes or no)?

   a. Chi-square
   b. *t* test
   c. ANOVA
   d. Correlation

18. Which inferential statistical analysis would be used if the IV was assault victims' gender (measured as male or female) and the DV was the length of prison terms given to their attackers (measured in months)?

   a. Chi-square
   b. *t* test
   c. ANOVA
   d. Correlation

KEY TERMS

Inferential analysis   Alternative hypothesis   Type II error

Null hypothesis   Type I error

GLOSSARY OF SYMBOLS AND ABBREVIATIONS INTRODUCED IN THIS CHAPTER

H_0	The null hypothesis
H_1	The alternative hypothesis
β	The symbol for the Type II error rate

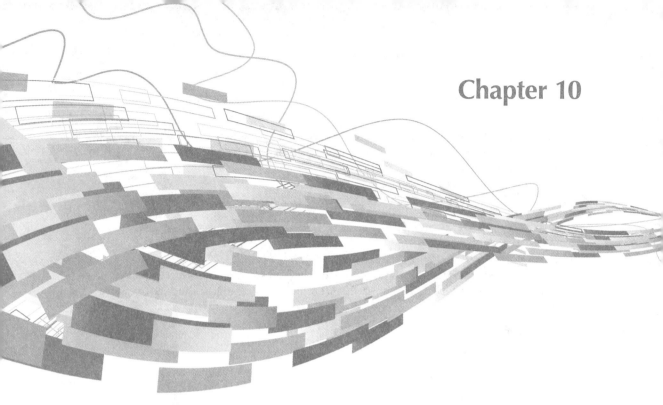

Chapter 10

Hypothesis Testing With Two Categorical Variables

Chi-Square

T he **chi-square test of independence** is used when the independent variable (IV) and dependent variable (DV) are both categorical (nominal or ordinal). The chi-square test is member of the family of **nonparametric statistics**, which are statistical analyses used when sampling distributions cannot be assumed to be normally distributed, which is often the result of the DV being categorical rather than continuous (we will talk in detail about this). Chi-square thus sits in contrast to **parametric statistics**, which are used when DVs are continuous and sampling distributions are safely assumed to be normal. The *t* test, analysis of variance, and correlation are all parametric. Before going into the theory and math behind the chi-square statistic, read the Research Examples for illustrations of the types of situations in which a criminal justice or criminology researcher would utilize a chi-square test.

Chi-square test of independence: The hypothesis-testing procedure appropriate when both the independent variable and the dependent variables are categorical.

Nonparametric statistics: The class of statistical tests used when dependent variables are categorical and the sampling distribution cannot be assumed to approximate normality.

Parametric statistics: The class of statistical tests used when dependent variables are continuous and normally distributed and the sampling distribution can be assumed to approximate normality.

In the study summarized in Research Example 10.1, *number of stops* is the IV and is ordinal. *Number of times called for assistance* and *number of times called to report neighborhood problems* are the DVs and are also ordinal. In the second study, *race or ethnicity* (the IV) and *sentence received* (the DV) are both nominal. The question each study attempted to answer was, "Are these two variables related? In other words, does the IV appear to exert an impact on the DV?" Answering this question requires the use of the chi-square test of independence because in these studies, the IVs and DVs are categorical.

RESEARCH EXAMPLE 10.1

Do Traffic Stops Alter People's Likelihood of Calling the Police?

Police rely on local community residents to call in when they see problematic people or conditions in their neighborhoods. Effective crime control and order maintenance depend, in part, on people's willingness to voluntarily make these types of reports.

There are many reasons, however, why people may be loath to call the police to

(Continued)

(Continued)

report problems. Gibson, Walker, Jennings, and Miller (2010) hypothesized that one factor that could deter people from reporting neighborhood problems is having had a recent negative encounter with a police officer. Using the Police-Public Contact Survey (PPCS), the researchers identified three variables. The primary IV was, "How many times in the past 12 months were you in a vehicle that was stopped by police?" Respondents' answers were coded as *none, once,* and *more than once.* Two DVs were used to tap into citizens' willingness to alert police to the presence of local issues. The first was "In the past 12 months, did you contact the police to ask for assistance or information?" and the second was "In the past 12 months, did you contact the police to report a neighborhood problem?" Both variables were coded as *not at all* and *one or more times.* The following are bivariate contingency tables displaying the overlap between the predictor and each of the outcome measures.[*] How can the researchers find out if the two variables are related?

Contingency Tables for Having Experienced a Traffic Stop and Having Called the Police for Assistance or to Report Neighborhood Problems

	Number of Times Called for Assistance		
Number of Stops	None	One or More	Row Marginal
None	6,068	1,433	7,501
One	5,639	404	6,043
More than One	1,289	136	1,425
Column Marginal	12,996	1,973	N = 14,969
	Number of Times Called to Report Problems		
Number of Stops	None	One or More	Row Marginal
None	6,409	1,095	7,504
One	5,724	323	6,047
More than One	1,335	92	1,427
Column Marginal	13,468	1,510	N = 14,978

[*]These are reanalyses of the same data used by the authors, not reproductions of the authors' analyses.

RESEARCH EXAMPLE 10.2

Do Waived Juvenile Defendants' Race/Ethnicity Affect the Sentences these Juveniles Receive?

Several criminal justice studies have demonstrated that black and Hispanic/Latino defendants are sentenced more harshly than their white counterparts, even when factors such as the severity of the instant offense and defendants' prior criminal records are accounted for. Attention has not been paid, however, to the effects of race and ethnicity on sentencing for juvenile defendants who are waived into criminal courts to be tried as adults. Jordan and Freiburger (2010) wished to address this gap in the literature by studying the sentences received by waived juveniles of multiple races and ethnicities. The authors selected the Juvenile Defendants in Criminal Courts data set (we will see this in Data Sources 11.1 in the next chapter), which offers information about juveniles in 40 urban counties who were charged with felonies and were either transferred or waived to adult court. The researchers' IV was *race and ethnicity* and was measured as *white, black,* or *Hispanic*. The DV was *sentence received* and was coded as *probation, jail,* or *prison*. (There were so few juveniles of other races and ethnicities that the authors decided to exclude them from the analysis.) The following crosstabs table displays these two variables' joint distribution.* How can the researchers find out if there is a relationship between the two variables?

Contingency Table for Juvenile Race or Ethnicity and Sentence Received

	Sentence Received			
Race or Ethnicity	Jail	Prison	Probation	Row Marginal
White	226	102	333	661
Black	398	295	917	1,610
Hispanic	177	83	195	455
Column Marginal	801	480	1,445	$N = 2,726$

*These are reanalyses of the same data used by the authors, not reproductions of the authors' analyses.

Conceptual Basis of the Chi-Square Test: Statistical Dependence and Independence

Two variables that are not related to one another are said to possess statistical independence. When two variables are related, they have statistical dependence. Statistical independence means that knowing which category an object falls into on the IV does not help predict its placement on the DV. When, conversely, two variables are statistically dependent, the independent does have predictive power over the outcome variable.

In Research Example 10.1, the IV was the number of traffic stops survey respondents reported having experienced in the past 12 months, and one of the DVs was whether or not respondents had called the police to request assistance. If these two variables are statistically independent, then having experienced a traffic stop will *not* influence respondents' likelihood of calling the police; if the variables are statistically dependent, then knowing whether or not someone has been the subject of a traffic stop will help predict whether that person has called the police for assistance or to report problems. When we want to know whether there is a relationship between two categorical variables, we turn to the chi-square test of independence.

Statistical independence: The condition in which two variables are not related to one another; that is, knowing what class persons or objects fall into on the independent variable does not help predict which class they will fall into on the dependent variable.

Statistical dependence: The condition in which two variables are related to one another; that is, knowing what class persons or objects fall into on the independent variable helps predict which class they will fall into on the dependent variable.

The Chi-Square Test of Independence

Let us work slowly through an example of a chi-square hypothesis test using the five steps described in Chapter 9 and discuss each step in detail along the way. For this example, we will turn to the 2012 General Social Survey (GSS; see Data Sources 2.2) and the issue of gender differences in attitudes about crime and punishment. Theory is somewhat conflicting as to whether women tend to be more forgiving of transgressions and to prefer leniency in punishment or whether they generally prefer harsher penalties out of the belief that offenders pose a threat to community safety. The GSS contains data on the sex of respondents and these persons' attitudes toward the death penalty. The joint frequency distribution is displayed in Table 10.1. We will test for a relationship between gender (the IV) and death-penalty attitudes (the DV). Both of these variables are nominal, so the chi-square test of independence is the correct analysis. Note that we are setting gender as the IV and death-penalty support as the DV. There is no mathematical requirement pertaining to the placement of the variables in the rows versus the columns, but it is customary to place the IV in the rows of the table and the DV in the columns.

You have seen tables like 10.1 before—it is a contingency (or crosstabs) table just like the ones we worked with in Chapter 3! Each cell of the table displays the number of people who fall into particular classes on each variable. (Ignore the superscripts for now; we will come back to these later.) For example, there are 385 GSS respondents who are female and who oppose the death penalty; 574 people are male and favor it. We can perform a cursory assessment of the possible relationship between gender and death-penalty support by calculating row percentages for each cell of the table (we use row percentages because the IV is in the rows). Approximately 61% (i.e., $\left[\dfrac{609}{994}\right]100$) of women

Table 10.1   GSS Respondents' Sex and Death-Penalty Attitudes

	Attitude Toward Death Penalty for Persons Convicted of Murder		
Sex	*Favor*	*Oppose*	*Row Marginal*
Female	609[A]	385[B]	994
Male	574[C]	256[D]	830
Column Marginal	1,183	641	$N = 1,824$

favor the death penalty, and 39% oppose it. Among men, there is 69% favorability and 31% opposition. Judging by the 8 percentage-point difference between men and women, it appears that there is a relationship between gender and attitudes about capital punishment. Recall from the previous chapter, however, that it would be erroneous to conclude on the basis of these percentages alone that there is a true difference between men and women in terms of their death-penalty attitudes—we have not yet ruled out the possibility that this seeming difference is the product of chance variation (i.e., sampling error) and is actually meaningless. A formal hypothesis test is required before we reach a conclusion about whether these variables are related.

Step 1. State the null (H_0) and alternative (H_1) hypotheses.

The null hypothesis (H_0) in chi-square tests is that there is no relationship between the independent and DVs. The chi-square test statistic is χ^2 (χ is the Greek letter *chi* and is pronounced "kye"). A χ^2 value of zero means that the variables are unrelated, so the null is formally written as

$$H_0: \chi^2 = 0.$$

The alternative hypothesis (H_1), on the other hand, predicts that there is a relationship. The chi-square statistic gets larger as the overlap or relationship between the IV and DV increases. The chi-square statistic has its own sampling distribution, as you will see soon, and the distribution contains only positive values; it is bounded at zero and has no negative side. This is because the statistic is a squared measure and, therefore, cannot take on negative values. As such, the alternative hypothesis is always expressed as

$$H_1: \chi^2 > 0.$$

Step 2. Identify the distribution and compute the degrees of freedom.

As mentioned, the χ^2 statistic has its own theoretical probability distribution—it is called the χ^2 distribution. The χ^2 table of critical values is located in Appendix D. Like the τ curve, the χ^2 distribution is a family of differently shaped curves, and each curve's shape is determined by degrees of freedom (*df*). At small *df* values, the distribution is extremely nonnormal; as the *df* increases, the distribution gradually normalizes. Unlike the t curve, df for χ^2 are based not on sample size but, rather, on the size of the crosstabs table (i.e., the number of rows and columns). Looking at Table 10.1, you can see that there are two rows (*female* and *male*) and two columns (*favor* and *oppose*). The marginals (row and column totals) are not included in the df calculation. The formula for degrees of freedom in a χ^2 distribution is

$$df = (r-1)(c-1),$$ Formula 10(1)

where r = the number of rows, excluding the marginal, and

   c = the number of columns, excluding the marginal.

χ^2 **distribution:** The sampling or probability distribution for chi-square tests.

Table 10.1 has two rows and two columns. Inserting these into the formula, the result is

$$df = (2 - 1)(2 - 1) = (1)(1) = 1.$$

Step 3. Identify the critical value of the test statistic and state the decision rule.

Remember in Chapter 8 when we used the α (alpha) level to find a particular value of z or t to plug into a confidence interval formula? We talked about α being the proportion of cases in the distribution that are out in the tail beyond a particular value of z or t. You learned that the critical value is the number that cuts α off the tail of the distribution. Alpha is the probability that a certain value will fall in the tail beyond the critical value. If $\alpha = .05$, for instance, then the values of the test statistic that are out in the tail beyond the critical value constitute just 5% of the entire distribution. In other words, these values have a .05 or less probability of occurring if, indeed, there is no relationship between the two variables being analyzed. These values, then, represent observed outcomes that are extremely unlikely if the null hypothesis is true.

The process of finding the critical value of χ^2 (symbolized χ^2_{crit}) employs the same logic as that for finding critical values of z or t. The value of χ^2_{crit} depends on two things: the α level and the df. Alpha must be set a priori so that the critical value can be determined before the test is run. Alpha can technically be set at any number, but .05 and .01 are the most commonly used α levels in criminal justice and criminology.

For the present example, we will choose $\alpha = .05$. Using Appendix D and finding the number at the intersection of $\alpha = .05$ and $df = 1$, it can be seen that $\chi^2_{crit} = 3.841$. This is the value that cuts .05 of the cases off the tail of the χ^2 distribution. The **obtained value** of χ^2 (symbolized χ^2_{obt}) that is calculated in Step 4 must exceed the critical value in order for the null to be rejected. Figure 10.1 illustrates this concept.

The decision rule is the a priori statement regarding the action you will take with respect to the null hypothesis based on the results of the statistical analysis that you are going to do in Step 4. The final product of Step 4 will be the obtained value of the test statistic. The null hypothesis will be rejected if the obtained value exceeds the critical value. If $\chi^2_{obt} > \chi^2_{crit}$, then the probability of

Figure 10.1 The Chi-Square Probability Distribution, α, $\chi^2_{crit,}$ and χ^2_{obt}

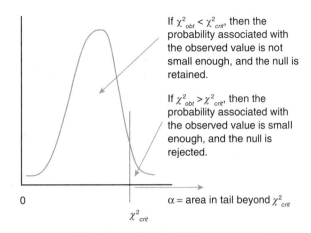

If $\chi^2_{obt} < \chi^2_{crit}$, then the probability associated with the observed value is not small enough, and the null is retained.

If $\chi^2_{obt} > \chi^2_{crit}$, then the probability associated with the observed value is small enough, and the null is rejected.

α = area in tail beyond χ^2_{crit}

0

χ^2_{crit}

obtaining this particular χ^2_{obt} value by chance alone is less than .05. Another way to think about it is that the probability of H_0 being true is less than .05. This is unlikely indeed! This would lead us to reject the null in favor of the alternative. The decision rule for the current test is the following: *If $\chi^2_{obt} > 3.841$, H_0 will be rejected.*

Obtained value: The value of the test statistic arrived at using the mathematical formulas specific to a particular test. The obtained value is the final product of Step 4 of a hypothesis test.

Step 4. Compute the obtained value of the test statistic.

Now that we know the critical value, it is time to complete the analytical portion of the hypothesis test. Step 4 will culminate in the production of the obtained value, or χ^2_{obt}. In substantive terms, χ^2_{obt} is a measure of the difference between observed frequencies (f_o) and expected frequencies (f_e). Observed frequencies are the empirical values that appear in the crosstabs table produced from the sample-derived data set. Expected frequencies are the frequencies that *would* appear if the two variables under examination were unrelated to one another. In other words, the expected frequencies are what you would see if the null hypothesis were true. The question is whether observed equals expected (indicating that the null is true and the variables are unrelated) or whether there is marked discrepancy between them (indicating that the null should be rejected because there is a relationship).

Observed frequencies: The empirical results seen in a contingency table derived from sample data. Symbolized f_o.

> **Expected frequencies:** The theoretical results that would be seen if the null were true, that is, if the two variables were, in fact, unrelated. Symbolized f_e.

Let's talk about observed and expected frequencies a little more before moving on. Table 10.2 is a crosstabs table for two hypothetical variables that are totally unrelated to one another. The 100 cases are spread evenly across the four cells of the table. The result is that knowing which class a given case falls into on the IV offers no information about which class that case is in on the DV. For instance, if you were faced with the question, "Who is more likely to fall into category Y on the DV, someone in category A or in category B?" your answer would be that they are equally likely. The distribution in Table 10.2 illustrates the null hypothesis in a chi-square test—the null predicts that the IV does not help us understand the DV.

Table 10.3 shows a distribution of hypothetical observed frequencies. There is a clear difference between this distribution and that in Table 10.2. Now, knowing what category a person is in on the IV does help predict their membership in a particular category on the DV. Someone in category A is more likely to be in category Y than in category X, whereas someone in category B is more likely to be in X than in Y. These observed frequencies represent a situation in which the null is false and the alternative is true: These variables are related to each other.

The chi-square analysis is, therefore, premised on a comparison of the frequencies that are observed in the data and the frequencies that would be expected, theoretically, if there were no

Table 10.2   Hypothetical Distribution of Expected Frequencies

| | **Dependent Variable** | | |
Independent Variable	*X*	*Y*	*Row Marginal*
A	25	25	50
B	25	25	50
Column Marginal	50	50	$N = 100$

Table 10.3   Hypothetical Distribution of Observed Frequencies

| | **Dependent Variable** | | |
Independent Variable	*X*	*Y*	*Row Marginal*
A	10	40	50
B	40	10	50
Column Marginal	50	50	$N = 100$

relationship between the two variables. If there is minimal difference between observed and expected, then the null is retained. If the difference is large, the null is rejected. We already know the observed frequencies, so the first task in Step 4 is to calculate the expected frequencies. This must be done for each cell of the crosstabs table.

The formula for an expected frequency count is

$$f_{e_i} = \frac{rm_i \cdot cm_i}{N},$$
Formula 10(2)

where f_{e_i} = the expected frequency for cell i,

rm_i = the row marginal of cell i,

$cm_{i=}$ the column marginal of cell i, and

N = the total sample size.

Since the expected frequency calculations must be done for each cell, it is a good idea to label them as a means of keeping track. This is the reason why the numbers in Table 10.1 are accompanied by superscripts. The letters A through D identify the cells. Using Formula 10(2) for each cell:

$$f_{e_A} = \frac{994 \cdot 1{,}183}{1{,}824} = \frac{1{,}175{,}902}{1{,}824} = 644.68$$

$$f_{e_B} = \frac{994 \cdot 641}{1{,}824} = \frac{637{,}154}{1{,}824} = 349.32$$

$$f_{e_C} = \frac{830 \cdot 1{,}183}{1{,}824} = \frac{981{,}890}{1{,}824} = 538.32$$

$$f_{e_D} = \frac{830 \cdot 641}{1{,}824} = \frac{532{,}030}{1{,}824} = 291.68$$

Once the expected frequencies have been calculated, χ^2_{obt} can be computed using the formula:

$$\chi^2_{obt} = \Sigma \frac{(f_o - f_e)^2}{f_{e_i}},$$
Formula 10(3)

where f_{o_i} = the observed frequency of cell i and

f_{e_i} = the expected frequency of cell i.

Formula 10(3) looks intimidating, but it is actually just a series of subtraction, multiplication, division, and addition. First, each cell's expected value will be subtracted from its observed frequency. Then each of these new terms will be squared and divided by the expected frequency. Then these terms will be summed. Recall that the uppercase sigma (Σ) is a symbol directing you to sum whatever is to the right of it.

The easiest way to complete the steps for Formula 10(3) is by using a table. We will rearrange the values from Table 10.1 into a format allowing for calculation of χ^2_{obt}. Table 10.4 shows this.

The obtained value of the test statistic is found by summing the final column of the table, as such:

$$\chi^2_{obt} = 1.97 + 3.64 + 2.36 + 4.36 = 12.33$$

There it is! The obtained value of the test statistic is 12.33.

Step 5. Make a decision about the null and state the substantive conclusion.

It is time to decide whether to retain or reject the null. To do this, revisit the decision rule laid out in Step 3. It was stated that the null would be rejected if the obtained value of the test statistic exceeded 3.841. The obtained value turned out to be 12.33, so $\chi^2_{obt} > \chi^2_{crit}$ and the null must be rejected. The alternative hypothesis is what we will take as being the true state of affairs. The technical term for this is **statistical significance**. A statistically significant result is one in which the obtained value exceeds the critical value and the variables are determined to be statistically related to one another.

Table 10.4   Calculating χ^2_{obt}

Cell	f_{oi}	f_{ei}	$\left(f_{o_i} - f_{e_i}\right)$	$\left(f_{o_i} - f_{e_i}\right)^2$	$\dfrac{\left(f_o - f_e\right)^2}{f_{e_i}}$
A	609	644.68	$644.68 - 609 = 35.68$	$35.68^2 = 1{,}273.06$	$\dfrac{1{,}273.06}{644.68} = 1.97$
B	385	349.32	$349.32 - 385 = -35.68$	$(-35.68)^2 = 1{,}273.06$	$\dfrac{1{,}273.06}{349.32} = 3.64$
C	574	538.32	$538.32 - 574 = -35.68$	$(-35.68)^2 = 1{,}273.06$	$\dfrac{1{,}273.06}{538.32} = 2.36$
D	256	291.68	$291.68 - 256 = 35.68$	$35.68^2 = 1{,}273.06$	$\dfrac{1{,}273.06}{291.68} = 4.36$
	$N = 1{,}824$	$N = 1{,}824$			

The final stage of hypothesis testing is to interpret the results. People who conduct statistical analyses are responsible for communicating their findings in a manner that effectively resonates with their audience, be that audience composed of scholars, practitioners, the general public, or the media. It is especially important when discussing statistical findings with lay audiences that clear explanations be provided about what a set of quantitative results actually *means* in a substantive, practical sense. This makes findings accessible to a wide array of audiences who may find criminological results interesting and useful.

Statistical significance: When the obtained value of a test statistic exceeds the critical value and the null is rejected.

In the context of the present example, rejecting the null leads to the conclusion that the independent and DVs are statistically related. More formally, we can state that there is a statistically significant relationship between people's gender and their attitudes about the death penalty. Another way of saying this is that there is a statistically significant difference between men and women in their attitudes toward capital punishment. Note that the chi-square test doesn't tell us about the precise nature of that difference. Nothing in χ^2_{obt} conveys information about which gender is more supportive or more opposed than the other. This is not a big problem with two-class IVs. Looking at the percentages, we know that a higher percentage of women than men oppose capital punishment, so we can conclude that women are significantly less supportive of the death penalty as compared to men. We will see later, when we use IVs that have more than two classes, that we are not able to so easily identify the location of the difference.

Note, as well, the language used in the conclusion—it is phrased as an association and there is no cause-and-effect assertion being advanced. This is because the relationship that seems to be present in this bivariate analysis may actually be the result of unmeasured omitted variables that are the real driving force behind the gender differences. We have not, for instance, measured age, race, political beliefs, or religiosity, all of which may relate to people's beliefs about the effectiveness and morality of capital punishment. If women differ from men systematically on any of these characteristics, then the gender-attitude relationship might be spurious, meaning it is the product of another variable that has not been accounted for in the analysis. It is best to keep your language toned down and to use words like *relationship* and *association* rather than *cause* or *effect*.

For the second example, let's use the General Social Survey again and this time test for a relationship between education level and death-penalty attitudes. To make it interesting, we will split the data by gender and analyze males and females in two separate tests. We will start with males (see Table 10.5). Using an alpha level of .01, we will test for a relationship between education level (the IV) and death-penalty attitudes (the DV). All five steps will be used.

Step 1. State the null (H_0) and alternative (H_1) hypotheses.

$$H_0: \chi^2 = 0$$

$$H_1: \chi^2 > 0$$

Table 10.5 Male Respondents' Education Level and Death-Penalty Attitudes

Education	Attitude Toward Death Penalty for Persons Convicted of Murder		Row Marginal
	Favor	*Oppose*	
High school or less	375[A]	155[B]	530
Some college	43[C]	14[D]	57
Bachelor's degree or higher	156[E]	87[F]	243
Column Marginal	574	256	$N = 830$

Step 2. Identify the distribution and compute the degrees of freedom.

The distribution is χ^2 and the $df = (r - 1)(c - 1) = (3 - 1)(2 - 1) = (2)(1) = 2$.

Step 3. Identify the critical value of the test statistic and state the decision rule.

With $\alpha = .01$ and $df = 2$, $\chi^2_{crit} = 9.210$. The decision rule is that *if $\chi^2_{obt} > 9.210$, H_0 will be rejected.*

Step 4. Compute the obtained value of the test statistic.

First, we need to calculate the expected frequencies using Formula 10(3). The frequencies for the first three cells (labeled A, B, and C, left to right) are as follows:

$$f_{e_A} = \frac{rm_i \cdot cm_i}{N} = \frac{530 \cdot 574}{830} = \frac{304,220}{830} = 366.53$$

$$f_{e_B} = \frac{530 \cdot 256}{830} = \frac{135,680}{830} = 163.47$$

$$f_{e_C} = \frac{57 \cdot 574}{830} = \frac{32,718}{830} = 39.42$$

Can you compute the rest? Try it out as practice.

Next, the computational table is used to calculate χ^2_{obt} (Table 10.6). As you can see in the summation cell in the last column, the obtained value of the test statistic is 4.50.

Before moving to Step 5, take note of a couple things about the chi-square calculation table. Both of these features will help you check your math as you work through the computation. First, the expected-frequency column always sums to the sample size. This is because we have not altered the number of cases in the sample; we have merely redistributed them throughout the table. After calculating the expected frequencies, sum them to make sure they add up to N. Second, the column created by subtracting the expected frequencies from the observed frequencies will always sum to

Table 10.6   Calculating χ^2_{obt}

Cell	f_{o_i}	f_{e_i}	$\left(f_{o_i} - f_{e_i}\right)$	$\left(f_{o_i} - f_{e_i}\right)^2$	$\dfrac{\left(f_o - f_e\right)^2}{f_{e_i}}$
A	375	366.53	8.47	71.74	
B	155	163.47	−8.47	71.74	.44
C	43	39.42	3.58	12.82	.33
D	14	17.58	−3.58	12.82	.73
E	156	168.05	−12.05	145.20	.86
F	87	74.95	12.05	145.20	1.94
	$N = 830$	$N = 830$	$\Sigma = .00$		$\Sigma = 4.50$

zero (or within rounding error of it). The reason for this is, again, no cases have been added to or removed from the sample. There are some cells that have observed frequencies that are less than expected and others where f_o is greater than f_e; in the end, these variations cancel each other out. Always sum both of these columns as you progress through a chi-square calculation. This will help you double-check your math.

   Step 5. Make a decision about the null and state the substantive conclusion.

The decision rule stated that the null would be rejected if the obtained value exceeded 9.210. Since χ^2_{obt} ended up being less than the critical value (i.e., 4.50 < 9.210), the null must be retained. There is not a statistically significant relationship between education and death-penalty attitudes among male respondents; it appears that men of all education levels are equally likely to support or oppose capital punishment. Remember that no claim is being made that gender is the only or main driving force behind death-penalty attitudes; what has been demonstrated here is a statistical association, nothing more.

   Finally, let's repeat the same analysis for female respondents. Again, we will set alpha at .01 and proceed through the five steps. See Table 10.7.

LEARNING CHECK

In the third example, no f_e calculations will be shown for the numbers displayed in Table 10.8. Check your mastery of the computation of expected frequencies by doing the calculations and making sure you arrive at the same answers shown in the text.

Table 10.7 Female Respondents' Education Level and Death-Penalty Attitudes

Education	Attitude Toward Death Penalty for Persons Convicted of Murder		Row Marginal
	Favor	*Oppose*	
High school or less	401[A]	233[B]	634
Some college	60[C]	22[D]	82
Bachelor's degree or higher	148[E]	130[F]	278
Column Marginal	609	385	$N = 994$

Step 1. State the null (H_0) and alternative (H_1) hypotheses.

$$H_0: \chi^2 = 0$$

$$H_1: \chi^2 > 0$$

Step 2. Identify the distribution and compute the degrees of freedom.

The distribution is χ^2 and $df = (3 - 1)(2 - 1) = 2$.

Step 3. Identify the critical value of the test statistic and state the decision rule.

With $\alpha = .01$ and $df = 2$, $\chi^2_{crit} = 9.210$. The decision rule is that *if $\chi^2_{obt} > 9.210$, H_0 will be rejected.*

Step 4. Compute the obtained value of the test statistic.

Table 10.8 Calculating χ^2_{obt}

Cell	f_{o_i}	f_{e_i}	$\left(f_{o_i} - f_{e_i}\right)$	$\left(f_{o_i} - f_{e_i}\right)^2$	$\dfrac{\left(f_o - f_e\right)^2}{f_{e_i}}$
A	401	388.44	12.56	157.75	.41
B	233	245.56	−12.56	157.75	.64
C	60	50.24	9.76	95.26	1.90
D	22	31.76	−9.76	95.26	3.00
E	148	170.32	−22.32	498.18	2.92
F	130	107.68	22.32	498.18	4.63
	$N = 994$	$N = 994$	$\Sigma = .00$		$\Sigma = 13.50$

Step 5. Make a decision about the null and state the substantive conclusion.

The decision rule stated that the null would be rejected if the obtained value exceeded 9.210. Since $\chi^2_{obt} = 13.50$, the null is rejected. There is a statistically significant relationship between education and death-penalty attitudes among female respondents; it appears that women's likelihood of favoring or opposing capital punishment changes with their education level. Another way to phrase this is that there are significant differences between women of varying levels of education. This is interesting, since education and attitudes were not related to one another among men. It appears that there is an "education effect" only among women.

A limitation of chi-square is its inability to identify the specific location of differences between categories. We know from the previous analysis that women differ depending on their education level, but we do not know which level(s) of education are different from the others. Row percentages can help speak to this. Interestingly, support for capital punishment increases from 63% to 73% for those who attended some college but drops to 53% among those who earned a bachelor's degree or higher. We are not able to say with certainty, however, whether all three groups are statistically significantly different from the others or whether only one of them stands apart. You can roughly estimate differences using row percentages, but you have to be cautious in your interpretation.

LEARNING CHECK

One criticism of the chi-square test for independence is that this statistic is sensitive to sample size. The problem lies in the specific way that χ^2_{obt} is calculated. Even with a substantively equivalent distribution of scores across the contingency table, the obtained value of the test statistic might not be statistically significant if the sample size is small and statistically significant if it is large. To see this for yourself, recalculate χ^2_{obt} using the death-penalty and gender data but with a sample size of 99 instead of 1,824. The distribution of this smaller table is identical to the larger one (i.e., all cell percentages are the same here as before). Make a decision about the null hypothesis, recalling that $\chi^2_{crit} = 3.841$.

Sex	Death Penalty		
	Favor	*Oppose*	*Row Marginal*
Female	33[A]	21[B]	54
Male	31[C]	14[D]	45
Column Marginal	64	35	N = 99

Are you surprised by the results? This demonstrates the untrustworthiness of statistical significance and the importance of being cautious in your conclusions.

Measures of Association

The chi-square test alerts you when there is a statistically significant relationship between two variables, but it is silent as to the strength or magnitude of that relationship. We know from the previous two examples, for instance, that gender is related to attitudes toward capital punishment and that convicted juveniles' race/ethnicity is related to the sentences they receive, but we do not know the magnitudes of these associations: They could be very strong, moderate, or quite weak. This question is an important one because a very slight relationship—even if statistically significant in a technical sense—is not of much substantive or practical importance. Large relationships are more meaningful in the "real world."

There are several **measures of association**, and this chapter covers four of them. The level of measurement of the IV and DV dictate which measures are appropriate for a given analysis. It is important to keep in mind that measures of association are computed only when the null hypothesis has been rejected—if the null is not rejected and you conclude that there is no relationship between the IV and DV, then it makes no sense to go on and try to interpret an association you just said does not exist. The following discussion will introduce four tests, and the next section will show you how to use SPSS to compute χ^2_{obt} and accompanying measures of association.

Measures of association: Procedures for determining the strength or magnitude of a relationship after a chi-square test has revealed a statistically significant association between two variables.

Cramer's V can be used when both of the variables are nominal or when one is ordinal and the other is nominal. It is symmetric, meaning that it always takes on the same value regardless of which variable is posited as the independent and which the dependent. This statistic ranges from 0.00 to 1.00, with higher values indicative of stronger relationships and values closer to 0.00 suggestive of weaker associations. Cramer's V is computed as

$$V = \sqrt{\frac{\chi^2_{obt}}{N \cdot m}},$$

Formula 10(4)

where χ^2_{obt} = the obtained value of the test statistic,

N = the total sample size, and

m = the smaller of either $(r-1)$ or $(c-1)$.

In the first example we saw in this chapter, where we found a statistically significant relationship between gender and death-penalty attitudes, $\chi^2_{obt} = 12.33$, $N = 1,824$, and there were two rows and two columns, so $m = 2 - 1 = 1$. Cramer's V is thus

$$V = \sqrt{\frac{12.33}{1,824 \cdot 1}} = \sqrt{.01} = .10$$

This value of V is not very robust and, therefore, represents a weak relationship. This demonstrates how statistical significance alone is not indicative of genuine importance or meaning—a relationship might be significant in a technical sense but still very *in*significant in practical terms. This is due in no small part to the chi-square test's sensitivity to sample size, as discussed earlier. Think back to the percentages we calculated for this table. Approximately 61% of women and 69% of men favored the death penalty. This is a difference, to be sure, but it is not very large. If any given respondent were randomly selected out of this sample, there would be a roughly two-thirds likelihood that the person would support capital punishment, irrespective of her or his gender. It is wise, then, to be cautious in interpreting statistically significant results—*statistical* significance does not always translate into *practical* significance.

When both variables under examination are nominal, lambda is an option. Like Cramer's V, lambda ranges from 0.00 to 1.00. Unlike Cramer's V, lambda is asymmetric, meaning that it requires that one of the variables be clearly identified as the independent and the other as the dependent. This is because lambda is a proportionate reduction in error measure.

Cramer's V: A symmetric measure of association for χ^2 when the variables are nominal or one is ordinal and the other is nominal. V ranges from 0.00 to 1.00 and indicates the strength of the relationship. Higher values represent stronger relationships. Identical to phi in 2×2 tables.

Lambda: An asymmetric measure of association for χ^2 when the variables are nominal. Lambda ranges from 0.00 to 1.00 and is a proportionate reduction in error measure.

Phi: A symmetric measure of association for χ^2 with nominal variables and a 2×2 table. Identical to Cramer's V.

Proportionate reduction in error (PRE) refers to the extent to which knowing a person or object's placement on an IV helps predict that person or object's classification on the dependent measure. Consider the gender and death-penalty attitudes example. If you were trying to predict a given individual's attitude toward capital punishment and the only piece of information you had was the frequency distribution of this DV (i.e., you knew that 1,183 people in the sample support capital punishment and 641 oppose it), then your best bet would be to guess the modal category (*mode* = support) because this would produce the fewest prediction errors. There would, though, be a substantial number of these errors—641, to be exact! Now, suppose that you know a given person's gender. To what extent does this knowledge improve your accuracy when you predict whether that person opposes or favors the death penalty? This is the idea behind PRE measures like lambda.

Lambda is symbolized as λ (the Greek lowercase letter lambda) and is calculated as

$$\lambda = \frac{E_1 - E_2}{E_1},$$ *Formula 10(5)*

where $E_1 = N_{total} - N_{mode}$

$$E_2 = \sum_{across\ DV categories} \left(N_{total} - N_{mode} \right)$$

Basically, E_1 represents the number of prediction errors made when the IV is ignored, and E_2 reflects the number of errors made when the IV is taken into account. Using the education and death-penalty data from Table 10.6, we can first calculate E_1 and E_2,

$$E_1 = 994 - 609 = 385$$

$$E_2 = (609 - 401) + (385 - 233) = 208 + 152 = 360,$$

and lambda is

$$\lambda = \frac{385 - 360}{385} = \frac{25}{385} = .06 \, .$$

Lambda is most easily interpreted by transforming it to a percentage. We can say that knowing women's education level reduces prediction errors by 6%. This is not very much! Again, we see a statistically significant but substantively modest association between variables.

There is a third measure for nominal data that bears brief mention, and that is **phi**. Phi can only be used on 2×2 tables (i.e., two rows and two columns) with nominal variables. It is calculated and interpreted just like Cramer's V with the exception that phi does not account for the number of rows or columns in the crosstabs table; since it can only be applied to 2×2 tables, m will always be equal to 1.00. For 2×2 tables, Cramer's V is identical to phi, but since Cramer's V can be used for tables of any size, it is more useful than phi is.

When both variables are ordinal or when one is ordinal and the other is dichotomous (i.e., has two classes), **Goodman and Kruskal's gamma** is an option. Gamma is a PRE measure but is symmetric—unlike lambda—and ranges from –1.00 to +1.00, with zero meaning no relationship, –1.00 indicating a perfect negative relationship (as one variable increases, the other decreases), and 1.00 representing a perfect positive relationship (as one increases, so does the other, and vice versa). Generally speaking, gamma values between 0 and ±.19 are considered weak, between ±.20 and ±.39 moderate, ±.40 to ±.59 strong, and ±.60 to ±1.00 very strong.

Two other measures available when both variables are ordinal are **Kendall's tau$_b$** and **Kendall's tau$_c$**. Both are symmetric. Tau$_b$ is for use when the crosstabs table has an equal number of rows and columns, and tau$_c$ is used when they are unequal. Both tau statistics range from –1.00 to +1.00. They measure the extent to which the order of the observations in the IV match the order in the DV; in other words, as cases increase in value on the IV, what happens to their scores on the DV? If their scores on the dependent measure decrease, tau will be negative; if they increase, tau will be positive; and if they do not display a clear pattern (i.e., the two variables have very little dependency), tau will be close to zero. Similar to the tau measures is **Somers' d**. This measure of association is asymmetric and for use when both variables are ordinal. Its range and interpretation mirror those of tau. The calculations of gamma, tau, and d are complicated, so we will refrain from doing them by hand and will instead use SPSS to generate these values.

None of the measures of association discussed here is perfect; each has limitations and weaknesses. The best strategy is to examine two or more measures for each analysis and use them to gain a comprehensive picture of the strength of the association. There will likely be variation among them, but the differences should not be wild and all measures should lean in a particular direction. If they are all weak or all are strong, then you can safely arrive at a conclusion about the level of dependency between the two variables.

Goodman and Kruskal's gamma: A symmetric measure of association used when both variables are ordinal or one is ordinal and the other is dichotomous. Ranges from −1.00 to +1.00.

Kendall's tau$_b$: A symmetric measure of association for two ordinal variables when the number of rows and columns in the crosstabs table are equal. Ranges from −1.00 to +1.00.

Kendall's tau$_c$: A symmetric measure of association for two ordinal variables when the number of rows and columns in the crosstabs table are unequal. Ranges from −1.00 to +1.00.

Somers' d: An asymmetric measure of association for two ordinal variables. Ranges from −1.00 to +1.00.

SPSS

The SPSS program can be used to generate χ^2_{obt}, determine statistical significance, and produce measures of association. The chi-square analysis is found via the sequence *Analyze → Descriptive Statistics → Crosstabs*. Let us first consider the gender and capital punishment example from earlier in the chapter. Figure 10.2 shows the dialog boxes involved in running this analysis in SPSS. Note that you must check the box labeled *Chi-square* in order to get a chi-square analysis; if you do not check this box, SPSS will merely give you a crosstabs table. This box is opened by clicking *Statistics* in the crosstabs window. By default, SPSS provides only observed frequencies in the crosstabs table. If you want expected frequencies or percentages, you must go into *Cells* and request them. Since both of these variables are nominal, lambda and Cramer's V are the appropriate measures of association. Figure 10.3 shows the output.

The obtained value of the χ^2_{obt} statistic is located on the line labeled *Pearson Chi-Square*. You can see in Figure 10.3 that $\chi^2_{obt} = 12.351$, which is very close to the value we obtained by hand. The output also tells you whether or not the null should be rejected, but it does so in a way that we have not seen before. The SPSS program gives you what is called a *p* value. The *p* value tells you the exact probability of the obtained value of the test statistic; the smaller *p* is, the more unlikely the χ^2_{obt} is if the null is true and, therefore, the probability that the null is, indeed, correct. The *p* value in SPSS χ^2 output is the number located at the intersection of the *Asymp. Sig. (2-sided)* column and the *Pearson Chi-Square* row. Here, $p = .000$. What you do is compare *p* to α. If *p* is less than α, it means that the obtained value of the test statistic exceeded the critical value, and the null is rejected; if *p* is greater than α, the null is retained. Since in this problem α was set at .05, the null hypothesis is rejected because .000 < .05. There is a statistically significant relationship between gender and death-penalty attitudes.

---

p value: In SPSS output, the probability associated with the obtained value of the test statistic. When $p < α$, the null hypothesis is rejected.

Figure 10.2 Running a Chi-Square Test and Measures of Association in SPSS

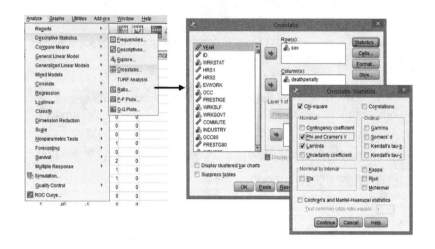

Figure 10.3 Chi-Square Output

Chi-Square Tests

	Value	df	Asymp. Sig. (2-sided)	Exact Sig. (2-sided)	Exact Sig. (1-sided)
Pearson Chi-Square	12.351[a]	1	.000		
Continuity Correction[b]	12.007	1	.001		
Likelihood Ratio	12.409	1	.000		
Fisher's Exact Test				.000	.000
Linear-by-Linear Association	12.344	1	.000		
N of Valid Cases	1824				

Symmetric Measures

		Value	Approx. Sig.
Nominal by Nominal	Phi	.082	.000
	Cramer's V	.082	.000
N of Valid Cases		1824	

Directional Measures

			Value	Asymp. Std. Error[a]	Approx. T	Approx. Sig.
Nominal by Nominal	Lambda	Symmetric	.000	.000	[b]	[b]
		Respondent sex Dependent	.000	.000	[b]	[b]
		Do you favor or oppose the death penalty for people convicted of murder? Dependent	.000	.000	[b]	[b]
	Goodman and Kruskal tau	Respondent sex Dependent	.007	.004		.000[c]
		Do you favor or oppose the death penalty for people convicted of murder? Dependent	.007	.004		.000[c]

As you know, though, rejection of the null hypothesis is only part of the story because the χ^2 statistic does not offer information about the magnitude or strength of the relationship between the variables. For this, we turn to measures of association.

Judging by both Cramer's *V* and lambda, this relationship is very weak. We actually already knew this because we calculated *V* by hand and arrived at .10, which is within rounding error of the .082 produced by SPSS. Lambda is zero, which means that knowing people's gender does not reduce the number of errors made in predicting their death-penalty attitudes. As noted earlier, using multiple tests of association helps provide confidence in the conclusion that the association between these two variables, while statistically significant, is very modest in a substantive sense.

CHAPTER SUMMARY

This chapter introduced the chi-square test of independence, which is the hypothesis-testing procedure appropriate when both of the variables under examination are categorical. The key elements of the χ^2 test are observed frequencies and expected frequencies. Observed frequencies are the empirical results seen in the sample, and expected frequencies are those that would appear if the null hypothesis were true and the two variables unrelated. The obtained value of chi-square is a measure of the difference between observed and expected, and comparing χ^2_{obt} to χ^2_{crit} for a set α level allows for a determination of whether the null hypothesis should be retained or rejected.

When the null is retained (i.e., when $\chi^2_{obt} < \chi^2_{crit}$), the substantive conclusion is that the two variables are not related. When the null is rejected (when $\chi^2_{obt} > \chi^2_{crit}$), the conclusion is that there is a relationship between them. *Statistical* significance, though, is only a necessary and not a sufficient condition for *practical* significance. The chi-square statistic does not offer information about the strength of a relationship and how substantively meaningful this association is.

For this, measures of association are turned to when the null has been rejected. Cramer's *V*, lambda, Goodman and Kruskal's gamma, Kendall's tau_a and tau_b, and Somers' *d* are appropriate in any given situation depending on the variables' levels of measurement and the size of the crosstabs table. SPSS can be used to obtain chi-square tests, *p* values for determining statistical significance, and measures of association. When $p < \alpha$, the null is rejected, and when $p > \alpha$, it is retained. You should always generate measures of association when you run χ^2 tests yourself, and you should always expect them from other people who run these analyses and present you with the results. Statistical significance is important, but the magnitude of the relationship tells you just how meaningful the association is in practical terms.

CHAPTER 10 REVIEW PROBLEMS

1. A researcher wants to test for a relationship between the number of citizen complaints that a police officer receives and whether or not that officer commits serious misconduct. He gathers a sample of officers and records the number of complaints that have been lodged against them (0–2, 3–5, 6+) and whether they have ever been written up for misconduct (yes or no). Can he use a chi-square to test for a relationship between these two variables? Why or why not?

2. A researcher wishes to test for a relationship between age and criminal offending. She gathers a sample and for each person, she collects his or her age (in years) and whether that person has ever committed a crime (yes or no). Can she use a chi-square to test for a relationship between these two variables? Why or why not?

3. A researcher is interested in finding out whether people who drive vehicles that are in bad condition are more likely than those driving better cars to get pulled over by police. She collects a sample and codes each person's vehicle's condition (good, fair, poor) and the number of times that person has been pulled over (measured by respondents writing in the correct number). Can she use a chi-square to test for a relationship between these two variables? Why or why not?

4. A researcher is studying the effectiveness of an in-prison treatment program in reducing post-release recidivism. He gathers a sample of recently released prisoners and records, for each person, whether he or she participated in a treatment program while incarcerated (yes or no) and whether that person committed a new crime within 6 months of release (yes or no). Can he use a chi-square to test for a relationship between these two variables? Why or why not?

5. Is a criminal defendant's gender related to the type of sentence she or he receives? A researcher collects data on defendants' gender (male or female) and sentence (jail, probation, fine).

   a. Which of these variables is the independent one, and which is the dependent?

   b. Identify each variable's level of measurement.

   c. How many rows and columns would the crosstabs table have?

6. Is the value of the goods stolen during a burglary related to the likelihood that the offender will be arrested? A researcher collects data on the value of stolen goods ($299 or less, $300–$599, $600 and more) and on whether the police arrested someone for the offense (yes or no).

    a. Which of these variables is the independent one, and which is the dependent?
    b. Identify each variable's level of measurement.
    c. How many rows and columns would the crosstabs table have?

7. Is the crime for which a person is convicted related to the length of the prison sentence she or he receives? A research gathers data on crime type (violent, property, drug) and sentence length (18 months or less, 19–30 months, 31 or more months).

    a. Which of these variables is the independent one, and which is the dependent?
    b. Identify each variable's level of measurement.
    c. How many rows and columns would the crosstabs table have?

8. Is a victim's gender related to whether or not the offender will be convicted for the crime? A researcher collects data on victim gender (male or female) and whether the offender was convicted (yes or no).

    a. Which of these variables is the independent one, and which is the dependent?
    b. Identify each variable's level of measurement.
    c. How many rows and columns would the crosstabs table have?

9. It might be expected that adult prisons that offer college courses to inmates are more likely than those that do not to also provide vocational training. The following table displays data from a random sample of adult correctional facilities. With an alpha level of .01, conduct a five-step chi-square hypothesis test to determine whether or not the two variables are independent.

	Vocational Training		
College Courses	Yes	No	Row Marginal
Yes	41[A]	9[B]	50
No	26[C]	74[D]	100
Column marginal	67	83	$N = 150$

10. Is there an association between the circumstances surrounding a violent altercation that results in a shooting and the type of firearm used? The Firearm Injury Surveillance Study records whether drugs were involved in the incident and the type of firearm used to cause the injury. With an alpha of .01, conduct a five-step hypothesis test to determine if the variables are independent.

	Firearm Type		
Drugs Involved	Handgun	Long gun	Row marginal
Yes	29	5^B	34
No	417^C	147^D	564
Column marginal	446	152	$N = 598$

11. One criticism of private prisons is that they are profitdriven and therefore have an incentive to cut corners. This may reduce opportunities for rehabilitation and self-improvement among persons incarcerated in these facilities. The Census of State and Federal Correctional Facilities data set contains information about whether a prison is publicly or privately operated and whether that institution offers vocational training to its inmates. The following table contains data from a random sample of prisons. With an alpha of .05, conduct a five-step hypothesis test to determine if the variables are independent.

	Prison Offers Vocational Training?		
Facility Type	No	Yes	Row marginal
Public	52^A	103^B	155
Private	38^C	12^D	50
Column marginal	90	115	$N = 205$

12. In the chapter, we saw that there was a statistically significant difference between men and women in terms of their attitudes about capital punishment. We can extend that line of inquiry and find out whether there is a gender difference in general attitudes about crime and punishment. The General Social Survey (GSS) asks respondents whether they think courts are too harsh, about right, or not harsh enough in dealing with criminal offenders. The following table contains the data. With an alpha level of .05, conduct a five-step chi-square hypothesis test to determine whether the two variables are independent.

	Attitude Toward Courts			
Sex	Too harsh	About right	Not harsh enough	Row marginal
Male	134^A	173^B	498^C	805
Female	135^D	207^E	630^F	972
Column marginal	269	380	1,128	$N = 1,777$

13. Do men and women differ on their attitudes toward drug laws? The GSS asks respondents to report whether they think marijuana should be legalized. The following table shows the frequencies, by gender, among black respondents. With an alpha level of .05, conduct a five-step chi-square hypothesis test to determine whether the two variables are independent.

	Should Marijuana Be Legalized?		
Sex	Yes	No	Row marginal
Male	38^A	33^B	71
Female	42^C	76^D	118
Column marginal	80	109	$N = 189$

14. The following table shows the support for marijuana legalization, by gender, among white respondents. With an alpha level of .01, conduct a five-step chi-square hypothesis test to determine whether the two variables are independent.

	Should Marijuana Be Legalized?		
Sex	Yes	No	Row marginal
Male	234^A	185^B	419
Female	227^C	268^D	496
Column marginal	461	453	$N = 914$

15. There is some concern that people of lower-income statuses are more likely to come in contact with the police as compared to higher-income individuals. The following table contains PPCS data on income and police contacts among respondents who were 21 years of age or younger. With an alpha of .01, conduct a five-step hypothesis test to determine if the variables are independent.

	Number of Contacts			
Annual Income	0–2	3–5	6+	Row marginal
Less than $20,000	315^A	42^B	15^C	372
$20,000–$49,999	196^D	31^E	9^F	236
$50,000 or more	266^G	32^H	9^I	307
Column marginal	777	105	33	$N = 915$

16. One criticism of racial profiling studies is that people's driving frequency is often unaccounted for. This is a problem because all else being equal, people who spend more time on the road are more likely to get pulled over eventually. The following table contains Police-Public Contact Survey (PPCS) data narrowed down to black male respondents. The variables measure driving frequency and whether or not these respondents had been stopped by police for traffic offenses within the past 12 months. With an alpha of .01, conduct a five-step hypothesis test to determine if the variables are independent.

Driving Frequency	Experienced a Traffic Stop?		Row marginal
	Yes	No	
Almost every day	214^A	946^B	1,160
Often	32^C	238^D	270
Rarely	6^E	360^F	366
Column marginal	252	1,544	$N = 1,796$

17. The companion website (http://www.sagepub.com/gau) contains the SPSS data file *CSFACF for Chapter 10.sav.* This file contains a random sample of state prisons and four variables: the gender of inmates that the facility houses, whether or not the facility offers adult basic education, the security level of the facility, and whether or not the facility was under court order for having poor conditions of confinement. Use SPSS to run a chi-square analysis to test for independence between *gender* (the IV) and *adult-basic* (the DV). Based on the variables' level of measurement, select appropriate measures of association. Then do the following:

   a. Identify the obtained value of the chi-square statistic.

   b. Make a decision about whether you would reject the null hypothesis of independence at an alpha level of .05 *and* explain how you arrived at that decision.

   c. State the conclusion that you draw from the results of each of these analyses in terms of whether or not there is a relationship between the two variables.

   d. *If you rejected the null hypothesis,* interpret the measures of association. How strong is the relationship? Would you say that this is a substantively meaningful relationship?

18. Using the *CSFACF for Chapter 10.sav* file, run a chi-square analysis to determine whether prisons vary in their court-order status (*courtorder*; the DV) depending on their level of physical security (*security*; the IV). Based on the variables' level of measurement, select appropriate measures of association. Then do the following:

   a. Identify the obtained value of the chi-square statistic.

   b. Make a decision about whether you would reject the null hypothesis of independence at an alpha level of .05 *and* explain how you arrived at that decision.

   c. State the conclusion that you draw from the results of each of these analyses in terms of whether there is a relationship between the two variables.

d. *If you rejected the null hypothesis*, interpret the measures of association. How strong is the relationship? Would you say that this is a substantively meaningful relationship?

19. A consistent finding in research on police-community relations is that there are racial differences in attitudes toward police. Although all racial groups express positive views of police overall, the level of support is highest for whites and tends to dwindle among persons of color. The companion website (http://www.sagepub.com/gau) contains variables from the Police-Public Contact Survey (*PPCS for Chapter 10.sav*). The sample has been narrowed to males who were stopped by the police while driving a car and were issued a traffic ticket. There are three variables in this data set: *race, income*, and *legitimacy*. The legitimacy variable measures whether respondents believed that the officer who pulled them over had a credible reason for doing so. Use SPSS to run a chi-square analysis to determine whether legitimacy judgments (the DV) differ by race (the IV). Based on the variables' level of measurement, select appropriate measures of association. Then do the following:

   a. Identify the obtained value of the chi-square statistic.

   b. Make a decision about whether you would reject the null hypothesis of independence at an alpha level of .01 *and* explain how you arrived at that decision.

   c. State the conclusion that you draw from the results of each of these analyses as to whether or not there is a difference between private and public prisons in terms of offering vocational training.

   d. *If you rejected the null hypothesis*, interpret the measures of association. How strong is the relationship? Would you say that this is a substantively meaningful relationship?

20. Using the *PPCS for Chapter 10.sav* file again (http://www.sagepub.com/gau), run a chi-square test to determine whether respondents' perceptions of stop legitimacy (the DV) vary across income levels (the IV). Based on the variables' level of measurement, select appropriate measures of association. Then do the following:

   a. Identify the obtained value of the chi-square statistic.

   b. Make a decision about whether you would reject the null hypothesis of independence at an alpha level of .01 *and* explain how you arrived at that decision.

   c. State the conclusion that you draw from the results of each of these analyses in terms of whether or not there is a difference between private and public prisons in terms of offering vocational training.

   d. *If you rejected the null hypothesis*, interpret the measures of association. How strong is the relationship? Would you say that this is a substantively meaningful relationship?

KEY TERMS

Chi-square test of independence	Observed frequencies	Goodman and Kruskal's gamma
Nonparametric statistics	Expected frequencies	Kendall's tau$_b$
Parametric statistics	Statistical significance	Kendall's tau$_c$
Statistical independence	Measures of association	Somers' d
Statistical dependence	Cramer's V	p value
χ^2 distribution	Lambda	
Obtained value	Phi	

χ^2	The Greek letter chi squared; a symbol for the test of independence and its associated sampling distribution
χ^2_{crit}	The critical value of the chi-square statistic
χ^2_{obt}	The obtained value of the chi-square statistic
f_o	Observed frequencies
f_e	Expected frequencies
p value	The obtained probability on SPSS output that is compared to the alpha level in order to make a decision about the null hypothesis

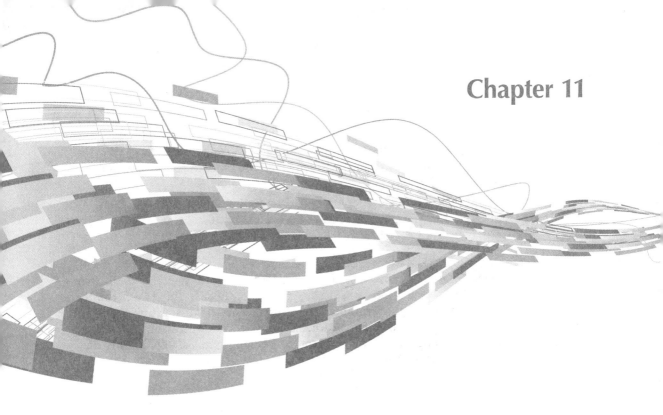

Chapter 11

Hypothesis Testing With Two Population Means or Proportions

(Continued)

- For *t* tests, identify the correct type of test (dependent or independent samples) and, for independent samples, the correct variance formula (pooled or separate).
- Select the correct equations for a given test type, and use them to conduct five-step hypothesis tests.
- In SPSS, identify the correct type of test, run that analysis, and interpret the output.

There are many situations in which criminal justice and criminology researchers work with categorical independent variables (IVs) and continuous dependent variables (DVs). They might want to know, for instance, whether male and female police officers differ in the number of arrests they make, whether criminal offenders who have children are given shorter jail sentences compared to those who do not, or whether prisoners who successfully complete a psychological rehabilitation program have a significant reduction in antisocial thinking. Research Example 11.1 illustrates another instance of a categorical IV and a continuous DV.

RESEARCH EXAMPLE 11.1

Do Multiple Homicide Offenders Specialize in Killing?

Serial killers and mass murderers capture the public's curiosity and imagination. Who can resist some voyeuristic gawking at a killer who periodically snuffs out innocent victims while outwardly appearing to be a regular guy or the tormented soul whose troubled life ultimately explodes in an episode of wanton slaughter? Popular portrayals of multiple homicide offenders (MHOs) lend the impression that these killers are fundamentally different from more ordinary criminals and from single homicide offenders (SHOs) in that they only commit homicide and lead otherwise crime-free lives. But is this popular conception true?

Wright, Pratt, and DeLisi (2008) decided to find out. They constructed an index measuring diversity of offending within a sample of homicide offenders. This index captured the extent to which homicide offenders committed only homicide and no other crimes versus the extent to which they engaged in various types of illegal acts. The researchers divided the sample into MHOs and SHOs and calculated each group's mean and standard deviation on the diversity index. They found the statistics located in the following table.

Diversity Index Means and Standard Deviations for Multiple Homicide Offenders and Single Homicide Offenders

	MHOs		SHOs	
	$\bar{x}$	s	$\bar{x}$	s
Diversity index	.36	.32	.37	.33

Source: Adapted from Table 1 in Wright, Pratt, and DeLisi (2008).

In Research Example 11.1, Wright et al. (2008) had two groups (MHOs and SHOs), each with their own mean and standard deviation, and the goal was to find out whether the groups' means differ significantly from one another. A significant difference would indicate that MHOs and SHOs do indeed differ in the variety of crimes they commit, whereas rough equivalency in the means would imply that these two types of homicide offenders are equally diverse in offending. What should the researchers do to find out whether MHOs and SHOs have significantly different diversity indices?

The answer is that they should conduct a two-population test for differences between means, or what is more commonly referred to as a *t* test. As you probably figured out, these tests rely on the *t* distribution. These types of tests are the subject of this chapter. We will also cover two-population tests for differences between proportions, which are conceptually similar to *t* tests but employ the *z* distribution.

---

t test: The test used with a two-class, categorical independent variable and a continuous dependent variable.

Both of these test types are appropriate only when the IV is categorical with exactly two classes or groups. Examples of two-class, categorical IVs include gender (*male* or *female*) and political orientation (*liberal* or *conservative*). The two test types differ, though, in terms of their dependent variables: *t* tests require continuous DVs, whereas tests for differences between proportions are for use with binary, categorical DVs. The diversity index that Wright et al. (2008) used is continuous, which is the reason they were able to compute a mean and a standard deviation, and the reason that a *t* test is the appropriate analytic strategy. In the review problems at the end of the chapter, you will conduct a *t* test to find out whether MHOs and SHOs differ significantly in offending diversity.

Two-Population Tests for Differences Between Means: *t* Tests

There are many situations in which people working in criminal justice and criminology would want to test for differences between two means. Someone might be interested in finding out whether offenders who are sentenced to a term of incarceration receive significantly different mean sentence lengths depending on whether they are male or female. A municipal police department might implement an innovative new policing strategy and want to know whether the program significantly reduced mean crime rates in the city. These types of studies require *t* tests.

In Chapter 7, you learned the difference between sample, sampling, and population distributions. Recall that sampling distributions are theoretical curves created when multiple or infinite samples are drawn from a single population and a statistic is computed and plotted for each sample. Over time, with repeated drawing, calculating, plotting, throwing back, and drawing again, the distribution of sample statistics builds up and, if the size of each sample is large (meaning $N \geq 100$), the statistics form a normal curve. There are also sampling distributions for differences between means. See Figure 11.1. You have seen in prior chapters how sampling distributions' midpoint is the population mean (symbolized μ). Sampling distributions for differences between means are similar in that they center on the true population difference, $\mu_1 - \mu_2$. A sampling distribution of differences between means is created by pulling infinite *pairs* of samples—rather than single samples. Imagine drawing two samples, computing both means, subtracting one mean from the other to form a difference score, and then plotting that difference score. Over time, the difference scores build up. If $N \geq 100$, the sampling distribution of differences between means is normal; if $N \leq 99$, then the distribution is more like "normalish" because it tends to be wide and flat. The *t* distribution, being flexible and able to accommodate various sample sizes, is the probability distribution of choice for tests of differences between means.

Figure 11.1   The Sampling Distribution of Differences Between Means

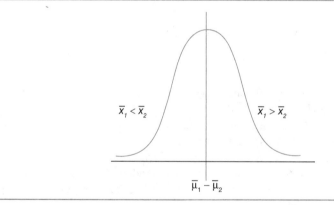

There are two general types of *t* tests, one for use with **independent samples** and one for use with **dependent samples**. The difference between them pertains to the method used to select the two samples under examination. In independent sampling designs, the selection of cases into one sample in no way affects, or is affected by, the selection of cases into the other sample. If a researcher is interested in the length of prison sentences received by male and female defendants, then that researcher would draw a sample of females and a sample of males. A researcher investigating the effects of judicial selection type on judges' sentencing decisions might draw a sample of judges who were elected and a sample of those who were appointed to their posts. In neither of these instances does the selection of one person into one sample have bearing on the selection of another into the other sample. They are independent because they have no influence on each other.

Independent samples: Pairs of samples in which the selection of people or objects into one sample in no way affected, or was affected by, the selection of people or objects into the other sample.

Dependent samples: Pairs of samples in which the selection of people or objects into one sample directly affected, or was directly affected by, the selection of people or objects into the other sample. The most common types are matched pairs and repeated measures.

In dependent-samples designs, by contrast, the two samples are related to each other in some way. The two major types of dependent-samples designs are matched pairs and repeated measures. **Matched-pairs designs** are used when researchers need an experimental group and a control group but are unable to use random assignment to create the groups. They therefore gather a sample from a treatment group and then construct a control group via the deliberate selection of cases that did not receive the treatment but that are similar to the treatment group cases on key characteristics. If the unit of analysis is people, participants in the control group might be matched to the treatment group on race, gender, age, and criminal history.

Repeated-measures designs are commonly used to evaluate program impacts. These are before-and-after designs wherein the treatment group is measured prior to the intervention of interest and then again afterward to determine whether the post-intervention scores differ significantly from the pre-intervention ones. In repeated measures, then, the "two" samples are actually the same people or objects measured twice.

Matched-pairs design: A research strategy where a second sample is created on the basis of each case's similarity to a case in an existing sample.

Repeated-measures design: A research strategy used to measure the effectiveness of an intervention by comparing two sets of scores (pre and post) from the same sample.

The first step in deciding what kind of *t* test to use is to figure out whether the samples are independent or dependent. It is sometimes easier to identify dependent designs than independent ones. The biggest clue to look for is a description of the research methods. If the samples were collected by matching individual cases on the basis of similarities between them, or if an intervention was being evaluated by collecting data before and after a particular event, then the samples are dependent and the dependent-samples *t* test is appropriate. If the methods do not detail a process of matching or of repeated measurement, if all that is said is that two samples were collected or a single sample was divided on the basis of a certain characteristic to form two subsamples, then you are probably dealing with independent samples and should use the independent-samples *t* test.

There is one more wrinkle. There are two types of independent-samples *t* tests: **pooled variances** and **separate variances**. The former is used when the two population variances are similar to one another, whereas the latter is used when the variances are significantly disparate. The rationale for having these two options is that when two samples' variances are similar, they can safely be combined (pooled) into a single estimate of the population variance. When they are markedly unequal, however, they must be mathematically manipulated before being combined. You will not be able to tell merely by looking at two samples' variances whether you should use a pooled-variance or separate-variance approach, but that is fine. In this book, you will always be told which one to use. When we get to SPSS, you will see that this program produces results from both of these tests, along with a criterion to use for deciding between them (more on this later). You will, therefore, always be able to figure out which type of test to use.

This has probably all gotten somewhat murky. Luckily, there is a simple set of steps you can follow anytime you encounter a two-population test that will help you determine which type of *t* test to use. This mental sequence is depicted in Figure 11.2.

Pooled variances: The type of *t* test appropriate when the samples are independent and the population variances are equal.

Figure 11.2   Steps for Deciding Which *t* Test to Use

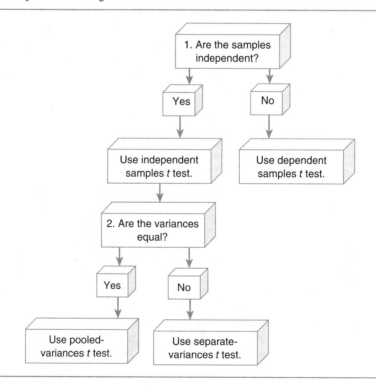

Separate variances: The type of *t* test appropriate when the samples are independent and the population variances are unequal.

In this chapter, we will encounter something we have touched on before but have not addressed in detail: **one-tailed tests** versus two-tailed tests. We discussed the *t* distribution in Chapters 7 and 8. The *t* distribution is symmetric and has positive and negative sides. In two-tailed tests, there are two critical values, one positive and one negative. You learned in Chapter 8 that confidence intervals are always two-tailed. In *t* tests, by contrast, some analyses will be two-tailed and some will be one-tailed. Two-tailed tests split alpha (α) in half such that half of α is in each tail of the distribution. One-tailed tests, by contrast, place all of α into a single tail. One-tailed tests may have α in the upper (or positive) tail or lower (or negative) tail, depending on the specific question under investigation.

The choice of a one-tailed test versus a two-tailed test is generally made on a case-by-case basis. It depends on whether a researcher has a good reason to believe that the relationship under examination should be positive or negative. Suppose that you are studying an in-prison treatment program that focuses on improving participants' literacy skills. You would measure their reading levels before the program began and then again after it had ended, and would expect to see an increase—you have good reason to predict that post-intervention literacy skills would be greater than pre-intervention ones. In this case, a one-tailed test would be in order (these are also called directional tests, since a prediction is being made about the direction of a relationship). Now suppose you want to know whether that literacy program works better for men or for women. You do not have any particular reason for thinking that it would be more effective for one group than the other, so you set out merely to test for any difference at all, regardless of direction. This would be cause for using a two-tailed test (also called a nondirectional test). Let us work our way through some examples and discuss one-tailed and two-tailed tests as we go.

One-tailed tests: Hypothesis tests in which the entire alpha is placed in either the upper (positive) or lower (negative) tail such that there is only one critical value of the test statistic. Also called directional tests.

LEARNING CHECK

Be very careful about order of operations! The formulas we will encounter in this chapter require multiple steps, and you have to do those steps in proper sequence or you will arrive at an erroneous result. Remember "*Please Excuse My Dear Aunt Sally*"? This mnemonic device reminds you to use the order parentheses, exponents, multiplication, division, addition, subtraction. Your calculator automatically employs proper order of operations, so you need to insert parentheses where appropriate so that you can direct the sequence. There is a big difference between, for instance, the numeric phrases *3 + 4/2* and *(3 + 4)/2*. Consult your operator's manual and your course instructor if you need assistance.

Independent-Samples *t* Tests

A Two-Tailed Test With Equal Population Variances: Does Transferred Female Juveniles' Mean Age of Arrest Differ Across Races/Ethnicities?

There is a theoretical and empirical connection between how old people are when they start committing delinquent offenses (this is called the *age of onset*) and their likelihood of continuing law-breaking behavior in adulthood. All else being equal, younger ages of onset are associated with greater risks of adult criminal activity. Using the Juvenile Defendants in Criminal Court data set (JDCC; Data Sources 11.1), we can test for a significant difference in the mean age at which juveniles were arrested for the offense that led to them being transferred to adult court. To address questions about gender and race, the sample is narrowed to females, and we will test for an age difference between Hispanics and whites in this subsample. Among Hispanic female juveniles in the JDCC sample ($N = 44$), the mean age of arrest was 15.89 years ($s = 1.45$). Among white females ($N = 31$), the mean age of arrest was 16.57 years ($s = 1.11$). To be clear, the IV is race (*Hispanic; white*) and the DV is age at arrest (*years*). A *t* test is therefore the proper analytic strategy. We will use an α level of .05, a presumption that the population variances are equal, and the five steps of hypothesis testing.

DATA SOURCES 11.1

Juvenile Defendants in Criminal Courts

The Juvenile Defendants in Criminal Courts (JDCC) is a subset of the Bureau of Justice Statistics' (BJS) State Court Processing series that gathers information on defendants convicted of felonies in large, urban counties. BJS researchers pulled information about juveniles charged with felonies in 40 of these counties in May 1998. Each case was tracked through disposition. Information about the juveniles' demographics, court processes, final dispositions, and sentences was recorded. Due to issues with access to and acquisition of data in some of the counties, the JDCC is a nonprobability sample, and conclusions drawn from it should therefore be interpreted cautiously (Bureau of Justice Statistics, 1998).

It is useful in an independent-samples *t* test to first make a table that lays out the relevant pieces of information that you will need for the test. Table 11.1 shows these numbers. It does not matter which sample you designate Sample 1 and which you call Sample 2 as long as you stick with your original designation throughout the course of the hypothesis test. Since it is easy to simply designate the samples in the order in which they appear in the problem, let us call Hispanic females Sample 1 and white females Sample 2.

We will use a two-tailed test because we have no solid theoretical reason for thinking that whites' mean would be greater than Hispanics' or vice versa. The alternative hypothesis will merely specify a

Table 11.1 Relevant Numbers for Example 1

Sample 1: Hispanic Females	Sample 2: White Females	Test
$\bar{x}_1 = 15.89$	$\bar{x}_2 = 16.57$	$\alpha = .05$
$s_1 = 1.45$	$s_1 = 1.11$	two-tailed test
$N_1 = 44$	$N_1 = 31$	equal population variances

difference (i.e., an inequality) between the means, with no prediction about which one is greater than or less than the other.

Step 1. State the null (H_0) and alternative (H_1) hypotheses.

In t tests, the null and alternative are phrased in terms of the population means. Recall that population means are symbolized μ (the Greek letter mu, pronounced "mew"). We use the population symbols rather than the sample symbols because the goal is to make a statement about the relationship, or lack thereof, between two variables in the population. The null hypothesis for a t test is that the means are equal:

$$H_0: \mu_1 = \mu_2$$

Equivalence in the means suggests that the IV is not exerting an impact on the DV. Another way of thinking about this is that H_0 predicts that the two samples came from the same population. In the context of the present example, retaining the null would indicate that race or ethnicity does not affect female juveniles' age of arrest (in other words, that all female juveniles are part of the same population, irrespective of race or ethnicity).

The alternative or research hypothesis is that there *is* a significant difference between the population means or, in other words, that there are two separate populations, each with its own mean:

$$H_1: \mu_1 \neq \mu_2$$

Rejecting the null would lead to the conclusion that the IV does affect the DV; here, it would mean that race and ethnicity does appear related to age of arrest. Note that this phrasing of the alternative hypothesis is specific to two-tailed tests—the "not equal" sign implies no prediction about the direction of the difference. The alternative hypothesis will be phrased slightly differently for one-tailed or directional tests.

Step 2. Identify the distribution and compute the degrees of freedom.

As mentioned earlier, two-population tests for differences between means employ the t distribution. The t distribution, you should recall, is a family of curves that changes shape depending on degrees of freedom (df). The t distribution is normal at large df and gets wider and flatter as df declines.

The df formula differs across the three types of t tests, so you have to identify the proper test before you can compute the df. Using the sequence depicted in Figure 11.2, we know (1) that the samples are independent because this is a random sample divided into two groups and (2) that the population variances are equal. This leads us to choose the pooled-variances t test. The df formula is

$$df = N_1 + N_2 - 2, \qquad\qquad \textit{Formula 11(1)}$$

where N_1 = the size of the first sample and

N_2 = the size of the second sample.

Pulling the sample sizes from Table 11.1,

$$df = 44 + 31 - 2 = 73.$$

Step 3. Identify the critical value and state the decision rule.

Three pieces of information are required to find the critical value of t (t_{crit}) using the t table: the number of tails in the test, the alpha level, and the df. The exact df value of 73 does not appear on the table, so we use the value that is closest to it, which is 60. With two tails, an α of .05, and 73 degrees of freedom, the absolute value of t_{crit} is 2.000.

This is not the end of finding the critical value, though, because we still have to figure out the sign or signs; that is, we need to determine whether t_{crit} is positive, negative, or both. A one-tailed test has only one critical value and it is either positive or negative. In two-tailed tests, there are always two critical values. Their absolute values are the same, but one is negative and one is positive. Figure 11.3 illustrates this.

Given that there are two tails in this current test and, therefore, two critical values, $t_{crit} = \pm 2.000$. The decision rule is stated thus: *If t_{obt} is either greater than 2.000 or less than –2.000,* H$_0$ *will be rejected.* The decision rule has to be stated as an "either/or" proposition because of the presence of two critical values. There are, in essence, two ways for the null to be rejected: t_{obt} could be out in the right tail beyond 2.000 or out in the left tail beyond –2.000.

Step 4. Calculate the obtained value of the test statistic.

The formulas for the obtained value of t (t_{obt}) vary across the three different types of t tests; however, the common thread is to have (1) a measure of the difference between means in the numerator and (2) an estimate of the standard error of the sampling distribution of differences between means in the denominator (remember that the standard error is the standard deviation of a sampling distribution). The estimated standard error is symbolized $\hat{\sigma}_{\bar{x}_1 - \bar{x}_2}$ and the formula for estimating it with pooled variances is

Figure 11.3 The Critical Values for a Two-Tailed Test With α = .05 and *df* = 73

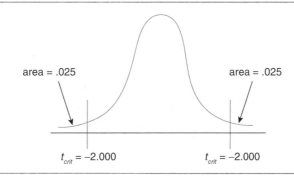

area = .025   area = .025

$t_{crit} = -2.000$ $t_{crit} = -2.000$

$$\hat{\sigma}_{\bar{x}_1 - \bar{x}_2} = \sqrt{\frac{(N_1 - 1)s_1^2 + (N_2 - 1)s_2^2}{N_1 + N_2 - 2}} \sqrt{\frac{N_1 + N_2}{N_1 N_2}}.$$ *Formula 11(2)*

This formula may look a bit daunting, but keep in mind that it is only composed of sample sizes and standard deviations, both of which are numbers you are accustomed to working with. The most important thing is to work through it carefully. Plug the numbers in correctly and use proper equation-solving techniques. Entering the numbers from our example yields

$$\hat{\sigma}_{\bar{x}_1 - \bar{x}_2} = \sqrt{\frac{(44 - 1)1.45^2 + (31 - 1)1.11^2}{44 + 31 - 2}} \sqrt{\frac{44 + 31}{44.31}}$$

$$= \sqrt{\frac{(43)2.10 + (30)1.23}{73}} \sqrt{\frac{75}{1,364}}$$

$$= \sqrt{\frac{90.30 + 36.90}{73}} \sqrt{.05}$$

$$= \sqrt{\frac{127.20}{73}} \sqrt{.05}$$

$$= \sqrt{1.74} \sqrt{.05}$$

$$= 1.32(.22)$$

$$= .29.$$

This is our estimate of the standard error of the sampling distribution. This is not t_{obt}! Be careful. What must be done is to plug the standard error into the t_{obt} formula. This formula is

$$t_{obt} = \frac{\overline{x}_1 - \overline{x}_2}{\hat{\sigma}_{\overline{x}_1 - \overline{x}_2}}.$$

Formula 11(3)

Using our numbers, we perform the calculation:

$$t_{obt} = \frac{15.89 - 16.57}{.29} = \frac{-.68}{.29} = -2.34$$

$$t_{obt} = \frac{15.89 - 16.57}{.29} = \frac{-.68}{.29} = -2.34$$

This is the final answer! The obtained value of t is −2.34. Step 4 is done.

Step 5. Make a decision about the null, and state the substantive conclusion.

We said in the decision rule that if t_{obt} was either greater than 2.000 or less than −2.000, the null would be rejected. So, what will we do? If you said, "Reject the null," you are correct. Since t_{obt} is less than −2.000, the null is rejected. The conclusion is that white and Hispanic female juveniles transferred to adult court differ significantly in terms of mean age of arrest for their instant offense. Another way to think about it is that there is a relationship between race/ethnicity and mean age of arrest.

Note that, strictly speaking, it is not permissible to draw a conclusion about the direction of this relationship. Since we employed a two-tailed test, we relinquished our right to state after rejecting the null that we found that one group's mean is greater than the other. This seems strange, since we can look at the two means and see that the mean age for the white sample is greater than that for this Hispanic sample—clearly, we know the direction! It might help to think about it this way. Our use of a two-tailed test implied that we did not have sufficient basis, on the grounds of theory or prior empirical evidence, to think that Hispanics' age of onset was significantly lower than that of whites. The fact that we found such an effect in the current sample is not, by itself, enough to conclude that this is the case. You should never let your data drive your thinking—do not construct a reality around an empirical finding. We need to lay out a logical rationale for thinking that Hispanics' age of onset is earlier than that of whites and then gather a sample and test this hypothesis.

A One-Tailed Test With Unequal Population Variances: Does the Length of an Incarceration Sentence Differ Depending on Whether It Was Imposed Pursuant to a Jury Trial or a Bench Trial?

For the second t-test example, we will again use the JDCC data on juveniles diverted to adult criminal courts. Let's consider whether the length of time it takes for a juvenile's case to be disposed of is affected by the type of attorney the juvenile has. The prediction will be that juvenile defendants who retain private counsel experience have significantly longer times-to-disposition compared to those who utilize the services of public defenders. This, theoretically, is because private attorneys might file more pretrial motions and spend more time negotiating with the prosecutor and the judge. The sample is narrowed to juveniles charged with violent offenses who were not released pending trial and who were ultimately sentenced to prison. Those with private attorneys ($N = 36$) had a mean of 7.93 months to disposition ($s = 4.53$), whereas those represented by public defenders ($N = 234$) experienced a mean of 6.36 months ($s = 3.66$). We will call the defendants who retained private attorneys Sample 1 and those who were represented by public defenders Sample 2. Using an alpha level of .01 and the assumption that the population variances are unequal, we will conduct a five-step hypothesis test to determine whether persons convicted by juries receive significantly longer prison sentences. Table 11.2 shows the numbers we will need for the analysis.

Step 1. State the null (H_0) and (H_1) alternative hypotheses.

The null hypothesis is the same as that used above (H_0: $\mu_1 = \mu_2$) and reflects the prediction that the two means do not differ. The alternative hypothesis used in Example 1, however, does not apply in the present context because this time, we are making a prediction about which mean will be greater than the other. The nondirectional sign ($\neq$ must therefore be replaced by a sign that indicates a specific direction. This will either be a greater than (>) or less than (<) sign. We are predicting that jury trials will result in significantly longer mean sentences, so we can conceptualize the hypothesis as *private attorney disposition time > public defender disposition time*. Since defendants represented by private attorneys are Sample 1 and those by public defenders Sample 2, the alternative hypothesis is

$$H_1\colon \mu_1 > \mu_2.$$

Step 2. Identify the distribution and compute the degrees of freedom.

The distribution is still *t*, but the *df* equation for unequal population variances differs sharply from that for equal variances because the situation of unequal variances mandates the use of the separate-variances *t* test. The *df* formula is obnoxious, but as with the prior formulas we have

Table 11.2   Relevant Numbers for Example 2

Sample 1: Private Attorney	Sample 2: Public Defender	Test
$\bar{x}_1 = 7.93$	$\bar{x}_2 = 6.36$	$\alpha = .01$
$s_1 = 4.53$	$s_2 = 3.66$	one-tailed test
$N_1 = 36$	$N_2 = 234$	unequal population variances

encountered, you have everything you need to solve it correctly—just take care to plug in the right numbers and use proper order of operations.

$$df = \dfrac{\left[\dfrac{\left(\dfrac{s_1^2}{N_1-1}+\dfrac{s_2^2}{N_2-1}\right)}{\left(\dfrac{s_1^2}{N_1-1}\right)^2\left(\dfrac{1}{N_1+1}\right)+\left(\dfrac{s_4^2}{N_2-1}\right)^2\left(\dfrac{1}{N_2+1}\right)}\right]}{} - 2 \qquad \text{Formula 11(4)}$$

Plugging in the correct numbers from the current example,

$$df = \left[\dfrac{\left(\dfrac{4.53^2}{36-1}+\dfrac{3.66^2}{234-1}\right)}{\left(\dfrac{4.53^2}{36-1}\right)^2\left(\dfrac{1}{36+1}\right)+\left(\dfrac{3.66^2}{234-1}\right)^2\left(\dfrac{1}{234+1}\right)}\right] - 2$$

$$= \left[\dfrac{\left(\dfrac{20.52}{35}+\dfrac{13.40}{233}\right)}{\left(\dfrac{20.52}{35}\right)^2\left(\dfrac{1}{37}\right)+\left(\dfrac{13.40}{233}\right)^2\left(\dfrac{1}{235}\right)}\right] - 2$$

$$= \left[\dfrac{(.59+.06)}{(.59)^2(.03)+(.06)^2(.004)}\right] - 2$$

$$= \left[\dfrac{.65}{.35(.03)+.004(.004)}\right] - 2$$

$$= \left[\dfrac{.65}{.01+.00002}\right] - 2$$

$$= \left[\dfrac{.65}{.010002}\right] - 2$$

$$= 64.99 - 2$$

$$= 62.99$$

Step 2 is complete; $df = 62.99$. The t table contains only whole numbers, so this has to be rounded to 63.

Step 3. Identify the critical value and state the decision rule.

With one tail, an α of .01, and 63 degrees of freedom, $t_{crit} = 2.390$. The sign of the critical value is positive because the alternative hypothesis predicts that $\bar{x}_1 > \bar{x}_2$. Revisit Figure 11.2 for an illustration. When the alternative predicts that $\bar{x}_1 < \bar{x}_2$, the critical value will be on the left (negative) side of the distribution and when the alternative is that $\bar{x}_1 > \bar{x}_2$, t_{crit} will be on the right (positive) side. The decision rule is that *if t_{obt} is greater than 2.390, H_0 will be rejected.*

Step 4. Compute the obtained value of the test statistic.

As before, the first step is to obtain an estimate of the standard error of the sampling distribution. Since the population variances are unequal, the separate variances version of independent-samples t must be used. The standard error formula for the difference between means in a separate-variance t test is

$$\hat{\sigma}_{\bar{x}_1 - \bar{x}_2} = \sqrt{\frac{s_1^2}{N_1 - 1} + \frac{s_2^2}{N_2 - 1}}. \qquad \text{Formula 11(5)}$$

Plugging in the numbers from the present example yields

$$\hat{\sigma}_{\bar{x}_1 - \bar{x}_2} = \sqrt{\frac{4.53^2}{36 - 1} + \frac{3.66^2}{234 - 1}} = \sqrt{\frac{20.52}{35} + \frac{13.40}{233}} = \sqrt{.59 + .06} = \sqrt{.65} = .81.$$

Now, the standard error estimate can be entered into the same t_{obt} formula used with the pooled-variances t test. Using Formula 11(3),

$$t_{obt} = \frac{7.93 - 6.36}{.81} = \frac{1.57}{.81} = 1.94.$$

Step 5. Make a decision about the null and state the substantive conclusion.

The decision rule stated that the null would be rejected if t_{obt} exceeded 2.390. Since t_{obt} ended up being 19.4, the null is retained. Juveniles who had privately retained attorneys did not experience a statistically significant increase in the amount of time it took for their cases to be resolved, compared to juveniles who had public defenders. Another way to say this is that there is no relationship between attorney type and disposition time.

Dependent-Samples *t* Tests

The foregoing discussion centered on the situation in which a researcher is working with two independently selected samples; however, as described earlier, there are times when the samples under examination are not independent. The main types of dependent samples are *matched pairs* and *repeated measures*. Dependent samples require a *t* formula different from that used when the study samples are independent because of the manipulation entailed in selecting dependent samples. With dependent-samples *t*, the sample size (N) is not the total number of people or objects in the sample but, rather, the number of *pairs* being examined. We will go through an example now to demonstrate the use of this *t* test.

RESEARCH EXAMPLE 11.2

Do Mentally Ill Offenders' Crimes Cost More?

There is ongoing debate about the precise role of mental illness in offending. Some individuals with mental illness (MI) are unstable, antisocial, or crime prone, but it would be wrong to stigmatize the entire group based on the behavior of a few members. One question that could be asked is whether mentally ill offenders' crimes exact a particularly heavy toll on taxpayers relative to offenders who do not have MI. Ostermann and Matejkowski (2014) collected data on all persons released from New Jersey prisons in 2006. The data included the number of times each ex-prisoner was rearrested within a 3-year follow-up period. The researchers did two things to analyze the effect of MI on crime cost. First, they divided the group according to whether or not each person had received a MI diagnosis and then calculated the average cost of each group's recidivism. The results showed that MI offenders' crimes were nearly three times more expensive compared to non-MI offenders. Next, however, the authors matched the sample of MI offenders to a subsample of non-MI offenders on the basis of each person's demographic characteristics and offense histories and then recalculated each group's average cost. The results changed dramatically. After the one-to-one matching procedure, the non-MI group's average cost was more than double that of the MI group. It turns out that the initial results—the ones suggesting that MI offenders' crimes are much more expensive—are misleading. It is not good policy to use the mere existence of MI as cause to enhance supervision or restrictions on ex-prisoners. What should be done instead is to focus on the risk factors that are associated with recidivisms among both MI and non-MI offenders. This policy focus would cut costs and create higher levels of social justice.

Dependent-Samples t Test: Are Female Correctional Officers a Threat to Institutional Security?

The traditionally male-dominated field of correctional security is gradually being opened to women who wish to work in jails and prisons, yet there are lingering concerns regarding how well female correctional officers can maintain order in male institutions. Criticism has been raised that women are not as capable as men when it comes to controlling male inmates, which could threaten the internal safety and security of the prison environment. Let us test the hypothesis that male maximum-security prisons with relatively small percentages of female security staff will have lower inmate-on-inmate assault rates relative to those institutions with high percentages of female security staff because security in the latter will be compromised. We will use data from the Census of State and Federal Adult Correctional Facilities (CSFACF; Data Sources 3.1) and an alpha level of .05. The first sample consists of five male, state-run, maximum-security prisons in Texas with below-average percentages of female security staff, and the second sample contains five prisons selected on the basis of each one's similarity to a prison in the first sample (in other words, the second sample's prisons are all male, state-run, maximum-security facilities in Texas with inmate totals similar to those of the first sample). The difference between the samples is that the second sample has above-average percentages of female security staff. Table 11.3 contains the raw data.

Table 11.3 Matched Samples of Male Maximum-Security Prisons in Texas

	Assault Rate	
	Low Percentage Female (x_1)	High Percentage Female (x_2)
Pair A	1.46	.63
Pair B	2.72	.76
Pair C	1.22	1.29
Pair D	.95	1.09
Pair E	1.26	1.72

Step 1. State the null (N_0) and (N_1) alternative hypotheses.

The null, as is always the case with t tests, is H_0: $\mu_1 = \mu_2$. It is being suggested in this problem that low-percentage female prisons (i.e., prisons with greater percentages of male staff) should have lower assault rates than high-percentage female (low male percentage) prisons do; hence, the alternative in words is *low < high* and in formal symbols is H_1: $\mu_1 < \mu_2$.

Step 2. Identify the distribution and compute the degrees of freedom.

The distribution is t. The degrees of freedom calculation for dependent-samples tests is different from those above—for dependent samples, the *df* is based on the number of pairs rather than on the size of each sample. The *df* for pairs is

$$df = N_{pairs} - 1.$$ *Formula 11(6)*

Using the data from Example 3,

$$df = 5 - 1 = 4.$$

Step 3. Identify the critical value and state the decision rule.

With an alpha of .05, a one-tailed test, and $df = 4$, the absolute value derived using the t table is 2.132. To determine whether this critical value is positive or negative, refer back to Figure 11.1. The phrasing of our alternative hypothesis makes the critical value negative, so $t_{crit} = -2.132$. The decision rule states that *if $t_{obt} < -2.132$, H_0 will be rejected.*

Step 4. Compute the obtained value of the test statistic.

The formulas required to calculate t_{obt} for dependent samples looks quite different from those for independent samples, but the logic is the same. The numerator contains a measure of the difference between means, and the denominator is an estimate of the standard error. Finding the standard error requires two steps. First, the standard deviation of the differences between means (s_D) is needed. In the independent-samples t tests we conducted earlier, we knew each sample's standard deviation and so we could plug those numbers directly into the standard-error formula. We do not yet know the standard deviation for the matched-pairs sample, however, so we have to obtain that number before tackling the standard error. The standard deviation for matched pairs is computed using the formula

$$s_D = \sqrt{\frac{\Sigma\left(x_D - \bar{x}_D\right)}{N_{pairs} - 1}},$$ *Formula 11(7)*

where x_D = the difference scores, and

$\bar{x}_D$ = the mean of the difference scores.

The standard deviation is then used to find the standard error of the sampling distribution, as follows:

$$\hat{\sigma}_{\bar{x}_1 - \bar{x}_2} = \frac{s_D}{\sqrt{N_{pairs}}}$$ *Formula 11(8)*

Finally, the obtained value of the test statistic is calculated as

$$t_{obt} = \frac{\bar{x}_D}{\hat{\sigma}_{\bar{x}_1 - \bar{x}_2}}.$$ *Formula 11(9)*

This computation process is substantially simplified by the use of Table 11.4. This table contains the raw scores and three additional columns. The first column to the right of the raw scores contains the difference scores (x_D), which are computed by subtracting each x_2 score from its corresponding x_1 value. The mean difference score ($\bar{x}_D$) is then needed and is calculated thus:

$$\bar{x}_D = \frac{\Sigma x_D}{N}$$ Formula 11(10)

The mean difference score is subtracted from each individual difference score—this is the $(x_D - \bar{x}_D)$ column—to form deviation scores. Finally, each of these scores is squared and the last column summed. The final product of Table 11.4 is the sum of the squared deviation scores, located in the lower right-hand corner. This number (here, 3.86) gets entered into the s_D formula and the calculations proceed through t_{obt} as such:

$$s_D = \sqrt{\frac{3.86}{5-1}} = \sqrt{.97} = .98$$

$$\hat{\sigma}_{\bar{x}_1 - \bar{x}_2} = \frac{.98}{\sqrt{5}} = \frac{.98}{2.24} = .44$$

$$t_{obt} = \frac{.42}{.44} = .95$$

Table 11.4 Matched Samples of Male Maximum-Security Prisons in Texas

	Assault Rate by Percentage Female				
	Low Percentage Female (x_1)	High Percentage Female (x_2)	$x_D = x_1 - x_2$	$(x_D - \bar{x}_D)$	$(x_D - \bar{x}_D)^2$
Pair A	1.46	.63	$1.46 - .63 = .83$	$.83 - .42 = .41$	$(.41)^2 = .17$
Pair B	2.72	.76	1.96	1.54	2.37
Pair C	1.22	1.29	−.07	−.49	.24
Pair D	.95	1.09	−.14	−.56	.31
Pair E	1.26	1.72	−.46	−.88	.77
			$\bar{x}_D = \dfrac{2.12}{5} = .42$		$\Sigma = 3.86$

And Step 4 is (finally) done! The obtained value of *t* is .95.

Step 5. Make a decision about the null and state the substantive conclusion.

The decision rule stated that the null would be rejected if the obtained value was less than −2.132. With t_{obt} = .95, the null is retained. The conclusion is that male maximum-security prisons with low levels of female security staff do not experience fewer inmate-on-inmate assaults relative to prisons with high levels of female security staff. Alternatively, we can say that there is no relationship between a prison's level of female staffing and its rate of inmate-on-inmate assaults. There is no support for the notion that female correctional officers compromise institutional security.

RESEARCH EXAMPLE 11.3

Pulling Levers: Targeted Interventions to Reduce Crime

The past two decades have seen a shift in criminal justice operations toward an emphasis on multiagency efforts designed to address the specific crime problems plaguing individual neighborhoods and communities. One strategy that has been devised is the "pulling levers" approach that entails identifying high-risk offenders and offering them a choice between tough prosecution and reform. Police and prosecutors explain the penalties these offenders would face if they continue their antisocial behavior, and community social service providers offer treatment and educational opportunities for those who want to put their lives on a better track. In 2007, the Rockford (Illinois) Police Department implemented a pulling levers approach in an attempt to reduce violent crime in the city. Corsaro, Brunson, and McGarrell (2013) evaluated the Rockford intervention. They measured the mean number of violent crimes that occurred in several areas of the city per month before and after the program. The following table shows these results. The target neighborhood is the one in which the pulling levers strategy was implemented.

Using a statistical analysis, the researchers found that the target neighborhood experienced a significant reduction in nonviolent crime as a result of the pulling levers program. The reduction in violent crime, though, was not statistically significant, so it appeared that the intervention did not affect these types of offenses. The researchers were able to attribute the target area's decline in nonviolent offenses to the pulling levers strategy because crime fell only in the target zone and nowhere else in the city. It thus appears from this analysis that pulling levers is a promising strategy for reducing nonviolent crimes such as drug, property, and nuisance offenses but is perhaps less useful with respect to violent crime.

Location	Number of Offenses per Month	
	Pre-Intervention	Post-Intervention
Target Neighborhood		
Nonviolent	29	22
Violent	21	18
Remainder of City		
Nonviolent	944	859
Violent	567	554
Overall City		
Nonviolent	1,013	881
Violent	588	573

Two-Population Tests for Differences Between Proportions

Two-population tests for differences between proportions follow the same logic as those for differences between means. The independent variable is still a two-class, categorical measure; however, the dependent variable is a proportion rather than a mean. Differences between proportions have their own sampling distribution, which looks very much like that for differences between means and can be drawn as Figure 11.4.

Population proportions are symbolized with the letter P and sample proportions with $\hat{p}$ (pronounced "p hat"). Like confidence intervals for proportions, two-population tests employ the z distribution. Thus, the sample size must be at least 100; these tests cannot be carried out on samples smaller than that. All the other fundamentals for proportion tests are the same as those for tests of differences between means, so we will dive right into an example.

Do community-based sex offender treatment programs significantly reduce recidivism?

Sex offenders are perhaps the most reviled class of criminal offenders, yet imprisoning low-level sex offenders is not necessarily the best option in terms of social and economic policy. These people might be good candidates for community-based treatment, which can be effective at reducing the likelihood of recidivism and is less expensive than imprisonment. Washington State has a program called the Special Sex Offender Sentencing Alternative (SSOSA) that separates low-risk from high-risk sex offenders and sentences the low-risk offenders to community-based supervision and treatment. Participants must maintain standards of good behavior, compliance with imposed conditions, and adherence to the required treatment regimen. Transgressors are removed from SSOSA

Figure 11.4 The Sampling Distribution of Differences Between Proportions

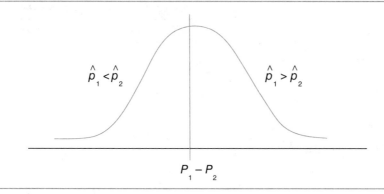

$\hat{P}_1 < \hat{P}_2$ $\hat{P}_1 > \hat{P}_2$

$P_1 - P_2$

and incarcerated. This program has raised questions about how well the SSOSA program reduces recidivism. It has also generated concerns among critics who fear that allowing convicted sex offenders to remain in the community jeopardizes public safety.

To address the issue of sex offender recidivism and the effectiveness of the SSOSA program, researchers from the Washington State Institute for Public Policy compared recidivism across sex offenders who were sentenced to SSOSA and those who were sentenced to jail or prison instead of to this community-based treatment program. Recidivism was measured as a conviction for a new crime within 5 years of release from prison or the program. Among the SSOSA group ($N = 1{,}097$), 10% were convicted of new crimes; among the non-SSOSA group that was incarcerated ($N = 2{,}994$), 30% were reconvicted (Barnoski, 2005). Using an alpha level of .05, let us test the null hypothesis that there is no difference between the population proportions against the alternative hypothesis that the SSOSA group's recidivism rate was significantly lower than the incarceration group's. The use of a directional hypothesis is justified because the SSOSA program is intended to lower recidivism.

Step 1. State the null (H_0) and (H_1) alternative hypotheses.

The null hypothesis for a two-population test for differences between proportions represents the prediction that the two proportions do not differ or, in other words, that the two population proportions are equal. The alternative hypothesis can take on the three forms discussed in the preceding section regarding two-population tests for means. Here, calling the SSOSA group Sample 1 and the incarceration group Sample 2, the hypotheses are

$$H_0: P_1 = P_2,$$

$$H_1: P_1 < P_2.$$

Step 2. Identify the distribution and compute the degrees of freedom.

The proper distribution for two-population tests of proportions is the z curve. It is important to note, though, that this distribution can only be used when the samples are large and independent; violation of either of these assumptions can be fatal to a test of this type. You should always have enough knowledge about the research design that produced the data you are working with to determine whether the independence assumption has been met. In the present case, it has, because the SSOSA and incarceration groups were unrelated to each other. Remember that the proportion test can only be conducted when $N \geq 100$; there is an additional requirement that both the proportion of cases that fall into the category of interest ($\hat{p}$) and the proportion that does not (symbolized $\hat{q}$) are both greater than or equal to five. Formally stated,

$$N_{\hat{p}_k} \geq 5 \qquad\qquad \textit{Formula 11(11)}$$

and

$$N_{\hat{q}_k} \geq 5, \qquad\qquad \textit{Formula 11(12)}$$

where $\hat{p}_k$ the sample proportion for each of Sample 1 and Sample 2 and

$\hat{q}_k = 1 - \hat{p}_k$ for each of Sample 1 and Sample 2.

In the current example, the SSOSA group meets the large sample criterion because $\hat{p} = .10$, which means that $\hat{q} = .90$. Therefore,

$$1,097(.10) = 109.70,$$

$$1,097(.90) = 987.30.$$

The incarceration group likewise succeeds, as $\hat{p} = .30$ and $\hat{q} = .70$ and

$$2,994(.30) = 898.20,$$

$$2,994(.70) = 2,095.80.$$

The z distribution can thus be used. There is no need to compute degrees of freedom because they are not applicable to z.

Step 3. Identify the critical value and state the decision rule.

It has been a while since we used the z distribution, but recall that a z value can be found using a known area. Here, alpha is that area. Since $\alpha = .05$ and the test is one-tailed, go to the z table and find the area closest to $.50 - .05 = .45$. There are actually two areas that fit this description (.4495 and .4505), so $z_{crit} = \dfrac{-1.64 + (-1.65)}{2} = -1.645$. The critical value is negative because the alternative hypothesis $(P_1 < P_2)$ tells us that we are working on the left (negative side) of the distribution (see Figure 11.5). The decision rule is thus: *If z_{obt} is less than -1.65, H_0 will be rejected.*

Step 4. Compute the obtained value of the test statistic.

For this portion of the test, you need to be very careful about symbols because there are a few that are similar to one another but actually represent very different numbers. Pay close attention to the following:

p = population proportion

$\hat{p}$ = pooled sample proportions as an estimate of the population proportion

$\hat{q}$ = 1.00 – the pooled sample proportions

$\hat{p}_1$ = Sample 1 proportion

$\hat{p}_2$ = Sample 2 proportion

There are a few analytical steps in the buildup to the z_{obt} formula. First, the sample proportions have to be pooled in order to form a single estimate of the proposed population proportion:

$$\hat{p} = \frac{N_1 \hat{p}_1 + N_2 \hat{p}_2}{N_1 + N_2} \qquad \textit{Formula 11(13)}$$

The complement of the pooled proportion ($\hat{q}$) is also needed. This is done using the formula

$$\hat{q} = 1.00 - \hat{p}. \qquad \textit{Formula 11(14)}$$

Next, the standard error of the sampling distribution of differences between proportions must be estimated using the formula

$$\hat{\sigma}_{\hat{p}_1 - \hat{p}_2} = \sqrt{\hat{p}\hat{q}}\sqrt{\frac{N_1 + N_2}{N_1 N_2}}. \qquad \textit{Formula 11(15)}$$

Finally, the obtained value of the test statistic is calculated as

$$z_{obt} = \frac{\hat{p}_1 - \hat{p}_2}{\hat{\sigma}_{\hat{p}_1 - \hat{p}_2}}. \qquad \textit{Formula 11(16)}$$

Now, we will plug in the numbers from the current example and solve the formulas all the way up to z_{obt}:

$$\hat{p} = \frac{1,097(.10) + 2,994(.30)}{1,097 + 2,994} = \frac{109.70 + 898.20}{4,091} = \frac{1,007.90}{4,091} = .25$$

$$\hat{q} = 1.00 - .25 = .75$$

$$\hat{\sigma}_{\hat{p}_1 - \hat{p}_2} = \sqrt{(.25)(.75)} \sqrt{\frac{1,097 + 2,994}{1,097 \times 2,994}} = \sqrt{.19} \sqrt{\frac{4,091}{3,284,418}} = \sqrt{.19} \sqrt{.001}$$

$$= (.44)(.03) = .01$$

$$z_{obt} = \frac{.10 - .30}{.01} = \frac{-.20}{.01} = -20.00$$

Step 5. Make a decision about the null and state the substantive conclusion.

Since $z_{obt} = -20.00$, which is far less than the critical value of -1.65, the null is rejected. The sex-offender group that went through the SSOSA program had a significantly lower recidivism rate compared to the group sentenced to jail or prison. Of course, we cannot say for sure that this is because the SSOSA program is effective, as the offenders selected to go through this program might be those who were at the lowest risk for reoffending anyway. What does seem clear is that, at the very least, the SSOSA program is not harming public safety, could be reducing recidivism rates, and, therefore, might be a useful cost-savings program.

SPSS

The SPSS program can run all of the *t* tests discussed in this chapter, though it cannot run tests for differences between proportions, so you would have to use SPSS to derive the proportions and then do the analysis by hand. Independent-samples *t* tests are located under the *Analyze* menu in the SPSS data screen. In this menu, find *Compare Means* and then *Independent-Samples T Test*. To demonstrate the use of SPSS, some of the examples we did by hand in the foregoing pages will be replicated. Note that the final answers obtained in SPSS may depart somewhat from those that we calculated by hand because we use only two decimal places and SPSS uses far more than that, so our hand-derived answers have rounding error.

First, let us run an independent-samples *t* test using the *race/ethnicity* and *age at arrest* variables that were under study in Example 1 earlier in this chapter. Figure 11.5 shows how to select these variables for an analysis. The IV is designated as the *Grouping Variable* and the DV goes into the *Test Variable(s)* space. You have to specify the values of the IV, as Figure 11.5 depicts. Click *OK* to obtain the output shown in Figure 11.6.

The first box in Figure 11.6 shows the descriptive statistics for each category. The second box contains the *t* test results. You will notice that there are two values reported for t_{obt}, along with two *p* values. This is because SPSS produces results for both pooled- and separate-variances tests. Remember at the beginning of the chapter when we said that SPSS would help you decide which of these tests you should use? Well, this is it! Levene's test for equality of variances is an analysis that SPSS runs automatically. Levene's *F* statistic is a hypothesis test. The null is that the variances are equal (meaning that they can be pooled). The "F" column displays the obtained value

Figure 11.5   Running a Dependent-Samples *t* Test in SPSS

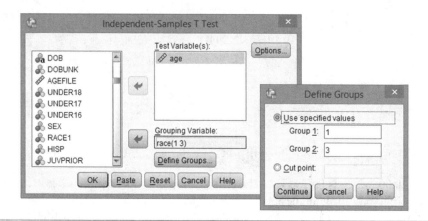

of the *F* statistic and the "Sig." column shows the *p* value for *F*. It is customary to use an alpha level of .05 when determining whether or not to reject the null of equivalence. If $p < .05$, the null is rejected, which means the variances are unequal and the "Equal variances not assumed" row is the one containing the correct *t* test results; if $p > .05$, the null is retained and the "Equal variances assumed" line is the one to look at. In Figure 11.6, $F = .126$ and $p = .724$, so the null is retained and the variances are equal. The obtained value of *t* is –2.203, which is close to the value we arrived at by hand (–2.34). The *p* value is .031, which is less than .05, so judging by this output, the null should be rejected. There is a relationship between race/ethnicity and age at arrest or, in other words, there is a significant difference between white and Hispanic girls in the age at which they were arrested.

The procedure for dependent-samples *t* tests is a little different. The SPSS file has to be set up so that the rows represent pairs and two columns contain the two sets of scores for each pair. When you go to *Analyze → Compare Means → Paired-Samples T Test*, you will see a variable list on the left and will need to select the two sets of scores that you wish to compare and move them to the right. Figure 11.7 demonstrates this.

Once you have moved the variables over, click *OK* and output like that in Figure 11.8 will appear.

Figure 11.8 contains the results of the matched sample of male, maximum-security prisons that we used for hand calculations in Example 3. The obtained value of *t* is .964, which differs only slightly from the value of .95 that our hand computations yielded. The *p* value is .390. This is well above the alpha level of .05, so the null is retained. There is no relationship between female staffing and inmate assault rates.

CHAPTER SUMMARY

In this chapter, you learned several types of analyses that can be conducted to test for differences between two populations. These can be used to test for differences between means or for

Figure 11.6   SPSS Output for Independent-Samples *t* Test

Group Statistics

	Race and ethnicity	N	Mean	Std. Deviation	Std. Error Mean
AGE AT ARREST	White	31	16.5745	1.10904	.19919
	Hispanic	44	15.8936	1.44616	.21802

Independent-Samples Test

| | | Levene's Test for Equality of Variances | | t test for Equality of Means | | | | | 95% Confidence Interval of the Difference | |
		F	Sig.	t	df	Sig. (2-tailed)	Mean Difference	Std. Error Difference	Lower	Upper
AGE AT ARREST	Equal variances assumed	.126	.724	-2.203	73	.031	-.68088	.30908	-1.29687	-.06489
	Equal variances not assumed			-2.306	72.421	.024	-.68088	.29531	-1.26951	-.09225

Figure 11.7 Running a Dependent-Samples *t* Test in SPSS

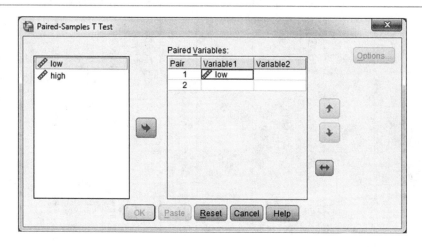

Figure 11.8 SPSS Output for Dependent (Paired) Samples *t* Test

Paired Samples Test

		Paired Differences							
					95% Confidence Interval of the Difference				
		Mean	Std. Deviation	Std. Error Mean	Lower	Upper	t	df	Sig. (2-tailed)
Pair 1	Assault rate—low-percentage female staff Assault rate—high-percentage female staff	.42400	.98333	.43976	−.79696	1.64496	.964	4	.390

differences between proportions; each type of difference has its own sampling distribution. The *t* distribution can be used for means tests and the *z* for proportions tests.

When you approach a hypothesis-testing question involving a two-class, categorical independent variable and a continuous dependent variable, you first have to ask yourself whether the two samples are independent. If they are not, the dependent-samples *t* test must be used. If they are independent, you must then decide whether the population variances are equal. If the DV at issue is measured as a proportion, then the two-population tests for differences in proportions should be used.

SPSS can be used to run *t* tests. You should use your knowledge of the research design to determine whether the samples are independent or dependent. If they are independent, Levene's *F* statistic is used to determine whether or not the population variances can be assumed equal. If *F* is not statistically significant (generally at an alpha of .05), then the null of equality is retained and you should use the equal/pooled variances *t*; if the null is rejected at .05, the unequal/separate variances test is the one to look at. Tests for differences in proportions must be done by hand.

As always, GIGO! It is your responsibility to make sure that you select the proper test and run that test correctly. SPSS is pretty unforgiving—it will not alert you to errors unless those errors are so serious that the requested analysis simply cannot be run at all. If you make a mistake, such as using dependent samples when you should use independent samples, SPSS will give you a result that resembles the serial killers (mentioned in Research Example 1) that opened this chapter: It looks normal on the surface, but it is actually untrustworthy and potentially dangerous.

Note: Answers to review problems in this and subsequent chapters may vary depending on the number of steps used and whether rounding is employed during the calculations. The answers provided in this book's key were derived using the procedures illustrated in the main text.

CHAPTER 11 REVIEW PROBLEMS

1. A researcher wants to test the hypothesis that defendants who plead guilty are sentenced more leniently than those who insist on going to trial. The researcher measures the plea decision as *guilty plea or trial* and the sentence as the number of months of incarceration to which defendants were sentenced.

   a. What is the independent variable?
   b. What is the level of measurement of the independent variable?
   c. What is the dependent variable?
   d. What is the level of measurement of the dependent variable?

2. A researcher wants to test the hypothesis that defendants who are released on bail are more likely to be convicted than those who are unable to post bail or are denied it. The researcher measures pretrial release as *released or detained* and calculates the proportion within each group that is convicted.

   a. What is the independent variable?
   b. What is the level of measurement of the independent variable?
   c. What is the dependent variable?
   d. What is the level of measurement of the dependent variable?

3. A researcher wants to test the hypothesis that male and female judges differ in the severity of the sentences they hand down. The researcher gathers a sample of judges and measures gender as *male or female* and sentence severity as the number of prison sentences they issue in 1 year.

   a. What is the independent variable?
   b. What is the level of measurement of the independent variable?
   c. What is the dependent variable?
   d. What is the level of measurement of the dependent variable?

4. A researcher wants to test the hypothesis that police are less likely to arrest a suspect if the suspect has a full-time job. The researcher gathers a sample and measures job status as *employed or unemployed* and records the proportion of each group that was arrested.

   a. What is the independent variable?
   b. What is the level of measurement of the independent variable?
   c. What is the dependent variable?
   d. What is the level of measurement of the dependent variable?

5. In Question 1, the researcher studying guilty pleas and sentence severity would use what kind of statistical test?

   a. Test for differences between means
   b. Test for differences between proportions

6. In Question 2, the researcher studying pretrial release and conviction likelihood would use what kind of statistical test?

   a. Test for differences between means
   b. Test for differences between proportions

7. In Question 3, the researcher studying judges' gender and sentencing behavior would use what kind of statistical test?

   a. Test for differences between means
   b. Test for differences between proportions

8. In Question 4, the researcher studying suspect unemployment status and arrest would use what kind of statistical test?

   a. Test for differences between means
   b. Test for differences between proportions

9. Tests for differences between two population means utilize the ____ distribution, and tests for differences between population proportions use the ____ distribution.

10. A researcher wishes to find out whether a new drug court program appears to be effective at reducing drug use among participants. He gathers a random sample of drug defendants who are about to enter the drug court's treatment regimen and measures the number of times per month that they use drugs. After the participants finish the program, the researcher again measures their monthly drug use. Which type of *t* test would be appropriate for analyzing the data?

a. Independent samples, pooled variances
b. Independent samples, separate variances
c. Dependent samples

11. A researcher is investigating the relationship between the restrictiveness of gun laws and gun-crime rates. She gathers a sample of states and divides them into two groups: *strict gun laws or lax gun laws*. She then calculates the gun crime rate in each state. She finds that the two groups have unequal variances. Which type of *t* test would be appropriate for analyzing the data?

a. Independent samples, pooled variances
b. Independent samples, separate variances
c. Dependent samples

12. A researcher wishes to test the hypothesis that attorney type affects the severity of the sentence a defendant receives. He gathers a sample of defendants and records attorney type (*publicly funded; privately retained*) and the number of days in the jail or prison sentence. He finds that the groups have equal variances. Which type of *t* test would be appropriate for analyzing the data?

a. Independent samples, pooled variances
b. Independent samples, separate variances
c. Dependent samples

13. In Research Example 11.1, you learned of a study by Wright et al. (2008) in which the researchers set out to determine whether multiple homicide offenders (MHOs) were diverse in the number and types of crimes they commit or whether, instead, they tend to specialize in killing. The researchers compared MHOs to single homicide offenders (SHOs) for purposes of this study. MHOs (Sample 1; $N = 155$) had a mean diversity index score of .36 ($s = .32$) and SHOs (Sample 2; $N = 463$) had a mean of .37 ($s = .33$). Using an alpha level of .05, test the hypothesis that the two groups' means are significantly different. Assume equal population variances. Use all five steps.

14. Are juvenile defendants who are released pending adjudication processed slower than those who are detained? The Juvenile Defendants in Criminal Courts (JDCC) data set records whether a juvenile was released and the number of months it took for that juvenile's case to reach a disposition. The sample will be narrowed to black female youth. Released juveniles (Sample 1) had a mean of 4.30 months to disposition ($s = 3.86$, $N = 123$) and detained juveniles (Sample 2) had a mean of 3.57 ($s = 4.20$, $N = 64$). Using an alpha level of .01, test the hypothesis that released juveniles' mean time-to-adjudication is significantly greater than detained juveniles' mean. Assume equal population variances. Use all five steps.

15. Do juveniles transferred to adult court get treated more, or less, harshly depending on their age? The JDCC data set contains information about juveniles' age at arrest and the sentence length received by those sent to jail pursuant to conviction. Those male juveniles who were younger than 16 at the time of arrest ($N = 85$) received a mean of 68.84 days in jail ($s = 125.59$) and those who were older than 16 at arrest ($N = 741$) had a jail sentence mean of 95.24 days ($s = 146.91$). Using an alpha level of .05, test the hypothesis that the over-16 group received a significantly longer mean sentence compared to those younger than 16 at the time of arrest. Assume unequal population variances. Use all five steps.

16. One critique of sentencing research is that it generally focuses on the differences between white defendants and defendants of color and rarely examines differences between minority groups. The JDCC data set can be used to test for differences between the sentences received by black and Hispanic juveniles convicted of property crimes. Black juveniles (Sample 1; $N = 229$) were sentenced to a mean of 31.09 months of probation ($s = 15.42$), and Hispanic juveniles (Sample 2; $N = 118$) received a mean of 40.84 months ($s = 16.45$). Using an alpha level of .01, test the hypothesis that there is a statistically significant difference between the two group means. Assume unequal population variances. Use all five steps.

17. Do property and drug offenders get sentenced differently? The JDCC data show that among male juveniles convicted and fined, those convicted of drug offenses (Sample 1) had a mean fine of $674.78 ($s = 867.94$; $N = 160$) and that those convicted of property offenses had a mean fine of $344.91 ($s = 251.91$; $N = 181$). Using an alpha level of .05, test the hypothesis that there is a statistically significant difference between the two groups' means. Assume equal population variances. Use all five steps.

18. In Question 16, you tested for a relationship between black and Hispanic juveniles in terms of the length of probation sentences received. Now let's find out whether there is a between-group difference among those sentenced to community service. The following table shows pairs of youths matched on gender (male) and offense type (weapons). Using an alpha level of .05, test the hypothesis that there is a statistically significant difference between the groups' means. Use all five steps.

Pair	Community-Service Sentence (Hours)	
	Black	Hispanic
Pair A	25	30
Pair B	50	40
Pair C	48	50
Pair D	100	110
Pair E	40	30

19. One of the most obvious potential contributors to the problem of assaults against police officers is exposure—all else being equal, jurisdictions wherein officers make more arrests may have elevated rates of officer assaults relative to lower-arrest jurisdictions. The Uniform Crime Reports (UCR) offer state-level information on arrest rates and officer assault rates. The states in the two samples in the following table were selected based on key similarities; that is, they are all in the western region of the country, have similar statewide violent crime rates, and have similar populations. The difference is that the states in the first sample have relatively low arrest rates and those in the second sample have relatively high arrest rates. The table shows the officer assault rate (number of officers assaulted per 1,000 officers) in each pair of states. Using an alpha level of .05, test the hypothesis that there is a statistically significant difference between the groups' means. Use all five steps.

Pair	Officer Assaults per 1,000 Officers	
	Low Arrest Rate	High Arrest Rate
Pair A	2.54	2.28
Pair B	4.72	4.08
Pair C	2.75	2.28
Pair D	2.55	2.13
Pair E	3.31	3.38

20. Are male juvenile gunshot victims older than female victims? The Firearm Injury Surveillance Study can be used to derive a set of pairs matched on juvenile status (younger than 18 years), firearm type (handgun), and circumstances of the incident (intentional assault involving drugs). The table lists the ages of each pair. Using an alpha level of .01, test the hypothesis that male victims are significantly older than female victims. Use all five steps.

Pair	Victim Age	
	Female	Male
Pair A	12	14
Pair B	17	17
Pair C	15	17
Pair D	16	14
Pair E	16	15
Pair F	13	13

21. The American Bar Association recommends that defendants who obtain pretrial release should have their cases disposed of within 180 days of their first court appearance. One question with regard to the speed of case processing is whether attorney type matters. Some evidence suggests that publicly appointed attorneys move cases faster than their privately retained counterparts do, other evidence points toward the opposite conclusion, and some studies find no difference. The Juvenile Defendants in Criminal Court (JDCC) data set contains information on attorney type, pretrial release, and days to adjudication. The sample consists of juveniles charged with drug felonies who were granted preadjudication release. Among those juveniles represented by public attorneys (Sample 1; $N = 509$), .64 had their cases disposed of in 180 days or less, while .32 of the juveniles who retained private attorneys (Sample 2; $N = 73$) were adjudicated within 180 days. Using an alpha level of .05, test the hypothesis that there is a significant difference between the proportions. Use all five steps.

22. Are male victims of crime-involved shootings more likely than female victims to be shot by a stranger? The Firearm Injury Surveillance Study captures data on the circumstances and on victims of shootings that took place in the course of a criminal event. Among males (Sample 1; $N = 402$), 68% were shot by strangers,

and among females (Sample 2; $N = 75$), 57% were shot by strangers. Using an alpha level of .05, test the hypothesis that males are significantly more likely than females to be shot by strangers. Use all five steps.

23. Do pedestrian stops vary in duration depending on the time of day at which they take place? The data set *PPCS Independent Samples for Chapter 11.sav* (http://www.sagepub.com/gau) contains the variables *time* and *minutes*, which measure whether a stop took place during the day or at night and the number of minutes the stop lasted. Run an independent-samples *t* test to determine whether these two variables are related.

    a. At an alpha level of .05, will you use the results for the pooled/equal variances *t* or that for separate/unequal variances? How did you make this decision?
    b. What is the obtained value of *t*?
    c. Would you reject the null at an alpha level of .01? Why or why not?
    d. What is your substantive conclusion? In other words, are there significant differences between the two IV groups? Are the IV and the DV related?

24. Do juveniles facing charges for violent crimes have more total charges filed against them compared to juveniles charged with property crimes? The Juvenile Defendants in Criminal Courts dataset contains information on charge type and total charges. The data file *JDCC Independent Samples for Chapter 11.sav* (http://www.sagepub.com/gau) contains the variables *offense* and *charges*. Run an independent-samples *t* test to determine whether offense type appears to be related to the total number of charges.

    a. At an alpha level of .05, will you use the results for the pooled/equal variances *t* or that for separate/unequal variances? How did you make this decision?
    b. What is the obtained value of *t*?
    c. Would you reject the null at an alpha level of .05? Why or why not?
    d. What is your substantive conclusion? In other words, are there significant differences between the two IV groups? Are the IV and the DV related?

25. Critics of the use of DNA evidence in criminal trials sometimes argue that DNA usage would clog up courts due to the delay caused by waiting for labs to return test results. Supporters claim, though, that any such delays would be justified by the improvement in the accuracy of felony convictions and acquittals. The Census of State Court Prosecutors is contained in the file *CSCP Independent Samples for Chapter 11.sav*. The variable *DNA* measures whether a prosecutor's office uses DNA evidence in plea negotiations or in criminal trials, and the variable *convictions* displays the number of felony convictions the office obtained within the past year. Run an independent-samples *t* test.

    a. At an alpha level of .05, will you use the results for the pooled/equal variances *t* or that for separate/unequal variances? How did you make this decision?
    b. What is the obtained value of *t*?
    c. Would you reject the null at an alpha level of .01? Why or why not?
    d. What is your substantive conclusion? In other words, are there significant differences between the two IV groups? Are the IV and DV related?

26. In Question 23, we did not account for PPCS respondents' demographic characteristics. We can ask the same question—whether stop duration varies across day and night—and this time narrow the sample down by gender and race to create a subsample of white males. This strategy removes any potentially

confounding effects of gender and race, and allows us to isolate the effects of the day/night variable. Using the dataset *PPCS Matched Pairs for Chapter 11.sav* (http://www.sagepub.com/gau), run a dependent-samples *t* test using the *day* and *night* variables.

a. What is the obtained value of *t*?
b. Would you reject the null at an alpha level of .05? Why or why not?
c. What is your substantive conclusion? In other words, are there significant differences between the two IV groups? Are the IV and the DV related?

KEY TERMS

t test	Matched-pairs design	Separate variances
Independent samples	Repeated-measures design	One-tailed tests
Dependent samples	Pooled variances	

GLOSSARY OF SYMBOLS AND ABBREVIATIONS INTRODUCED IN THIS CHAPTER

t_{crit}	The critical value of *t*
t_{obt}	The obtained value of *t*
$\hat{\sigma}_{\bar{x}_1 - \bar{x}_2}$	The standard error of the sampling distribution of differences between means
s_D	The standard deviation of the differences; used with dependent-samples *t*
x_D	The raw difference scores; used with dependent-samples *t*
$\bar{x}_D$	The mean of the difference scores; used with dependent-samples *t*
$\hat{q}$	The complement of $\hat{p}$; used with tests for differences between proportions

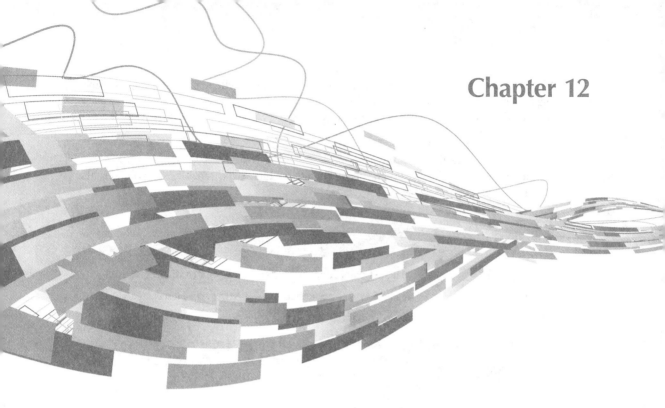

Hypothesis Testing With Three or More Population Means

Analysis of Variance

Learning Objectives

- Identify situations in which, based on the levels of measurement of the independent and dependent variables, ANOVA is appropriate.
- Explain between- and within-group variances and how they can be compared to make a judgment about the presence or absence of group effects.
- Explain the *F* statistic conceptually.

- Explain what the null and alternative hypotheses predict.
- Use raw data to solve equations and conduct five-step hypothesis tests.
- Explain measures of association and why they are necessary.
- Use SPSS to run ANOVA and interpret the output.

In Chapter 11, you learned how to determine whether a two-class categorical variable exerts an impact on a continuous outcome measure: This is a case in which a two-population t test for differences between means is appropriate. In many situations, though, a categorical independent variable (IV) has more than two classes. The proper hypothesis-testing technique to use when the IV is categorical with three or more classes and the dependent variable (DV) is continuous is analysis of variance (ANOVA).

Analysis of variance (ANOVA): The analytic technique appropriate when an independent variable is categorical with three or more classes and a dependent variable is continuous.

As its name suggests, ANOVA is premised on variance. Why do we care about variance when testing for differences between means? Consider the hypothetical distributions displayed in Figure 12.1. The distributions have the same mean but markedly disparate variances—one curve is wide and flat, indicating a fair amount of variance, whereas the other is taller and thinner, indicating less variance.

Figure 12.1   Hypothetical Distributions With the Same Mean and Different Variances

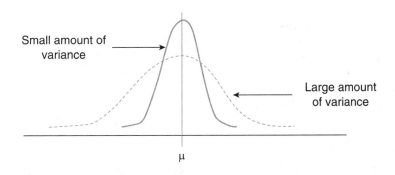

In any analysis of differences between means, the variance associated with each mean must be accounted for. This is what ANOVA does. It combines means and variances into a single test for significant differences between means. A rejected null indicates the presence of a relationship between an independent and a DV.

You might be wondering why, if we have a categorical IV and a continuous DV, we do not just use a series of *t* tests to find out if one or more of the means are different from the others. Family-wise error is the primary reason that this is not a viable analytic strategy. Every time that you run a *t* test, there is a certain probability that the null is true (i.e., that there is no relationship between the IV and the DV) but will be rejected erroneously. This probability, as we saw in Chapter 9, is alpha, and the mistake is called a Type I error. Alpha (the probability of incorrectly rejecting a true null) attaches to each *t* test, so in a series of *t* tests, the Type I error rate increases exponentially until the likelihood of mistake reaches an unacceptable level. This is the familywise error rate, and it is the reason that you should not run multiple *t* tests on a single sample.

Another problem is that multiple *t* tests get messy. Imagine a categorical IV with classes A, B, C, and D. You would have to run a separate *t* test for each combination (AB, AC, AD, BC, BD, CD). That is a lot of *t* tests! The results would be cumbersome and difficult to interpret.

The ANOVA test solves the problems of familywise error and overly complicated output because ANOVA analyzes all classes on the IV simultaneously. One test is all it takes. This simplifies the process and makes for cleaner results.

Familywise error: The increase in the likelihood of a Type I error (i.e., erroneous rejection of a true null hypothesis) that results from running repeated statistical tests on a single sample.

Between-group variance: The extent to which a set of groups or classes are similar to or different from one another. This is a measure of true group effect, or a relationship between the independent and dependent variables.

Within-group variance: The amount of diversity that exists among the people or objects in a single group or class. This is a measure of random fluctuation, or error.

ANOVA: Different Types of Variances

There are two types of variance analyzed in ANOVA. Both are based on the idea of groups, which are the classes on the IV. If an IV was *political orientation* measured as *liberal, moderate,* or *conservative*, then liberals would be a group, moderates would be a group, and conservatives would be a group. Groups are central to ANOVA.

The first type of variance is between-group variance. This is a measure of the similarity among or difference between the groups. It assesses whether groups are markedly different from one another or whether the differences are trivial and meaningless. This is a measure of true group effect. Figure 12.2 illustrates the concept of between-group variance. The groups on the left cluster closely together, while those on the right are distinctly different from one another.

The second kind of variance is **within-group variance** and measures the extent to which people or objects differ from their fellow group members. Within-group variance is driven by random variations between people or objects and is a measure of error. Figure 12.3 depicts the conceptual idea behind within-group variance. The cases in the group on the left cluster tightly around their group's mean, whereas the cases in the right-hand group are scattered widely around their mean. The left-hand group, then, would be said to have much smaller within-group variability than the right-hand group.

The ANOVA test statistic—called the *F statistic* because the theoretical probability distribution for ANOVA is the *F distribution*—is a ratio that compares the amount of variance between groups to that within groups. When true differences between groups substantially outweigh the random fluctuations present within each group, the *F* statistic will be large and the null hypothesis that there is no IV–DV relationship will be rejected in favor of the alternative hypothesis that there is an association between the two variables. When between-group variance is small relative to within-group variance, the *F* statistic will be small and the null will be retained.

Figure 12.2   Small and Large Between-Group Variability

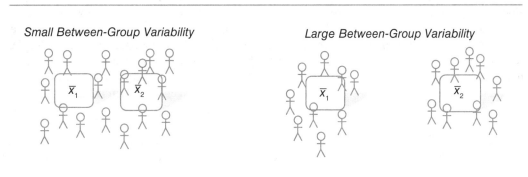

Small Between-Group Variability   Large Between-Group Variability

Figure 12.3   Small and Large Within-Group Variability

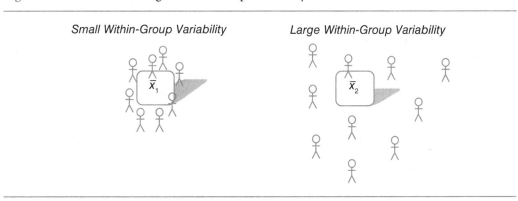

Small Within-Group Variability   Large Within-Group Variability

An example might help illustrate the concept behind the F statistic. Suppose we wanted to test the effectiveness of a mental-health treatment program on recidivism rates in a sample of probationers. We gather three samples: treatment-program completers, people who started the program and dropped out, and those who did not participate in the program at all. Our DV is the number of times each person is rearrested within 2 years of the end of the probation sentence. There will be some random fluctuations within each of the groups; not everybody in each group is going to have the same recidivism score. This is white noise or, more formally, within-group variance—in any sample of people, places, or objects, there will be variation. What we are attempting to discern, though, is whether the difference *between* the groups outweighs the random variance among the people within each group. If the program is effective, then the treatment-completion group should have significantly lower recidivism scores than the other two groups. The impact of the program should be large relative to the random white noise. We might even expect the dropout group's recidivism to be significantly less than the no-treatment group (though probably not as low as the treatment completers). Figure 12.4 diagrams the two possible sets of results.

The xs in the figure represent recidivism scores under two possible scenarios: that within-group variance trumps between-group variance and that between-group variance is stronger than that within groups. The overlap depicted on the left side suggests that the treatment program was ineffective, since it failed to pull one or two groups away from the others. On the right side, the separation between the groups indicates that they are truly different; this implies that the treatment program did work and that those who completed or started and dropped out are significantly different from each other and from the group that did not participate. An ANOVA test for the left side would yield a small F statistic, because the between-group variance is minimal compared to the within-group variance. An ANOVA for the right side, though, would produce a large (statistically significant) F because the ratio of between-to-within is high.

F statistic: The statistic utilized in ANOVA; a ratio of the amount of between-group variance present in a sample relative to the amount of within-group variance.

F distribution: The sampling distribution for ANOVA. The distribution is bounded at zero on the left and extends to positive infinity; all values in the F distribution are thus positive.

Figure 12.4   Recidivism Scores

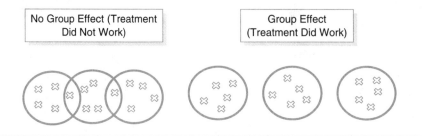

The *F* distribution is bounded on the left at zero, meaning it does not have a negative side. As a result, all critical and obtained values of *F* are positive; it is impossible for a correctly calculated *F* to be negative. This is because *F* is based on variance and variance cannot be negative.

Take a moment now to read Research Example 12.1, which describes a situation in which researchers would use ANOVA to test for a difference between groups or, in other words, would attempt to discover whether there is a relationship between a multiple-class IV and a continuous DV.

Franklin and Fearn's (2010) IV (*race* coded as *white; black; Hispanic; Asian*) was a four-class, categorical variable. Their DV (*sentence length*, measured in months) was continuous. ANOVA is the correct bivariate analysis in this situation.

RESEARCH EXAMPLE 12.1

Race-Based Sentencing Disparities: Do Asian Defendants Benefit from a "Model Minority" Stereotype?

Numerous studies have found racially based sentencing disparities that are not attributable to differences in defendants' prior records or the severity of their instant offenses. Most such studies have focused on white, black, and Hispanic/Latino defendants. One area of the race-and-sentencing research that has received very little scholarly attention is the effect of race on sentencing among Asians. Franklin and Fearn (2010) set out to determine whether Asian defendants are treated differently from those of other races. They predicted that Asians would be sentenced more leniently due to the stereotype in the United States that Asians are a "model minority" in that they are widely presumed to be an economically, academically, and socially productive group.

To test the hypothesis that Asian defendants are given lighter sentences relative to similarly situated defendants of other races, Franklin and Fearn employed the dependent variable *sentence length,* which was coded as the number of months of incarceration imposed on offenders sentenced to jail or prison. The authors reported the statistics shown in the table below with respect to the mean sentence length across race in this sample.

So, what did the researchers find? It turned out that there were no statistically significant differences between the groups. Franklin and Fearn retained the null hypothesis that there is no relationship between race and sentencing, and concluded that Asian defendants do not, in fact, receive significantly shorter jail or prison sentences relative to other racial groups once relevant legal factors (e.g., offense type) are taken into account.

	Defendant Race				
	White	Black	Hispanic	Asian	Total
Mean Sentence Length (Months)	11.80	17.40	16.50	16.10	15.50

Source: Adapted from Table 1 in Franklin and Fearn (2010).

Let's get into an example to see the ANOVA steps and calculations in action. We will use the Juvenile Defendants in Criminal Courts (JDCC; see Data Sources 11.1). We can examine whether attorney type (measured as public defender, assigned counsel, or private attorney) affects the jail sentences received by male youth convicted of weapons offenses. Table 12.1 shows the youths' sentences in months.

We will conduct a five-step hypothesis test to determine whether defendants' conviction histories affect their sentences. Alpha will be set at .01.

Step 1. State the null (H_0) and alternative (H_1) hypotheses.

The null hypothesis in ANOVA is very similar to that in t tests, the only difference being that now there are more than two means. The null is phrased as

$$H_0: \mu_1 = \mu_2 = \mu_3.$$

The structure of the null is dependent on the number of groups—if there were four groups, there would be a μ_4 as well, and five groups would require the addition of a μ_5.

The alternative hypothesis in ANOVA is a bit different from what we have seen before because the only information offered by this test is whether at least one group is significantly different from at least one other group. The F statistic indicates neither the number of differences nor the specific group or groups that stand out from the others. The alternative hypothesis is, accordingly, rather nondescript. It is phrased as

$$H_1: some\ \mu_i \neq some\ \mu_j.$$

If the null is rejected in an ANOVA test, the only conclusion possible is that at least one group is markedly different from at least one other group—there is no way to tell which group is different

Table 12.1   Jail Sentences (Months) of Male Juveniles
Convicted of Weapons Offenses, by Attorney Type

	Attorney Type	
Public Defender (x_1)	Assigned Counsel (x_2)	Private Attorney (x_3)
1	4	3
2	1	12
9	3	10
3	6	9
6		12
		11
$n_1 = 5$	$n_2 = 4$	$n_3 = 6$

or how many between-group differences there are. This is the reason for the existence of post hoc tests, which will be covered later in the chapter.

Post hoc tests: Analyses conducted when the null is rejected in ANOVA in order to determine the number and location of differences between groups.

Step 2. Identify the distribution, and compute the degrees of freedom.

As aforementioned, ANOVA relies on the F distribution. This distribution is bounded on the left at zero (meaning it has only positive values) and is a family of curves whose shapes are determined by alpha and the degrees of freedom. There are two types of degrees of freedom in ANOVA: between-group (df_B) and within-groups (df_W). They are computed as

$$df_B = k - 1 \qquad\qquad\qquad \textit{Formula 12(1)}$$

$$df_W = N - k, \qquad\qquad\qquad \textit{Formula 12(2)}$$

where N = the total sample size across all groups and

k = the number of groups.

The total sample size N is derived by summing the number of cases in each group, the latter of which are called *group sample sizes* and are symbolized n_k. In the present example, there are three groups ($k = 3$) and $N = n_1 + n_2 + n_3 = 5 + 5 + 5 = 15$. The degrees of freedom are therefore

$$df_B = 3 - 1 = 2,$$

$$df_W = 15 - 3 = 12.$$

Step 3. Identify the critical value and state the decision rule.

The F distribution is located in Appendix E. There are different distributions for different alpha levels, so take care to ensure that you are looking at the correct one! You will find the between-group df across the top of the table and the within-group df down the side. The critical value is located at the intersection of the proper column and row. With $\alpha = .01$, $df_B = 2$, and $df_W = 12$, $F_{crit} = 6.93$. The decision rule is that *if* $F_{obt} > 6.93$, H_0 *will be rejected.* The decision rule in ANOVA is always phrased using a *greater than* inequality because the F distribution contains only positive values, so the critical region is always in the right-hand tail.

Step 4. Compute the obtained value of the test statistic.

Step 4 entails a variety of symbols and abbreviations, all of which are listed and defined in Table 12.2. Stop for a moment and study this chart. You will need to know these symbols and what they mean in order to understand the concepts and formulas about to come.

Table 12.2 Elements of ANOVA

Sample Sizes	Means	Sums of Squares	Mean Squares
n_k = the sample size of group k; the number of cases in each group	$\bar{x}_k$ = a group mean; each group's mean on the DV	SS_B = between-groups sums of squares	MS_B = between-groups mean squares
N = the total sample size across all groups	$\bar{x}_G$ = the grand mean; the mean for the entire sample regardless of group	SS_W = within-groups sums of squares SS_T = total sums of squares; $SS_B + SS_W = SS_T$	MS_W = within-groups mean squares

You already know that each group has a sample size (n_k) and that the entire sample has a total sample size (N). Each group also has its own mean $(\bar{x}_k)$ and the entire sample has a grand mean $(\bar{x}_G)$. These sample sizes and means, along with other numbers that will be discussed shortly, are used to calculate the three types of sums of squares. The sums of squares are then used to compute mean squares, which, in turn, are used to derive the obtained value of F. We will first take a look at the formulas for the three types of sums of squares: total (SS_T), between-group (SS_B), and within-group (SS_W).

$$SS_T = \sum_i \sum_k x^2 - \frac{\left(\sum_i \sum_k x\right)^2}{N},$$

Formula 12(3)

where $\sum_i$ = the sum of all scores i in group k,

$\sum_k$ = the sum of each group total across all groups in the sample,

x = the raw scores, and

N = the total sample size across all groups.

$$SS_B = \sum_k n_k \left(\bar{x}_k - \bar{x}_G\right)^2,$$

Formula 12(4)

where n_k = the number of cases in group k,

$\bar{x}_k$ = the mean of group k, and

$\bar{x}_G$ = the grand mean across all groups.

$$SS_W = SS_T - SS_B$$

Formula 12(5)

The double summation signs in the SS_T formula look a bit intimidating, but they are just instructing you to sum sums. The i subscript denotes individual scores and k signifies groups, so the double sigmas direct you to first sum the scores within each group and to then add up all the group sums to form a single sum representing the entire sample.

Sums of squares are measures of variation. They calculate the amount of variation that exists within and between the groups' raw scores, squared scores, and means. The SS_B formula should look somewhat familiar—in Chapters 4 and 5, we calculated deviation scores by subtracting the sample mean from each raw score. Here, we are going to subtract the grand mean from each group mean. See the connection? This strategy produces a measure of variation. The sums of squares provide information about the level of variability within each group and between the groups.

The easiest way to compute the sums of squares is to use a table. What we ultimately want from the table are (a) the sums of the raw scores for each group, (b) the sums of each group's *squared* raw scores, and (c) each group's mean. All of these numbers are displayed in Table 12.3.

Table 12.3   ANOVA Computation Table for *Attorney Type* and *Jail Sentence*

			Attorney Type		
Public Defender (x_1)	x_1^2	**Assigned Counsel** (x_2)	x_2^2	**Private Attorney** (x_3)	x_3^2
1	1	4	16	3	9
2	4	2	4	8	64
9	81	3	9	10	100
3	9	6	36	9	81
6	36			12	144
				11	121
$n_1 = 5$		$n_2 = 4$		$n_3 = 6$	
$\sum x_1 = 21$	$\sum x_1^2 = 131$	$\sum x_2 = 15$	$\sum x_2^2 = 65$	$\sum x_3 = 53$	$\sum x_3^2 = 519$
$\bar{x}_1 = \dfrac{21}{5} = 4.20$		$\bar{x}_2 = \dfrac{15}{4} = 3.75$		$\bar{x}_3 = \dfrac{53}{6} = 8.33$	

We also need the grand mean, which is computed by summing all of the raw scores across groups and dividing by the total sample size N, as such:

$$\bar{x}_G = \frac{\sum_i \sum_k x}{N} \qquad \text{Formula 12(6)}$$

Here,

$$\bar{x}_G = \frac{21+15+53}{5+4+6} = \frac{89}{15} = 5.93.$$

With all of this information, we are ready to compute the three types of sums of squares, as follows. The process begins with SS_T:

$$SS_T = \sum_i \sum_k x^2 - \frac{\left(\sum_i \sum_k x\right)^2}{N} = (131+65+519) - \frac{(21+15+53)^2}{15}$$

$$= 715 - \frac{89^2}{15}$$

$$= 715 - \frac{7{,}921}{15}$$

$$= 715 - 528.07$$

$$= 186.93$$

Then it is time for the between-groups sums of squares:

$$SS_B = \sum_k n_k \left(\bar{x}_k - \bar{x}_G\right)^2 = 5(4.20 - 5.93)^2 + 4(3.75 - 5.93)^2 + 6(8.83 - 5.93)^2$$

$$= 5(-1.73)^2 + 4(-2.18)^2 + 6(2.90)^2$$

$$= 5(2.99) + 4(4.75) + 6(8.41)$$

$$= 14.95 + 19.00 + 50.46$$

$$= 84.41$$

Next, we calculate the within-groups sums of squares:

$$SS_W = SS_T - SS_B = 186.93 - 84.41 = 102.52$$

A great way to help you check your math as you go through Step 4 of ANOVA is to remember that the final answers for any of the sums of squares, mean squares, or F_{obt} will never be negative. If you get a negative number for any of your final answers in Step 4, you will know immediately that you made a calculation error and you should go back and locate the mistake. Can you identify the reason why all final answers are positive? Hint: The answer is in the formulas.

We now have what we need to compute the mean squares (symbolized *MS*). Mean squares transform sums of squares (measures of variation) into variances by dividing SS_B and SS_w by their respective degrees of freedom, df_B and df_w. This is a method of standardization. The mean squares formulas are

$$MS_B = \frac{SS_B}{k-1},$$ *Formula 12(7)*

$$MS_W = \frac{SS_W}{N-k}.$$ *Formula 12(8)*

Plugging in our numbers,

$$MS_B = \frac{84.41}{3-1} = 42.21,$$

$$MS_W = \frac{102.52}{15-3} = 8.54,$$

we now have what we need to calculate F_{obt}. The F statistic is the ratio of between-group variance to within-group variance and is computed as

$$F_{obt} = \frac{MS_B}{MS_W}.$$ *Formula 12(9)*

Inserting the numbers from the present example,

$$F_{obt} = \frac{42.21}{8.54} = 4.94,$$

Step 4 is done! $F_{obt} = 4.94$.

Step 5. Make a decision about the null hypothesis and state the substantive conclusion.

The decision rule stated that if the obtained value exceeded 6.93, the null would be rejected. With an F_{obt} of 4.94, the null is retained. The substantive conclusion is that there is no significant difference between the groups in terms of sentence length received. In other words, male juvenile weapons offenders' jail sentences do not vary as a function of the type of attorney they had. That is, attorney type does not influence jail sentences. This finding makes sense, as existing research on attorney types and defendants' court outcomes is mixed with regard to whether privately retained attorneys (who cost defendants a lot of money) really are better than publicly funded defense attorneys (who are provided to poor defendants for free).

We will go through another ANOVA example. If you are not already using your calculator to work through the steps as you read and make sure you can replicate the results obtained here in the book, start doing so. This is an excellent way to learn the material.

For the second example, we will study handguns and murder rates. Handguns are a prevalent murder weapon and, in some locations, they account for more deaths than all other modalities combined. In criminal justice and criminology researchers' ongoing efforts to learn about violent crime, the question arises as to whether there are geographical differences in handgun-involved murders. Uniform Crime Report data can be used to find out whether there are significant regional differences in handgun murder rates (calculated as the number of murders by handgun per 100,000 residents in each state). A random sample of states was drawn, and the selected states were divided by region. Table 12.4 contains the data in the format that will be used for computations. Alpha will be set at .05.

Step 1. State the null (H_0) and alternative (H_1) hypotheses.

$$H_0: \mu_1 = \mu_2 = \mu_3 = \mu_4$$

$$H_1: some\ \mu_i \neq some\ \mu_j$$

Step 2. Identify the distribution and compute the degrees of freedom.

This being an ANOVA, the F distribution will be employed. There are four groups, so $k = 4$. The total sample size is $N = 5 + 5 + 7 + 6 = 23$. Using Formulas 12(1) and 12(2), the degrees of freedom are

$$df_B = 4 - 1 = 3$$

$$df_W = 23 - 4 = 19$$

Step 3. Identify the critical value and state the decision rule.

With $\alpha = .05$ and the above-derived df values, $F_{crit} = 3.13$. The decision rule states that *if $F_{obt} > 3.13$, H_0 will be rejected.*

Table 12.4 Handgun Murder Rate by Region

		Region					
Northeast		Midwest		South		West	
(x_1)	$(x_1)^2$	(x_2)	$(x_2)^2$	(x_3)	$(x_3)^2$	(x_4)	$(x_4)^2$
1.45	2.10	2.12	4.49	4.16	17.31	.14	.02
.30	.09	.10	.01	1.87	3.50	1.09	1.19
.71	.50	1.35	1.82	3.29	10.82	.92	.85
2.17	4.71	.66	.44	2.82	7.95	2.50	6.25
.00	.00	.15	.02	2.52	6.35	1.13	1.28
				2.67	7.13	.19	.04
$\sum x_1 = 4.63$	$\sum x_1^2 = 7.40$	$\sum x_2 = 4.38$	$\sum x_2^2 = 6.78$	1.37	1.88	$\sum x_4 = 5.97$	$\sum x_4^2 = 9.63$
$n_1 = 5$		$n_2 = 5$		$\sum x_3 = 18.70$	$\sum x_3^2 = 54.94$	$n_4 = 6$	
$\bar{x}_1 = .93$		$\bar{x}_2 = .88$		$n_3 = 7$		$\bar{x}_4 = 1.00$	
				$\bar{x}_3 = 2.67$			

Step 4. Calculate the obtained value of the test statistic.

We begin by calculating the total sums of squares:

$$SS_T = (7.40 + 6.78 + 54.94 + 9.63) - \frac{(4.63 + 4.38 + 18.70 + 5.97)^2}{23}$$

$$= 78.75 - \frac{33.68^2}{23}$$

$$= 78.75 - \frac{1134.34}{23}$$

$$= 78.75 - 49.32$$

$$= 29.43$$

Before computing the between-groups sums of squares, we need the grand mean:

$$\overline{x}_G = \frac{4.63 + 4.38 + 18.70 + 5.97}{23} = \frac{33.68}{23} = 1.46$$

Now SS_B can be calculated:

$$SS_B = 5(.93 - 1.46)^2 + 5(.88 - 1.46)^2 + 7(2.67 - 1.46)^2 + 6(1.00 - 1.46)^2$$

$$= 5(-.53)^2 + 5(-.58)^2 + 7(1.21)^2 + 6(-.46)^2$$

$$= 5(.28) + 5(.34) + 7(1.46) + 6(.21)$$

$$= 1.40 + 1.70 + 10.22 + 1.26$$

$$= 14.58$$

Next, we calculate the within-groups sums of squares:

$$SS_w = 29.43 - 14.58 = 14.85$$

Plugging our numbers into Formulas 12(7) and 12(8) for mean squares:

$$MS_B = \frac{14.58}{4 - 1} = 4.86$$

$$MS_W = \frac{14.85}{23 - 4} = .78$$

Finally, using Formula 12(9) to derive F_{obt},

$$F_{obt} = \frac{4.86}{.78} = 6.23,$$

$$F_{obt} = \frac{4.86}{.78} = 6.23,$$

this is the obtained value of the test statistic. $F_{obt} = 6.23$, and Step 4 is complete.

Step 5. Make a decision about the null and state the substantive conclusion.

In Step 3, the decision rule stated that if F_{obt} turned out to be greater than 3.13, the null would be rejected. F_{obt} ended up being 6.23, so the null is indeed rejected. The substantive interpretation is that there is a significant difference across regions in the handgun-murder rate. Which region or regions differ from which other regions, you ask? The F statistic is silent with respect to the location and number of differences, so post hoc tests are used to get this information. The next section covers post hoc tests and measures of association that can be used to gauge relationship strength.

When the Null Is Rejected: A Measure of Association and Post Hoc Tests

If the null is not rejected in ANOVA, then the analysis stops because the conclusion is that the independent and dependent variables are not related. If the null is rejected, however, it is customary to explore the statistically significant results in more detail using *measures of association* (MA) and *post hoc tests*. MAs permit an assessment of the strength of the relationship between the IV and DV, and post hoc tests allow researchers to determine which groups are significantly different from which other ones. The MA that will be discussed here is fairly easy to calculate by hand, but the post hoc tests will be discussed and then demonstrated in the SPSS section, as they are computationally intensive.

Omega squared (ω^2) is an MA for ANOVA that is expressed as the proportion of the total variability in the sample that is due to between-group differences. Omega squared can be left as a proportion or multiplied by 100 to form a percentage. Larger values of ω^2 indicate stronger IV–DV relationships, whereas smaller values signal weaker associations. Omega squared is computed as

$$\omega^2 = \frac{SS_B - (k-1)MS_w}{MS_w + SS_T}. \qquad \text{Formula 12(10)}$$

There are many different types of post hoc tests, so two of the most popular ones are presented here. The first is Tukey's honest significant difference (HSD). Tukey's test compares each group to all the others in a series of two-variable hypothesis tests. The null hypothesis in each comparison is that the two group means are equal; rejection of the null means that there is a significant difference between the means. In this way, Tukey's is conceptually similar to a series of t tests, though the HSD method sidesteps the problem of familywise error.

Bonferroni is another commonly used test and owes its popularity primarily to the fact that it is fairly conservative. This means that it minimizes Type I error (erroneously rejecting a true null) at the cost of increasing the likelihood of a Type II error (erroneously retaining a false null). The Bonferroni, though, has been criticized for being too conservative. In the end, the best method is to select both Tukey's and Bonferroni in order to garner a holistic picture of your data and make an informed judgment.

Omega squared: A measure of association used in ANOVA when the null has been rejected in order to assess the magnitude of the relationship between the independent and dependent variables. This measure shows the proportion of the total variability in the sample that is attributable to between-group differences.

Tukey's honest significant difference: A widely used post hoc test used in ANOVA when the null is rejected as a means of determining the number and location of differences between groups.

Bonferroni: A widely used and relatively conservative post hoc test used in ANOVA when the null is rejected as a means of determining the number and location of differences between groups.

LEARNING CHECK

Would it be appropriate to compute omega squared and post hoc tests for the ANOVA in Example 1 pertaining to juvenile defendants' sentences? Why or why not?

We will now turn to SPSS. You will first learn how to run an ANOVA using this program and the data used in Example 2 (presented earlier). We will then look at omega squared and post hoc tests.

RESEARCH EXAMPLE 12.2

Are Juveniles Transferred to Adult Courts Seen as More Threatening?

Recent decades have seen a shift in juvenile-delinquency policy. There has been an increasing "zero tolerance" sentiment with respect to juveniles who commit serious offenses. The reaction by most states has been to make it easier for juveniles to be tried as adults, which allows their sentences to be more severe than they would be in juvenile court. The potential problem with this strategy is that there is a prevalent stereotype about juveniles who get transferred or waived to adult court: They are often viewed as vicious, coldhearted predators. Judges, prosecutors, and jurors might be biased against transferred juveniles, simply because they got transferred. This means that a juvenile and an adult could commit the same offense and yet be treated very differently by the court, potentially even ending up with different sentences.

Tang, Nunez, and Bourgeois (2009) tested mock jurors' perceptions about the dangerousness of 16-year-olds who were transferred to adult court, 16-year-olds who were kept in the juvenile justice system, and 19-year-olds in adult court. They found that mock jurors rated transferred 16-year-olds as committing more serious crimes, being more dangerous, and having

a greater likelihood of chronic offending relative to non-transferred juveniles and to 19-year-olds. The following table shows the means, standard deviations, and F tests.

As you can see, all of the F statistics were large; the null was rejected for each test. The transferred juveniles' means are higher than the other two groups' means for all measures. These results suggest that transferring juveniles to adult court could have serious implications for fairness. In some cases, prosecutors have discretion in deciding whether or not to waive a juvenile over to adult court, which means that two juveniles guilty of similar crimes could end up being treated very differently. Even more concerning is the disparity between transferred youths and 19-year-olds—it appears that juveniles who are tried in adult court could face harsher penalties than adults, even when their crimes are the same.

	16-Year-Olds Transferred	16-Year-Olds Not Transferred	19-Year-Olds	F
	mean (sd)	mean (sd)	mean (sd)	
Serious	7.44 (.24)	5.16 (.23)	5.66 (.24)	26.30
Dangerous	6.92 (.25)	4.76 (.25)	5.47 (.25)	19.45
Chronic	7.18 (.25)	5.74 (.24)	5.87 (.25)	10.22

Adapted from Table 1 in Tang, Nunez, and Bourgeois (2009).

SPSS

Let us revisit the question asked in Example 2 regarding whether handgun murder rates vary by region. To run an ANOVA in SPSS, follow the steps depicted in Figure 12.5. Use the *Analyze* → *Compare Means* → *One-Way ANOVA* sequence to bring up the dialog box on the left side in Figure 12.5 and then select the variables you want to use. Move the IV to the *Factor* space and the DV to the *Dependent List*. Then click *Post Hoc* and select the Bonferroni and Tukey tests. Click *Continue* and *OK* to produce the output shown in Figure 12.6.

The first box of the output shows the results of the hypothesis test. You can see the sums of squares, *df*, and mean squares for within groups and between groups. There are also total sums of squares and total degrees of freedom. The number in the *F* column is F_{obt}; here, you can see that $F_{obt} = 6.329$. When we did the calculations by hand, we got 6.23. Our hand calculations had some rounding error, but this did not affect the final decision regarding the null because you can also see that the significance value (the *p* value) is .004, which is less than .05, the value at which α was set. The null hypothesis is rejected in the SPSS context just like it was in the hand calculations.

The next box in the output shows the Tukey and Bonferroni post hoc tests. The difference between these tests is in the *p* values in the *Sig.* column. In the present case, those differences are immaterial because the results are the same across both types of tests. Based on the asterisks that flag significant results and the fact that the *p* values associated with the flagged numbers are less than .05, it is apparent that the South is the region that stands out from the others. Its mean is significantly greater than all three of the other regions' means. The Northeast, West, and Midwest do not differ significantly from one another, as evidenced by the fact that all of their *p* values are greater than .05.

Now it is time to find out just how strong the relationship between region and handgun-murder rates is. To find out, we can use ω^2 from Formula 12(10):

$$\omega^2 = \frac{14.67 - (4-1)(.77)}{.77 + 29.36} = \frac{14.67 - 2.31}{30.13} = \frac{12.36}{30.13} = .41$$

Omega squared shows that 41% of the total variability in the states' handgun-murder rates is a function of regional characteristics. Region appears to be a very important determinate of the prevalence of handgun murders. In the ongoing effort to reduce firearm violence, it would be useful to identify the characteristics of regions that exert impact on handgun murders.

Figure 12.5   Running an ANOVA in SPSS

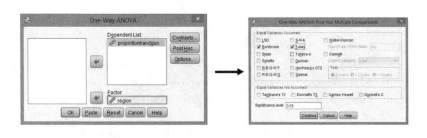

Figure 12.6 ANOVA Output

Handgun murders per 100,000

	Sum of Squares	df	Mean Square	F	Sig
Between Groups	14.674	3	4.891	6.329	.004
Within Groups	14.684	19	.773		
Total	29.358	22			

Post Hoc Tests

Multiple Comparisons

Dependent Variable:Handgun murders per 100,000

	(I) Region	(J) Region	Mean Difference (I– J)	Std. Error	Sig.	95% Confidence interval	
						Lower Bound	Upper Bound
TukeyHSD	Northeast	Midwest	.05037	.55600	1.000	−1.5130	1.6138
		South	−1.74371*	.51475	.015	−3.1911	−.2963
		west	−0.6898	.53233	.999	−1.5658	1.4278
	Midwest	Northeast	−.05037	.55600	1.000	−1.6138	1.5130
		South	−1.79408*	.51475	.012	−3.2415	−.3467
		west	−.11935	.53233	.996	−1.6162	1.3775
	South	Northeast	1.74371*	.51475	.015	.2963	3.1911
		Midwest	1.79408*	.51475	.012	.3467	3.2415
		west	1.67473*	.48909	.014	.2995	3.0500
	west	Northeast	.06898	.53233	.999	−1.4278	1.5658
		Midwest	.11935	.53233	.996	−1.3775	1.6162
		South	−1.67473*	.48909	.014	−3.0500	−.2995
Bonferroni	Northeast	Midwest	.05037	.55600	1.000	−1.5864	1.6872
		South	−1.74371*	.51475	.019	−3.2591	−.2283
		west	−.06899	.53233	1.000	−1.6361	1.4991
	Midwest	Northeast	−05037	.55600	1.000	−1.6872	1.5864
		South	−1.79408*	.51475	.015	−3.3095	−.2787
		west	−.11935	.53233	1.000	−1.6865	1.4478
	South	Northeast	1.74371*	.51475	.019	.2283	3.2591
		Midwest	1.79408*	.51475	.015	.2787	3.3095
		West	1.67473*	.48909	.017	.2349	3.1146
	West	Northeast	.06898	.53233	1.000	−1.4981	1.6361
		Midwest	.11935	.53233	1.000	−1.4478	1.6865
		South	−1.67473*	.48909	.017	−3.1146	−.2349

*The mean difference is significant at the 0.05 level.

This chapter taught you what to do when you have a categorical IV with three or more classes and a continuous DV. A series of *t* tests in such a situation is not viable because of the family-wise error rate. Analysis of variance (ANOVA) conducts multiple between-group comparisons in a single analysis. ANOVA's *F* statistic compares between-group variance to within-group variance to determine whether between-group variance (a measure of true effect) substantially outweighs within-group variance (a measure of error). If it does, the null is rejected; if it does not, the null is retained.

The ANOVA *F*, though, does not indicate the size of the effect, so this chapter introduced you to a measure of association that allows for a determination of the strength of a relationship. This measure is omega squared (ω^2), and it is used only when the null has been rejected—there is no sense in examining the strength of an IV–DV relationship that you just said does not exist! Omega squared is interpreted as the proportion of the variability in the DV that is attributable to the IV. It can be multiplied by 100 to be interpreted as a percentage rather than a proportion.

The *F* statistic also does not offer information about the location or number of differences between groups. When the null is retained, this is not a problem because a retained null means that there are no differences between groups; however, when the null is rejected, it is desirable to gather more information about which group or groups differ from which others. This is the reason for the existence of post hoc tests. This chapter covered Tukey's HSD and Bonferroni, which are two of the most commonly used post hoc tests in criminal justice and criminology research. Bonferroni is a conservative test, meaning that it is more difficult to reject the null hypothesis of no difference between groups. It is a good idea to run both tests and, if they produce discrepant information, make a reasoned judgment based on your knowledge of the subject matter and data. Together, measures of association and post hoc tests can help you glean a comprehensive and informative picture of the relationship between the independent and dependent variables.

CHAPTER 12 REVIEW PROBLEMS

1. A researcher wants to know whether judges' gender (measured as *male; female*) affects the severity of sentences they impose on convicted defendants (measured as *months of incarceration*). Answer the following questions:
   a. What is the independent variable?
   b. What is the level of measurement of the independent variable?
   c. What is the dependent variable?
   d. What is the level of measurement of the dependent variable?
   e. What type of hypothesis test should the researcher use?

2. A researcher wants to know whether judges' gender (measured as *male; female*) affects the types of sentences they impose on convicted criminal defendants (measured as *jail; prison; probation; fine; other*). Answer the following questions:
   a. What is the independent variable?
   b. What is the level of measurement of the independent variable?

c. What is the dependent variable?
d. What is the level of measurement of the dependent variable?
e. What type of hypothesis test should the researcher use?

3. A researcher wishes to find out whether arrest deters domestic violence offenders from committing future acts of violence against intimate partners. The researcher measures arrest as *arrest; mediation; separation; no action* and recidivism as *number of arrests for domestic violence within the next 3 years*. Answer the following questions:

   a. What is the independent variable?
   b. What is the level of measurement of the independent variable?
   c. What is the dependent variable?
   d. What is the level of measurement of the dependent variable?
   e. What type of hypothesis test should the researcher use?

4. A researcher wishes to find out whether arrest deters domestic violence offenders from committing future acts of violence against intimate partners. The researcher measures arrest as *arrest; mediation; separation; no action* and recidivism as whether or not these offenders were arrested for domestic violence within the next 2 years (measured as *arrested; not arrested*). Answer the following questions:

   a. What is the independent variable?
   b. What is the level of measurement of the independent variable?
   c. What is the dependent variable?
   d. What is the level of measurement of the dependent variable?
   e. What type of hypothesis test should the researcher use?

5. A researcher wants to know whether poverty affects crime. The researcher codes neighborhoods as being *lower-class, middle-class*, or *upper-class* and obtains the crime rate for each area (measured as the number of index offenses per 10,000 residents). Answer the following questions:

   a. What is the independent variable?
   b. What is the level of measurement of the independent variable?
   c. What is the dependent variable?
   d. What is the level of measurement of the dependent variable?
   e. What type of hypothesis test should the researcher use?

6. A researcher wants to know whether the prevalence of liquor-selling establishments (such as bars and convenience stores) in neighborhoods affects crime in those areas. The researcher codes neighborhoods as having *0–1, 2–3, 4–5,* or *6+* liquor-selling establishments. The researcher also obtains the crime rate for each area (measured as the number of index offenses per 10,000 residents). Answer the following questions:

   a. What is the independent variable?
   b. What is the level of measurement of the independent variable?
   c. What is the dependent variable?
   d. What is the level of measurement of the dependent variable?
   e. What type of hypothesis test should the researcher use?

7. Explain within-groups variance and between-groups variance. What does each of these concepts represent or measure?

8. Explain the F statistic in conceptual terms. What does it measure? Under what circumstances will F be small? Large?

9. Explain why the F statistic can never be negative.

10. When the null hypothesis in an ANOVA test is rejected, why are measures of association and post hoc tests necessary?

11. The Omnibus Crime Control and Safe Streets Act of 1968 requires state and federal courts to report information on all wiretaps sought by and authorized for law enforcement agencies (Duff, 2010). One question of interest to someone studying wiretaps is whether wiretap use varies by crime type; that is, we might want to know whether law enforcement agents use wiretaps with greater frequency in certain types of investigations than in other types. The following table contains data from the U.S. courts website (www.uscourts.gov/Statistics.aspx) on the number of wiretaps sought by law enforcement agencies in a sample of states. The wiretaps are broken down by offense type, meaning that each number in the table represents the number of wiretap authorizations received by a particular state for a particular offense. Using an alpha level of .05, test the null hypothesis of no difference between the group means against the alternative hypothesis that at least one group mean is significantly different from at least one other. Use all five steps. If appropriate, compute and interpret omega squared.

Offense Type		
Homicide and Assault (x_1)	Narcotics (x_2)	Racketeering (x_3)
2	25	1
0	1	1
0	4	0
1	2	3
14	21	0
1	3	0
2	12	0
$n_1 = 7$	$n_2 = 7$	$n_3 = 7$

12. Does the inmates-to-staff ratio vary across prisons as a function of security level? The following table contains data from the Census of State and Federal Adult Correctional Facilities (CSFACF). A sample of prisons is broken down by security level, and for each one the number of inmates per correctional staff member is recorded. Using an alpha level of .05, test the null hypothesis of no difference between the group means against the alternative hypothesis that at least one group mean is significantly different from at least one other. Use all five steps. If appropriate, compute and interpret omega squared.

Security Level			
Minimum (x_1)	Medium (x_2)	Maximum (x_3)	Super Maximum (x_4)
1	3	3	6
8	4	6	9
5	8	6	11
3	7	5	12
9	5	4	10
2	10	5	8
$n_1 = 6$	$n_2 = 6$	$n_3 = 6$	$n_4 = 6$

13. In the ongoing effort to reduce police injuries and fatalities resulting from assaults, one issue is the technology of violence against officers or, in other words, the type of implements offenders use when attacking police. Like other social events, weapon use might vary across regions. The Uniform Crime Reports collect information on weapons used in officer assaults. These data can be used to find out whether the percentage of officer assaults committed with firearms varies by region. The following table contains the data. Using an alpha level of .01, test the null of no difference between means against the alternative that at least one region is significantly different from at least one other. Use all five steps. If appropriate, compute and interpret omega squared.

Region			
Northeast (x_1)	Midwest (x_2)	South (x_3)	West (x_4)
.76	1.05	2.86	3.55
1.53	5.28	2.41	4.52
2.65	4.92	3.49	3.64
.00	.96	2.12	2.29
.23	1.41	3.39	3.88
$n_1 = 5$	1.50	$n_3 = 5$	4.90
	$n_2 = 6$		.68
			$n_4 = 7$

14. An ongoing source of question and controversy in the criminal court system are the possible advantages that wealthier defendants may have over poorer ones, largely as a result of the fact that the former can pay to hire their own attorneys, whereas the latter must accept the services of court-appointed counsel. There is a common perception that privately retained attorneys are more skilled and dedicated than their publicly appointed counterparts. Let us examine this issue using a sample of property defendants from the Juvenile Defendants in Criminal Courts (JDCC) data set. The independent variable is *attorney type* and the dependent variable is *days to pretrial release*, which measures the number of days between arrest and pretrial release for those rape defendants who were released pending trial. (Those who did not make bail or were denied bail are not included.) Using an alpha level of .05, test the null of no difference between means against the alternative that at least one region is significantly different from at least one other. Use all five steps. If appropriate, compute and interpret omega squared.

Attorney Type		
Public Defender (x_1)	Assigned Counsel (x_2)	Private Attorney (x_3)
2	0	0
42	0	0
5	6	0
4	51	1
8	5	3
1	5	24
0	$n_2 = 6$	5
$n_1 = 7$		34
		$n_3 = 8$

15. In Research Example 12.1, we read about a study that examined whether Asian defendants were sentenced more leniently than offenders of other races. Let us run a similar test using data from the JDCC. The following table contains a sample of juveniles convicted of property offenses and sentenced to probation. The independent variable is *race* and the dependent variable is each person's *probation sentence in months*. Using an alpha level of .01, test the null of no difference between means against the alternative that at least one region is significantly different from at least one other. Use all five steps. If appropriate, compute and interpret omega squared.

	Race		
Asian (x_1)	Black (x_2)	White (x_3)	Other (x_4)
3	12	6	2
9	10	18	6
14	2	3	18
8	6	2	12
24	72	24	$n_3 = 4$
12	$n_2 = 5$	$n_3 = 5$	
$n_1 = 6$			

16. Does the number of juveniles held in an adult correctional facility vary according to the gender of inmates housed in that prison? The following table contains a random sample of prisons drawn from the CSFACF. Using an alpha level of .01, test the null of no difference between means against the alternative that at least one facility type is significantly different from at least one other. Use all five steps. If appropriate, compute and interpret omega squared.

	Gender of Inmates	
Male Only (x_1)	Female Only (x_2)	Both (x_3)
1	15	1
0	0	1
15	0	0
0	0	0
7	1	8
1	0	2
3	4	0
2	0	0
$n_1 = 8$	1	$n_3 = 8$
	3	
	$n_2 = 10$	

17. Does the gender of inmates housed in a prison affect the inmate-on-inmate assault rate in that facility? The following table contains a random sample of prisons drawn from the CSFACF. Using an alpha level of .01, test the null of no difference between means against the alternative that at least one facility type is significantly different from at least one other. Use all five steps. If appropriate, compute and interpret omega squared.

Facility Type		
Male Only (x_1)	Female Only (x_2)	Both (x_3)
5.12	.00	.09
6.57	.00	.17
1.21	1.91	.00
10.15	2.64	.00
1.21	.00	.00
3.16	2.10	1.67
2.07	1.19	5.53
9.96	.00	.00
1.18	3.27	.28
$n_1 = 9$	.23	.00
	$n_2 = 10$	3.57
		$n_3 = 11$

18. Prisons sometimes come under court scrutiny and receive judicial orders to reduce capacity or improve conditions of confinement. The CSFACF asks facilities whether they were under court order and, if so, the maximum number of inmates they were permitted to hold. The following table shows the inmate-maximum data, broken down by the gender of inmates the prison houses. Using an alpha level of .05, test the null of no difference between means against the alternative that at least one facility type is significantly different from at least one other. Use all five steps. If appropriate, compute and interpret omega squared.

Gender of Inmates		
Male Only (x_1)	Female Only (x_2)	Both (x_3)
36	20	29
248	312	58
50	150	35
61	100	208
712	60	$n_3 = 4$
84	$n_2 = 5$	
$n_1 = 6$		

19. Are there race differences among juvenile defendants with respect to the length of time it takes them to acquire pretrial release? The data set *JDCC for Chapter 12.sav* (http://www.sagepub.com/gau) can be used to test for whether time-to-release varies by race for juveniles accused of property crimes. The variables are *race* and *days*. Using SPSS, run an ANOVA with *race* as the IV and *days* as the DV. Select the appropriate post hoc tests.

   a. Identify the obtained value of *F*.
   b. Would you reject the null at an alpha of .01? Why or why not?
   c. State your substantive conclusion about whether there is a relationship between race and days to release for juvenile property defendants.
   d. If appropriate, interpret the post hoc tests to identify the location and total number of significant differences.
   e. If appropriate, compute and interpret omega squared.

20. Are juvenile property offenders sentenced differently depending on the file mechanism used to waive them to adult court? The data set *JDCC for Chapter 12.sav* (http://www.sagepub.com/gau) contains the variables *file* and *jail*, which measure the mechanism used to transfer each juvenile to adult court (discretionary, direct file, or statutory) and the number of months in the sentences of those sent to jail on conviction. Using SPSS, run an ANOVA with *file* as the IV and *jail* as the DV. Select the appropriate post hoc tests.

   a. Identify the obtained value of *F*.
   b. Would you reject the null at an alpha of.05? Why or why not?
   c. State your substantive conclusion about whether there is a relationship between attorney type and days to release for juvenile defendants.
   d. If appropriate, interpret the post hoc tests to identify the location and total number of significant differences.
   e. If appropriate, compute and interpret omega squared.

Analysis of variance (ANOVA)	*F* statistic	Tukey's honest significant difference
Familywise error	*F* distribution	
Between-group variance	Post hoc tests	Bonferroni
Within-group variance	Omega squared	

GLOSSARY OF SYMBOLS AND ABBREVIATIONS INTRODUCED IN THIS CHAPTER

F	The statistic and sampling distribution for ANOVA
n_k	The sample size of group k
N	The total sample size across all groups
$\bar{x}_k$	The mean of group k
$\bar{x}_G$	The grand mean across all cases in all groups
SS_B	Between-groups sums of squares; a measure of true group effect
SS_W	Within-groups sums of squares; a measure of error
SS_T	Total sums of squares; equal to $SS_B + SS_W$
MS_B	Between-group mean square; the variance between groups and a measure of true group effect
MS_W	Within-group mean square; the variance within groups and a measure of error
ω^2	A measure of association that indicates the proportion of the total variability that is due to between-group differences

Chapter 13

Hypothesis Testing With Two Continuous Variables

Correlation

(Continued)

Learning Objectives

- Identify situations in which, based on the levels of measurement of the independent and dependent variables, correlation is appropriate.
- Define positive and negative correlations.
- Use graphs or hypotheses to determine whether a bivariate relationship is positive or negative.

(Continued)

- Explain the difference between linear and nonlinear relationships.
- Explain the *r* statistic conceptually.
- Explain what the null and alternative hypotheses predict about the population correlation.
- Use raw data to solve equations and conduct five-step hypothesis tests.
- Explain the sign, magnitude, and coefficient of determination and use them in the correct situations.
- Use SPSS to run correlation analyses and interpret the output.

T hus far, we have learned the hypothesis tests for use when the two variables under examination are both categorical (chi-square), when the independent variable (IV) is categorical and the dependent variable (DV) is a proportion (two-population *z* test for proportions), when the IV is a two-class categorical measure and the DV is continuous (*t* tests), and when the IV is categorical with three or more classes and the DV is continuous (ANOVA). In the current chapter, we will address the technique that is proper when both of the variables are continuous. This technique is **Pearson's correlation** (sometimes also called Pearson's *r*), because it was developed by Karl Pearson, who was instrumental in advancing the field of statistics.

Pearson's correlation: The bivariate statistical analysis used when both independent and dependent variables are continuous.

Positive correlation: When a one-unit increase in the independent variable produces an increase in the dependent variable.

Negative correlation: When a one-unit increase in the independent variable produces a reduction in the dependent variable.

The question asked in a correlation analysis is, "When the IV increases by one unit, what happens to the DV?" The DV might also increase (a **positive correlation**), it might decrease (a **negative correlation**), or it might do nothing at all (no relationship). Figure 13.1 depicts these possibilities.

A positive correlation might be found between variables such as drug use and violence in neighborhoods—since drug markets often fuel violence, it would be expected that neighborhoods with high levels of drug activity would be more likely to also display elevated rates of violent crime (i.e., as drug activity increases, so does violence). A negative correlation would be anticipated between the amount of collective efficacy in an area and the crime rate. Researchers have found that neighborhoods where residents know one another, are organized, and are willing to take action to protect their areas from disorderly conditions have lower crime rates (meaning that an increase in collective efficacy is associated with a reduction in crime).

Figure 13.1 Three Types of Correlations Between a Continuous IV and a Continuous DV

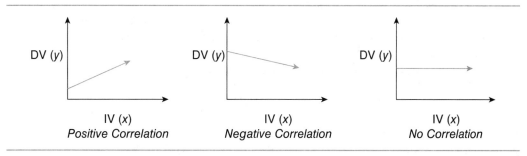

The bivariate associations represented by correlations are linear relationships. This means that the amount of change in the DV that is associated with an increase in the IV remains constant across all levels of the IV and is always in the same direction (positive or negative). Linear relationships can be contrasted to nonlinear or curvilinear relationships such as those displayed in Figure 13.2. You can see in this figure how a one-unit change in the IV is associated with varying changes in the DV. Sometimes the DV increases, sometimes it decreases, and sometimes it does nothing at all. These nonlinear relationships cannot be modeled using correlational analyses.

Linear relationship: A relationship wherein the change in the dependent variable associated with a one-unit increase in the independent variable remains static or constant at all levels of the independent variable.

r coefficient: The test statistic in a correlation analysis.

The statistic representing correlations is called the r coefficient. This coefficient ranges from −1.00 to +1.00. The population correlation coefficient is ρ, which is the Greek letter *rho* (pronounced

Figure 13.2 Examples of Nonlinear Relationships

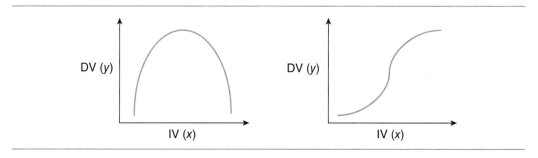

"row"). A correlation of ±1.00 signals a perfect relationship where a one-unit increase in x (the IV) is always associated with exactly the same unit increase of x, across all values of both variables. Correlations of zero indicate that there is no relationship between the two variables. Coefficients less than zero signify negative relationships, whereas coefficients greater than zero represent positive relationships. Figure 13.3 depicts the sampling distribution for r.

Figures 13.4, 13.5, and 13.6 exemplify perfect, strong, and weak positive relationships, respectively. These scatterplots all show that as y increases, so does x, but you can see how the association breaks down from one figure to the next. Each scatterplot contains what is called a line of best fit—this is the line that minimizes the distance between itself and each value in the data. In other words, no line would come closer to all the data points than this one. The more tightly the data points cluster around the line, the better the line represents the data and the stronger the r coefficient will be. When the data points are scattered, then there is a lot of error (i.e., distance between the line and the data points) and the r coefficient will be smaller.

Figure 13.3 The Sampling Distribution of Correlation Coefficients

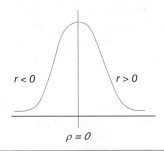

Figure 13.4 A Perfect Linear, Positive Relationship Between x and y

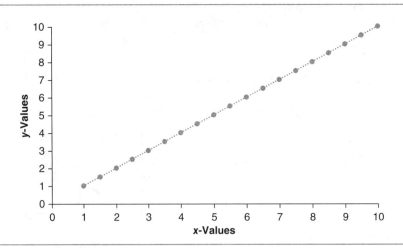

Figure 13.5 A Strong Linear, Positive Relationship Between *x* and *y*

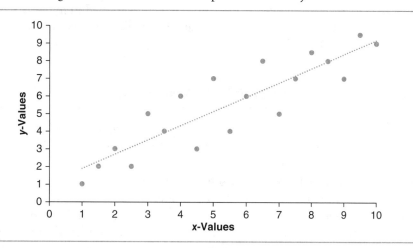

Figure 13.6 A Weak Linear, Positive Relationship Between *x* and *y*

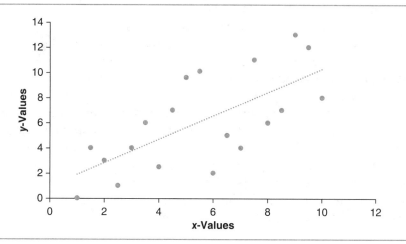

There are no set rules regarding what constitutes a "strong" or "weak" value of *r*. Researchers use general guidelines to assess magnitudes. In criminal justice and criminology research, values between 0 and ±.29 are generally considered weak, from about ±.30 to ±.49 are moderate, ±.50 to ±.69 are strong, and anything beyond ±.70 is very strong. These are guidelines only, not rules, but we will use them throughout the chapter when assessing the magnitude of the relationship suggested by a certain *r* value.

As always, it must be remembered that correlation is not causation. A large correlation between two variables means that there is a linear association between them, but it does not provide proof that the independent variable causes the dependent variable. There could be another variable that accounts for the DV better than the IV does but that has been omitted from the analysis. It could also be the case that both the IV and the DV are caused by a third, omitted variable. Proceed with caution when interpreting correlation coefficients.

RESEARCH EXAMPLE 13.1

Part 1: Is Perceived Risk of Internet Fraud Victimization Related to Online Purchases?

Many researchers have addressed the issue of perceived risk with regard to people's behavioral adaptations. Perceived risk has important consequences at both the individual and the community level, because people who believe their likelihood of victimization to be high are less likely to connect with their neighbors, less likely to utilize public spaces in their communities, and more likely to stay indoors to avoid the frightening environment of the outside world. What has not been addressed with much vigor in the criminal justice and criminology literature is the issue of perceived risk of Internet theft victimization. Given how integral the Internet is to American life and the enormous volume of commerce that takes place online every year, it is important to study the online shopping environment as an arena ripe for theft and fraud.

Reisig, Pratt, and Holtfreter (2009) examined this issue in the context of Internet theft victimization. They used self-report data from a survey administered to a random sample of citizens. Their research question was whether perceived risk of Internet theft victimization would dampen people's tendency to shop online because of the vulnerability created when credit cards are used to make Internet purchases. They also examined whether people's financial impulsivity (the tendency to spend money rather than save it and to possibly spend more than one's income provides for) affected perceived risk. Reisig et al. ran a correlation analysis. Was their hypothesis supported? We will revisit this study later in the chapter to find out.

Correlation analyses employ the t distribution because this probability distribution adequately mirrors the sampling distribution of r at small and large sample sizes (see Figure 13.3). The method for conducting a correlation analysis is to first calculate r and then test for the statistical significance of r by comparing t_{crit} and t_{obt}. Keep this two-step procedure in mind so that you understand the analytic technique in Step 4.

For our first example, we will use the Census of State and Federal Adult Correctional Facilities (CSFACF; see Data Sources 3.1). Let's examine the possible impact of prison crowding on institutional security; specifically, let us test for a correlation between the extent to which a prison's actual inmate population exceeds its rated capacity and the number of major disturbances the prison experienced in the past year. Table 13.1 shows the data for a random sample of seven prisons. We will set alpha at .05.

Table 13.1   Prison Overcapacity and Major Disturbances

Number Overcapacity (x)	Major Disturbances (y)
50	3
70	6
0	1
46	6
20	2
75	4
10	1

Step 1. State the null (H_0) and alternative (H_1) hypotheses.

In a correlation analysis, the null hypothesis is that there is no correlation between the two variables. The null is phrased in terms of ρ, the population correlation coefficient. Recall that a correlation coefficient of zero signifies an absence of a relationship between two variables; therefore, the null is

$$H_0\text{: } \rho = 0.$$

Three options are available for the phrasing of the alternative hypothesis. Since correlations use the t distribution, these three options are the same as those in t tests. There is a two-tailed option (phrased as $H_1\text{: } \rho \neq 0$) that predicts a correlation of unspecified direction. This is the option used when a researcher does not wish to make an a priori prediction about whether the correlation is positive or negative. There are also two one-tailed options. The first predicts that the correlation is negative ($H_1\text{: } \rho < 0$) and the second predicts that it is positive ($H_1\text{: } \rho > 0$).

In the present example, it is expected that prison overcrowding will be linked to more disturbances, so the alternative hypothesis predicts a positive correlation coefficient:

$$H_1\text{: } \rho > 0$$

This is a directional or one-tailed test. As with t tests, the selection of a one- versus a two-tailed research hypothesis will affect the critical value of the test statistic.

Step 2. Identify the distribution and compute the degrees of freedom.

The t distribution is the probability curve used in correlation analyses. This curve is symmetric and, unlike the χ^2 and F distributions, has both a positive and a negative side. The degrees of freedom in correlation are computed as

$$df = N - 2.$$ *Formula 13 (1)*

In the present example, there are five prisons in the sample, so

$$df = 5 - 2 = 3.$$

Step 3. Identify the critical value, and state the decision rule.

With a one-tailed test with $\alpha = .05$ and $df = 3$, the value of t_{crit} is 2.353. The decision rule is that if t_{obt} is > 2.353, H_0 will be rejected.

Step 4. Compute the obtained value of the test statistic.

There are two parts to Step 4 in correlation analyses: First, the correlation coefficient r is calculated, and second, the statistical significance of r is tested by plugging r into the t_{obt} formula. The formula for r looks complex, but we will solve it step by step.

$$r = \frac{N\Sigma xy - \Sigma x \Sigma y}{\sqrt{\left[N\Sigma x^2 - (\Sigma x)^2\right]\left[N\Sigma y^2 - (\Sigma y)^2\right]}}$$ *Formula 13(2)*

The formula requires several different sums. These sums must be calculated and then entered into the equation. The easiest way to obtain these sums is to use a table. Table 13.2 reproduces the raw data from Table 13.1 and adds three columns to the right that allow us to compute the needed sums. Enter the sums into Formula 13(2):

$$r = \frac{7(1,196) - (271)(23)}{\sqrt{\left[7(15,641) - 271\right]\left[7(103) - 23\right]}}$$

$$= \frac{8,372 - 6,233}{\sqrt{\left[109,487 - 73,441\right]\left[721 - 529\right]}}$$

$$= \frac{2,139}{\sqrt{\left[36,046\right]\left[192\right]}}$$

$$= \frac{2,139}{\sqrt{6,920,832}}$$

Table 13.2 Correlation Computation Table for Example 1

Number Overcapacity (x)	Major Disturbances (y)	xy	x^2	y^2
50	3	150	2,500	9
70	6	420	4,900	36
0	1	0	0	1
46	6	276	2,116	36
20	2	40	400	4
75	4	300	5,625	16
10	1	10	100	1
$\Sigma_x = 271$	$\Sigma_y = 23$	$\Sigma_{xy} = 1,196$	$\Sigma_x^2 = 15,641$	$\Sigma_y^2 = 103$

$$= \frac{2,139}{2,630.75}$$

$$= .81$$

The first part of Step 4 is thus complete. We now know that $r = .81$. This is a high value suggestive of a strong relationship between these variables. It appears that overcrowding is closely related to disturbances; however, we do not yet know whether the null hypothesis will be rejected because we have not computed t_{obt}. Until we either reject or retain the null, we cannot reach any conclusions about r. To make a decision about the null, the following equation is used:

$$t_{obt} = r\sqrt{\frac{N-2}{1-r}} \qquad \textit{Formula 13(3)}$$

Plugging our numbers in,

$$t_{obt} = .81\sqrt{\frac{7-2}{1-.81}}$$

$$= .81\sqrt{\frac{5}{1-.66}}$$

$$= .81\sqrt{\frac{5}{.34}}$$

$$= .81\sqrt{14.71}$$

$$= .81(3.84)$$

$$= 3.11$$

Step 4 is complete! We know that $r = .81$ and $t_{obt} = 3.11$.

Step 5. Make a decision about the null and state the substantive conclusion.

In the decision rule, we said that the null would be rejected if t_{obt} were greater than 2.353 and t_{obt} meets this condition, so the null is rejected. The conclusion is that there is a correlation between prisons being over capacity and the number of major disturbances they experience. In other words, as overcrowding increases, so, too, does the number of disturbances.

For a second example, let's continue exploring factors that could be related to major disturbances in prisons. We now know that overcrowding is one contributor, but what about staffing levels? All else being equal, prisons with higher staff-to-inmate ratios should have fewer disturbances compared to relatively poorly staffed institutions. This suggests a negative correlation. We will use a random sample of 10 prisons from the CSFACF and will set alpha at .01.

Step 1. State the null (H_0) and alternative (H_1) hypotheses.

$$H_0: \rho = 0$$

$$H_1: \rho < 0$$

Step 2. Identify the distribution and compute the degrees of freedom.

The distribution is t, and the df are computed using Formula 13(1):

$$df = 10 - 2 = 8$$

Step 3. Identify the critical value and state the decision rule.

Table 13.3   Security Staff per 100 Inmates and the Number of Major Disturbances in the Past Year

Staff per 100 Inmates (x)	*Major Disturbances* (y)	xy	x^2	y^2
4	0	0	16	0
7	0	0	49	0
12	1	12	144	1
3	2	6	9	4
14	3	42	196	9
17	1	17	289	1
38	0	0	1,444	0
15	2	30	225	4
14	0	0	196	0
39	1	39	1,521	1
$\Sigma_x = 163$	$\Sigma_y = 10$	$\Sigma_{xy} = 146$	$\Sigma_x^{\,2} = 4{,}089$	$\Sigma_y^{\,2} = 20$

With a one-tailed test, an alpha of .01, and $df = 8$, $t_{crit} = $ -2.896. The critical value is negative because the alternative hypothesis predicts that the correlation is less than zero. The decision rule is that if $t_{obt} < -2.896$, H_0 will be rejected.

Step 4. Compute the obtained value of the test statistic.

Using Formula 13(2) and the sums from Table 13.3,

$$r = \frac{N\Sigma xy - \Sigma x \Sigma y}{\sqrt{\left[N\Sigma x^2 - (\Sigma x)^2\right]\left[N\Sigma y^2 - (\Sigma y)^2\right]}} = \frac{10(146) - (163)(10)}{\sqrt{\left[10(4{,}089) - 163^2\right]\left[10(20) - 10^2\right]}}$$

$$= \frac{1{,}460 - 1{,}630}{\sqrt{\left[40{,}890 - 26{,}569\right]\left[200 - 100\right]}}$$

$$= \frac{-170}{\sqrt{\left[14{,}321\right]\left[100\right]}}$$

$$= \frac{-170}{\sqrt{1{,}432{,}100}}$$

$$= \frac{-170}{1196.70}$$

$$= -.14 \, .$$

This is a fairly weak value of r, suggesting that there is not much overlap between these two variables. Nonetheless, r might be statistically significant, so we proceed to finding t_{obt} using Formula 13(3):

$$t_{obt} = -.14\sqrt{\frac{10-2}{1-(-.14)^2}} = -.41\sqrt{\frac{8}{1-.02}} = -.14\sqrt{\frac{8}{.80}} = -.14\sqrt{10} = -.14(3.16) = -.44$$

And Step 4 is done! $t_{obt} = -.44$.

Step 5. Make a decision about the null and state the substantive conclusion.

The decision rule stated that the null would be rejected if t_{obt} was less than -2.896. Since $-.44$ does not meet this requirement, the null must be retained. There is not a statistically significant correlation between the staff-to-inmate ratio and the number of major disturbances facilities experience. In other words, as the number of staff members per inmate increases, the number of major disturbances does not decline in a consistent or predictable manner. The lack of statistical significance is not surprising in light of the fact that our r value ($-.14$) was quite weak.

RESEARCH EXAMPLE 13.2

Do Good Recruits Make Good Cops?

The purpose of police training academies is to prepare recruits for work on the street; however, it is not known to what extent academy training relates to on-the-job performance. Henson, Reyns, Klahm, and Frank (2010) attempted to determine whether, and to what extent, recruits' academy performance is associated with their later effectiveness as police officers. They used three dependent variables: the evaluations new officers received from their supervisors, the number of complaints that were lodged against those new officers, and the number of commendations the officers received for exemplary actions. The independent variables consisted of various measurements of academy performance.

Henson et al. obtained the following correlations. Note that the authors did not report correlation coefficients that were not statistically significant; these coefficients are labeled *ns* for *nonsignificant*.

Were the authors' predictions supported? Is academy performance related to the quality of the job those recruits do once they are on the street? The results were mixed. You can see in the table that many of the correlations were statistically significant, but nearly as many were not. It would appear from this analysis that academy performance and on-the-job performance are not as closely related as would be expected or hoped. These findings have implications for police training procedures.

	Evaluation	Complaints	Commendations
Civil Service Exam	ns	−.14**	ns
Physical Agility Rating	.19*	.13*	ns
Overall Academy Score	.12*	ns	.12*

Source: Adapted from Table 3 in Henson, Reyns, Klahm, and Frank (2010).

*p < .01; **p < .001.

For a third example, we will draw from the data set Juvenile Defendants in Criminal Courts (JDCC; Data Sources 11.1). A question we might ask is whether there is a correlation between juveniles' ages at the time that charges are filed against them and the amount of time it takes for their cases to reach disposition. We can measure age in years and time-to-disposition in months. Table 13.4 shows the data for a sample of eight male juveniles. We do not have a specific reason to predict that the correlation will be positive or negative, so this will be a two-tailed (nondirectional) test. Alpha will be .05.

Step 1. State the null (H_0) and alternative (H_1) hypotheses.

$$H_0: \rho = 0$$

$$H_1: \rho \neq 0$$

Table 13.4   Male Juveniles' Ages at File Date and Time to Case Disposition

Age (x)	Time (y)	xy	x^2	y^2
16	5	80	256	25
17	6	102	289	36
15	7	105	225	49
16	4	64	256	16
12	3	36	144	9
15	9	135	225	81
16	3	48	256	9
11	5	55	121	25
$\Sigma_x = 118$	$\Sigma_y = 42$	$\Sigma_{xy} = 625$	$\Sigma_x^2 = 1,772$	$\Sigma_y^2 = 250$

Step 2. Identify the distribution and compute the degrees of freedom.

The distribution is t, and the df are computed using Formula 13(1):

$$df = 8 - 2 = 6$$

Step 3. Identify the critical value and state the decision rule.

With a two-tailed test, an alpha of .05, and $df = 6$, the critical value of t is 2.441. There are two critical values, though, because this is a two-tailed test, so $t_{obt} = \pm 2.441$. The decision rule is that *if t_{obt} is either less than –2.441 or greater than 2.441, H_0 will be rejected.*

Step 4. Compute the obtained value of the test statistic.

Using Formula 13(2) and the sums from Table 13.4,

$$r = \frac{N\Sigma xy - \Sigma x \Sigma y}{\sqrt{\left[N\Sigma x^2 - (\Sigma x)^2\right]\left[N\Sigma y^2 - (\Sigma y)^2\right]}} = \frac{8(625) - (118)(42)}{\sqrt{\left[8(1772) - 118^2\right]\left[8(250) - 42^2\right]}}$$

$$= \frac{5000 - 4956}{\sqrt{[14176 - 13924][2000 - 1764]}}$$

$$= \frac{44}{\sqrt{[252][236]}}$$

$$= \frac{44}{\sqrt{59472}}$$

$$= \frac{44}{243.87}$$

$$= .18.$$

This r value is small, so we can see already that there is not much of a correlation between the variables, if indeed there is any correlation at all. The t test will tell us that.

$$t_{obt} = .18\sqrt{\frac{8 - 2}{1 - .18^2}} = .18\sqrt{\frac{6}{1 - .03}} = .18\sqrt{\frac{6}{.97}} = .18\sqrt{6.19} = .18(2.49) = .45$$

Step 5. Make a decision about the null and state the substantive conclusion.

The decision rule stated that the null would be rejected if t_{obt} ended up being either less than −2.441 or greater than 2.441, and .45 is neither. The null is retained. There is no statistically significant correlation between male juveniles' ages and the amount of time it takes for their cases to reach disposition. In other words, it does not appear that male juveniles' time in the court system changes as a function of whether they were younger or older at the time charges were brought against them.

Beyond Statistical Significance: Sign, Magnitude, and Coefficient of Determination

When the null hypothesis is rejected in a correlation hypothesis test, the correlation coefficient r can be examined with respect to its substantive meaning. We have touched on the topic of magnitude versus statistical significance already; note that in all three examples of correlation tests, we made a preliminary assessment of the magnitude of r before moving on to the t_{obt} calculations. In each one, though, we had to do that last step to check for statistical significance before formally interpreting the strength or weakness of r, and we only interpreted r if the null was rejected. On the other hand, the reverse is also true: A rejected null is not in and of itself an indication that the variables are strongly correlated. The null can be rejected even when a correlation is of little practical importance. The biggest culprit of misleading significance is sample size: correlations that are substantively weak can result in rejected nulls simply because the sample is large enough to drive up the value of t_{obt}. When the null is rejected, criminal justice and criminology researchers turn to three interpretive measures to assess the substantive importance of a statistically significant r: *sign*, *magnitude*, and *coefficient of determination*.

The sign of the correlation coefficient indicates whether the correlation between the IV and the DV is negative or positive. Take another look at Figure 13.1 to refresh your memory as to what negative and positive correlations look like. A positive correlation means that a unit increase in the independent variable is associated with an increase in the dependent variables, and a negative correlation indicates that as the independent variable increases, the dependent variable declines.

The magnitude is an evaluation of the strength of the relationship based on the value of r. As noted in the outset of the chapter, there are no set-in-stone rules for determining whether a given r value is strong, moderate, or weak in magnitude; this judgment is based on a researcher's knowledge of the subject matter. A very general guideline is that values between 0 and ±.29 are weak, from about ±.30 to ± .49 are moderate, ±.50 to ±.69 are strong, and those beyond ±.70 are very strong.

Third, the coefficient of determination is calculated as the obtained value of r, squared (i.e., r^2). The result is a proportion that can be converted to a percentage and interpreted as the percentage of the variance in the DV that is attributable to the IV. As a percentage, the coefficient ranges from 0 to 100, with higher numbers signifying stronger relationships and numbers closer to zero representing weaker associations.

Let us interpret the sign, magnitude, and coefficient of determination for the correlation coefficient computed in the first example. Since we retained the null in the second and third examples, we cannot apply the three interpretive measures to these r values. Recall that in the first example pertaining to prison overcrowding and disturbances, $r = .81$.

First, the sign of the correlation coefficient is positive, meaning that more overcrowding is associated with more disturbances. Second, the magnitude is quite strong, as .81 well exceeds the .70 threshold. Third, the coefficient of determination is $r^2 = .81^2 = .66$. This means that 66% of the variance in the dependent variable (major disturbances) can be explained by the independent variable (overcrowding). This is really good! Of course, we cannot draw causal conclusions—there might be an additional characteristic of overcrowded prisons that is to blame for disturbances (e.g., they might house particularly rowdy inmates or tend to be older facilities that prevent effective supervision of prisoners), or there could be an underlying variable that causes both of these problems (such as budget troubles that create overcrowding while simultaneously cutting prisoners off from needed resources and causing them to feel anxious and angry). Anytime you interpret the outcome of a correlation hypothesis test, keep in mind that statistical significance is not, by itself, enough to demonstrate a practically significant or substantively meaningful relationship between two variables; moreover, even a strong association does not mean that one variable truly causes the other.

SPSS

Correlations are run in SPSS using the *Analyze → Correlation → Bivariate* sequence. Once the dialog box shown in Figure 13.7 appears, select the variables of interest and move them into the analysis box as shown. Then click *OK*. The variables shown in Figure 13.7 are those that were used

Figure 13.7   Running a Correlation Analysis in SPSS

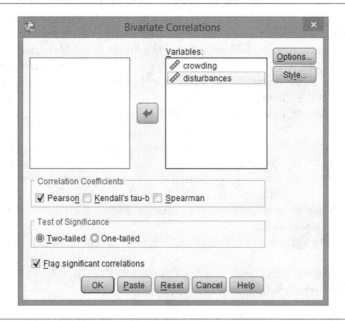

in the first example pertaining to prison overcrowding and major disturbances. Figure 13.8 shows the output.

The result is what is called a correlation matrix, meaning that it is split by what is called a diagonal (here, the cells in the upper left and lower right corners of the matrix) and is symmetric on both of the off-diagonal sides. The numbers in the diagonal are always 1.00 because they represent each variable's correlation with itself. The numbers in the off-diagonals are the ones to look at. The number associated with Pearson's correlation is the value of r. In Figure 13.8, you can see that $r = .813$, which is what we arrived at by hand. The *Sig.* value is, as always, the obtained significance level or p value. This number is compared to alpha to determine whether or not the null will be rejected: If $p < \alpha$, the null is rejected; if $p > \alpha$, the null is retained. In this example, $\alpha = .05$ and $p = .026$, so the null is rejected. The conclusion is that the two variables are correlated. Moreover, the sign is positive, the magnitude is strong, and the coefficient of determination is .66.

Figure 13.8   SPSS Output

Correlations

		Crowding	Disturbances
Crowding	Pearson Correlation	1	.813*
	Sig. (2-tailed)		.026
	N	7	7
Disturbances	Pearson Correlation	.813*	1
	Sig. (2-tailed)	.026	
	N	7	7

*Correlation is significant at the 0.05 level (2-tailed).

Let's add another variable to the mix. In the second example, we examined whether staffing levels were related to disturbances. It was predicted that greater numbers of staff (per 100 inmates) would be negatively correlated with the number of major disturbances. We ended up retaining the null and concluding that the two variables are unrelated. We can analyze staffing among the prisons analyzed in the first example. Figure 13.9 shows the SPSS output containing all three variables. When you run a correlation analysis with three or more variables, all the variables are placed into the same correlation matrix.

You can see that staffing's correlation with disturbances is −.614 and with crowding is −.435. Both of these correlations seem strong, but neither of them is statistically significant ($p = .329$ and $p = .143$, respectively), so we cannot conclude that there is a relationship between staffing and either disturbances or crowding. The sample only has seven prisons in it; it is possible that with a larger sample, we would see these correlations reach statistical significance.

Figure 13.9 SPSS Output

Correlations

		Crowding	Disturbances	Staffing
Crowding	Pearson Correlation	1	.813*	−.435
	Sig. (2-tailed)		.026	.329
	N	7	7	7
Disturbances	Pearson Correlation	.813*	1	−.614
	Sig. (2-tailed)	.026		.143
	N	7	7	7
Staffing	Pearson Correlation	−.435	−.614	1
	Sig. (2-tailed)	.329	.143	
	N	7	7	7

*Correlation is significant at the 0.05 level (2-tailed).

RESEARCH EXAMPLE 13.1

Part 2

Recall that Reisig et al. (2009) predicted that people's perceived likelihood of falling victim to Internet theft would lead to less frequent engagement in the risky practice of purchasing items online using credit cards. They also thought that financial impulsivity, as an indicator of low self-control, would affect people's perceptions of risk. The following table is an adaptation of the correlation matrix obtained by these researchers.

Were the researchers' hypotheses correct? The results were mixed. On one hand, they were correct in that the correlations between the IVs and the DV

	Perceived Risk	Financial Impulsivity	Online Purchases
Perceived Risk	1.00		
Financial Impulsivity	.11*	1.00	
Online Purchases	−.12*	.05	1.00

Source: Adapted from Table 1 in Reisig et al. (2009).

*$p < .05$.

were statistically significant. You can see the significance of these relationships indicated by the asterisks that flag both of these correlations as being statistically significant at an alpha level of .05. Since the null was rejected, it is appropriate to interpret the coefficients. Regarding sign, perceived risk was negatively related to online purchases (i.e., greater perceived risk meant less online purchasing activity), and financial impulsivity was positively related to perceived risk (in other words, financially impulsive people were likely to see themselves as facing an elevated risk of victimization).

The reason the results were mixed, however, is that the correlations—though statistically significant—were not strong.

Using the magnitude guidelines provided in this chapter, it can be seen that −.12 and .11 are very weak. The coefficient of determination for each one is $(-.12)^2 = .01$ and $.11^2 = .01$, so only 1% of the variance in online purchases was attributable to perceived risk, and only 1% was due to financial impulsivity, respectively. This illustrates the potential discrepancy between statistical significance and substantive importance: Both of these correlations were statistically significant, but neither meant much in terms of substantive or practical implications. As always, though, it must be remembered that these analyses were bivariate and that the addition of more IVs may alter the IV–DV relationships observed here.

CHAPTER SUMMARY

This chapter introduced you to Pearson's correlation, the hypothesis-testing technique that is appropriate in studies employing two continuous variables. The correlation coefficient is symbolized r and ranges from −1.00 to +1.00. The value of r represents the amount of linear change in the DV that accompanies a one-unit increase in the IV. Values of r approaching ±1.00 are indicative of strong relationships, whereas values close to zero signify weak correlations. The statistical significance of r is tested using the t distribution because the sampling distribution of r is normal in shape.

When the null hypothesis is rejected in a correlation test, the sign, magnitude, and coefficient of determination should be examined in order to determine the substantive, practical meaning of r. The sign indicates whether the correlation is positive or negative. The magnitude can be assessed using general guidelines and subject-matter expertise. The coefficient of determination is computed by squaring r to produce a proportion (or percentage, when multiplied by 100) that represents the amount of variance in the dependent variable that is attributable to the independent variable.

Correlation analyses can be run in SPSS. The program provides the calculated value of the correlation coefficient r and its associated significance value (its p value). When p is less than alpha, the null is rejected and the correlation coefficient can be interpreted for substantive meaning; when p is greater than alpha, the null is retained and r is not interpreted because the conclusion is that the two variables are not correlated.

1. A researcher wishes to test the hypothesis that parental incarceration is a risk factor for lifetime incarceration of the adult children of incarcerated parents. She measures parental incarceration as *had a parent in prison; did not have a parent in prison* and adult children's incarceration as *incarcerated; not incarcerated*.

    a. Identify the independent variable.
    b. Identify the level of measurement of the independent variable.
    c. Identify the dependent variable.
    d. Identify the level of measurement of the dependent variable.
    e. What type of inferential analysis should the researcher run to test for a relationship between these two variables?

2. A researcher wishes to test the hypothesis that coercive control can actually increase, rather than reduce, subsequent criminal offending among persons who have been imprisoned. He gathers a sample of people who have spent time in prison and measures coercive control as *number of years spent in prison* and recidivism as *number of times rearrested after release from prison*.

    a. Identify the independent variable.
    b. Identify the level of measurement of the independent variable.
    c. Identify the dependent variable.
    d. Identify the level of measurement of the dependent variable.
    e. What type of inferential analysis should the researcher run to test for a relationship between these two variables?

3. A researcher hypothesizes that a new policing strategy involving community meetings designed to educate residents on the importance of self-protective measures will increase the use of such measures. He gathers a sample of local residents and finds out whether they have participated in an educational session (*have participated; have not participated*). Among each group, he computes the *proportion of residents who now take self-protective measures*.

    a. Identify the independent variable.
    b. Identify the level of measurement of the independent variable.
    c. Identify the dependent variable.
    d. Identify the level of measurement of the dependent variable.
    e. What type of inferential analysis should the researcher run to test for a relationship between these two variables?

4. A researcher thinks that there may be a relationship between neighborhood levels of socioeconomic disadvantage and the amount of violent crime that occurs in those neighborhoods. She measures socioeconomic disadvantage as the *percentage of neighborhood residents that live below the poverty line,* and she measures violent crime as the *number of violent offenses reported to police per 1,000 neighborhood residents*.

    a. Identify the independent variable.
    b. Identify the level of measurement of the independent variable.
    c. Identify the dependent variable.
    d. Identify the level of measurement of the dependent variable.
    e. What type of inferential analysis should the researcher run to test for a relationship between these two variables?

5. Explain what it means for a relationship to be linear.

6. Explain what it means for a relationship to be nonlinear.

7. Explain the concept of the line of best fit.

8. When a correlation is _____, increases in the independent variable are associated with increases in the dependent variable.

   a. positive
   b. negative
   c. zero

9. When a correlation is _____, increases in the independent variable are not associated with any predictable or consistent change in the dependent variable.

   a. positive
   b. negative
   c. zero

10. When a correlation is _____, increases in the independent variable are associated with decreases in the dependent variable.

    a. positive
    b. negative
    c. zero

11. Is there a correlation between the amount of money states spend on prisons and those states' violent crime rates? There could be a negative correlation insofar as prisons may suppress crime, in which case money invested in incarceration produces a reduction in violence; however, there could also be a positive correlation if prison expenditures do not reduce crime but, rather, merely reflect the amount of violence present in a state. Morgan, Morgan, and Boba (2010) offer information on the dollars spent per capita on prison expenditures in 2009, and the Uniform Crime Reports (UCR) provide 2009 violent crime data. The following table contains dollars spent per capita and violent crime rates per 1,000 citizens for a random sample of five states. Using an alpha level of .05, test for a correlation between the variables (note that no direction is being specified). Use all five steps. If appropriate, interpret the sign, the magnitude, and the coefficient of determination.

State	Prison Dollars per Capita (x)	Violent Crime Rate (y)	
Florida	140	6.12	= 856.8
Idaho	135	2.28	= 307.8
Maine	99	1.20	= 118.8
Nebraska	120	2.82	= 338.4
Texas	133	4.91	= 653.03
N = 5			2276.83

627   17.33

12. One aspect of deterrence theory predicts that punishment is most effective at preventing crime when would-be criminals know that they stand a high likelihood of being caught and penalized for breaking the law. When certainty breaks down, by contrast, crime rates may increase because offenders feel more confident that they will not be apprehended. The following table contains UCR data on the clearance rate for property crimes in 2010 and the property crime rate per 100 in 2011. The prediction is that higher clearance rates in 1 year will be associated with lower property crime rates the following year. Using an alpha of .01, test for a negative correlation between the variables. Use all five steps. If appropriate, interpret the sign, the magnitude, and the coefficient of determination.

Region	Percent of Property Crimes Cleared (x)	Property Crime Rate (y)
New England	15.40	2.33
Mid-Atlantic	22.80	2.05
East North Central	16.30	2.93
West North Central	19.40	2.84
South Atlantic	19.10	3.50
East South Central	17.60	3.34
West South Central	15.80	3.92
Mountain	16.90	3.10
Pacific	14.50	2.90
N = 9		

13. Are there more police agencies in areas with higher crime rates? We will find out using data from Morgan et al. (2010). The independent variable is *crimes per square mile* and the dependent variable is *law enforcement agencies per 1,000 square miles*. Using an alpha level of .05, test for a positive correlation between the variables. Use all five steps. If appropriate, interpret the sign, the magnitude, and the coefficient of determination.

State	Crime per Sq. Mile (x)	Police Agencies per 1,000 Sq. Miles (y)
Georgia	7.30	9.40
Iowa	1.40	7.20
Kansas	1.30	4.40
Maine	1.00	3.90
Minnesota	1.90	5.30

(Continued)

(Continued)

State	Crime per Sq. Mile (x)	Police Agencies per 1,000 Sq. Miles (y)
Missouri	3.50	8.40
Nebraska	.70	3.20
South Carolina	6.90	8.40
Washington	3.80	3.70
N = 9		

14. In police agencies—much like in other types of public and private organizations—there are concerns over disparities in pay; in particular, lower-ranking officers might feel undercompensated relative to higher-ranking command staff and administrators. Let us investigate whether there is a correlation between the pay of those at the top of the police hierarchy (chiefs) and those at the bottom (officers). We will use a random sample of six agencies from the Law Enforcement Management and Administrative Statistics data set. The following table shows the minimum annual salaries of chiefs and officers among the agencies in this sample. (The numbers represent thousands; for instance, 57.5 means $57,500.) Using an alpha level of .05, test for a correlation between the two variables (no direction specified). Use all five steps. If appropriate, interpret the sign, the magnitude, and the coefficient of determination.

Agency	Minimum Chief Salary (x)	Minimum Officer Salary (y)	
A	57.50 3306.25	28.40 806.56	1633
B	20.40 416.16	14.50 210.25	295.8
C	57.60 3317.76	31.60 998.56	1820.16
D	70.00 4900	21.50 462.25	1505
E	21.70 470.89	16.50 272.25	358.05
F	75.50 5700.25	33.80 1142.44	2551.9
N = 6	$\Sigma x^2 = 18111.31$	$\Sigma y^2 = 3892.51$ $\Sigma xy = 8163.91$	

$\Sigma x = 502.7$ $\Sigma y = 146.3$ 7354.5

15. It is well known that handguns account for a substantial portion of murders. This has led some people to claim that stricter handgun regulations would help curb the murder rate in the United States. Others, though, say that tougher gun laws would not work because people who are motivated to kill but who cannot obtain a handgun will simply find a different weapon instead. This is called a *substitution effect*. If the substitution effect is operative, then there should be a negative correlation between handgun and knife murders. The following table contains data from a random sample of states. For each state, the handgun and knife murder rates (per 100,000 state residents) are shown. Using an alpha level of .01, test for a negative correlation between the variables. Use all five steps. If appropriate, interpret the sign, magnitude, and coefficient of determination.

State	Handgun Murder Rate (x)	Knife Murder Rate (y)
Nebraska	1.22	.45
Wisconsin	1.15	.39
Arkansas	1.87	.73
North Carolina	2.59	.52
Virginia	1.37	.52
California	2.77	.79
Washington	1.13	.53
$N = 10$		

16. Does it take defendants who face multiple charges longer to get through the adjudication process? The following table contains data on a random sample of juveniles from the Juvenile Defendants in Criminal Courts data set. The variables are *number of charges* and *months to adjudication*, the latter of which measures the total amount of time that it took for these juveniles to have their cases disposed of. Using an alpha level of .05, test for a positive correlation between the variables. Use all five steps. If appropriate, interpret the sign, the magnitude, and the coefficient of determination.

Juvenile	Charges (x)	Months (y)
A	5	7.13
B	3	5.50
C	3	2.47
D	2	1.20
E	4	.47
F	3	.80
G	2	.07
H	1	.00
I	1	.93
J	1	.67
$N = 10$		

17. Earlier in the chapter, we tested for a correlation between age at file date and time to disposition among a sample of male juveniles. We found no significant results (i.e., the null was retained). Now let us conduct the same test for a sample of female juveniles. The following table contains the data. Using an alpha level of .05, test for a correlation between the variables (no direction specified). Use all five steps. If appropriate, interpret the sign, the magnitude, and the coefficient of determination.

Juvenile	Age (x)	Time (y)
A	17	4
B	14	5
C	16	5
D	17	8
E	13	2
F	15	6
G	16	3
H	13	4
N = 8		

18. Is there a relationship between age and attitudes about crime and punishment? The General Social Survey asks respondents whether they oppose or favor the death penalty and whether they think courts are too harsh, about right, or not harsh enough on offenders. These two variables can be summed to form a scale measuring people's general preferences for harsher or more lenient penalties (higher values represent harsher attitudes). The data are displayed in the table. Using an alpha level of .01, test for a correlation between the variables (no direction specified). Use all five steps. If appropriate, interpret the sign, the magnitude, and the coefficient of determination.

Respondent	Age (x)	Sentence Severity (y)
A	18	4
B	46	5
C	63	2
D	19	3
E	22	2
F	35	3
G	39	2
H	74	5
I	68	4
N = 9		

19. Is there a relationship between age and the types of experiences people have with police? The file *PPCS for Chapter 13.sav* contains data from the Police-Public Contact Survey. The sample is narrowed to male Asian respondents and contains the variables *age* (respondents' ages in years), *contacts* (total number of face-to-face contacts respondents had in the past year), and *length* (the number of minutes in a traffic stop, for those respondents who had been stopped in the past year). Run a correlation analysis using all three variables.

   a. Identify the obtained values of the correlation coefficient *r* for the three tests.
   b. For each, state whether you would reject the null hypothesis at an alpha of .05 and how you reached that decision.
   c. State the substantive conclusion for each of the three tests.
   d. As appropriate, interpret the sign, the magnitude, and the coefficient of determination for each test.

20. Let's revisit the variable measuring attitudes toward criminal punishment. The file *GSS for Chapter 13.sav* (http://www.sagepub.com/gau) contains data from the General Social Survey, narrowed down to female respondents. The variable *severity* measures how harshly respondents feel toward persons convicted of crimes (higher values indicate greater preferences for severe punishment). The other variables are *children, age,* and *education.* We want to find out whether there are any statistically significant correlations among these variables. Run a correlation analysis using all four variables.

   a. Identify the obtained values of the correlation coefficient *r*.
   b. For each of the *r* values, state whether you would reject the null hypothesis at an alpha of .05 and how you reached that decision.
   c. State the substantive conclusion for each test.
   d. As appropriate, interpret the sign, the magnitude, and the coefficient of determination for each test.

KEY TERMS

Pearson's correlation	Negative correlation	*r* coefficient
Positive correlation	Linear relationship	

GLOSSARY OF SYMBOLS AND ABBREVIATIONS INTRODUCED IN THIS CHAPTER

r	The correlation coefficient for a sample
ρ	The correlation coefficient for a population
r^2	The coefficient of determination

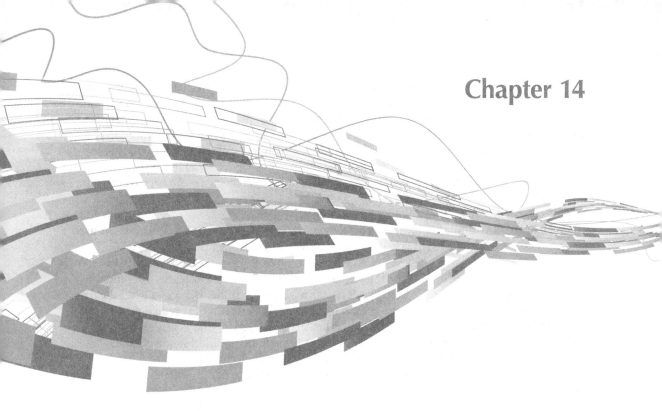

Chapter 14

Introduction to Regression Analysis

Learning Objectives

- Explain the benefits of regression's ability to predict values on the dependent variable (*y*) and explain how regression differs from the tests covered in previous chapters.
- Explain the difference between bivariate and multiple regression, including the importance of controlling for additional independent variables.
- Calculate each element of an ordinary least squares regression model, and compile the elements into an equation predicting *y*.
- Use an ordinary least squares regression equation to find the predicted value of *y* given a certain value of *x*.
- Read and interpret SPSS regression output, including identifying each key element of the equation and forming a conclusion about the statistical significance and substantive strength of relationships.

In Chapter 13, you learned about correlation analyses. Correlation is a statistical procedure for finding two pieces of information: (1) whether two continuous variables are statistically related in a linear fashion and (2) the strength of that relationship. In most criminal justice and criminology research, however, merely finding out whether or not two variables are correlated is not sufficient. Researchers want, instead, to find out whether one of the variables (the independent variable [IV]) can be used to *predict* the other one (the dependent variable [DV]). Regression analysis does this. Regression goes a step beyond correlation by allowing researchers to determine the extent to which the IV predicts the DV.

This chapter will discuss two types of regression analyses. Bivariate regression employs one IV and one DV. It is similar to bivariate correlation in many respects. Multiple regression uses several IVs to predict the DV. The specific type of regression modeling discussed here is ordinary least squares (OLS) regression. This is a fundamental form of regression modeling that is used frequently in criminology and criminal justice research. The OLS form of regression produces a line of best fit (just like we talked about with regard to correlation) that is as close to all the data points as it can possibly get. In other words, it minimizes the errors in the prediction of the DV. There are other types of regression, but OLS is the default procedure that is generally employed unless there is good reason for departing from it and using a different technique instead. OLS is the starting point for understanding regression, and so it is the technique covered here. In OLS, the dependent variable must be continuous and normally distributed. The independent variables can be of any level of measurement.

Regression analysis: A technique for modeling linear relationships between one or more independent variables and one dependent variable wherein each independent variable is evaluated on the basis of its ability to accurately predict the values of the dependent variable.

Bivariate regression: A regression analysis that uses one independent and one dependent variable.

Multiple regression: A regression analysis that uses two or more independent variables and one dependent variable.

Ordinary least squares regression: A common procedure for estimating regression equations that minimizes the errors in predicting the dependent variable.

One Independent Variable and One Dependent Variable: Bivariate Regression

Bivariate regression is an extension of bivariate correlations; therefore, we will use the data from the first example in Chapter 13. These data were from a sample drawn from the Census of State and Federal Adult Correctional Facilities (CSFACF; see Data Sources 3.1). They measure the number of prisoners each prison has that is more than what the facility was rated to house and the number of major disturbances the facility experienced in the past year. The data from Table 13.1 are reproduced in Table 14.1. They are sorted in ascending order according to the overcrowding score (the IV).

Table 14.1   Number of Inmates Over Rated Capacity and Major Disturbances in a Sample of Prisons

Number Overcapacity (x)	Major Disturbances (y)
0	1
10	1
20	2
46	6
50	3
70	6
75	4

Every x score in Table 14.1 has a corresponding y score. These scores form the graphing coordinates (x, y). These coordinates can be graphed on a scatterplot like that in Figure 14.1. You can find each prison on the graph according to that person's x and y scores.

Figure 14.1   Scatterplot of Prison Overcrowding and Disturbances

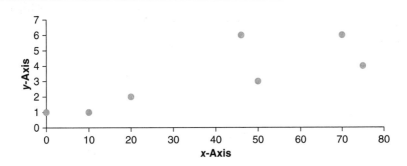

LEARNING CHECK

Can you create a scatterplot using a set of data points? Try plotting the data found in Table 13.4.

We already know that these two variables are correlated, but now we want to know how well age of onset *predicts* lifetime arrests. In other words, we want to know the extent to which knowing a woman's age of onset helps us predict the number of times she has been arrested. Correlation does not allow us to do this, but regression does.

Think about drawing a line in the scatterplot in Figure 14.1. You want the line to come close to as many of the data points as possible. What would this line look like? Would it have a positive or a negative slope? Where would it cross the y (vertical) axis? How steep would it be? Answering these questions will inform us as to how well x predicts y. The line of best fit is the line that comes closer to each of the data points than would any other line that could possibly be drawn. The following formula is that for a line. You might recognize it from prior algebra classes.

$$\hat{y} = a + bx, \qquad\qquad Formula\ 14(1)$$

where $\hat{y}$ = the predicted value of y at x,

  a = the y intercept,

  b = the slope coefficient, and

  x = the raw values of the independent variable.

The predicted values of y—symbolized $\hat{y}$ (pronounced "y hat")—are made up of the intercept (a) and a certain slope coefficient (b) that is constant across all values of x. The intercept is the point at which the line of best fit crosses the y axis. Another way to think of the intercept is as the value of y when x is zero. The slope coefficient conveys information about the steepness of that line.

Once the line given by Formula 14(1) is estimated, you have two different sets of DV scores: the actual, empirical scores (these are the y values); and the predicted values (the $\hat{y}$ scores). If the IV is a good predictor of the DV, these two sets of numbers will be very similar to one another. If the IV does not predict the DV very well, the predicted values will differ substantially from the empirical ones. The difference between a predicted value and an empirical value is called a residual (often also called an error term).

Intercept: The point at which the regression line crosses the y axis; also the value of y when $x = 0$.

Slope: The steepness of the regression line and a measure of the change in the dependent variable produced by a one-unit increase in an independent variable.

Residual: The difference between a predicted value and an empirical value on a dependent variable.

Ordinary least squares regression provides the formula that minimizes the residuals. If you were to add up all the error terms in a data set after running an OLS model, the total amount of error will be smaller than that you could get using any other regression approach.

To construct the regression line, b and a must be calculated. In OLS, the slope coefficient b is calculated as

$$b = \frac{N\Sigma xy - \Sigma x \Sigma y}{N\Sigma x^2 - \left(\Sigma x\right)^2}. \qquad\qquad Formula\ 14(2)$$

If you feel a sense of déjà vu when you look at Formula 14(2), that is good! This formula is very similar to that used to calculate the correlation coefficient r. Go back briefly and revisit Formula 13(2) to compare.

Once b is known, a can be calculated from the following formula:

$$a = \bar{y} - bx, \qquad\qquad Formula\ 14(3)$$

where $\bar{y}$ = the mean of the DV,

b = the slope coefficient, and

$\bar{x}$ = the mean of the IV.

Now we can construct the regression equation for our data. The first step is to calculate the slope coefficient b. In Chapter 13, Table 13.2, we computed the sums required by Formula 14(2), so these numbers can be pulled from that table and entered into the formula:

$$b = \frac{7(1,196) - (271)(23)}{7(15,641) - 271^2} = \frac{8,372 - 6,233}{109,487 - 73,441} = \frac{2,139}{36,046} = .06$$

The slope b is .06, meaning that for every one-prisoner increase in overcrowding, a prison experiences .06 more disturbances. Now let us find a. We first need the DV and IV means. These are found using the mean formula with which you are familiar:

$$\bar{y} = \frac{\sum y}{N} = \frac{23}{7} = 3.29$$

$$\bar{x} = \frac{\sum x}{N} = \frac{271}{7} = 38.71$$

Plugging the means and b into Formula 14(3) yields

$$a = 3.29 - .06(38.71) = 3.29 - 2.32 = .97.$$

Now the entire regression equation can be constructed using the pieces we just computed:

$$\hat{y} = .97 + .06x$$

This equation can be used to predict each prison's disturbances on the basis of its level of over-crowding. This is accomplished by entering a given value for x and solving the equation. One of the prisons was over capacity by 20 inmates. Substituting in for x,

$$\hat{y} = .97 + .06(20) = .97 + 1.20 = 2.17.$$

This is the predicted number of disturbances for a prison that has 20 prisoners over the limit. If you look at the actual data, you see that the empirical value is 2, so this prediction is pretty close!

LEARNING CHECK

Try calculating the predicted values of y for the remaining values in the data set. Compare each predicted value to its corresponding empirical value. How close are they?

Notice how the predicted value of any score can be calculated even without any knowledge of the empirical values of either x or y. That is, we do not need to know what is actually in the data set to be able to posit a particular x and find the corresponding $\hat{y}$. This is the unique and useful thing about regression! With all of the previous hypothesis-testing procedures, we were limited to what the data provided; we could use the empirical values and nothing else. With regression, we can go outside the scope of the empirical values. For example, how many disturbances would we expect to occur in a prison that is 15 people over capacity? There is no actual value of 15 in the independent variable, but we can find the $\hat{y}$ value nonetheless:

$$\hat{y} = .97 + .06(15) = .97 + .90 = 1.87$$

A prison that was overcrowded by 15 inmates would be expected to have 1.87 disturbances per year.

Inferential Regression Analysis: Testing for the Significance of b

The most common use of regression analysis in criminal justice and criminology research is in the context of hypothesis testing. Just like the correlation coefficient r, the slope coefficient b does not itself determine whether or not the null hypothesis should be rejected. The slope coefficient b is also unstandardized. This means that it is presented in the dependent variables' original units. This makes it impossible to figure out whether b is "large" or "small." If the dependent variable is measured in dollars, for instance, then a one-unit increase in this DV is only one dollar—that is not much! The value of b could be fairly large and still not represent a meaningful change in the DV. On the other hand, if the dependent variable is measured as the number of crimes a person has committed, then a one-unit increase represents an additional crime. This is meaningful. Even a small b could represent a relationship of practical importance. We will take a look at a solution to the issue of unstandardized b later. For now, bear in mind that you cannot judge the strength of a slope coefficient based on b alone.

To figure out whether b is significant, a five-step hypothesis test must be conducted. We will conduct this test on the b from above using $\alpha = .05$.

Step 1. State the null (H_0) and alternative (H_1) hypotheses.

The null hypothesis in regression is generally that there is no relationship between the IV and DV and, therefore, that the slope coefficient is zero. The alternative hypothesis is usually two-tailed; one-tailed tests are used only when there is a compelling reason to do so. Here, we will use a two-tailed test because this is the more customary course of action. The null and alternative hypotheses are, as always, phrased in terms of the population parameters. The default assumption (i.e., the null) is always that $B = 0$. What we are looking for in an inferential test is evidence to lead us to believe that b is insignificantly different from zero. In regression, B symbolizes the population slope coefficient. The hypotheses are

$$H_0: B = 0,$$

$$H_1: B \neq 0.$$

Step 2. Identify the distribution and compute the degrees of freedom.

The t distribution is the one typically used in regression. When the sample size is large, z can be used instead; however, since t can accommodate any sample size, it is more efficient to simply use that distribution in all circumstances. In bivariate regression, the degrees of freedom are calculated as

$$df = N - 2. \hspace{3cm} \textit{Formula 14(4)}$$

Here,

$$df = 7 - 2 = 5.$$

Step 3. Identify the critical value and state the decision rule.

With a two-tailed test, $\alpha = .05$, and $df = 5$, $t_{crit} = \pm 2.571$. The decision rule states that *if* t_{obt} *is either* < -2.571 *or* > 2.571, H_0 *will be rejected.*

Step 4. Compute the obtained value of the test statistic.

The first portion of this step entails calculating b and a in order to construct the regression equation in Formula 14(1). We have already done this; recall that the regression equation is $\hat{y} = .97 + .06x$. Just like all other statistics, b has a sampling distribution. See Figure 14.2. The distribution centers on zero because the null predicts that the variables are not related. We need to find out whether b is either large enough or small enough to lead us to believe that B is actually greater than or less than zero, respectively.

Finding out whether b is statistically significant is a two-step process. First, we compute this coefficient's standard error, symbolized SE_b. The standard error is the standard deviation of the sampling distribution depicted in Figure 14.2. The standard error is important because all else being equal, slope coefficients with larger standard errors are less trustworthy than those with smaller standard errors. A large standard error means that there is substantial uncertainty as to the accuracy of the sample slope coefficient b as an estimate of the population slope B. SE_b is computed as

$$SE_b = \frac{s_y}{s_x} \sqrt{\frac{1 - r^2}{N - 2}}, \hspace{3cm} \textit{Formula 14(5)}$$

Figure 14.2 The Sampling Distribution of Slope Coefficients

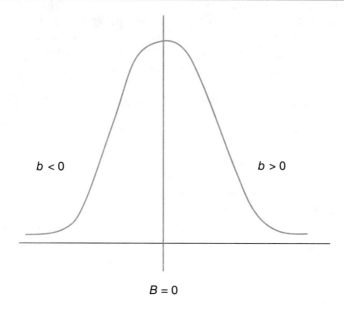

where s_x = the standard deviation of x (the IV),

s_y = the standard deviation of y (the DV), and

r = the correlation between x and y.

Since you already know how to compute standard deviations, they will simply be provided here rather than the entire process being shown. The standard deviation of y (the DV, number of disturbances) is 2.14 and the standard deviation of x (the IV, crowding) is 29.30. From Chapter 13, we know that $r = .81$. Plugging all of these numbers in to Formula 14(5) yields

$$SE_b = \frac{2.14}{29.30}\sqrt{\frac{1-.81^2}{7-2}} = .07\sqrt{\frac{1-.55}{5}} = .07\sqrt{\frac{.45}{5}} = .07\sqrt{.09} = .07(.30) = .02.$$

Now SE_b can be entered into the t_{obt} formula, which is

$$t_{obt} = \frac{b}{SE_b}. \qquad\qquad \textit{Formula 14(6)}$$

The obtained value of t is the ratio between the slope coefficient and its standard error. Entering our numbers into the equation results in

$$t_{obt} = \frac{.06}{.02} = 3.00.$$

Step 4 is complete! The obtained value of *t* is 3.00. We can now make a decision about the statistical significance of *b*.

Step 5. Make a decision about the null and state the substantive conclusion.
The decision rule stated that the null would be rejected if t_{obt} ended up being either less than –2.571 or greater than 2.571. Since 3.00 is greater than 2.571, the null is rejected. The slope is statistically significant at an alpha of .05. There is a positive relationship between the extent to which a prison is over capacity and the number of major disturbances that occur in that institution. In other words, knowing how many inmates a prison has beyond its rated capacity helps predict the number of major disturbances that a prison will experience in a year.

As with correlation, rejecting the null requires further examination of the IV–DV relationship to determine the strength and quality of that connection. In the context of regression, a rejected null indicates that the IV exerts some level of predictive power over the DV; however, it is desirable to know the magnitude of this predictive capability. The following section describes two techniques for making this assessment.

Beyond Statistical Significance: How Well Does the Independent Variable Perform as a Predictor of the Dependent Variable?

There are two ways to assess model quality. The first is to create a standardized slope coefficient or beta weight (symbolized β, the Greek letter beta) so the slope coefficient's magnitude can be gauged. The second is to examine the coefficient of determination. Each will be discussed in turn. Remember that these techniques should be used only when the null hypothesis has been rejected—if the null is retained, the analysis stops because the conclusion is that there is no relationship between the independent and dependent variables.

Beta weight: A standardized slope coefficient that ranges from –1.00 to +1.00 and can be interpreted similarly to a correlation so that the magnitude of an IV–DV relationship can be assessed.

Standardized Slope Coefficients: Beta Weights

As noted earlier, the slope coefficient *b* is unstandardized, which means that it is specific to the units in which the IV and DV are measured. There is no way to "eyeball" an unstandardized slope coefficient and assess its strength because there are no boundaries or benchmarks that can be used with unstandardized statistics—they are specific to whatever metric the dependent variable is measured in. The way to solve this is to standardize *b*. Beta weights range between 0.00 and ±1.00 and, like correlation coefficients, rely more on guidelines than rules for interpretation of their strength. Generally speaking, betas between 0 and ±.19 are generally considered weak, from about ±.20 to ± .29 are moderate, ±.30 to ±.39 are strong, and anything beyond ±.40 is very strong. These ranges can vary by topic, though; subject-matter experts must decide whether a beta weight is weak or strong within the customs of their fields of study.

Standardization is accomplished as follows:

$$\beta = b \left(\frac{s_x}{s_y} \right)$$

Formula 14(7)

We have all the numbers needed for Formula 14(7), so we can plug them in and solve:

$$\beta = .06 \left(\frac{29.30}{2.14} \right) = .06(13.69) = .82$$

The beta weight is .82. If this number seems familiar, it is! The correlation between these two variables is .81. Beta weights will equal correlations (within rounding error) in the bivariate context and can be interpreted the same way. A beta of .81 is very strong. Overcrowding appears to be robustly associated with disturbances.

LEARNING CHECK

You just learned that standardized beta weights are equal to regression coefficients in bivariate regression models. As we will see soon, however, this does not hold true when there is more than one independent variable. Why do you think this is? If you are not sure of the answer now, continue reading and then come back to this question.

The Quality of Prediction: The Coefficient of Determination

Beta weights help assess the magnitude of the relationship between an IV and a DV, but they do not provide information about how well the IV performs at predicting the DV. This is a substantial limitation because prediction is the heart of regression—it is the reason researchers use this technique. The coefficient of determination addresses the issue of the quality of prediction. It does this by comparing the actual, empirical values of y to the predicted values ($\hat{y}$). A close match between these two sets of scores indicates that x does a good job predicting y, whereas a poor correspondence signals that x is not a useful predictor. The coefficient of determination is given by

$$r_{y\hat{y}}^2,$$

Formula 14(8)

where $r_{y\hat{y}}$ = the correlation between the actual and predicted values of y.

The correlation between the y and $\hat{y}$ values is computed the same way that correlations between IVs and DVs are and so will not be shown here. In real life, you will have SPSS generate this value for you. The correlation in this example is .81. This makes the coefficient of determination

$$.81^2 = .66.$$

This means that 66% of the variance in y can be attributed to the influence of x. In the context of the present example, 66% of the variance in disturbances is explained by the extent to which a prison is above capacity. Again, this value looks familiar—it is the same as the coefficient of determination in Chapter 13! This illustrates the close connection between correlation and regression at the bivariate level. Things get a bit more complicated when more independent variables are added to the model, as we will see next.

Adding More Independent Variables: Multiple Regression

The problem with bivariate regression—indeed, with all bivariate hypothesis tests—is that social phenomena are usually the product of many factors, not just one. There is not just one, single reason why a person commits a crime, a police officer uses excessive force, or a prison experiences a riot or other major disturbance. Bivariate analyses risk overlooking variables that might be important predictors of the dependent variable. For instance, in the bivariate context, we could test for whether having a parent incarcerated increase's one's propensity for crime commission. This is probably a significant factor, but it is certainly not the only one. We can add having experienced violence as a child, suffering from a substance-abuse disorder, and being unemployed, too. Each of these independent variables might help improve our ability to understand (i.e., predict) a person's involvement in crime. The use of only one IV virtually guarantees that important predictors have been erroneously excluded and that the results of the analysis are therefore suspect, and it prevents us from conducting comprehensive, in-depth examinations of social phenomena.

Multiple regression is the answer to this problem. Multiple regression is an extension of bivariate regression and takes the form

$$\hat{y} = a + b_1 x_1 + b_2 x_2 + \ldots + b_k x_k.$$ *Formula 14(9)*

Revisit Formula 14(1) and compare it to Formula 14(9) to see how 14(9) expands on the bivariate equation by including multiple independent variables instead of just one. The subscripts show that each IV has its own slope coefficient. With k IVs in a given study, $\hat{y}$ is the sum of each $b_k x_k$ term and the y intercept.

In multiple regression, the relationship between each IV and the DV is assessed while controlling for the effect of the other IV or IVs. The slope coefficients in multiple regression are called **partial slope coefficients** because for each one, the relationship between the other IVs and the DV has been removed so that each partial slope represents the "pure" relationship between an IV and the DV. Each partial slope coefficient is calculated while holding all other variables in the model at their means, so researchers can see how the dependent variable would change with a one-unit increase in the IV of interest, while holding all other variables constant. The ability to incorporate multiple predictors and to assess each one's unique contribution to $\hat{y}$ is what makes multiple regression so useful.

RESEARCH EXAMPLE 14.1

Does Childhood Intelligence Predict the Emergence of Self-Control?

Theory suggests—and research has confirmed—that low self-control is significantly related to delinquency and crime. People with low self-control tend to be impulsive and to have trouble delaying gratification and considering possible long-term consequences of their behavior. Self-control is said to be learned during the formative years of a child's life. Parenting is critical to the development of self-control; parents who provide clear rules and consistent, fair punishment help instill self-discipline in their children. But what about children's innate characteristics, such as their intelligence level? Petkovsek and Boutwell (2014) set out to test whether children's intelligence significantly affected their development of self-control, net of parenting, and other environmental factors. They ran OLS regression models and found the following results (note that SE = standard error).

Independent Variable	b (SE)	β
Intelligence	−1.21** (.122)	−.318
Global positive parenting	−.080 (.049)	−.056
Maternal self-control	.064 (.099)	.022
Paternal self-control	.246* (.094)	.089
Spanking	.745 (.410)	.061
Child's sex (male)	4.82** (.713)	.228
Child's age	.189 (1.131)	.006

Source: Adapted from Table 2 in Petkovsek and Boutwell (2014).

$*p < .01; **p < .001$.

It is interesting and surprising that intelligence outweighed parenting in predicting children's self-control. Intelligence was, in fact, by far the strongest predictor of low self-control: More intelligent children had more self-control relative to their peers who scored lower on intelligence tests. Paternal low self-control significantly predicted children's low self-control, but the beta was very small. The only other significant variable is sex, with boys displaying higher levels of low self-control compared to girls. The model $R^2 = .225$, meaning that the entire set of predictors explained 22.5% of the variance in children's self-control. Clearly, childhood intelligence is integral in the development of self-control and, ultimately, in the prevention of delinquency and crime.

Partial slope coefficient: A slope coefficient that measures the individual impact of an independent variable on a dependent variable while holding other independent variables constant.

Before getting into more complex examples, let us work briefly with a hypothetical regression equation containing two independent variables, x_1 and x_2. Suppose the line is

$$\hat{y} = 1.00 + .80x_1 + 1.50x_2.$$

We can substitute various values for x_1 and x_2 to find $\hat{y}$. Let's find the predicted value of the dependent variable when $x_1 = 4$ and $x_2 = 2$:

$$\hat{y} = 1.00 + .80(4) + 1.50(2) = 1.00 + 3.20 + 3.00 = 7.20$$

There it is! If $x_1 = 4$ and $x_2 = 2$, the dependent variable is predicted to be 7.20.

LEARNING CHECK

Use the hypothetical formula in the text to find the predicted value of y when . . .

a. $x_1 = 2$ and $x_2 = 3$

b. $x_1 = 1.50$ and $x_2 = 3$

c. $x_1 = .86$ and $x_2 = -.67$

d. $x_1 = 12$ and $x_2 = 20$

The formulas involved in multiple regression are complex and are rarely used in the typical criminal justice and criminology research setting because of the prevalence of statistical software. We will, therefore, dispense with the hand calculations for this topic and instead turn to SPSS. We will keep analyzing institutional security in a sample of prisons derived from the Census of State and Federal Adult Correctional Facilities, but we will switch to the dependent variable *inmate-on-inmate assaults.*

Ordinary Least Squares Regression in SPSS

Before launching the analysis, we should revisit the null and alternative hypotheses. In multiple regression, the null and alternative each apply to every independent variable. For each IV, the null predicts that the population slope coefficient B_k is zero and the alternative predicts that it is significantly different from zero. Since the analysis in the current example has two independent variables, the null and alternative are

$$H_0: B_1 = 0 \text{ and } B_2 = 0,$$
$$H_1: B_1 \text{ and/or } B_2 \neq 0.$$

Since each IV has its own null, it is possible for the null to be rejected for one of the variables and not for the other.

To run a regression analysis in SPSS, go to *Analyze* → *Regression* → *Linear*. This will produce the dialogue box shown in Figure 14.3. Move the DV and IVs into their proper locations in the right-hand spaces and then press *OK*. This will produce an output window containing the elements displayed in the following figures.

The first portion of regression output you should look at is the ANOVA box. This may sound odd since we are running a multiple regression analysis, not an ANOVA, but what this box tells you is whether the set of IVs included in the model explains a statistically significant amount of the variance in the DV. If F is not significant (meaning if $p > .05$), then the model is no good. In the event of a nonsignificant F, you should not go on to interpret and assess the remainder of the

Figure 14.3 Running a Multiple Regression Analysis in SPSS

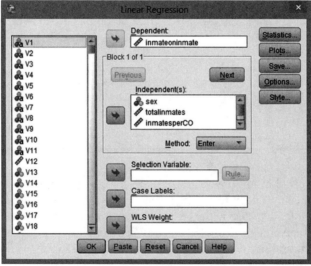

Figure 14.4 SPSS Regression Output

Model Summary

Model	R	R Square	Adjusted R Square	Std. Error of the Estimate
1	.377[a]	.142	.140	31.103

[a]Predictors: (Constant), Number of inmates over rated capacity, Prison houses males only, Number of inmates per security staff member, Inmate total.

ANOVA[a]

Model		Sum of Squares	df	Mean Square	F	Sig.
1	Regression	210908.535	4	52727.134	54.506	.000[b]
	Residual	1273054.566	1316	967.367		
	Total	1483963.101	1320			

[a]Dependent variable: Between 1/1/2005 and 12/30/2005 how man inmate-on-inmate assaults.

[b]Predictors: (Constant), Number of inmates over rated capacity, Prison houses males only, Number of inmates per security staff member, Inmate total.

Coefficients[a]

Model		Unstandardized Coefficients		Standardized Coefficients	t	Sig.
		B	Std. Error	Beta		
1	(Constant)	8.334	3.024		2.756	.006
	Prison houses males only	.292	2.816	.003	.104	.918
	Inmate total	.016	.001	.366	13.293	.000
	Number of inmates per security staff member	-1.065	.271	-.103	-3.934	.000
	Number of inmates over rated capacity	.004	.004	.028	1.014	.311

[a]Dependent variable: Number of inmate-on-inmate assaults in the past year.

model. Your analysis is over at that point and what you must do is revisit your data, your hypothesis, or both, to find out what went wrong.

In Figure 14.4, you can see that $F = 54.506$ and $p = .000$, so the amount of the variance in the DV variance that is explained by the IVs is significantly greater than zero. Note that a significant

F is not by itself proof that the model is good—this is a necessary but insufficient condition for a high-quality regression model.

Second, look at the R Square column in the Model Summary box. This number tells you the proportion of the variance in the dependent variable that is explained by all the independent variables combined. It is an indication of the overall explanatory power of the model. It is a proportion that can be converted to a percentage, and it indicates how much of the variance in the DV is explained by the IVs collectively. There are no specific rules for evaluating R square. Generally, values up to .20 are considered fairly low, .21 to .30 are moderate, .31 to .40 are good, and anything beyond .41 is very good. Here, R square is .142, meaning the independent variables that we selected explain 14.2% of the variance in assaults. This is pretty low; we would hope for better. There are definitely important variables that have been omitted from this model.

Third, go to the Coefficients box to see the unstandardized *b* values, standardized beta weights, and significance results. The Unstandardized Coefficients: B column contains the slope for each variable (the constant is the intercept). All of the variables except the number of inmates per staff have positive signs; the staffing variable is negatively associated with assaults. Notice that one of these variables (the one measuring whether an institution houses only males or only females) is categorical and dichotomous. The interpretation of dichotomous independent variables (also sometimes called dummy variables) in OLS is a little different than that for continuous IVs. The slope coefficient for the male–female dummy variable measures whether male prisons have more assaults relative to female prisons. For continuous IVs, the slope coefficient tells you what happens to the DV when the IV increases by one unit; for dichotomous IVs, *b* offers information about the value of the DV on one class of the IV as compared to the other class.

The Beta column shows the standardized values. The utility of beta weights over *b* values is readily apparent—you can compare the three independent variables' individual impacts on the dependent variable to figure out which ones seem to be stronger or weaker than the others. Two betas—the one for the inmate total (.366) and the one for inmates per staff member (−.103)—are noticeably larger than the others.

Before drawing any conclusions about which independent variables are important, you must examine the Sig. column where the *p* values are located. As would be expected from the beta weights, total inmates and inmates per staff member are significant ($p = .000$ for both) and the other two variables, which had very small betas, are not statistically significant (both *p* values well exceed .05).

RESEARCH EXAMPLE 14.2

Does Having a Close Black Friend Reduce Whites' Concerns About Crime?

In Chapter 1, you read about a study by Mears, Mancini, and Stewart (2009) in which the researchers sought to uncover whether whites' concerns about crime as a local and as a national problem were affected by whether or not those whites had at least one close friend who was black. Concern about crime was the DV in this study. White respondents expressed their attitudes about crime on a 4-point scale where higher values indicated greater concern. The researchers ran an OLS regression model and arrived at the following results with respect to whites' concerns about local crime.

The authors found, contrary to what they had hypothesized, that having a close friend who was black actually *increased* whites' concerns about crime. You can see this in the fact that the slope coefficient for *have a black friend* is statistically significant ($p < .05$) and positive. Age was also related to concern, with older respondents expressing more worry about local crime. Income had a negative slope coefficient such that a one-unit increase in annual income was associated with a .06 reduction in concern. Finally, living in an urban area substantially heightened whites' worry about crime—looking at the beta weights, you can see that *urban* is the strongest IV in the model. The researchers concluded that for whites living in urban areas, having black friends may make the crime problem seem more real and immediate because they are exposed to it vicariously through these friends.

IV	DV: Whites' Concern About Local Crime		
	b	SE_b	b
Have a black friend	.15*	.07	.08
Age	.06**	.02	.10
Sex	−.05	.06	−.03
Education	−.01	.03	−.01
Income	−.06*	.03	−.08
Urban	.48***	.09	.20
Intercept	1.80***	.13	
$R^2 = .256$			

Source: Adapted from Table 2 in Mears, Mancini, and Stewart (2009).

*$p < .05$; **$p < .01$; ***$p < .001$.

Recall that a benefit of regression is that it can be used to predict values of the DV. Let us see how this works with multiple regression. Using Formula 14(9) and the numbers from the SPSS output, the regression equation can be written as

$$\hat{y} = 8.334 + .292x_{male} + .016x_{total} + (-1.065)x_{inmatesper} + .004x_{overcap} \, .$$

Suppose we want to predict the number of assaults for a prison that contains 750 inmates. We will use 750 as the value of x for this variable and will substitute the other x values with their means, as such:

$$\hat{y} = 8.334 + .292(.88) + .016(750) + (-1.065)5.74 + .004(15.86)$$

$$= 8.334 + .26 + 12 + (-6.11) + .06$$

$$= 14.54$$

We would expect a prison with 750 inmates to have 14.54 inmate-on-inmate assaults per year, all other variables held constant.

RESEARCH EXAMPLE 14.3

Do Multiple Homicide Offenders Specialize in Killing?

In Chapter 11, you read about a study by Wright, Pratt, and DeLisi (2008) wherein the researchers examined whether multiple homicide offenders (MHOs) differed significantly from single homicide offenders (SHOs) in terms of the diversity of offending. Diversity was measured as a continuous variable with higher values indicating a greater spectrum of offending.

We saw in Chapter 11 that Wright et al. first ran a t test to check for differences between the group means for MHOs and SHOs; that test showed that the difference was not statistically significant. Given that bivariate results are untrustworthy for the reasons discussed in this chapter, Wright et al. ran a multiple OLS regression model. They found the following results.

IV	DV: Diversity Index		
	b	SE_b	b
Offender type: SHO	.004	.163	.001
Age	.068*	.008	.355
Age of onset	−.156*	.011	−.551
White	−.375*	.145	−.090
Constant	−1.346		
$R^2 = .256$			

Source: Adapted from Table 2 in Wright, Pratt, and DeLisi (2008).

$*p < .05; **p < .01.$

Offenders' current age, the age at which they started offending, and their race were statistically significant predictors of offending diversity. As foreshadowed by the nonsignificant t test, the coefficient for *Offender type: SHO* was not statistically significant. A dichotomous IV like that used here, where people in the sample were divided into two groups classified as either *MHOs* or *SHOs*, is called a **dummy variable**. The slope is interpreted just as it is with a continuous IV: It is the amount of predicted change in the DV that occurs with a one-unit increase in the IV. Here, you can see that being an SHO increased offending diversity by only .004 of a unit. This is a very trivial change and was not statistically significant. Race is also a dummy variable, as offenders in the sample were classified as either *nonwhite* or *white*. Can you interpret this slope coefficient with respect to what it means about race as a predictor of the diversity index? If you said that white offenders score significantly lower on the diversity index, you are correct.

Wright et al.'s multiple regression model confirmed that MHOs and SHOs do not differ in terms of offending diversity. This suggests that multiple homicide offenders do not specialize in killing; to the contrary, they display as much diversity as other types of homicide offenders. The theoretical implication of this finding is that the theories that have been developed to help explain violent offending may be applicable to MHOs because these people are similar to other offenders.

Dummy variable: A dichotomous independent variable.

When the Dependent Variable Is Not Continuous and Normally Distributed: Alternatives to OLS

This chapter has focused on ordinary least squares regression because it is the most basic regression-modeling strategy and is generally the starting point for the study of regression. Recall that OLS can only be used when a dependent variable is continuous and (reasonably) normally distributed. As you might have already guessed, researchers often confront dependent variables that do not meet one or both of these criteria. A dependent variable might be nominal or dichotomous, or it could be heavily skewed.

Various regression techniques are available for situations when the DV violates the OLS assumptions. We will not go into them in detail, but it is worth knowing the names of at least some of the most common models. Each one is specific to a certain kind of dependent variable.

When a DV is dichotomous (i.e., categorical with two classes), binary logistic regression is used. Binary logistic regression calculates the probability of a certain case in the data set falling into the category of interest. The DV might be, for instance, whether a defendant was sentenced to prison. Binary logistic regression would tell the user whether and to what extent each of the IVs (offense

Is Police Academy Performance a Predictor of Effectiveness on the Job?

In Chapter 13, you encountered a study by Henson, Reyns, Klahm, and Frank (2010). The researchers sought to determine whether recruits' performance while at the academy significantly influenced their later success as police officers. Henson et al. measured success in three ways: the scores new officers received on the annual evaluations conducted by those officers' supervisors, the number of complaints lodged against these new officers, and the number of commendations they earned. These three variables are the DVs in this study.

You saw in Chapter 13 that the bivariate correlations indicated mixed support for the prediction that academy performance was related to on-the-job performance; however, to fully assess this possible link, the researchers ran an OLS regression model. They obtained the following results.

	Dependent Variables		
	Evaluation	Complaints	Commendations
IV	b (SE_b)	b (SE_b)	b (SE_b)
Civil service exam	−.07	−.01	.00
	(.02)	(.01)	(.01)
Overall academy score	.06*	−.004	−.003
	(.03)	(.01)	(.01)
Physical agility rating	−.01	.02	.00
	(.03)	(.02)	(.02)
Gender	−.40	−.32*	−.07
	(.25)	(.12)	(.14)
Age	−.04	−.02*	.01
	(.02)	(.01)	(.01)
Race	.13	−.10	.14
	(.23)	(.11)	(.13)
Education	−.02	−.15	.14
	(.29)	(.14)	(.16)
	$R^2 = .048$	$R^2 = .098$	$R^2 = .000$

Source: Adapted from Table 5 in Henson et al. (2010).

*p < .01.

The results from the three OLS models showed that recruits' civil service exam scores, physical agility exam scores, and overall academy ratings were—with only one exception—unrelated to on-the-job performance. The exception was the positive slope coefficient between overall academy ratings and evaluation scores ($b = .06$; $p < .01$). The demographic variables gender, age, race, and education also bore limited and inconsistent relationships with the three performance measures. These results seem to indicate that the types of information and training that recruits receive are not as clearly and directly related to on-the-job performance as would be ideal. There may be a need for police agencies to revisit their academy procedures to ensure that recruits are receiving training that is current, realistic, and practical in the context in which these recruits will be working once they are out on the street.

type, prior record, and so on) increases the odds of a given defendant being sentenced to prison. Additionally, a heavily skewed DV can sometimes be dichotomized (i.e., split in half) and put through binary logistic rather than OLS. Binary logistic regression is very popular. There are two other types of logistic regression that are used for categorical DVs. For a nominal DV with three or more classes, multinomial logistic is available. For an ordinal DV with three or more classes, ordered logistic can be employed. Each of these types of models functions by sequentially comparing pairs of classes.

A technique called Poisson regression is used when a dependent variable is composed of count data (sometimes also called event data). Count data are phenomena such as the number of times a person has been arrested or the number of homicides that occur in a city in 1 year. Throughout this book, we have treated count data as being part of the continuous level of measurement, and this is often perfectly fine to do, but it can cause problems if done so in the regression realm. Part of the problem is that count data are usually highly skewed, because most of the DVs that are studied are relatively rare events (violent crimes, criminal convictions, and the like). In a data set containing the number of homicides experienced by a sample of cities, the vast majority of cities will cluster at the low end of the distribution, a few will be in the middle, and a small minority will extend out in the tail. Additionally, OLS assumes that the dependent variable can take on any value, including negatives and decimals, but count data can only be positive and can only be whole numbers (integers). For these reasons, OLS is inappropriate for count data. The Poisson distribution is a probability distribution that works well for count data. Poisson regression is based off this probability distribution. This type of regression is quite common in criminal justice and criminology research.

There are also modeling strategies for use when none of the previously discussed techniques is adequate given the type of hypothesis being tested or the type of data a researcher is working with. A technique called structural equation modeling can be applied when a researcher has multiple dependent variables rather than just one. A researcher might posit that one variable causes another and that this second variable, in turn, causes a third one. Standard regression can only accommodate one DV, but structural equation modeling can handle a more complex causal structure. Multilevel modeling (also called hierarchical linear modeling) is appropriate when data are measured at two units of analysis (such as people nested within neighborhoods or prisoners nested within institutions). Basic regression assumes that all data are of the same unit of analysis, and when that is not the case, the standard-error estimates can be inaccurate and the significance tests thrown off as a result. Both structural equation modeling and multilevel modeling are based in regression.

This has been a brief overview of regression and regression-based alternatives to ordinary least squares. There are many options available to accommodate hypotheses and data of all types. More information on these and other techniques is readily available in advanced statistics textbooks and online.

CHAPTER SUMMARY

This chapter introduced you to the basics of bivariate and multiple regression analysis. Bivariate regression is an extension of bivariate correlation and is useful because correlation allows only for a determination of the association between two variables, but bivariate regression permits an examination of how well the IV acts as a predictor of the DV. When an IV emerges as a statistically significant predictor of the DV, the IV can then be assessed for magnitude using the standardized beta weight, β, and the coefficient of determination, r^2.

The problem with bivariate analyses of all types, though, is that every phenomenon that is studied in criminal justice and criminology is the result of a combined influence of multiple factors. In bivariate analyses, it is almost certain that one or more important independent variables have been omitted. Multiple regression addresses this by allowing for the introduction of several IVs so that each one can be examined while controlling for the others' impacts. In the bivariate regression example conducted in this chapter, age of onset significantly predicted lifetime arrests; however, when education was entered into the regression model, age lost its significance and education emerged as a significant and strong predictor of lifetime arrests. This exemplifies the omitted variable bias: Failing to consider the full gamut of relevant IVs can lead to erroneous results and conclusions.

This also brings us to the end of the book. You made it! You struggled at times, but you stuck with it and now you have a solid grasp on the fundamentals of criminology and criminal justice research. You know how to calculate univariate and bivariate statistics and how to conduct hypothesis tests. Just as important, you know how to evaluate the statistics and tests conducted by other people. You know to be critical, ask questions, and always be humble in arriving at conclusions because every statistical test contains some level of error, be it the Type I or Type II error rate, omitted variables, or some other source of mistake. Proceed with caution and a skeptical mind when approaching statistics as either a producer or a consumer. Make GIGO a part of your life—when the information being input into the system is deficient, the conclusions are meaningless or possibly even harmful. The bottom line: Question everything!

CHAPTER 14 REVIEW PROBLEMS

1. You learned in this chapter that the key advantage of bivariate regression over correlation is that regression can be used for prediction. Explain this. How is it that regression can be used to predict values not in the data set, but correlation cannot?

2. Identify the two criteria that a dependent variable must meet for ordinary least squares regression to be used.

3. Does OLS regression place restrictions on the levels of measurement of the independent variables?

4. Explain the advantage of multiple regression over bivariate regression. What does multiple regression do that bivariate regression does not? Why is this important?

5. In a hypothetical example of five prison inmates, let us find out whether prior incarcerations influence in-prison behavior. The following table contains data on the prior incarcerations and the number of disciplinary reports filed against each inmate. Use the data to do the following.

Person	Incarcerations (x)	Disciplinary Reports (y)
A	14	4
B	1	3
C	2	8
D	5	1
E	2	3
$N = 5$		

a. Calculate the slope coefficient b.
b. Calculate the intercept a. (Note that $[\bar{x}] = 4.80$ and $[\bar{y}] = 3.80$.)
c. Write out the full regression equation.
d. Calculate the number of disciplinary reports you would expect to be received by a person with

   i. 3 prior incarcerations
   ii. 15 prior incarcerations

e. Using an alpha level of .05 and two-tailed alternative hypothesis, conduct a five-step hypothesis test to determine whether b is statistically significant. Note that $s_x = 5.36$, $s_Y = 2.59$, and $r = -.09$.
f. If appropriate (i.e., if you rejected the null in Part e), calculate the beta weight.

6. Does the amount of crime in an area predict the level of police presence? The following table displays data on the number of crimes per square mile and the number of police agencies per 1,000 square miles in a sample of states. Use the data to do the following.

State	Crime per Sq. Mile (x)	Police Agencies per 1,000 Sq. Miles (y)
Georgia	7.30	9.40
Iowa	1.40	7.20
Kansas	1.30	4.40
Maine	1.00	3.90
Minnesota	1.90	5.30
Missouri	3.50	8.40

(Continued)

(Continued)

State	Crime per Sq. Mile (x)	Police Agencies per 1,000 Sq. Miles (y)
Nebraska	.70	3.20
Pennsylvania	7.60	24.90
South Carolina	6.90	8.40
Washington	3.80	3.70
$N = 10$		

a. Calculate the slope coefficient b.

b. Calculate the intercept a. (Note that $\bar{x} = 3.54$ and $\bar{y} = 7.88$.)

c. Write out the full regression equation.

d. Calculate how many police agencies per 1,000 square miles you would expect in a state with

    i. 5 crimes per square mile

    ii. 10 crimes per square mile

e. Using an alpha level of .05 and two-tailed alternative hypothesis, conduct a five-step hypothesis test to determine whether the IV is a significant predictor of the DV. (Note that $s_x = 2.76$, $s_y = 6.39$, and $r = .71$.)

f. If appropriate (i.e., if you rejected the null in Part e), calculate the beta weight.

7. Research has found that socioeconomic disadvantage is one of the strongest and most consistent predictors of crime. Negative socioeconomic factors such as poverty and unemployment have been shown to profoundly impact crime rates. The following table contains a random sample of states. The independent variable consists of 2009 data from the U.S. Census on the percentage of adults in the civilian labor force that was unemployed. The DV is UCR-derived violent crime rates per 1,000 persons. Use the data to do the following.

State	Unemployed (x)	Violent Crime Rate (y)
Alaska	8.70	6.33
Arkansas	7.30	5.18
Kentucky	7.60	2.59
Louisiana	7.60	6.20
Montana	5.60	2.54
New Jersey	6.90	3.11
Pennsylvania	6.80	3.81
Virginia	5.40	2.27
Vermont	5.60	1.31
Wyoming	4.50	2.28
$N = 10$		

a. Calculate the slope coefficient b.

b. Calculate the intercept a. ($\bar{x} = 6.60$ and $\bar{y} = 3.56$.)

c. Write out the full regression equation.

d. Calculate how many violent crimes per 1,000 citizens you would expect in a state with

   i. A 4% unemployment rate

   ii. An 8% unemployment rate

e. Using an alpha level of .05 and two-tailed alternative hypothesis, conduct a five-step hypothesis test to determine whether the IV is a significant predictor of the DV. Note that $s_x = 1.29$, $s_Y = 1.76$, and $r = .79$.

f. If appropriate (i.e., if you rejected the null in Part e), calculate the beta weight.

8. Deterrence theory suggests that as the number of crimes that police solve goes up, crime should decrease because would-be offenders are scared by the belief that there is a good chance that they would be caught and punished if they committed an offense. The following table contains regional data from the UCR. The independent variable is *clearance* and is the percentage of violent crimes that were cleared by arrest or exceptional means in one year. The dependent variable is *violent crime rate* and is the number of violent crimes that occurred in the following year (rate per 1,000 residents). Use the data to do the following.

Region	Clearance (x)	Violent Crime Rate (y)
New England	48.00	2.37
Mid-Atlantic	51.30	3.59
East North Central	35.40	3.83
West North Central	47.70	2.98
South Atlantic	47.30	4.83
East South Central	45.60	4.14
West South Central	43.70	5.32
Mountain	44.50	3.74
Pacific	44.10	3.93
N = 9		

a. Calculate the slope coefficient b.

b. Calculate the intercept a. (Note that $\bar{x} = 45.29$ and $\bar{y} = 3.86$.)

c. Write out the full regression equation.

d. Calculate the rate of violent crimes per 1,000 citizens you would expect in a region where

   i. 30% of violent crimes were cleared.

   ii. 50% of violent crimes were cleared.

e. Using an alpha level of .05 and two-tailed alternative hypothesis, conduct a five-step hypothesis test to determine whether the IV is a significant predictor of the DV. Note that $s_x = 4.41$, $s_Y = .88$, and $r = -.25$.

f. If appropriate (i.e., if you rejected the null in Part e), calculate the beta weight.

9. Following the theme in Question 3, let us now consider the possible relationship between poverty and crime. The following table contains a random sample of states and the violent crime rate DV used in Question 3, but the independent variable is now the percentage of families living below the poverty line. Use the table to do the following.

State	Poverty (x)	Violent Crime Rate (y)
Pennsylvania	8.30	3.81
Vermont	6.90	1.31
Florida	9.50	6.12
Hawaii	6.80	2.75
Iowa	7.30	2.79
Missouri	9.80	4.92
Mississippi	9.90	2.81
South Carolina	11.90	6.71
Tennessee	12.20	6.68
Texas	13.20	4.91
N = 10		

a. Calculate the slope coefficient b.

b. Calculate the intercept α. (Note that $\bar{x} = 9.58$ and $\bar{y} = 4.28$.)

c. Write out the full regression equation.

d. Calculate the rate of violent crimes per 1,000 citizens would you expect in a state with

   i. a 5% poverty rate.

  ii. a 10% poverty rate.

e. Using an alpha level of .05 and two-tailed alternative hypothesis, conduct a five-step hypothesis test to determine whether the IV is a significant predictor of the DV. Note that $s_x = 2.29$, $s_Y = 1.87$, and $r = .78$.

f. If appropriate (i.e., if you rejected the null in Part e), calculate the beta weight.

10. In the Chapter 13 Review Problems, you determined whether there was a correlation between prison dollars spent by states per capita and those states' violent crime rates. Let us use the same concept to fit a regression line.

a. Calculate the slope coefficient b.

b. Calculate the intercept α. ($\bar{x} = 1.85$ *and* $\bar{y} = .56$.) ($\bar{x}_x = 1.85$; $\bar{x}_y = .56$.)

c. Write out the full regression equation.

State	Handgun Murder Rate (x)	Knife Murder Rate (y)
Nebraska	1.22	.45
Wisconsin	1.15	.39
Arkansas	1.87	.73
North Carolina	2.59	.52
Virginia	1.37	.52
California	2.77	.79
Washington	1.13	.53
N = 10		

d. Calculate the rate of knife murders per 1,000 citizens would you expect in a state with

   i. a handgun murder rate of 3.00.
   ii. a handgun murder rate of 1.75.

e. Using an alpha level of .05 and two-tailed alternative hypothesis, conduct a five-step hypothesis test to determine whether the IV is a significant predictor of the DV. Note that $s_x =.70$, $s_Y =.15$, and $r = .68$.

f. If appropriate (i.e., if you rejected the null in Part e), calculate the beta weight.

11. The data set *JDCC for Chapter 14.sav* at http://www.sagepub.com/gau contains data from the Juvenile Defendants in Criminal Courts survey. The sample has been narrowed to those facing drug charges who were convicted and sentenced to probation. The DV (probation) is the number of months to which convicted juveniles were sentenced. The IVs are the number of charges filed against each defendant (*charges*) and whether the defendant had a prior record of juvenile arrests or convictions (*priors*). Run a bivariate regression using the DV *probation* and the IV *charges* to determine whether the number of charges significantly predicts the severity of the probation sentence at the bivariate level. Do not include the other variable. Then do the following.

   a. Report the value of the ANOVA F and determine whether you would reject the null at an alpha of .05. What does the rejection or retention of F mean?
   b. Report the R-square value. Using the guidelines provided in the text, interpret the strength of the explanatory power of the IV.
   c. Using the numbers in the output, write out the bivariate regression equation for $\hat{y}$.
   d. Determine whether b is statistically significant at $\alpha = .05$, and explain how you arrived at this decision.
   e. If appropriate, identify the value of the beta weight.
   f. What is your substantive conclusion? Do the number of charges to predict probation sentences? Explain your answer.

12. Keeping the same data set and model from Question 11, add *priors* to the model to account for whether or not each defendant had a prior record of arrests or convictions as a juvenile. Note that this is a binary (dummy) variable with "yes" coded as 1 and "no" as zero, so what you will be looking for in the output is a comparison between those who had and had not been arrested or convicted before. The slope coefficient will tell you the impact of having a prior record as opposed to not having one (the larger the slope, the stronger the impact).

   a. Report the value of the ANOVA F and determine whether you would reject the null at an alpha of .05. What does the rejection or retention of F mean?
   b. Report the R square value. Using the guidelines provided in the text, interpret the strength of the explanatory power of the IVs.
   c. Using the numbers in the output, write out the multiple regression equation for $\hat{y}$.
   d. Determine whether each b is statistically significant at $\alpha = .05$, and explain how you arrived at these decisions.
   e. If appropriate, identify the value of the beta weight for each significant IV and compare them. Which one is stronger? Weaker?
   f. What is your substantive conclusion? Do age and/or number of charges seem to be strong predictors of probation sentences? Explain your answer.

13. Using the multiple regression equation you wrote in Question 12, do the following:

   a. Setting *charges* at its mean (2.09), calculate the predicted probation sentence for a juvenile who does not have a prior record (i.e., $x_{priors} = 0$ in the equation).
   b. Holding *charges* constant at its mean, calculate the predicted probation sentence for a juvenile who does have a prior record (i.e., $x_{priors} = 1$).
   c. By how much did the predicted sentence change? Was this change an increase or decrease?

14. Using the multiple regression equation you wrote in Question 12, do the following:

   a. Setting *priors* at its mean (.79), calculate the predicted probation sentence for a juvenile facing two charges.
   b. Holding *age* constant at its mean, calculate the predicted probation sentence for a juvenile facing five charges.
   c. By how much did the predicted sentence change? Was this change an increase or decrease?

15. The data file *Socioeconomics and Violence for Chapter 14.sav* at http://www.sagepub.com/gau contains a sample of states. Violent crime rates (the variable *violentrate*) is the DV. The IVs are percentage of households receiving food stamps or SNAP (snap); the percentage of the adult civilian workforce that is unemployed (unemployed); and the percentage of families that are below poverty (poverty). Run a bivariate regression using the DV *violentrate* and the IV *unemployed* to test for a relationship between unemployment and violent crime. Do not include the other variables. Then do the following:

   a. Report the value of the ANOVA F and determine whether you would reject the null at an alpha of .05. What does the rejection or retention of F mean?
   b. Report the R-square value. Using the guidelines provided in the text, interpret the strength of the explanatory power of the IV.
   c. Using the numbers in the output, write out the bivariate regression equation for $\hat{y}$.

d. Determine whether b is statistically significant at $\alpha = .05$, and explain how you arrived at this decision.

e. If appropriate, identify the value of the beta weight.

f. What is your substantive conclusion? Does the unemployment rate seem to be a strong predictor of violent crime? Explain your answer.

16. Using the data file *Socioeconomics and Violence for Chapter 14. sav*, run a multiple regression using all three IVs. Then do the following:

a. Report the value of the ANOVA F and determine whether you would reject the null at an alpha of .05. What does the rejection or retention of F mean?

b. Report the R-square value. Using the guidelines provided in the text, interpret the strength of the explanatory power of the IVs.

c. Using the numbers in the output, write out the multiple regression equation for $\hat{y}$.

d. Determine whether each b is statistically significant at $\alpha = .05$, and explain how you arrived at these decisions.

e. Identify the beta weights for each significant IV and compare them. Which one is strongest? Weakest?

f. What is your substantive conclusion? Do these variables seem to be strong predictors of violent crime rates? Explain your answer.

17. Using the multiple regression equation you wrote in Question 16, find the predicted violent crime rate for a state where 15% of households receive benefits, 10% of people are unemployed, and 16% of families live below poverty.

18. Using the multiple regression equation you wrote in Question 16, do the following:

a. Setting *snap* at its mean (8.25) and *poverty* at its mean (8.94), calculate the predicted violent crime rate for a state with a 4% unemployment rate.

b. Holding *snap* and *poverty* constant at their means, calculate the predicted violent crime rate for a state with a 10% unemployment rate.

c. By how much did the predicted rate change? Was this change an increase or decrease?

19. Using the multiple regression equation you wrote in Question 16, do the following:

a. Setting *unemployment* at its mean (6.77) and *poverty* at its (8.94), calculate the predicted violent crime rate for a state where 11% of households receive benefits.

b. Holding *unemployment* and *poverty* constant at their means, calculate the predicted violent crime rate for a state where 6% of households receive benefits.

c. By how much did the predicted rate change? Was this change an increase or decrease?

20. Using the multiple regression equation you wrote in Question 16, do the following.

a. Setting *unemployment* at its mean (6.77) and *snap* at its (8.25), calculate the predicted violent-crime rate for a state where 15% of families live below poverty.

b. Holding *unemployment* and *snap* constant at their means, calculate the predicted violent-crime rate for a state where 20% of families live below poverty.

c. By how much did the predicted rate change? Was this change an increase or decrease?

Regression analysis	Ordinary least squares regression	Residual
Bivariate regression	Intercept	Beta weight
Multiple regression	Slope	Partial slope coefficient

GLOSSARY OF SYMBOLS AND ABBREVIATIONS INTRODUCED IN THIS CHAPTER

y	A given empirical value of the dependent variable
$\hat{y}$	A given predicted value of the dependent variable
a	The y intercept
b	In a sample, the slope of the regression line
B	In a population, the slope of the regression line
SE_b	The standard error of the slope
β	Beta weight; a standardized slope coefficient
$r_{y\hat{y}}^2$	The coefficient of determination in a bivariate regression analysis
R^2	The coefficient of determination in a multiple regression analysis

Appendix A. Review of Basic Mathematical Techniques

I n order to succeed in this class, you must have a solid understanding of basic arithmetic and algebra. This appendix is designed to help you review and brush up on your math skills.

Section 1: Division

You will be doing a lot of dividing throughout this book. The common division sign "÷" will not be used. Division will always be presented in fraction format. Instead of "6 ÷ 3," for example, you will see "$\frac{6}{3}$." For example,

$$\frac{20}{4} = 5 \qquad \frac{90}{10} = 9$$

Try the following as practice.

a. $\frac{6}{2} =$

b. $\frac{14}{2} =$

c. $\frac{15}{3} =$

d. $\frac{9}{3} =$

Section 2: Multiplication

Multiplication is another oft-used technique in this book. The common multiplication sign "×" will not be used, as the symbol "x" is meaningful in statistics and use of this symbol in multiplication as well could result in confusion. The signs that will be used to designate multiplication are

"( )" and "·" Also, when operands or variables are right next to one another, this is an indication that you should use multiplication. For example,

$$7(3) = 21 \qquad 7 \cdot 4 = 28 \qquad 10(3)(4) = 120$$

Try the following as practice.

    a. $3(4) =$

    b. $9 \cdot 8 =$

    c. $12(2) =$

    d. $4 \cdot 5 \cdot 3 =$

Section 3: Order of Operations

Solving equations correctly requires the use of proper order of operations. The correct order is parentheses; exponents; multiplication; division; addition; subtraction. Using any other order could result in erroneous final answers. For example,

$$3(5) + 2 = 15 + 2 = 17 \qquad (4 + 7) - 6 = 11 - 6 = 5 \qquad \left(\frac{8}{2}\right)^2 = (4)^2 = 16$$

Try the following as practice.

    a. $3 + 2 - 4 =$

    b. $4(5) + 7 =$

    c. $\dfrac{19 - 4}{5} =$

    d. $5 \cdot 6 - \dfrac{16}{4} =$

    e. $\left(\dfrac{16}{8}\right)\left(\dfrac{14}{2}\right) =$

    f. $2^2 + 3^3 =$

    g. $(3 + 2)^2 =$

Section 4: Variables

The formulas in this book require you to plug numbers into equations and solve those equations. You must, therefore, understand the basic tenets of algebra, wherein a formula contains variables, you are told the values of those variables, and you plug the values into the formula. For example,

$$\text{If } x = 9 \text{ and } y = 7, \text{ then } x + y = 9 + 7 = 16$$

$$\text{If } x = 10 \text{ and } y = 7, \text{ then } xy = 10(7) = 70$$

$$\text{If } x = 2, y = 5, \text{ and } z = 8, \text{ then } \left(\frac{z}{x}\right)y = \left(\frac{8}{2}\right)5 = 4 \cdot 5 = 20$$

Try the following as practice.

a. $\dfrac{x}{y}$, where $x = 12$ and $y = 3$

b. xy, where $x = 1$ and $y = 1$

c. $x + y + z$, where $x = 1$, $y = 19$, and $z = 4$

d. $\dfrac{x}{y} + 2$, where $x = 6$ and $y = 3$

e. $\left(\dfrac{x}{6}\right)y + 5$, where $x = 36$ and $y = 11$

Section 5: Negatives

There are several rules with respect to negatives. Negative numbers and positive numbers act differently when they are added, subtracted, multiplied, and divided. Positive numbers get larger as the number line is traced away from zero and toward positive infinity. Negative numbers, by contrast, get smaller as the number line is traced toward negative infinity. Adding a negative number is equivalent to subtracting a positive number. When a positive number is multiplied or divided by a negative number, the final answer is negative. When two negative numbers are multiplied or divided, the answer is positive. For example,

$$5 + (-2) = 5 - 2 = 3 \qquad -5 + (-2) = -5 - 2 = -7 \qquad -10(9) = -90 \qquad \frac{-90}{-9} = 10$$

Try the following as practice.

a. $-3 + (-2) =$

b. $-3 - 4 =$

c. $-5 + 3 =$

d. $3 - 8 =$

e. $(-2)^2 =$

f. $-2^2 =$

g. $(-4)(-5) =$

h. $\dfrac{-9}{3} =$

Section 6: Decimals and Rounding

This book requires you to round. Two decimal places are used here; however, your instructor may require more or fewer, so pay attention to directions. When rounding to two decimal places, you should look at the number in the third decimal place to decide whether you will round up or whether you will truncate. When the number in the third (thousandths) position is 5 or greater, you should round the number in the second (hundredths) position up. When the number in the thousandths position is 4 or less, you should truncate. The diagram below shows these positions pictorially.

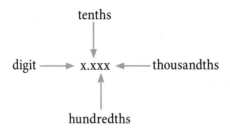

Examples:

.506 rounded to two decimal places = .51   .632 rounded to two decimal places = .63

$.50 + .70 = 1.20$ $(.42)(.80) = .336 \approx .34$ $\sqrt{14} = 3.742 \approx 3.74$ $\left(\dfrac{12}{9}\right)5 = (1.33)5 = 6.65$

Try the following as practice.

a. $.50 + .55 =$

b. $\dfrac{39}{5} =$

c. $2.23 - .34 =$

d. $\sqrt{12}$

e. $1 - .66 =$

f. $(.20)(.80) =$

g. $\dfrac{1.90}{1.20} =$

h. $-3\left(\dfrac{19}{8}\right) + 10 =$

i. Round this number to two decimal places: .605

j. Round this number to two decimal places: .098

If these operations all looked familiar to you and you were able to do them with little or no difficulty, then you are ready for the course! If you struggled with them, you should speak with your course instructor regarding recommendations and options.

Answers to Appendix A Problems

Section 1

a. 3   b. 7   c. 5   d. 3

Section 2

a. 12   b. 72   c. 24   d. 60

Section 3

a. 1   b. 27   c. 3   d. 26   e. 4   f. 13   g. 25

Section 4

a. 4   b. 1   c. 24   d. 4   e. 71

Section 5

a. −5   b. −7   c. −2   d. −5   e. 4   f. −4   g. 20   h. −3

Section 6

a. 1.05   b. 7.80   c. 1.89   d. 3.46   e. .34   f. .16   g. 1.58   h. 2.88   i. .61   j. .10

Appendix B. Standard Normal (z) Distribution

Area Between the Mean and z

z: tenths and hundredths → z: digits and tenths ↓	.00	.01	.02	.03	.04	.05	.06	.07	.08	.09
0.0	.0000	.0040	.0080	.0120	.0160	.0199	.0239	.0279	.0319	.0359
0.1	.0398	.0438	.0478	.0517	.0557	.0596	.0636	.0675	.0714	.0753
0.2	.0793	.0832	.0871	.0910	.0948	.0987	.1026	.1064	.1103	.1141
0.3	.1179	.1217	.1255	.1293	.1331	.1368	.1406	.1443	.1480	.1517
0.4	.1554	.1591	.1628	.1664	.1700	.1736	.1772	.1808	.1844	.1879
0.5	.1915	.1950	.1985	.2019	.2054	.2088	.2123	.2157	.2190	.2224
0.6	.2257	.2291	.2324	.2357	.2389	.2422	.2454	.2486	.2517	.2549
0.7	.2580	.2611	.2642	.2673	.2704	.2734	.2764	.2794	.2823	.2852
0.8	.2881	.2910	.2939	.2967	.2995	.3023	.3051	.3078	.3106	.3133
0.9	.3159	.3186	.3212	.3238	.3264	.3289	.3315	.3340	.3365	.3389
1.0	.3413	.3438	.3461	.3485	.3508	.3531	.3554	.3577	.3599	.3621
1.1	.3643	.3665	.3686	.3708	.3729	.3749	.3770	.3790	.3810	.3830
1.2	.3849	.3869	.3888	.3907	.3925	.3944	.3962	.3980	.3997	.4015
1.3	.4032	.4049	.4066	.4082	.4099	.4115	.4131	.4147	.4162	.4177
1.4	.4192	.4207	.4222	.4236	.4251	.4265	.4279	.4292	.4306	.4319
1.5	.4332	.4345	.4357	.4370	.4382	.4394	.4406	.4418	.4429	.4441
1.6	.4452	.4463	.4474	.4484	.4495	.4505	.4515	.4525	.4535	.4545
1.7	.4554	.4564	.4573	.4582	.4591	.4599	.4608	.4616	.4625	.4633
1.8	.4641	.4649	.4656	.4664	.4671	.4678	.4686	.4693	.4699	.4706
1.9	.4713	.4719	.4726	.4732	.4738	.4744	.4750	.4756	.4761	.4767
2.0	.4772	.4778	.4783	.4788	.4793	.4798	.4803	.4808	.4812	.4817

z: tenths and hundredths →	.00	.01	.02	.03	.04	.05	.06	.07	.08	.09
z: digits and tenths ↓										
2.1	.4821	.4826	.4830	.4834	.4838	.4842	.4846	.4850	.4854	.4857
2.2	.4861	.4864	.4868	.4871	.4875	.4878	.4881	.4884	.4887	.4890
2.3	.4893	.4896	.4898	.4901	.4904	.4906	.4909	.4911	.4913	.4916
2.4	.4918	.4920	.4922	.4925	.4927	.4929	.4931	.4932	.4934	.4936
2.5	.4938	.4940	.4941	.4943	.4945	.4946	.4948	.4949	.4951	.4952
2.6	.4953	.4955	.4956	.4957	.4959	.4960	.4961	.4962	.4963	.4964
2.7	.4965	.4966	.4967	.4968	.4969	.4970	.4971	.4972	.4973	.4974
2.8	.4974	.4975	.4976	.4977	.4977	.4978	.4979	.4979	.4980	.4981
2.9	.4981	.4982	.4982	.4983	.4984	.4984	.4985	.4985	.4986	.4986
3.0	.4987	.4987	.4987	.4988	.4988	.4989	.4989	.4989	.4990	.4990
3.5	.4998									
4.0	.4999									

Appendix C. *t* Distribution

df	Level of Significance for One-Tailed Test					
	.10	**.05**	**.025**	**.01**	**.005**	**.0005**
	Level of Significance for Two-Tailed Test					
	.20	**.10**	**.05**	**.02**	**.01**	**.001**
1	3.078	6.314	12.706	31.821	63.657	636.619
2	1.886	2.920	4.303	6.965	9.925	31.598
3	1.638	2.353	3.182	4.541	5.841	12.941
4	1.533	2.132	2.776	3.747	4.604	8.610
5	1.476	2.015	2.571	3.365	4.032	6.859
6	1.440	1.943	2.447	3.143	3.707	5.959
7	1.415	1.895	2.365	2.998	3.499	5.405
8	1.397	1.860	2.306	2.896	3.355	5.041
9	1.383	1.833	2.262	2.821	3.250	4.781
10	1.372	1.812	2.228	2.764	3.169	4.587
11	1.363	1.796	2.201	2.718	3.106	4.437
12	1.356	1.782	2.179	2.681	3.055	4.318
13	1.350	1.771	2.160	2.650	3.012	4.221
14	1.345	1.761	2.145	2.624	2.977	4.140
15	1.341	1.753	2.131	2.602	2.947	4.073
16	1.337	1.746	2.120	2.583	2.921	4.015
17	1.333	1.740	2.110	2.567	2.898	3.965
18	1.330	1.734	2.101	2.552	2.878	3.922
19	1.328	1.729	2.093	2.539	2.861	3.883
20	1.325	1.725	2.086	2.528	2.845	3.850
21	1.323	1.721	2.080	2.518	2.831	3.819
22	1.321	1.717	2.074	2.508	2.819	3.792

	Level of Significance for One-Tailed Test					
	.10	.05	.025	.01	.005	.0005
	Level of Significance for Two-Tailed Test					
df	.20	.10	.05	.02	.01	.001
23	1.319	1.714	2.069	2.500	2.807	3.767
24	1.318	1.711	2.064	2.492	2.797	3.745
25	1.316	1.708	2.060	2.485	2.787	3.725
26	1.315	1.706	2.056	2.479	2.779	3.707
27	1.314	1.703	2.052	2.473	2.771	3.690
28	1.313	1.701	2.048	2.467	2.763	3.674
29	1.311	1.699	2.045	2.462	2.756	3.659
30	1.310	1.697	2.042	2.457	2.750	3.646
40	1.303	1.684	2.021	2.423	2.704	3.551
60	1.296	1.671	2.000	2.390	2.660	3.460
120	1.289	1.658	1.980	2.358	2.617	3.373
∞	1.282	1.645	1.960	2.326	2.576	3.291

Source: Abridged from R. A. Fisher and F. Yates, *Statistical Tables for Biological, Agricultural and Medical Research*, 6th ed. Copyright © R. A. Fisher and F. Yates 1963. Reprinted by permission of Pearson Education Limited.

Appendix D. Chi-Square Distribution

df	α				
	.10	.05	.02	.01	.001
1	2.706	3.841	5.412	6.635	10.827
2	4.605	5.991	7.824	9.210	13.815
3	6.251	7.815	9.837	11.341	16.268
4	7.779	9.488	11.668	13.277	18.465
5	9.236	11.070	13.388	15.086	20.517
6	10.645	12.592	15.033	16.812	22.457
7	12.017	14.067	16.622	18.475	24.322
8	13.362	15.507	18.168	20.090	26.125
9	14.684	16.919	19.679	21.666	27.877
10	15.987	18.307	21.161	23.209	29.588
11	17.275	19.675	22.618	24.725	31.264
12	18.549	21.026	24.054	26.217	32.909
13	19.812	22.362	25.472	27.688	34.528
14	21.064	23.685	26.873	29.141	36.123
15	22.307	24.996	28.259	30.578	37.697
16	23.542	26.296	29.633	32.000	39.252
17	24.769	27.587	30.995	33.409	40.790
18	25.989	28.869	32.346	34.805	42.312
19	27.204	30.144	33.687	36.191	43.820
20	28.412	31.410	35.020	37.566	45.315
21	29.615	32.671	36.343	38.932	46.797
22	30.813	33.924	37.659	40.289	48.268

df	α				
	.10	.05	.02	.01	.001
23	32.007	35.172	38.968	41.638	49.728
24	33.196	36.415	40.270	42.980	51.179
25	34.382	37.652	41.566	44.314	52.620
26	35.563	38.885	42.856	45.642	54.052
27	36.741	40.113	44.140	46.963	55.476
28	37.916	41.337	45.419	48.278	56.893
29	39.087	42.557	46.693	49.588	58.302
30	40.256	43.773	47.962	50.892	59.703

Source: R. A. Fisher & F. Yates, Statistical Tables for Biological, Agricultural and Medical Research, 6th ed. Copyright © R. A. Fisher and F. Yates 1963. Reprinted by permission of Pearson Education Limited.

Appendix E. *F* Distribution

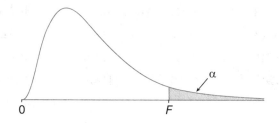

				$\alpha = .05$						
					df_B					
df_W	1	2	3	4	5	6	8	12	24	∞
1	161.4	199.5	215.7	224.6	230.2	234.0	238.9	243.9	249.0	254.3
2	18.51	19.00	19.16	19.25	19.30	19.33	19.37	19.41	19.45	19.50
3	10.13	9.55	9.28	9.12	9.01	8.94	8.84	8.74	8.64	8.53
4	7.71	6.94	6.59	6.39	6.26	6.16	6.04	5.91	5.77	5.63
5	6.61	5.79	5.41	5.19	5.05	4.95	4.82	4.68	4.53	4.36
6	5.99	5.14	4.76	4.53	4.39	4.28	4.15	4.00	3.84	3.67
7	5.59	4.74	4.35	4.12	3.97	3.87	3.73	3.57	3.41	3.23
8	5.32	4.46	4.07	3.84	3.69	3.58	3.44	3.28	3.12	2.93
9	5.12	4.26	3.86	3.63	3.48	3.37	3.23	3.07	2.90	2.71
10	4.96	4.10	3.71	3.48	3.33	3.22	3.07	2.91	2.74	2.54
11	4.84	3.98	3.59	3.36	3.20	3.09	2.95	2.79	2.61	2.40
12	4.75	3.88	3.49	3.26	3.11	3.00	2.85	2.69	2.50	2.30
13	4.67	3.80	3.41	3.18	3.02	2.92	2.77	2.60	2.42	2.21
14	4.60	3.74	3.34	3.11	2.96	2.85	2.70	2.53	2.35	2.13
15	4.54	3.68	3.29	3.06	2.90	2.79	2.64	2.48	2.29	2.07
16	4.49	3.63	3.24	3.01	2.85	2.74	2.59	2.42	2.24	2.01
17	4.45	3.59	3.20	2.96	2.81	2.70	2.55	2.38	2.19	1.96
18	4.41	3.55	3.16	2.93	2.77	2.66	2.51	2.34	2.15	1.92

$\alpha = .05$

df_B

df_W	1	2	3	4	5	6	8	12	24	∞
19	4.38	3.52	3.13	2.90	2.74	2.63	2.48	2.31	2.11	1.88
20	4.35	3.49	3.10	2.87	2.71	2.60	2.45	2.28	2.08	1.84
21	4.32	3.47	3.07	2.84	2.68	2.57	2.42	2.25	2.05	1.81
22	4.30	3.44	3.05	2.82	2.66	2.55	2.40	2.23	2.03	1.78
23	4.28	3.42	3.03	2.80	2.64	2.53	2.38	2.20	2.00	1.76
24	4.26	3.40	3.01	2.78	2.62	2.51	2.36	2.18	1.98	1.73
25	4.24	3.38	2.99	2.76	2.60	2.49	2.34	2.16	1.96	1.71
26	4.22	3.37	2.98	2.74	2.59	2.47	2.32	2.15	1.95	1.69
27	4.21	3.35	2.96	2.73	2.57	2.46	2.30	2.13	1.93	1.67
28	4.20	3.34	2.95	2.71	2.56	2.44	2.29	2.12	1.91	1.65
29	4.18	3.33	2.93	2.70	2.54	2.43	2.28	2.10	1.90	1.64
30	4.17	3.32	2.92	2.69	2.53	2.42	2.27	2.09	1.89	1.62
40	4.08	3.23	2.84	2.61	2.45	2.34	2.18	2.00	1.79	1.51
60	4.00	3.15	2.76	2.52	2.37	2.25	2.10	1.92	1.70	1.39
120	3.92	3.07	2.68	2.45	2.29	2.17	2.02	1.83	1.61	1.25
∞	3.84	2.99	2.60	2.37	2.21	2.09	1.94	1.75	1.52	1.00

Source: R. A. Fisher and F. Yates, *Statistical Tables for Biological, Agricultural and Medical Research*, 6th ed. Copyright © R. A. Fisher and F. Yates 1963. Reprinted by permission of Pearson Education Limited.

$\alpha = .01$

df_B

df_W	1	2	3	4	5	6	8	12	24	∞
1	4052	4999	5403	5625	5764	5859	5981	6106	6234	6366
2	98.49	99.01	99.17	99.25	99.30	99.33	99.36	99.42	99.46	99.50
3	34.12	30.81	29.46	28.71	28.24	27.91	27.49	27.05	26.60	26.12
4	21.20	18.00	16.69	15.98	15.52	15.21	14.80	14.37	13.93	13.46
5	16.26	13.27	12.06	11.39	10.97	10.67	10.27	9.89	9.47	9.02
6	13.74	10.92	9.78	9.15	8.75	8.47	8.10	7.72	7.31	6.88
7	12.25	9.55	8.45	7.85	7.46	7.19	6.84	6.47	6.07	5.65
8	11.26	8.65	7.59	7.01	6.63	6.37	6.03	5.67	5.28	4.86
9	10.56	8.02	6.99	6.42	6.06	5.80	5.47	5.11	4.73	4.31

	$\alpha = .01$									
	df_B									
df_w	1	2	3	4	5	6	8	12	24	∞
10	10.04	7.56	6.55	5.99	5.64	5.39	5.06	4.71	4.33	3.91
11	9.65	7.20	6.22	5.67	5.32	5.07	4.74	4.40	4.02	3.60
12	9.33	6.93	5.95	5.41	5.06	4.82	4.50	4.16	3.78	3.36
13	9.07	6.70	5.74	5.20	4.86	4.62	4.30	3.96	3.59	3.16
14	8.86	6.51	5.56	5.03	4.69	4.46	4.14	3.80	3.43	3.00
15	8.68	6.36	5.42	4.89	4.56	4.32	4.00	3.67	3.29	2.87
16	8.53	6.23	5.29	4.77	4.44	4.20	3.89	3.55	3.18	2.75
17	8.40	6.11	5.18	4.67	4.34	4.10	3.79	3.45	3.08	2.65
18	8.28	6.01	5.09	4.58	4.25	4.01	3.71	3.37	3.00	2.57
19	8.18	5.93	5.01	4.50	4.17	3.94	3.63	3.30	2.92	2.49
20	8.10	5.85	4.94	4.43	4.10	3.87	3.56	3.23	2.86	2.42
21	8.02	5.78	4.87	4.37	4.04	3.81	3.51	3.17	2.80	2.36
22	7.94	5.72	4.82	4.31	3.99	3.76	3.45	3.12	2.75	2.31
23	7.88	5.66	4.76	4.23	3.94	3.71	3.41	3.07	2.70	2.26
24	7.82	5.61	4.72	4.22	3.90	3.67	3.36	3.03	2.66	2.21
25	7.77	5.57	4.68	4.18	3.86	3.63	3.32	2.99	2.62	2.17
26	7.72	5.53	4.64	4.14	3.82	3.59	3.29	2.96	2.58	2.13
27	7.68	5.49	4.60	4.11	3.78	3.56	3.26	2.93	2.55	2.10
28	7.64	5.45	4.57	4.07	3.75	3.53	3.23	2.90	2.52	2.06
29	7.60	5.42	4.54	4.04	3.73	3.50	3.20	2.87	2.49	2.03
30	7.56	5.39	4.51	4.02	3.70	3.47	3.17	2.84	2.47	2.01
40	7.31	5.18	4.31	3.83	3.51	3.29	2.99	2.66	2.29	1.80
60	7.08	4.98	4.13	3.65	3.34	3.12	2.82	2.50	2.12	1.60
120	6.85	4.79	3.95	3.48	3.17	2.96	2.66	2.34	1.95	1.38
∞	6.64	4.60	3.78	3.32	3.02	2.80	2.51	2.18	1.79	1.00

Glossary

Alpha level: The opposite of the confidence level; that is, the probability that a confidence interval does not contain the true population parameter. Symbolized α.

Alternative hypothesis: In an inferential test, the hypothesis predicting that there is a relationship between the independent and dependent variables. Symbolized H_1. Sometimes referred to as a research hypothesis.

Analysis of variance (ANOVA): The analytic technique appropriate when an independent variable is categorical with three or more classes and a dependent variable is continuous.

Beta weight: A standardized slope coefficient that ranges from -1.00 to $+1.00$ and can be interpreted similarly to a correlation so that the magnitude of an IV–DV relationship can be assessed.

Between-group variance: The extent to which a set of groups or classes are similar to or different from one another. This is a measure of true group effect, or a relationship between the independent and dependent variables.

Binomial: A trial with exactly two possible outcomes. Also called a dichotomous or binary variable empirical outcome.

Binomial coefficient: The formula used to calculate the probability for each possible outcome of a trial and to create the binomial probability distribution.

Binomial probability distribution: A numerical or graphical display showing the probability associated with each possible outcome of a trial.

Bivariate: Analysis involving two variables. Usually, one is designated the independent variable and the other the dependent variable.

Bivariate regression: A regression analysis that uses one independent and one dependent variable.

Bonferroni: A widely used and relatively conservative post hoc test used in ANOVA when the null is rejected as a means of determining the number and location of differences between groups.

Bounding rule: The rule stating that all proportions range from 0.00 to 1.00.

Categorical variable: A variable that classifies people or objects into groups. Two types: nominal and ordinal.

Cell: The place in a table where a row and column meet.

Central limit theorem: The property of the sampling distribution that guarantees that this curve will be normally distributed when infinite samples of large size have been drawn.

χ^2 distribution: The sampling or probability distribution for chi-square tests.

Chi-square test of independence: The hypothesis-testing procedure appropriate when both the independent variable and the dependent variables are categorical.

Classes: The categories or groups on a categorical variable.

Combination: The total number of ways that a success r can occur over N trials.

Confidence interval: A range of values spanning a point estimate that is calculated so as to have a certain probability of containing the population parameter.

Constant: A characteristic that describes people, objects, or places and takes on only one value in a sample or population.

Contingency table: A table showing the overlap between two variables.

Continuous variable: A variable that numerically measures the presence of a particular characteristic. Two types: interval and ratio.

Cramer's V: A symmetric measure of association for χ^2 when the variables are nominal or when one is ordinal and the other is nominal. V ranges from 0.00 to 1.00 and indicates the strength of the relationship. Higher values represent stronger relationships. Identical to phi in 2×2 tables.

Critical value: The value of z or t associated with a given alpha level. Symbolized z_a or t_a.

Cumulative: A frequency, proportion, or percentage obtained by adding a given number to all numbers below it.

Dependent samples: Pairs of samples in which the selection of people or objects into one sample directly affected, or was directly affected by, the selection of people or objects into the other sample. The most common types are matched pairs and repeated measures.

Dependent variable: The phenomenon that a researcher wishes to study, explain, or predict.

Descriptive research: Studies done solely for the purpose of describing a particular phenomenon as it occurs in a sample.

Deviation score: The distance between the mean of a data set and any given raw score in that set.

Dispersion: The amount of spread or variability among the scores in a distribution.

Dummy variable: A dichotomous independent variable.

Empirical: Having the qualities of being measurable, observable, or tangible. Empirical phenomena are detectable with senses such as sight, hearing, or touch.

Empirical outcome: A numerical result from a sample, such as a mean or frequency. Also called an observed outcome.

Evaluation research: Studies intended to assess the results of programs or interventions for purposes of discovering whether those programs or interventions appear to be effective.

Expected frequencies: The theoretical results that would be seen if the null were true, that is, if the two variables were, in fact, unrelated. Symbolized f_e.

Exploratory research: Studies that address issues that not been examined much or at all in prior research and that therefore may lack firm theoretical and empirical grounding.

F distribution: The sampling distribution for ANOVA. The distribution is bounded at zero on the left and extends to positive infinity; all values in the F distribution are thus positive.

F statistic: The statistic utilized in ANOVA; a ratio of the amount of between-group variance present in a sample relative to the amount of within-group variance.

Factorial: Symbolized $!$, the mathematical function whereby the first number in a sequence is multiplied successively by all numbers below it down to 1.00.

Failure: Any outcome other than success or the event of interest.

Familywise error: The increase in the likelihood of a Type I error (i.e., erroneous rejection of a true null hypothesis) that results from running repeated statistical tests on a single sample.

Frequency: A raw count of the number of times a particular characteristic appears in a data set.

Goodman and Kruskal's gamma: A symmetric measure of association used when both variables are ordinal or one is ordinal and the other is dichotomous. Ranges from -1.00 to $+1.00$.

Hypothesis: A single proposition, deduced from a theory, that must hold true in order for the theory itself to be considered valid.

Independent samples: Pairs of samples in which the selection of people or objects into one sample in no way affected, or was affected by, the selection of people or objects into the other sample.

Independent variable: A factor or characteristic that is used to try to explain or predict a dependent variable.

Inferential analysis: The process of generalizing from a sample to a population; the use of a sample statistic to estimate a population parameter. Also called hypothesis testing.

Inferential statistics: The field of statistics in which a descriptive statistic derived from a sample is employed probabilistically to make a generalization or inference about the population from which the sample was drawn.

Intercept: The point at which the regression line crosses the y-axis; also the value of y when $x = 0$.

Interval variable: A quantitative variable that numerically measures the extent to which a particular characteristic is present or absent and does not have a true zero point.

Kendall's tau$_b$: A symmetric measure of association for two ordinal variables when the number of rows and columns in the crosstabs table are equal. Ranges from −1.00 to +1.00.

Kendall's tau$_c$: A symmetric measure of association for two ordinal variables when the number of rows and columns in the crosstabs table are unequal. Ranges from −1.00 to +1.00.

Kurtosis: A measure of how much a distribution curve's width departs from normality.

Lambda: An asymmetric measure of association for χ^2 when the variables are nominal. Lambda ranges from 0.00 to 1.00 and is a proportionate reduction in error measure.

Leptokurtosis: A measure of how peaked or clustered a distribution is.

Level of confidence: The probability that a confidence interval contains the population parameter. Commonly set at 95% or 99%.

Level of measurement: A variable's specific type or classification. Four types: nominal, ordinal, interval, and ratio.

Linear relationship: A relationship wherein the change in the dependent variable associated with a one-unit increase in the independent variable remains static or constant at all levels of the independent variable.

Longitudinal variables: Variables measured repeatedly over time.

Matched-pairs design: A research strategy where a second sample is created on the basis of each case's similarity to a case in an existing sample.

Mean: The arithmetic average of a set of data.

Measures of association: Procedures for determining the strength or magnitude of a relationship after a chi-square test has revealed a statistically significant association between two variables.

Measures of central tendency: Descriptive statistics that offer information about where the scores in a particular data set tend to cluster. Examples include the mode, median, and mean.

Median: The score that cuts a distribution exactly in half such that 50% of the scores are above that value and 50% are below it.

Methods: The procedures used to gather and analyze scientific data.

Midpoint of the magnitudes: The property of the mean that causes all deviation scores based on the mean to sum to zero.

Mode: The most frequently occurring category or value in a set of scores.

Multiple regression: A regression analysis that uses two or more independent variables and one dependent variable.

Negative correlation: When a one-unit increase in the independent variable produces a reduction in the dependent variable.

Negative skew: A clustering of scores in the right-hand side of a distribution with some relatively small scores that pull the tail toward the negative side of the number line.

Nominal variable: A classification that places people or objects into different groups according to a particular characteristic that cannot be ranked in terms of quantity.

Nonparametric statistics: The class of statistical tests used when dependent variables are categorical and the sampling distribution cannot be assumed to approximate normality.

Normal curve: A distribution of raw scores from a sample or population that is symmetric, unimodal, and has an area of 1.00. Normal curves are expressed in raw units and differ from one another in metrics, means, and standard deviations.

Normal distribution: A set of scores that clusters in the center and tapers off to the left (negative) and right (positive) sides of the number line.

Null hypothesis: In an inferential test, the hypothesis predicting that there is no relationship between the independent and dependent variables. Symbolized H_0.

Observed frequencies: The empirical results seen in a contingency table derived from sample data. Symbolized f_o.

Obtained value: The value of the test statistic arrived at using the mathematical formulas specific to a particular test. The obtained value is the final product of Step 4 of a hypothesis test.

Omega squared: A measure of association used in ANOVA when the null has been rejected in order to assess the magnitude of the relationship between the independent and dependent variables. This measure shows the proportion of the total variability in the sample that is attributable to between-group differences.

One-tailed tests: Hypothesis tests in which the entire alpha is placed in either the upper (positive) or lower (negative) tail such that there is only one critical value of the test statistic. Also called directional tests.

Ordinal variable: A classification that places people or objects into different groups according to a particular characteristic that can be ranked in terms of quantity.

Ordinary least squares regression: A common procedure for estimating regression equations that minimizes the errors in predicting the dependent variable.

p value: In SPSS output, the probability associated with the obtained value of the test statistic. When $p < \alpha$, the null hypothesis is rejected.

Parameter: A number that describes a population from which samples might be drawn.

Parametric statistics: The class of statistical tests used when dependent variables are continuous and normally distributed and the sampling distribution can be assumed to approximate normality.

Partial slope coefficient: A slope coefficient that measures the individual impact of an independent variable on a dependent variable while holding other independent variables constant.

Pearson's correlation: The bivariate statistical analysis used when both independent and dependent variables are continuous.

Percentage: A standardized form of a frequency that ranges from 0.00 to 100.00.

Phi: A symmetric measure of association for chi-square with nominal variables and a 2×2 table. Identical to Cramer's V.

Platykurtosis: A measure of how flat or spread out a distribution is.

Point estimate: A sample statistic, such as a mean or proportion.

Pooled variances: The type of t test appropriate when the samples are independent and the population variances are equal.

Population: The universe of people, objects, or locations that researchers wish to study. These groups are often very large.

Population distribution: An empirical distribution made of raw scores from a population.

Positive correlation: When a one-unit increase in the independent variable produces an increase in the dependent variable.

Positive skew: A clustering of scores in the left-hand side of a distribution with some relatively large scores that pull the tail toward the positive side of the number line.

Post hoc tests: Analyses conducted when the null is rejected in ANOVA in order to determine the number and location of differences between groups.

Probability: The likelihood that a certain event will occur.

Probability distribution: A table or graph showing the entire set of probabilities associated with every possible empirical outcome.

Probability sampling: A sampling technique in which all people, objects, or areas in a population have a known chance of being selected into the sample.

Probability theory: Logical premises that form a set of predictions about the likelihood of certain events or the empirical results that one would expect to see in an infinite set of trials.

Proportion: A standardized form of a frequency that ranges from 0.00 to 1.00.

r coefficient: The test statistic in a correlation analysis.

Range: A measure of dispersion for continuous variables that is calculated by subtracting the smallest score from the largest. Symbolized as R.

Ratio variable: A quantitative variable that numerically measures the extent to which a particular characteristic is present or absent and has a true zero point.

Regression analysis: A technique for modeling linear relationships between one or more independent variables and one dependent variable wherein each independent variable is evaluated on the basis of its ability to accurately predict the values of the dependent variable.

Replication: The repetition of a particular study that is conducted for purposes of determining whether the original study's results hold when new samples or measures are employed.

Repeated-measures design: A research strategy used to measure the effectiveness of an intervention by comparing two sets of scores (pre and post) from the same sample.

Residual: The difference between a predicted value and an empirical value on a dependent variable.

Restricted multiplication rule for independent events: A rule of multiplication that allows the probability that two events will both occur to be calculated as the product of each event's probability of occurrence: that is, $p(A \text{ and } B) = p(A) \cdot p(B)$.

Rule of the complement: Based on the bounding rule, the rule stating that the proportion of cases that are not in a certain category can be found by subtracting the proportion that are in that category from 1.00.

Sample: A subset pulled from a population with the goal of ultimately using the people, objects, or places in the sample as a way to generalize to the population.

Sample distribution: An empirical distribution made of raw scores from a sample.

Sampling distribution: A theoretical distribution made out of an infinite number of sample statistics.

Sampling error: The uncertainty introduced into a sample statistic by the fact that any given sample is only one of many samples that could have been drawn from that population.

Science: The process of gathering and analyzing data in a systematic and controlled way using procedures that are generally accepted by others in the discipline.

Separate variances: The type of t test appropriate when the samples are independent and the population variances are unequal.

Slope: The steepness of the regression line and a measure of the change in the dependent variable produced by a one-unit increase in an independent variable.

Somers' d: An asymmetric measure of association for χ^2 when the variables are nominal. Somers' d ranges from −1.00 to +1.00.

Standard deviation: Computed as the square root of the variance, a measure of dispersion that is the mean of the deviation scores. Notated as s or sd.

Standard error: The standard deviation of the sampling distribution.

Standard normal curve: A distribution of z scores. The curve is symmetric and unimodal and has a mean of zero, a standard deviation of 1.00, and an area of 1.00.

Statistic: A number that describes a sample that has been drawn from a larger population.

Statistical dependence: The condition in which two variables are related to one another; that is, knowing what class persons/objects fall into on the independent variable helps predict which class they will fall into on the dependent variable.

Statistical independence: The condition in which two variables are not related to one another; that is, knowing what class persons or objects fall into on the independent variable does not help predict which class they will fall into on the dependent variable.

Statistical significance: When the obtained value of a test statistic exceeds the critical value and the null is rejected.

Success: The outcome of interest in a trial.

t distribution: A family of curves whose shapes are determined by the size of the sample. All t curves are unimodal, symmetric, and have an area of 1.00.

t test: The test used with a two-class, categorical independent variable and a continuous dependent variable.

Theoretical prediction: A prediction, grounded in logic, about whether or not a certain event will occur.

Theory: A set of proposed and testable explanations about reality that are bound together by logic and evidence.

Trends: Patterns that indicate whether something is increasing, decreasing, or staying the same over time.

Trial: An act that has several different possible outcomes.

Tukey's honest significant difference: A widely used post hoc test used in ANOVA when the null is rejected as a means of determining the number and location of differences between groups.

Two-tailed test: A statistical test in which alpha is split in half and placed into both tails of the z or t distribution.

Type I error: The erroneous rejection of a true null hypothesis.

Type II error: The erroneous retention of a false null hypothesis.

Unit of analysis: The object or target of a research study.

Univariate: Involving one variable

Variable: A characteristic that describes people, objects, or places and takes on multiple values in a sample or population.

Variance: A measure of dispersion calculated as the mean of the squared deviation scores. Notated as s^2.

Variation ratio: A measure of dispersion for variables of any level of measurement that is calculated as the proportion of cases located outside the modal category. Symbolized as VR.

Within-group variance: The amount of diversity that exists among the people or objects in a single group or class. This is a measure of random fluctuation, or error.

z score: A standardized version of a raw score that shows that offers two pieces of information about the raw score: (1) how close it is to the distribution mean and (2) whether it is greater than or less than the mean.

z table: A table containing a list of z scores and the area of the curve that is between the distribution mean and each individual z score.

Answers to Learning Checks

Chapter 1

1. a. sample
    b. sample
    c. population
    d. sample

2. a. descriptive
    b. evaluation
    c. theory testing
    d. exploratory

Chapter 2

1. The variable *offense type* could be coded as either a nominal or an ordinal variable because it could be purely descriptive, or it could represent a ranking of severity. An example of a nominal coding scheme is "violent offense, weapons offense, sex offense, property offense." This coding approach does not lend itself to clear ranking in terms of the severity of the crime. An example of ordinal coding is "property offense, violent offense (non-homicide), homicide."

This approach allows for a moderate comparison of crime severity across the different categories.

2. Zip codes are nominal variables. They are composed of numbers, but these numbers are not meaningful from a statistical standpoint; that is, zip codes cannot be added, subtracted, multiplied, or divided. Zip codes are merely placeholders designating particular locations. They offer no information about ranking or quantification.

Chapter 3

1. A sum greater than 1.00 (for proportions) or 100.00 (for percentages) would suggest that one or more cases in the table or data set got counted twice or that there is an error in the count of the total cases. If the result is less than 1.00 or 100.00, then the opposite has occurred; that is, one or more cases in the sample have been undercounted or the total has been overestimated.

2. *Hispanic male* is a nominal variable; it is categorical with no ranking or quantification properties. *Number of violent victimizations* is ratio; it is a continuous, quantitative variable with a true zero.

3. Rates measure the prevalence of a certain event or characteristic in a population or sample. Percentages

break samples or populations down into elements that either do or do not possess a certain characteristic. The calculation of rates requires information about the total population, something not needed for percentages. Rates do not sum to 100 because they are a ratio-level variable that can range from 0 to infinity (theoretically); that is, there is no maximum value that a rate cannot exceed. Percentages are confined to the range 0 to 100.

4. In Table 3.8, column percentages would show the percentages of college-offering prisons that house males only, house females only, or house both, and the percentage of prisons not offering college courses that house males, females, or both. The column percentages for the prisons offering courses would be

male = (497/642)100 = 77.41; female = (76/642)100 = 11.84; and both = (69/642)100 = 10.75. The column percentages for prisons not providing courses is male = (861/1,179)100 = 73.03; female = (111/1,179)100 = 9.41; and both = (207/1,179)100 = 17.56. This means that 77.41% of prisons that offer college courses house males only, 11.84% house females only, and 10.75% house both. The same interpretations would also apply to the non-college prisons.

5. Pie charts can only be composed of percentages because the idea behind them is that the entire "pie" represents 100% of the total available options, categories, or cases. The total is then partitioned into its constituent parts, with the "slices" representing percentages. This would not work with rates, because rates are independent numbers that have no maximum values and do not sum to 100% when combined with other rates.

6. The histogram in Figure 3.8 and the frequency polygon in Figure 3.9 probably would not benefit from grouping. Their ungrouped distributions display clear, interpretable shapes; they are distinctly different from the flat, shapeless histogram in Figure 3.12. The data in 3.8 and 3.9 appear to be fine ungrouped.

7. Rates are advantageous compared to raw counts because rates are standardized according to the size of the population. For instance, a police department with 25 officers serving a town of 1,000 residents is much different than a department of 25 officers in a city of 100,000 residents. Rates are more informative and useful than raw counts are in this type of situation.

Chapter 4

1. The positively skewed distribution should look similar to Figure 4.2, and the negatively skewed one should look like Figure 4.3.

2. The modal number of victimizations is zero. Of the 725 people in the sample, 639 experienced no victimizations; thus, this is the most frequently occurring number.

3. First, rearrange the categories so that they are in order from *Never* to *Every day or almost every day*. Next, sum the frequencies until the cumulative sum is equal to or greater than 772.5. Since 457 + 37 + 82 + 217 = 793, we reach the same conclusion as before: *A few days a week* is the modal driving frequency.

4. Formula 4(3) would be used to calculate the mean for Table 2.3. This is because the numbers are arranged so that the left-hand column (*Number Executed*) contains the values in the data set and the right-hand column (*Frequency*) displays the number of times each value occurs. The mean formula with the f in the numerator (i.e., Formula 4[3]) is therefore the correct one. Using this formula, the fx column and sum would be: 0 + 2 + 2 + 6 + 18 + 15 = 43. Divided by the sample size (n = 50), the mean is 43/50 = .86. Across all 50 states, the mean number of executions per state in 2012 was .86. Since Table 2.3 includes all 50 states, including the 14 that do not authorize the death penalty, there are several more zeroes (14, to be exact!) than there would be if only those 36 states that authorize capital punishment were included in the calculations. As a result, the mean for all 50 states is much lower than it would be if only the 36 authorizing states were analyzed; specifically, the mean increases to 43/36 = 1.19 if the 14 states are dropped from the analysis. Similarly, the mean calculated on the data in Table 4.6, which contains only the 36 authorizing states, would be lower if the 14 non-authorizing states were added; the new calculation would be 78/50 = 1.56.

5. Subtracting 24.98 from each of the raw scores in Table 4.2 produces the deviation scores –7.16, 20.55, 17.36, –19.47, and –11.28. The sum of the deviation scores is 0.00.

Chapter 5

1. 45% is male; 4% were not convicted; and 10% received fines.

2. This distribution would be leptokurtic because the majority of the values cluster within a small range and

only a few values are outside of that range. Thus, the distribution's shape or curve would be tall and thin.

3. The values should sum to 0.00, as shown in Table 5.6b.

4. The sample with 10 cases would have a mean of $100/10 = 10$, whereas the sample with 50 cases would have a mean of $100/50 = 2$. The first sample's mean is much larger than the second sample's mean because in the first sample, the sum of 100 is spread across just 10 cases; in the second sample, the 100 is spread across 50 cases. Thus, two samples can have the same sum but very different means. This is why sample size matters.

5. The reason is mathematical: Since variances and squared deviation scores are calculated by squaring numbers, and since any number squared is positive (even if the original number was negative), variances and squared deviations have to be positive, by definition.

6. The mean salary is $732,644.99/8 = 91,580.62$. The deviation scores are $-4,007.62$; 47.98; $-25,069.56$; $5,919.38$; $6,419.38$; $5,279.71$; $5,991.38$; and $5,419.38$. Squaring and summing the deviation scores produces $813,935,309.50$, and dividing by $n - 1$ (i.e., $8 - 1 = 7$) gives us the variance $813,935,309.50/7 = 116,276,472.79$. The standard deviation is the square root of the variance and is $10,783.16$.

7. The upper and lower limits, in the order they appear in the table, are $2.14 - 74.12$; $-7.65 - 64.61$; $-.39 - .87$; $-.31 - 9.69$; $-8.05 - 15.43$; $-.68 - 8.24$; $1.16 - 7.84$; and $2.17 - 7.51$.

Chapter 6

1. a. The probability of the die landing on 3 is $1/6 = .17$. This probability remains the same no matter what the original prediction was.
   b. The probability of drawing the Ace of Hearts is $1/52 = .02$. Again, the probability is not dependent on the original prediction.
   a. The probability of the die landing on any value except 1 is $5/6 = .83$. This calculation would apply to any initial predicted outcome.
   b. The probability that the drawn card is anything other than the Nine of Spades is $51/52 = .98$. Again, this would apply to any predicted outcome.

2. Homicide $= 100.00 - 62.50 = 37.50$, so there is a $.62$ probability of clearance and a $.38$ probability that no arrest will be made. For rape, 59.90% are not cleared, so the probability of clearance is $.40$ and the probability of no clearance is $.60$. For robbery, 71.90% are not cleared, so the clearance probability is $.28$, and non-clearance probability is $.72$. For aggravated assault, the numbers are, in order, 44.20, .56, and .44. For larceny-theft, 78%, .22, and .78. For motor vehicle theft, 88.1%, .12, and .88.

3. It is in Hospital B that the sex ratio of babies born in a single day would be expected to roughly mirror the gender breakdown in the general population. This is because 20 is a larger sample size than 6 and, therefore, is less likely to produce anomalous or atypical results. In Hospital A, it would be relatively easy to have a day wherein 4 (67%), 5 (83%), or even all 6 (100%) babies were of the same gender. In Hospital B, however, it would be highly unlikely to see a result such as 16 of 20 babies being the same sex. Over the course of a year, though, it would be expected that both hospitals would produce gender ratios of approximately 50% female and 50% male. This is because the sample size in both hospitals would be large enough so that the variations seen on a day-to-day basis would even out over time.

4. With a clearance probability of $p = .63$, $q = 1.00 - .63 = .37$, and $N = 6$, the resulting probabilities are: $p(0) = .003$; $p(1) = .04$; $p(2) = .12$; $p(3) = .25$; $p(4) = .34$; $p(5) = .22$; and $p(6) = .06$. Increasing N to 10: $p(0) = .00005$; $p(1) = .0006$; $p(2) = .01$; $p(3) = .03$; $p(4) = .10$; $p(5) = .18$; $p(6) = .25$; $p(7) = .24$; $p(8) = .13$; $p(9) = .07$; and $p(10) = .01$. Some of these numbers are very small, so your answer might differ from these numbers a little bit depending on how you did your rounding.

5. The four types of deviation from normality are composed of two types of skew (positive and negative) and two types of kurtosis (leptokurtosis and platykurtosis).

6. Conceptually, a standard deviation is the mean of the deviation scores; in other words, it is the average distance between the raw data points and the mean. The mean

offers information about the location of the center of the distribution, and the standard deviation describes the amount of spread or variability in the scores.

7. a. area between = .4162; area beyond = .50 − .4162 = .0838
    b. area between = .2422; area beyond = .2578
    c. area between = .4931; area beyond = .0069
    d. area between = .4990; area beyond = .001

8. In the chapter, it was discovered that z scores greater than 2.33 are in the upper 1% of the distribution. Since the standard normal curve is symmetric, then the corresponding z score for the bottom 1% is -2.33,

and we can say that scores less than −2.33 are in the bottom 1% of the distribution.

9.

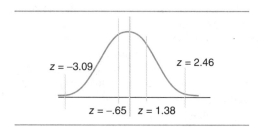

Chapter 8

1. The 99% confidence interval (with $z_\alpha = \pm2.58$) will produce a wider confidence interval than the 95% level ($z_\alpha = \pm1.96$). Mathematically, this is because the 99% level's z score is larger and will therefore create a larger interval. Conceptually, this is an illustration of the trade-off between confidence and precision: A higher confidence level means a wider (i.e., less precise) interval.

2. a. $t = \pm2.228$
    b. $t = \pm1.725$
    c. $t = \pm2.660$

3. The reason that critical values of t change depending on sample size is that t is not a single, static curve like z is; instead, t is a family of curves that are taller and more normal shaped at larger sample sizes and smaller and flatter at smaller sample sizes.

4. Two options to shrink the interval and increase the precision of the estimate are (1) to reduce the confidence level and (2) to increase the sample size.

5. 99% CI: $.44 \leq P \leq .54$. The interval shrunk (became more precise) when the confidence level was reduced. This exemplifies the trade-off between confidence and precision.

Part III: Hypothesis Testing

1. a. ratio
    b. ordinal
    c. nominal
    d. ordinal
    e. nominal
    f. interval

Chapter 9

1. The probability of a coin flip resulting in heads is .50. Results of flips will vary.

2. Security level is the independent variable and assault rate is the dependent variable.

Chapter 10

1. Expected-frequency final answers should match Table 10.8.

2. The expected frequencies, from cell A to cell D, are 34.91, 19.09, 29.09, and 15.91. The obtained value of

chi-square is .10 + .19 + .13 + .23 = .65. The obtained value is smaller than the critical value (3.841), so the null is retained. This is the opposite of the conclusion reached in the chapter, where the obtained value exceeded the critical value and the null was rejected. This illustrates the sensitivity of chi-square tests to sample size.

Chapter 12

1. The final answers to all the elements of the F_{obt} calculations can only be positive because SS_T and SS_B formulas require squaring. This eliminates negative signs and ensures that the final answers will be positive.

2. In the first example, it was determined that juvenile defendants' attorney types (public, private, or assigned) did not significantly influence the jail sentences that these defendants received on conviction. Since the null was retained, omega squared would not be computed and post hoc tests would not be examined; all of these posttest procedures are appropriate only when the null is rejected.

Chapter 13

1. The reason why there will always be correspondence between the sign of the r value and the sign of the t statistic lies in the sampling distribution for r. The negative values of r are located on the left side of the sampling distribution (i.e., the negative side), and the positive values are on the right side (i.e., the positive side). Therefore, r and t will always have the same sign.

Chapter 14

1. You must first organize the x values in ascending order. Then they can be plotted along with their y counterparts.

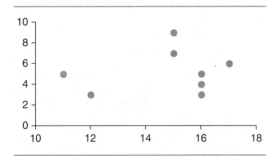

2. Using the formula $\hat{y} = .97 + .06x$, the predicted major disturbances are as follows: For $x = 0$, $\hat{y} = .97$; for $x = 10$, $\hat{y} = 1.57$; for $x = 20$, $\hat{y} = 2.17$; for $x = 46$, $\hat{y} = 3.73$; for $x = 50$, $\hat{y} = 3.97$; for $x = 70$, $\hat{y} = 5.17$; and for $x = 75$, $\hat{y} = 5.47$. Comparing these predicted values to the empirical values in Table 14.1, it appears that there is a close correspondence between the two. In other words, the formula seems to do a pretty good job predicting major disturbances on the basis of overcapacity counts.

3. The reason is that adding more variables to the model changes the estimation of the relationship between each IV and the DV. For example, a relationship that appears strong at the bivariate level can become weaker when more IVs are added. Multiple regression, unlike bivariate regression, estimates each IV's influence on the DV while controlling for the impact of other variables.

4. a. $\hat{y} = 7.10$
   b. $\hat{y} = 6.7$
   c. $\hat{y} = .68$
   d. $\hat{y} = 40.60$

Answers to Review Problems

Chapter 1

1. Science is a systematic and controlled way of gathering information about the world. Methods are integral to science because scientific results are only trustworthy when the procedures used to reach them are considered correct by others in the scientific community.

3. Samples are subsets of populations. Researchers draw samples because populations are too large to be studied directly. Samples are smaller and therefore more feasible to work with.

5. Hypothesis testing is used to test individual components of theories as a means of determining the validity of those theories. Samples are used to make inferences about populations. Evaluation research assesses the effectiveness of a program or intervention. People, places, or objects are measured before and after an intervention, or a control group is used for comparison to the treatment group. Exploratory research delves into new areas of study about which little is known. Hypotheses are generally not possible, as researchers usually do not have theory or prior evidence to guide them. Descriptive research analyzes a sample and provides basic information about those people, places, events, or objects. No inferences are made to the population.

7. Any three programs or policies; the correctness of students' responses is up to the instructor's judgment.

9. This would be descriptive research, because that type of research focuses solely on a sample rather than using a sample to draw conclusions about a population.

Chapter 2

1.
   a. education
   b. crime
   c. people

3.
   a. poverty
   b. violent crime
   c. neighborhoods

5.
   a. money spent on education, health, and welfare
   b. violent crime
   c. countries

7.
   a. police department location
   b. entry-level pay
   c. police departments

9. The researcher has failed to consider additional variables. A statistical relationship between ice cream and crime is not proof that one causes the other; one or more variables have been erroneously omitted from the analysis. In the present case, the missing variable is probably ambient temperature—both ice cream sales and crime might be higher in warmer months.

11.
   a. nominal
   b. interval (age is generally not considered to be ratio because everything that exists has some amount of age, so there is no true zero point)

c. nominal

d. ratio

e. ratio

f. ordinal

g. nominal

13.

a. The first would produce a ratio variable, the second would create an ordinal variable, and the third would make a nominal variable.

b. The phrasing that yields a ratio-level variable is best. Researchers who collect data should always use the highest level of measurement possible. Continuous variables can be made into categorical ones later on, but categorical data can never be made continuous.

15.

a. nominal

b. ratio

17.

a. victim advocacy (presence or absence of witness office)

b. nominal

c. sentencing (months of incarceration imposed)

d. ratio (the sample includes all offender in each court, not just those sentenced to prison, so there is a zero point)

e. courts

19.

a. homicide rate (homicides per population)

b. ratio

c. handgun ownership (own or not)

d. nominal

e. cities for homicide rates and people for gun ownership

Chapter 3

1.

a.

Charge	f	cf	p	cp	pct	$cpct$
Violent Offense	13,938	13,938	.25	.25	24.93	24.93
Property Offense	16,241	30,179	.29	.54	29.05	53.98
Drug Offense	18,220	48,399	.33	.87	32.59	86.57
Public-Order Offense	7,504	55,903	.13	1.00	13.42	99.99
	$N = 55,903$		1.00		99.99	

b. Since this variable is nominal, a pie chart or a bar graph would be appropriate. The pie chart requires percentages be used, whereas the bar graph can be percentages or frequencies. (Frequencies shown here.)

c.

Arrest Charge Among Convicted Felons

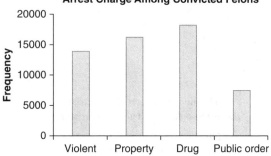

3.

a. The data are ratio, so a histogram is the correct chart type.

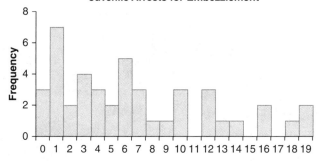

b. The range is 53 − 0 = 53. With 10 intervals,

the width of each would be $width = \dfrac{53}{10} = 5.30$.

Rounding to the nearest whole number, the width is 5.00.

Stated Class Limits	f
0–4	19
5–9	12
10–14	8
15–19	5
20–24	3

Stated Class Limits	f
25–29	0
30–34	0
35–39	1
40–44	1
45–49	0
50–54	1
	N = 50

c. Grouped data are technically ordinal, but the underlying scale is continuous and so a histogram is correct.

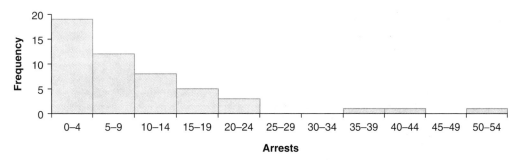

Number of Juvenile Arrests for Embezzlement

5. The line chart displays an upward trend, meaning that support has been increasing over time.

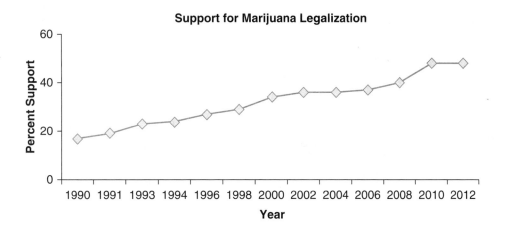

Support for Marijuana Legalization

7.

a.

City	Rate per 1,000
Birmingham, AL	15.18
Portland, ME	2.62
San Francisco, CA	7.04

City	Rate per 1,000
Tampa, FL	6.16
Ann Arbor, MI	1.97
Washington, DC	11.78

b. The variable *city* is nominal and rates cannot be used for pie charts, so a bar graph is correct.

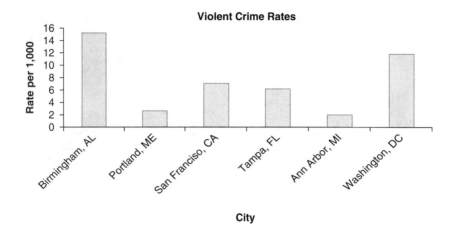

Violent Crime Rates

9.

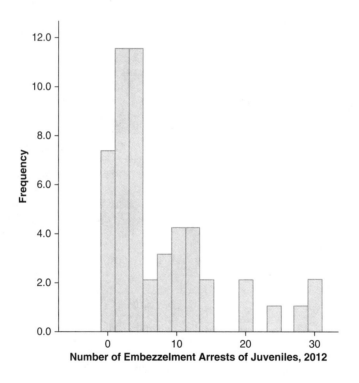

11. [No answer; SPSS exercise]

13. The variable is nominal, so a pie chart (percentages) or bar chart (percentages or frequencies) can be used.

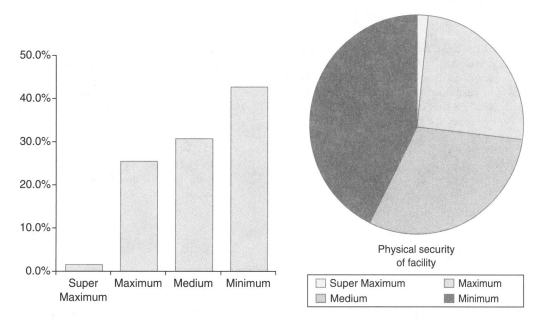

Gender of inmates facility is authorized to house * Does facility operate a work-release program? Crosstabulation			Does facility operate a work-release program?		Total
			Yes	No	
Gender of inmates facility is authorized to house	Male	Count	200	866	1066
		% within Gender of inmates facility is authorized to house	18.8%	81.2%	100.0%
	Female	Count	41	87	128
		% within Gender of inmates facility is authorized to house	32.0%	68.0%	100.0%
	Both	Count	44	49	93
		% within Gender of inmates facility is authorized to house	47.3%	52.7%	100.0%
Total		Count	285	1002	1287
		% within Gender of inmates facility is authorized to house	22.1%	77.9%	100.0%

Chapter 4

● ●

Note: Rounding, where applicable, is to two decimal places in each step of calculations and in the final answer.

1.
a. ratio
b. mode, median, mean

3.

a. nominal

b. mode

5. The mean is the midpoint of the magnitudes because it is the value that perfectly balances the deviation scores. Deviation scores are produced by subtracting the mean from each raw score; deviation scores measure the distance between raw scores and the mean. They always sum to zero.

7. c

9. a

11.

a. nominal; mode

b. mode = acquaintance

13.

a.

1. rank order: 170, 176, 211, 219, 220, 258, 317, 345

2. $MP = (8 + 1)/2 = 4.5$

3. $md = (219 + 220)/2 = 439/2 = 219.5$

b. mean = $(317 + 170 + 211 + 258 + 219 + 345 + 176 + 220)/8 = 1916/8 = 239.5$

15.

a. mean = $((0 \cdot 7) + (1 \cdot 7) + (2 \cdot 4) + (3 \cdot 7) + (4 \cdot 4) + (5 \cdot 1) + (6 \cdot 1) + (8 \cdot 3) + (9 \cdot 2) + (10 \cdot 2) + (11 \cdot 1) + (12 \cdot 3) + (13 \cdot 1) + (14 \cdot 1) + (19 \cdot 1) + (20 \cdot 1) + (23 \cdot 1) + (27 \cdot 1) + (29 \cdot 1) + (30 \cdot 1))/50 = (0 + 7 + 8 + 21 + 16 + 5 + 6 + 24 + 18 + 20 + 11 + 36 + 13 + 14 + 19 + 20 + 23 + 27 + 29 + 30)/50 = 347/50 = 6.94$

b. The mean (6.94) is greater than the median (3.50), so this distribution is positively skewed.

17.

a. $md = 15$

b. mean = $(13 + 9 + 32 + 23 + 17 + 15 + 8)/7 = 117/7 = 16.71$

c. Alaska = $13 - 16.71 = -3.71$; Arkansas = $9 - 16.71 = -7.71$; Connecticut = $32 - 16.71 = 15.29$; Kansas = $23 - 16.71 = 6.29$; Montana = $17 - 16.71 = .29$; South Dakota = $15 - 16.71 = -1.71$; Vermont = $8 - 16.71 = -8.71$; sum = .03

19. smallest mode = 5; median = 5.60; mean = 6.21

Chapter 5

• •

Note: Rounding, where applicable, is to two decimal places in each step of calculations and in the final answer. For numbers close to zero, decimals are extended to the first nonzero number.

1. Measures of central tendency offer information about the middle of the distribution (i.e., where scores tend to cluster), but they do not provide a picture of the amount of variability present in the data. Measures of dispersion show whether the data cluster around the mean or whether they are very spread out.

3. two-thirds

5. $VR = 1 - (969/1821) = 1 - .53 = .47$

7. $VR = 1 - (3131/4364) = 1 - .72 = .18$

9.

a. $R = 139 - 3 = 136$

b. mean = $(12 + 9 + 47 + 11 + 139 + 3)/6 = 221/6 = 36.83$

c. variance = $13744.84/(6 - 1) = 2748.97$

d. $sd = \sqrt{2748.97} = 52.43$

11.

a. $R = 15.80 - 10.00 = 5.80$

b. mean = (12.60 + 16.60 + 10.00 + 12.20 + 15.80 + 13.20 + 10.40 + 10.20 + 11.80)/9 = 112.80/9 = 12.53

c. variance = 44.72/(9 − 1) = 5.59

d. $sd = \sqrt{5.59} = 2.36$

13.

a. 63.10 + 18.97 = 82.07 and 63.10 − 18.97 = 44.13

b. 1.75 + .35 = 2.10 and 1.75 − .35 = 1.40

Chapter 6

Note: Rounding, where applicable, is to two decimal places in each step of calculations and in the final answer. For numbers close to zero, decimals are extended to the first nonzero number. Areas are reported using all four decimal places.

1.

a. N = 8

b. r = 2

c. 28

3.

a. N = 7

b. r = 3

c. 35

5.

a. N = 8

b. r = 4

c. 70

7.

a. standard normal

b. standard normal

c. binomial

c. 450.62 + 36.48 = 487.10 and 450.62 − 36.48 = 414.14

15. The standard deviation is the mean of the deviation scores. It represents the mean distance between the mean and the individual raw scores.

17. range = 42; variance = 67.15; standard deviation = 8.19

19. range = 64585; variance = 12294723.87; standard deviation = 3506.38

9.

a. With $p = .62$, $q = .38$, and $N = 6$: $p(0) = .003$; $p(1) = .04$; $p(2) = .11$; $p(3) = .24$; $p(4) = .32$; $p(5) = .21$; $p(6) = .06$

b. $r = 4$, or 4 of the 6 charges would be for assault

c. $r = 0$, or none of the 6 charges would be for assault

d. $p(2) + p(1) + p(0) = .11 + .04 + .003 = .15$

e. $p(5) + p(6) = .21 + .06 = .27$

11.

a. With $p = .61$, $q = .39$, and $N = 5$: $p(0) = .01$; $p(1) = .06$; $p(2) = .22$; $p(3) = .35$; $p(4) = .27$; $p(5) = .08$

b. $r = 3$, or 3 of the 5 murders committed with firearms

c. $r = 0$, or none of the 5 murders committed with firearms

d. $p(1) + p(0) = .06 + .01 = .07$

e. $p(4) + p(5) = .27 + .08 = .35$

13.

a. $z_{4.28} = (4.28 − 1.99)/.84 = 2.29/.84 = 2.73$

b. area between the mean and $z = 2.73$ is .4968

c. area in the tail beyond the mean and $z = 2.73$ is .50 − .4968 = .0032

15.

    a. $z_{1.29} = (1.29 - 1.99)/.84 = -.70/.84 = -.83$

    b. area between the mean and $z = -.83$ is .2967

    c. area in the tail beyond the mean and $z = -.83$ is
       $.50 - .2967 = .2033$

17. $.50 - .03 = .47$. The closest area on the table is .4699, which corresponds to a z score of 1.88. This is the upper tail, so $z = 1.88$.

19. $.50 - .10 = .40$. The closest area on the table is .3997, which corresponds to a z score of 1.28. This is the lower tail, so $z = -1.28$.

Chapter 7

. . . .

1. a

3. b

5. sampling

7. b

9. z

11. a

13. c

15. b

Chapter 8

. . . .

Note: Rounding, where applicable, is to two decimal places in each step of calculations and in the final answer. Calculation steps are identical to those in the text. For numbers close to zero, decimals are extended to the first nonzero number.

1. At least 100

3. The z distribution

5. The z distribution (or standard normal curve) is fixed; it cannot change shape to accommodate small samples. Small samples violate the assumption that the scores are perfectly normally distributed, so z cannot be used in these instances.

7. $df = 17$, $t = \pm 2.110$.

$$CI = 13.00 \pm 2.110 \left(\frac{12.10}{\sqrt{18-1}} \right)$$

$$= 13.00 \pm 2.110 \left(\frac{12.10}{4.12} \right)$$

$$= 13.00 \pm 2.110 (2.94)$$

$$= 13.00 \pm 6.20$$

95% CI: $6.80 \leq \mu \leq 19.20$

There is a 95% chance that the interval 6.80 to 19.20, inclusive, contains the population mean.

9. $z = 1.96$.

$$CI = 1.14 \pm 1.96 \left(\frac{.36}{\sqrt{2033-1}} \right)$$

$$= 1.14 \pm 1.96 \left(\frac{.36}{45.08} \right)$$

$$= 1.14 \pm 1.96 (.01)$$

$$= 1.14 \pm .02$$

95% CI: $1.12 \leq \mu \leq 1.16$

There is a 95% chance that the interval 1.11 to 1.17, inclusive, contains the population mean.

11. $z = 2.58$

$$CI = 3.06 \pm 2.58 \left(\frac{2.62}{\sqrt{707-1}} \right)$$

$$= 3.06 \pm 2.58 \left(\frac{2.62}{26.57} \right)$$

$$= 3.06 \pm 2.58 (.10)$$

$$= 3.06 \pm .26$$

99% CI: $2.80 \leq \mu \leq 3.32$

There is a 99% chance that the interval 2.80 to 3.32, inclusive, contains the population mean.

13. $df = 22$, $t = \pm 2.819$

$$CI = 3.30 \pm 2.819\left(\frac{2.24}{\sqrt{23-1}}\right)$$

$$= 3.30 \pm 2.819\left(\frac{2.24}{4.69}\right)$$

$$= 3.30 \pm 2.819(.48)$$

$$= 3.30 \pm 1.35$$

99% CI: $1.95 \leq \mu \leq 4.65$

There is a 99% chance that the interval 1.95 to 4.65, inclusive, contains the population mean.

15. $z = 1.96$

$$CI = .34 \pm 1.96\sqrt{\frac{.34(1-.34)}{1281}}$$

$$= .34 \pm 1.96\sqrt{\frac{.22}{1281}}$$

$$= .34 \pm 1.96\sqrt{.0002}$$

$$= .34 \pm 1.96(.01)$$

$$= .34 \pm .02$$

95% CI: $.34 \leq \mu \leq .36$
There is a 95% chance that the interval .34 to .36, inclusive, contains the population mean.

17. $z = 1.96$

$$CI = .31 \pm 1.96\sqrt{\frac{.31(1-.31)}{1967}}$$

$$= .31 \pm 1.96\sqrt{\frac{.21}{1967}}$$

$$= .31 \pm 1.96\sqrt{.0001}$$

$$= .31 \pm 1.96(.01)$$

$$= .31 \pm .02$$

95% CI: $.29 \leq \mu \leq .33$
There is a 95% chance that the interval .29 to .33, inclusive, contains the population mean.

19. $z = 1.96$

$$CI = .29 \pm 1.96\sqrt{\frac{.29(1-.29)}{295}}$$

$$= .29 \pm 1.96\sqrt{\frac{.21}{295}}$$

$$= .29 \pm 1.96\sqrt{.001}$$

$$= .29 \pm 1.96(.03)$$

$$= .29 \pm .06$$

95% CI: $.23 \leq \mu \leq .35$
There is a 95% chance that the interval .23 to .35, inclusive, contains the population mean.

Chapter 9

1. One possible explanation for the difference is sampling error. There might have been males with unusually long sentences, or females with atypically short sentences, and these extreme values might have pulled males' mean upward, females' mean downward, or both. The other possible explanation is that men truly are given longer sentences than women, on average. It could be that there is a real difference between the two population's means.

3. The symbol is H_1 and it predicts that there is a difference between populations; in other words,

it predicts that the observed differences between two or more samples' statistics reflects a genuine difference in the population.

5. A Type I error is the erroneous rejection of a true null (also called false positive). This occurs when a researcher concludes that two or more variables are related when, in fact, they are not.

7. Reducing the likelihood of one type of error increases the probability that the other one will occur. Preventing a Type I error requires increasing

the amount of evidence needed to reject the null, which raises the chances that a false null will not be rejected as it should be (Type II error). Preventing a Type II error requires a reduction in the amount of evidence needed to reject the null, thus increasing the probability that a true null will be wrongly rejected (Type I error).

9.

Step 1: State the null (N_0) and alternative (N_1) hypotheses. These are the competing predictions about whether or not there is a true difference between population values.

Step 2: Identify the distribution and calculate the degrees of freedom. Each type of statistical test utilizes a particular sampling distribution, so the correct one (and correct table) must be identified at the outset. With the exception of the z distribution, sampling distributions are families of curves and the degrees of freedom determine the shape of the curve that will be used.

Step 3: Identify the critical value of the test statistic and state the decision rule. The critical value is located by using the table associated with the selected distribution. The decision rule states what the

obtained value (calculated in Step 4) must be in order for the null to be rejected.

Step 4: Calculate the obtained value of the test statistic. This is the mathematical part of the test. Sample means, proportions, standard deviations, and sizes are entered into formulas, which are then solved to produce the obtained value.

Step 5: Make a decision about the null and state the substantive conclusion. In this final step, the obtained value is evaluated according to the decision rule (Step 3). If the criteria are met, the null is rejected; if they are not, it is retained. The substantive conclusion is the interpretation of the statistical outcome in the context of the specific variables and samples being analyzed.

11.

   a. True effect. Events with low probabilities are atypical. They are unlikely to occur by chance alone.

   b. Reject

13. b (categorical IV with two classes and continuous DV)

15. d (continuous IV and continuous DV)

17. a (categorical IV and categorical DV)

Chapter 10

Note: Rounding, where applicable, is to two decimal places in each step of calculations and in the final answer. For numbers close to zero, decimals are extended to the first nonzero number. Calculation steps are identical to those in the text; using alternative sequences of steps might result in answers different from those presented here. These differences might or might not alter the final decision regarding the null.

1. Yes. The IV and the DV are both categorical, so chi-square can be used.

3. No. The IV is categorical, but the DV is continuous, so chi-square cannot be used.

5.

   a. The IV is gender and the DV is sentence received.

   b. Both are nominal.

   c. Two rows and three columns

7.

   a. The IV is crime type and the DV is sentence length.

   b. The IV is nominal and the DV is ordinal.

   c. Three rows and three columns

9. Step 1: $H_0: \chi^2 = 0; H_1: \chi^2 > 0$

   Step 2: χ^2 distribution with $df = (2 - 1)(2 - 1) = 1$

   Step 3: $\chi^2_{crit} = 6.635$. Decision rule: If $\chi^2_{obt} > 6.635$, the null will be rejected.

Step 4: Expected frequencies are 22.33 for cell A, 27.67 for B, 44.67 for C, and 55.33 for D. χ^2_{obt} = 15.61 + 12.60 + 7.80 + 6.30 + 42.31 = 42.31

Step 5: The obtained value is greater than 6.635, so the null is rejected. There is a relationship between whether or not a prison offers college courses and whether it offers vocational training. Row percentages can be used to show that 82% of prisons that offer college also offer vocational training, and 74% of those that do not offer college also do not provide vocational training. It appears that most prisons provide either both of these services or neither of them; relatively few provide only one.

11. Step 1: H_0: $\chi^2 = 0$; H_1: $\chi^2 > 0$

Step 2: χ^2 distribution with $df = (2 - 1)(2 - 1) = 1$

Step 3: $\chi^2_{crit} = 3.841$. Decision rule: If $\chi^2_{obt} > 3.841$, the null will be rejected.

Step 4: Expected frequencies are 68.05 for cell A, 86.95 for B, 21.95 for C, and 28.05 for D. χ^2_{obt} = 3.79 + 2.96 + 11.74 + 9.18 = 27.67

Step 5: The obtained value is greater than 3.841, so the null is rejected. There is a relationship between facility type and the provision of vocational training. Row percentages show that 66% of publicly operated prisons, but just 24% of privately run facilities, offer vocational training, so private prisons are significantly less likely to provide this service to inmates.

13. Step 1: H_0: $\chi^2 = 0$; H_1: $\chi^2 > 0$

Step 2: χ^2 distribution with $df = (2 - 1)(2 - 1) = 1$

Step 3: $\chi^2_{crit} = 3.841$. Decision rule: If $\chi^2_{obt} > 3.841$, the null will be rejected.

Step 4: Expected frequencies are 30.05 for cell A, 40.95 for B, 49.95 for C, and 68.05 for D. χ^2_{obt} = 2.10 + 1.54 + 1.27 + .93 = 5.84.

Step 5: The obtained value is greater than 3.841, so the null is rejected. There is a relationship between gender and support for marijuana legalization among black Americans. Looking at row percentages, 54% of men but only 36% of women believe that marijuana should be made legal.

There appears to be more support for legalization by men than by women.

15. Step 1: H_0: $\chi^2 = 0$; H_1: $\chi^2 > 0$

Step 2: χ^2 distribution with $df = (3 - 1)(3 - 1) = 4$

Step 3: $\chi^2_{crit} = 13.277$. Decision rule: If $\chi^2_{obt} > 13.277$, the null will be rejected.

Step 4: Expected frequencies are 315.90 for cell A, 42.69 for B, 13.42 for C, 200.41 for D, 27.08 for E, 8.51 for F, 260.70 for G, 35.23 for H, and 11.07 for I. χ^2_{obt} = .003 + .01+ .19 + .10 + .57 + .03 + .11 + .30 + .39 = 1.70

Step 5: The obtained value is less than 13.277, so the null is retained. There is no relationship between annual income and the frequency of contact with police. Row percentages show that 85% of people in the lowest-income category, 83% of those in the middle-income category, and 87% of those in the highest-income group had between zero and two recent contacts. The vast majority of people have very few annual contacts with officers, irrespective of their income.

17.

a. The SPSS output shows $\chi^2_{obt} = 4.314$.

b. The null is retained at an alpha of .05 because $p = .116$, and $.116 > .05$.

c. There is no relationship between the gender of inmates institutions are authorized to house and whether those institutions offer adult basic education. Asking SPSS for row percentages shows that the majority of all three kinds of institutions offer adult basic education, irrespective of the gender of the inmates the facility houses (73.7%, 84.1%, and 64.1%).

d. The null was retained, so measures of association cannot be computed.

19.

a. The SPSS output shows $\chi^2_{obt} = 25.759$.

b. The null is rejected at an alpha of .05 because $p = .003$, and $.003 < .05$.

c. There is a relationship between race and perceived stop legitimacy. Asking SPSS for row percentages shows that 84.4% of white drivers, 71.3% of black drivers, and 85.5% of drivers of other races thought the stop was for a legitimate reason. Black drivers appear to stand out from nonblack drivers in that they are less likely to believe their stop was legitimate.

d. The null was rejected, so measures of association can be examined. Since both variables are nominal and there is a clear independent

and dependent designation, Cramer's V and lambda are both available. The SPSS output shows that lambda = .000, meaning that the relationship between race and stop legitimacy, while statistically significant, is substantively meaningless. Cramer's V = .107, also signaling a very weak relationship. This makes sense looking at the percentages from Part C. A clear majority of all drivers believed their stop was for a legitimate reasons. Black drivers deviated somewhat, but a large majority still endorsed stop legitimacy.

Chapter 11

Note: Rounding, where applicable, is to two decimal places in each step of calculations and in the final answer. For numbers close to zero, decimals are extended to the first nonzero number. Calculation steps are identical to those in the text; using alternative sequences of steps might result in answers different from those presented here. These differences might or might not alter the final decision regarding the null.

1.

   a. whether the defendant plead guilty or went to trial

   b. nominal

   c. sentence

   d. ratio (there is no indication that the sample was narrowed only to those who were incarcerated, so theoretically, zeroes are possible)

3.

   a. judge gender

   b. nominal

   c. sentence severity

   d. ratio

5. a

7. a

9. $t; z$

11. b

13. Step 1: $H_0: \mu_1 = \mu_2$; $H_0: \mu_1 \neq \mu_2$ (*Note:* No direction of the difference was specified, so the alternative is $\neq$.)

Step 2: t distribution with $df = 155 + 463 - 2 = 616$

Step 3: $t_{crit} = \pm 1.960$ (± 1.980 would also be acceptable). The decision rule is that if t_{obt} is greater than 1.960 or less than -1.960, the null will be rejected.

Step 4:

$$\hat{\sigma}_{\bar{x}_1 + \bar{x}_2} = \sqrt{\frac{15.40 + 50.82}{616}} \sqrt{\frac{618}{71765}}$$
$$= \sqrt{.11}\sqrt{.01} = .33(.10) = .03, \text{ and}$$

$$t_{obt} = \frac{-.01}{.03} = -.33$$

Step 5: Since t_{obt} is not greater than 1.960 or less than -1.960, the null is retained. There is no difference between MHOs and SHOs in the diversity of the crimes they commit. In other words, there does not appear to be a relationship between offenders' status as MHOs or SHOs and the variability in their criminal activity.

15. Step 1: $H_0: \mu_1 = \mu_2$; $H_0: \mu_1 < \mu_2$

Step 2: t distribution with

$$df = \frac{(187.77 + 29.17)^2}{35257.57(.01) + 850.89(.001)} - 2$$
$$= \frac{47062.96}{352.58 + .85} - 2$$
$$= 131.16$$

Step 3: $t_{crit} = -1.658$ (−1.645 would also be acceptable). The decision rule is that if t_{obt} is less than −1.658, the null will be rejected.

Step 4: $\sigma_{\bar{x}_1 - \bar{x}_2} = 14.73$ and $t_{obt} = -1.79$

Step 5: Since t_{obt} is less than −1.658, the null is rejected. Juveniles younger than 16 at the time of arrest received significantly shorter mean jail sentences relative to juveniles who were older than 16 at arrest. In other words, there appears to be a relationship between age at arrest and sentence severity for juveniles transferred to adult court.

17. **Step 1:** $H_0: \mu_1 = \mu_2; H_0: \mu_1 > \mu_2$

Step 2: t distribution with $df = 160 + 181 - 2 = 339$

Step 3: $t_{crit} = \pm 1.960$ (± 1.980 would also be acceptable). The decision rule is that if t_{obt} is greater than 1.960 or less than −1.960, the null will be rejected.

Step 4:

$$\hat{\sigma}_{\bar{x}_1 + \bar{x}_2} = \sqrt{\frac{119777854.56 + 11422557}{339}} \sqrt{\frac{341}{28960}}$$

$$= \sqrt{387021.86}\sqrt{.01} = 622.11(.10) = 62.21, \text{ and}$$

$$t_{obt} = \frac{329.87}{62.21} = 5.30$$

Step 5: Since t_{obt} is greater than 1.960, the null is rejected. There is a statistically significant difference between property and drug offenders' mean fines. In other words, there does not appear to be a relationship between crime type and fine amount.

19. **Step 1:** $H_0: \mu_1 = \mu_2; H_0: \mu_1 \neq \mu_2$

Step 2: t distribution with $df = 5 - 1 = 4$

Step 3: $t_{crit} = \pm 2.776$. The decision rule is that if t_{obt} is greater than 2.776 or less than −2.776, the null will be rejected.

Step 4:

$$\bar{x}_D = .34; s_D = \sqrt{\frac{.30}{4}} = \sqrt{.08} = .28;$$

$$\hat{\sigma}_{\bar{x}_1 - \bar{x}_2} = \frac{.28}{\sqrt{5}} = \frac{.28}{2.24} = .13; \text{ and}$$

$$t_{obt} = \frac{.34}{.13} = 2.62$$

Step 5: Since t_{obt} is not greater than 2.776 or less than −2.776, the null is retained. There is no difference between states with high and low arrest rates in terms of officer assault. In other words, there does not appear to be a relationship between arrest rates and officer assaults.

21. **Step 1:** $H_0: P_1 = P_2; H_0: P_1 \neq P_2$

Step 2: z distribution

Step 3: $z_{crit} = \pm 1.96$ (recall that $.50 - .025 = .475$). The decision rule is that if z_{obt} is less than −1.96 or greater than 1.96, the null will be rejected.

Step 4:

$$\hat{p} = \frac{325.76 + 23.36}{582} = \frac{349.12}{582} = .60;$$

$$\hat{q} = .40, \hat{\sigma}_{\hat{p}_1 - \hat{p}_2} = \sqrt{.60(.40)}\sqrt{\frac{582}{37157}}$$

$$= \sqrt{.24}\sqrt{.02} = (.49)(.14) = .07; \text{ and}$$

$$z_{obt} = \frac{.32}{.07} = 4.57$$

Step 5: Since z_{obt} is greater than 1.96, the null is rejected. There is a significant difference between juveniles represented by public attorneys and those represented by private counsel in terms of the time it takes for their cases to reach disposition. In other words, there appears to be a relationship between attorney type and time-to-disposition among juvenile drug defendants.

23.

a. Equal/pooled variances. Levene's $F = 2.810$ with a p value of .095. Since $.095 > .05$, the F statistic is not significant at alpha = .05 (i.e., the null of equal variances is retained).

b. $t_{obt} = .977$

c. No. The p value for t_{obt} is .330, which well exceeds .01; therefore, the null is retained.

d. There is no statistically significant difference between daytime and nighttime stops in terms of duration. That is, there seems to be no relationship between whether a stop takes place at day or night and the length of time the stop lasts.

25.

a. Unequal/separate variances. Levene's $F = 36.062$ with a p value of .000. Since $.000 < .05$, the F statistic is significant at alpha = .05 (i.e., the null of equal variances is rejected).

b. $t_{obt} = 8.095$

c. Yes. The p value for t_{obt} is .000, which is less than .01; therefore, the null is retained.

d. There is a statistically significant difference between prosecutors' offices that do and do not use DNA in plea negotiations and trials in the total number of felony convictions obtained each year. In other words, there is a relationship between DNA usage and total felony convictions. (Though one would suspect, of course, that this relationship is spurious and attributable to the fact that larger prosecutors' offices process more cases and are more likely to use DNA as compared to smaller offices.)

Chapter 12

. . . .

Note: Rounding, where applicable, is to two decimal places in each step of calculations and in the final answer. For numbers close to zero, decimals are extended to the first nonzero number. Calculation steps are identical to those in the text; using alternative sequences of steps might result in answers different from those presented here. These differences might or might not alter the final decision regarding the null.

1.

a. judges' gender

b. nominal

c. sentence severity

d. ratio

e. independent-samples t test

3.

a. arrest

b. nominal

c. recidivism

d. ratio

e. ANOVA

5.

a. poverty

b. ordinal

c. crime rate

d. ratio

e. ANOVA

7. Within-groups variance measures the amount of variability present among different members of the same group. This type of variance is akin to white noise; it is the random fluctuations inevitably present in any group of people, objects, or places. Between-groups variance measures the extent to which groups differ from one another. This type of variance conveys information about whether or not there are actual differences between groups.

9. The F statistic can never be negative because it is a measure of variance and variance cannot be negative. Mathematically, variance is a squared measure; all negative numbers are squared during the course of calculations. The final result, then, is always positive.

11. Step 1: $H_0: \mu_1 = \mu_2 = \mu_3$ and H_0: some $\mu_i \neq$ some μ_j

Step 2: F distribution with $df_B = 3 - 1 = 2$ and $df_W = 21 - 3 = 18$

Step 3: $F_{crit} = 3.55$ and the decision rule is that if F_{obt} is greater than 3.55, the null will be rejected.

Step 4: $SS_T = (206 + 1240 + 11) - \dfrac{(20 + 68 + 5)^2}{21}$

$= 1457 - 411.86;$

$= 1045.14$

$SS_B = 7(2.86 - 4.43)^2 + 7(9.71 - 4.43)^2 + 7(.71 - 4.43)^2 = 7(2.46) + 7(27.88) + 7(13.84) = 309.26; SS_w = 1045.14 - 309.26 = 735.88;$

$MS_B = \dfrac{309.26}{2} = 154.63$

$MS_W = \dfrac{735.88}{18} = 40.88$

$F_{obt} = \dfrac{154.63}{40.88} = 3.78$

Step 5: Since F_{obt} is greater than 3.55, the null is rejected. There is a statistically significant difference in the number of wiretaps authorized per crime type. In other words, wiretaps vary significantly across crime types. Since the null was rejected, it is appropriate to examine

omega squared: $\omega^2 = \dfrac{309.26 - 2(40.88)}{40.88 + 1045.14} = .21.$

This means that 21% of the variance in wiretap authorizations is attributable to crime type.

13. **Step 1:** $H_0: \mu_1 = \mu_2 = \mu_3 = \mu_4$ and $H_0:$ some $\mu_i \ne$ some μ_j

Step 2: F distribution with $df_B = 4 - 1 = 3$ and $df_W = 23 - 4 = 19$

Step 3: $F_{crit} = 5.01$ and the decision rule is that if F_{obt} is greater than 5.01, the null will be rejected.

Step 4: $SS_T = (9.99 + 58.35 + 42.15 + 91.04)$

$- \dfrac{(5.17 + 15.12 + 14.27 + 23.46)^2}{23}$

$= 201.53 - 146.36 = 55.17;$

$SS_B = 5(1.03 - 2.52)^2 + 6(2.52 - 2.52)^2 + 5(2.85 - 2.52)^2 + 7(3.35 - 2.52)^2 = 5(2.22) + 6(0) + 5(.11) + 7(.69) = 16.48; SS_w = 55.17 - 16.48 = 38.69$

$MS_B = \dfrac{16.48}{3} = 5.49$

$MS_W = \dfrac{38.69}{19} = 2.04$

$F_{obt} = \dfrac{5.49}{2.04} = 2.69$

Step 5: Since F_{obt} is less than 5.01, the null is retained. There are no statistically significant differences between regions in terms of the percentage of officer assaults committed with firearms. In other words, there is no apparent relationship between region and firearm involvement in officer assaults. Since the null was retained, it is not appropriate to calculate omega squared.

15. **Step 1:** $H_0: \mu_1 = \mu_2 = \mu_3 = \mu_4$ and $H_0:$ some $\mu_i \ne$ some μ_j

Step 2: F distribution with $df_B = 4 - 1 = 3$ and $df_W = 20 - 4 = 16$

Step 3: $F_{crit} = 5.29$ and the decision rule is that if F_{obt} is greater than 5.29, the null will be rejected.

Step 4:

$SS_T = (1070 + 5468 + 949 + 508)$

$- \dfrac{(70 + 102 + 53 + 38)^2}{20}$

$= 7995 - 3458.45$

$= 4536.55$

$SS_B = 6(11.67 - 13.15)^2 + 5(20.40 - 13.15)^2 + 5(10.60 - 13.15)^2 + 4(9.50 - 13.15)^2 = 6(2.19) + 5(52.56) + 5(6.50) + 4(13.32) = 361.72; SS_w = 4536.55 - 361.72 = 4174.83$

$MS_B = \dfrac{361.72}{3} = 120.57$

$MS_W = \dfrac{4174.83}{16} = 260.93$

$F_{obt} = \dfrac{120.57}{260.93} = .46$

Step 5: Since F_{obt} is less than 5.29, the null is retained. There are no statistically significant differences between juveniles of different races in the length of probation sentences they receive. In other words, there is no apparent relationship between race and probation sentences among juvenile property offenders. Since the null was retained, it is not appropriate to calculate omega squared.

17. **Step 1:** $H_0: \mu_1 = \mu_2 = \mu_3$ and $H_0:$ some $\mu_i \neq$ some μ_j

Step 2: F distribution with $df_B = 3 - 1 = 2$ and $df_W = 30 - 3 = 27$

Step 3: $F_{crit} = 5.49$ and the decision rule is that if F_{obt} is greater than 5.49, the null will be rejected.

Step 4:

$$SS_T = \left(290.17 + 27.19 + 46.23\right)$$
$$- \frac{\left(40.63 + 11.34 + 11.31\right)^2}{30}$$
$$= 363.59 - 133.48 = 230.11;$$

$SS_B = 9(4.51 - 2.11)^2 + 10(1.13 - 2.11)^2 + 11(1.03 - 2.11)^2 = 9(5.76) + 10(.96) + 11(1.17) = 74.31;$

$SS_W = 230.11 - 74.31 = 155.80;$

$$MS_B = \frac{74.31}{2} = 37.16;$$

$$MS_W = \frac{155.80}{27} = 5.77;$$

$$F_{obt} = \frac{37.16}{5.77} = 6.44$$

Step 5: Since F_{obt} is greater than 5.49, the null is rejected. There is a statistically significant difference in prisons' assault rates depending on facility gender. In other words, assault rates vary significantly across facilities that house males only,

females only, or both. Since the null was rejected, it is appropriate to examine omega squared:

$$\omega^2 = \frac{74.31 - 2(5.77)}{5.77 + 230.11} = .27. \text{ This means}$$

that 27% of the variance in assault rates is attributable to facility gender.

19.

a. $F_{obt} = 9.631$

b. Yes. The p value is .000, which is less than .01, so the null is rejected.

c. Among juvenile property defendants, there are significant differences between different racial groups in the amount of time it takes to acquire pretrial release. In other words, there is a relationship between race and time-to-release.

d. Since the null was rejected, post hoc tests can be examined. Tukey and Bonferroni post hoc tests show that there is one difference, and it lies between black and white youth. Group means reveal that black youths' mean time-to-release is 40.36 and white youths' is 20.80. Hispanics, with a mean of 30.30, appear to fall in the middle and are not significantly different from either of the other groups.

e. Since the null was rejected, it is correct to calculate omega squared:

$$\omega^2 = \frac{49125.707 - 2(2550.431)}{2550.431 + 1599787.836} = .027.$$ Only

about 2.7% of the variance in time-to-release is attributable to race. (This means that important variables are missing! Knowing, for instance, juveniles' offense types and prior records would likely improve our understanding of the timing of their release.)

Chapter 13

· ·

Note: Rounding, where applicable, is to two decimal places in each step of calculations and in the final answer. For numbers close to zero, decimals are extended to the first nonzero number. Calculation steps are identical to those in the text; using alternative sequences of steps might result in answers different from those presented here. These differences might or might not alter the final decision regarding the null.

1.

   a. parental incarceration

   b. nominal

   c. lifetime incarceration

   d. nominal

   e. chi-square

3.

   a. participation in community meetings

   b. nominal

   c. self-protective measures

   d. nominal (taking the proportion turns self-protective measures into a binary measure)

   e. two-population z test for a difference between proportions

5. A linear relationship is one in which a single-unit increase in the independent variable is associated with a constant change in the dependent variable. In other words, the magnitude and the direction of the relationship remain constant across all levels of the independent variable. When graphed, the IV-DV overlap appears as a straight line.

7. The line of best fit is the line that minimizes the distance from that line to each of the raw values in the data set. That is, it is the line that produces the smallest deviation scores (or error). No other line would come closer to all of the data points in the sample.

9. c

11. <u>Step 1</u>: $H_0: \rho = 0$ and $H_1: \rho \neq 0$

    <u>Step 2</u>: t distribution with $df = 5 - 2 = 3$

    <u>Step 3</u>: $t_{crit} = \pm 3.182$ and the decision rule is: If t_{crit} is greater than 3.182 for less than −3.182, the null will be rejected.

    <u>Step 4</u>:

$$r = \frac{5(2156.03) - 528(17.33)}{\sqrt{\left[5(69914) - 528^2\right]\left[5(7615) - 17.33\right]}}$$

$$= \frac{10780.15 - 9150.24}{\sqrt{[349570 - 278784][380.75 - 300.33]}}$$

$$= \frac{1629.91}{\sqrt{5692610.12}} = .68$$

$$t_{obt} = .68\sqrt{\frac{5 - 2}{1 - .68^2}} = .68\sqrt{\frac{3}{.54}} = .68(2.36) = 1.60$$

<u>Step 5</u>: Since t_{obt} is not greater than 3.182, the null is retained. There is no correlation between prison expenditures and violent crime rates. In other words, prison expenditures do not appear to impact violent crime rates. As the null was retained, it is not appropriate to examine the sign, the magnitude, or the coefficient of determination.

13. <u>Step 1</u>: $H_0: \rho = 0$ and $H_1: \rho > 0$

    <u>Step 2</u>: t distribution with $df = 9 - 2 = 7$

    <u>Step 3</u>: $t_{crit} = 1.895$ and the decision rule is that if t_{crit} is greater than 1.895, the null will be rejected.

    <u>Step 4</u>:

$$r = \frac{9(202.05) - 27.80(53.90)}{\sqrt{\left[9(136.34) - 27.80^2\right]\left[9(367.91) - 53.90^2\right]}}$$

$$= \frac{1818.45 - 1498.42}{\sqrt{[1227.06 - 772.84][3311.19 - 2905.21]}}$$

$$= \frac{320.03}{\sqrt{184404.24}} = .75$$

$$t_{obt} = .75\sqrt{\frac{9 - 2}{1 - .75^2}} = .75\sqrt{\frac{7}{.44}}$$

$$= .75(15.91) = 11.93$$

<u>Step 5</u>: Since t_{obt} is greater than 1.895, the null is rejected. There is a positive correlation between crime concentration and concentration of police agencies. In other words, where there is more crime, there also appears to be more police agencies. Since the null was rejected, the sign, the magnitude, and the coefficient of determination can be examined. The sign is positive, meaning that a one-unit increase in the IV is associated with an increase in the DV. The magnitude is very strong, judging by the guidelines offered in the text (where values between 0 and ±.29 are weak, from about ±.30 to ±.49 are moderate, ±.50 to ±.69 are strong, and those beyond ±.70 are very strong).

The coefficient of determination is $.75^2 = .56$. This means that 56% of the variance in police agencies can be attributed to crime rates.

15. Step 1: $H_0: \rho = 0$ and $H_1: \rho < 0$

Step 2: t distribution with $df = 7 - 2 = 5$

Step 3: $t_{crit} = -3.365$ and the decision rule is that if t_{crit} is less than -3.365, the null will be rejected.

Step 4:

$$r = \frac{7(7.22) - 12.10(3.93)}{\sqrt{\left[7(23.85) - 12.10^2\right]\left[7(2.32) - 3.93^2\right]}}$$

$$= \frac{50.54 - 47.55}{\sqrt{\left[166.95 - 146.41\right]\left[16.24 - 15.44\right]}}$$

$$= \frac{2.99}{\sqrt{16.43}} = .74$$

$$t_{obt} = .74\sqrt{\frac{7-2}{1-.74}} = .74\sqrt{\frac{5}{.45}} = .74(3.33) = 2.46$$

Step 5: Since t_{obt} is not less than -3.365, the null is retained. There is no correlation between handgun and knife murder rates. In other words, murder handgun rates do not appear to affect knife murder rates. As the null was retained, it is not appropriate to examine the sign, the magnitude, or the coefficient of determination.

17. Step 1: $H_0: \rho = 0$ and $H_1: \rho \neq 0$

Step 2: t distribution with $df = 8 - 2 = 6$

Step 3: $t_{crit} = \pm 2.447$ and the decision rule is that if t_{crit} is less than -2.447 or greater than 2.447, the null will be rejected.

Step 4:

$$r = \frac{8(570) - 121(37)}{\sqrt{\left[8(1849) - 121^2\right]\left[8(195) - 37^2\right]}}$$

$$= \frac{4560 - 4477}{\sqrt{\left[14792 - 14641\right]\left[1560 - 1369\right]}}$$

$$= \frac{83}{\sqrt{2884}} = .49$$

$$t_{obt} = .49\sqrt{\frac{8-2}{1-.49^2}} = .49\sqrt{\frac{6}{.76}} = .49(2.81) = 1.38$$

Step 5: Since t_{obt} is not greater than 2.447, the null is retained. There is no correlation between age and time-to-disposition among female juveniles. In other words, girls' ages do not appear to affect the time it takes for their cases to reach adjudication. As the null was retained, it is not appropriate to examine the sign, the magnitude, or the coefficient of determination.

19.

a. For age and contacts, $r = .044$; for age and length, $r = -.113$; for contacts and length, $r = .312$.

b. For age and contacts, the null is retained because $.5556 > .05$; for age and length, the null is retained because $.308 > .05$; for contacts and length, the null is rejected because $.004 < .05$.

c. There is no correlation between age and the number of contacts male Asian respondents had with police in the past year; there is no correlation between age and the duration of traffic stops for those who had been stopped while driving; the number of recent contacts with police is significantly correlated with the duration of traffic stops.

d. The only test for which it is appropriate to examine the sign, the magnitude, and the coefficient of determination is that for contacts and length. The sign is positive, meaning that a one-unit increase in one of these variables is associated with an increase in the other one. This suggests that those who experience more contacts also have longer encounters with officers. The magnitude is moderate. The coefficient of determination is $.312^2 = .097$, meaning that only 9.7% of the variance in stop length is attributable to number of contacts (or 9.7% of these variables' variance is shared). This suggests that although the variables are statistically related, the relationship is of very modest substantive importance.

Chapter 14

Note: Rounding, where applicable, is to two decimal places in each step of calculations and in the final answer. For numbers close to zero, decimals are extended to the first nonzero number. Calculation steps are identical to those in the text; using alternative sequences of steps might result in answers different from those presented here. These differences might or might not alter the final decision regarding the null. Numbers gleaned from SPSS output are presented using three decimal places.

1. Regression's advantage over correlation is its ability to predict values of the DV (y) using specified values of the IV (x). Because regression fits a line to the data, any value of y can be predicted using any value of x. Values of x can be plugged into the formula for the line of best fit ($\hat{y} = a + bx$, at the bivariate level), and the equation can be solved to produce the predicted value of y at the given value of x.

3. No. The OLS model can accommodate IVs of any level of measurement.

5.

a. $b = \dfrac{5(86) - 24(19)}{5(230) - 24^2} = \dfrac{430 - 456}{1150 - 576} = -.05$

b. $a = 3.80 - (-.05)4.80 = 3.80 - (-.24) = 4.04$

c. $\hat{y} = 4.04 - .05x$

d. i. For $x = 3$, $\hat{y} = 4.04 - .05(3) = 3.89$

ii. For $x = 15$, $\hat{y} = 4.04 - .05(15) = 3.26$

e. Step 1: H_0: B = 0 and H_1: B ≠ 0

Step 2: t distribution with $df = 5 - 2 = 3$

Step 3: $t_{crit} = \pm 3.182$ and the decision rule is that if t_{obt} is greater than 3.182 or less than −3.182, the null will be rejected.

Step 4:

$SE_b = \dfrac{2.59}{5.36}\sqrt{\dfrac{1 - (-.09)^2}{5 - 2}} = .48\sqrt{\dfrac{.99}{3}} = .48(.57) = .27$

$t_{obt} = \dfrac{-.05}{.27} = -.19$

Step 5: Since t_{obt} is not less than -3.182, the null is retained. There is not a statistically significant relationship between prisoners' prior incarcerations and their in-prison behavior. That is, prior incarceration history does not appear to significantly predict in-prison behavior.

5f. The null was not rejected, so the beta weight should not be calculated.

7.

a. $b = \dfrac{10(251.13) - 66(35.62)}{10(450.48) - 66^2}$

$= \dfrac{2511.30 - 2350.92}{4504.80 - 4356} = 1.08$

b. $a = 3.56 - (1.08)6.60 = -3.57$

c. $\hat{y} = -3.57 + .70x$

d. i. For $x = 4$, $\hat{y} = -3.57 + 1.08(4) = .75$

ii. For $x = 8$, $\hat{y} = -3.57 + 1.08(8) = 5.07$

e. Step 1: H_0: B = 0 and H_1: B ≠ 0

Step 2: t distribution with $df = 10 - 2 = 8$

Step 3: $t_{crit} = \pm 2.306$ and the decision rule is that if t_{obt} is greater than 2.306 or less than −2.306, the null will be rejected.

Step 4:

$SE_b = \dfrac{1.76}{1.29}\sqrt{\dfrac{1 - .79^2}{10 - 2}} = 1.36\sqrt{\dfrac{.38}{8}} = 1.36(.22) = .30$

$t_{obt} = \dfrac{1.08}{.30} = 3.60$

Step 5: Since t_{obt} is greater than 2.306, the null is rejected. There is a statistically significant relationship between unemployment rates and violent crime. That is, the concentration of unemployment in a state appears to help predict that state's violent crime rate.

f. $\beta = 1.08\left(\dfrac{1.29}{1.76}\right) = 1.08(.73) = .79$

9.

a. $b = \dfrac{10(440.07) - 95.80(42.81)}{10(965.02) - 95.80^2}$

$= \dfrac{4400.70 - 4101.20}{9650.20 - 9177.64} = .63$

b. $a = 4.28 - (.63)9.58 = -1.76$

c. $\hat{y} = -1.76 + .63x$

d. *i.* For $x = 5$, $\hat{y} = -1.76 + .63(5) = 1.39$

   ii. For $x = 10$, $\hat{y} = -1.76 + .63(10) = 4.54$

e. <u>Step 1</u>: H_0: B = 0 and H_1: B ≠ 0

   <u>Step 2</u>: t distribution with $df = 10 - 2 = 8$

   <u>Step 3</u>: $t_{crit} = \pm 2.306$ and the decision rule is that if t_{obt} is greater than 2.306 or less than −2.306, the null will be rejected.

   <u>Step 4</u>: $SE = \dfrac{1.87}{2.29}\sqrt{\dfrac{1 - .78}{10 - 2}}$

   $= .82\sqrt{\dfrac{.39}{8}} = .82(.22) = .18$

   $t_{obt} = \dfrac{.63}{.18} = 3.50$

   <u>Step 5</u>: Since t_{obt} is greater than 2.306, the null is rejected. There is a statistically significant relationship between poverty rates and violent crime. That is, the concentration of poverty in a state appears to help predict that state's violent crime rate.

f. $\beta = .63\left(\dfrac{2.29}{1.87}\right) = .63(1.22) = .77$

11.

a. $F = 19.176$. The p value is .000. Since .000 < .05, the null is rejected. The model is statistically significant, meaning that the IV explains a statistically significant proportion of the variance in the DV. This means that it is appropriate to continue on and examine the slope coefficient. (Recall that an F value that is not statistically significant means that you should not move on and examine the specifics of the model because the model is not useful.)

b. $R^2 = .042$. This means that *charges* explains 4.2% of the variance in *probation*. This is a very small amount of variance explained.

c. $\hat{y} = 23.947 + 1.170x$

d. The slope coefficient's p value is .000, which is less than .05, so b is statistically significant.

e. Since b is statistically significant, it is appropriate to examine the beta weight. Here, beta = .205.

f. The number of charges juvenile drug defendants face is a statistically significant predictor of the length of their probation sentences; however, this relationship is weak and the number of charges is not a substantively meaningful predictor. Clearly, important variables have been omitted from the model.

13.

a. $\hat{y} = 27.438 + 1.079(2.09) - 4.322(0) = 29.69$

b. $\hat{y} = 27.438 + 1.079(2.09) - 4.322(1) = 25.37$

c. The predicted sentence decreased by 4.322 units—exactly the slope coefficient for the *priors* variable! The decrease means that juveniles with prior records received probation sentences that were, on average, 4.322 months shorter compared to juveniles without records. This seems counterintuitive, but there are possible explanations (such as judges treating first-time offenders more harshly in order to "teach them a lesson") that we are not able to explore with the present data.

14.

a. $\hat{y} = 27.438 + 1.079(2) - 4.322(.79) = 26.18$

b. $\hat{y} = 27.438 + 1.079(5) - 4.322(.79) = 29.42$

c. The predicted sentence increased by 3.24 units. This means that a juvenile facing five charges should receive, on average, a sentence that is 3.24 months longer than a juvenile facing two charges.

15.

a. $F = 14.270$. Since $p = .001$, which is less than .05, the F statistic is significant. The IV explains a statistically significant amount of variance in the model, so it is appropriate to continue on and examine the slope coefficient.

b. $R^2 = .302$. This means that the IV explains 30.2% of the variance in the DV. This is a strong relationship, suggesting that unemployment is a meaningful predictor of violent crime rates.

c. $\hat{y} = -.410 + .637x$

d. The p value for the slope coefficient is .001, which is less than .05, so b is statistically significant.

e. Since b is significant, it is appropriate to examine beta. Beta = .549.

f. Unemployment rates are statistically significant and substantively meaningful predictors of violent crime. Knowing the unemployment rate in an area significantly improves the ability to predict that area's violent crime rate.

17. $\hat{y} = -1.437 + .648(10) - .231(15) + .320(16) = 6.70$

19.

a. $\hat{y} = -1.437 + .648(6.77) - .231(11) + .320(8.94)$
$= 3.27$

b. $\hat{y} = -1.437 + .648(6.77) - .231(6) + .320(8.94)$
$= 4.42$

c. The rate declined by 1.15 units. This means that states with 11% of the population receiving SNAP benefits should have violent crime rates that are, on average, 1.15 points lower than states where 6% of the population receives benefits. The negative association between SNAP benefit rates and violent crime might seem backwards but it makes sense if SNAP is viewed as a measure of social support. Research has found that states and countries that provide greater levels of social support to disadvantaged citizens have less violent crime compared to those states or countries that do not provide as much social support.

References

Chapter 1

Bureau of Justice Statistics. (2006). *National crime victimization survey, 2004: Codebook*. Washington, DC: U.S. Department of Justice.

Corsaro, N., Brunson, R. K., & McGarrell, E. F. (2013). Problem-oriented policing and open-air drug markets: Examining the Rockford pulling levers deterrence strategy. *Crime & Delinquency, 59*(7), 1085–1107.

Kerley, K. R., Hochstetler, A., & Copes, H. (2009). Self-control, prison victimization, and prison infractions. *Criminal Justice Review, 34*(4), 553–568.

Mears, D. P., Mancini, C., & Stewart, E. A. (2009). Whites' concern about crime: The effects of interracial contact. *Journal of Research in Crime and Delinquency, 46*(4), 524–552.

Muftić, L. R., Bouffard, L. A., & Bouffard, J. A. (2007). An exploratory analysis of victim precipitation among men and women arrested for intimate partner violence. *Feminist Criminology, 2*(4), 327–346.

Paoline, E. A., III, Terrill, W., & Ingram, J. R. (2012). Police use of force and officer injuries: Comparing conducted energy devices (CEDs) to hands- and weapons-based tactics. *Police Quarterly, 15*(2), 115–136.

White, M. D., Ready, J., Riggs, C., Dawes, D. M., Hinz, A., & Ho, J. D. (2013). An incident-level profile of TASER device deployments in arrest-related deaths. *Police Quarterly, 16*(1), 85–112.

Chapter 2

Bouffard, L. A., & Piquero, N. L. (2010). Defiance theory and life course explanations of persistent offending. *Crime & Delinquency, 56*(2), 227–252.

Bureau of Justice Statistics. (2011). *The police-public contact survey, 2011*. Ann Arbor, MI: Inter-University Consortium for Political and Social Research.

Dass-Brailsford, P., & Myrick, A. C. (2010). Psychological trauma and substance abuse: The need for an integrated approach. *Trauma, Violence, & Abuse, 11*(4), 202–213.

Davis, J. A., & Smith, T. W. (2009). *General social surveys, 1972–2008*. Chicago: National Opinion Research Center, producer, 2005; Storrs, CT: Roper Center for Public Opinion Research, University of Connecticut.

Gau, J. M., Mosher, C., & Pratt, T. C. (2010). An inquiry into the impact of suspect race on police use of Tasers. *Police Quarterly, 13*(1), 27–48.

Hart, T. C., & Miethe, T. D. (2009). Self-defensive gun use by crime victims: A conjunctive analysis of its situational contexts. *Journal of Contemporary Criminal Justice, 25*(1), 6–19.

Haynes, S. H. (2011). The effects of victim-related contextual factors on the criminal justice system. *Crime & Delinquency, 57*(2), 298–328.

Kleck, G., & Kovandzic, T. (2009). City-level characteristics and individual handgun ownership: Effects of collective security and homicide. *Journal of Contemporary Criminal Justice, 25*(1), 45–66.

Logan, E. (1999). The wrong race, committing crime, doing drugs, and maladjusted for motherhood: The nation's fury over "crack babies." *Social Justice, 26*(1), 115–138.

Smith, C. M. (2014). The influence of gentrification on gang homicides in Chicago neighborhoods, 1994 to 2005. *Crime & Delinquency, 60*(4), 569–591.

Snell, T. L. (2014). *Capital punishment, 2012—Statistical tables* (BJS Publication No. NCJ 245789). Washington, DC: U.S. Department of Justice.

Stults, B. J. (2010). Determinants of Chicago neighborhood homicide trajectories: 1965–1995. *Homicide Studies, 14*(3), 244–267.

U.S. Department of Justice. (2012). *National Crime Victimization Survey, 2012.* Ann Arbor, MI: Inter- University Consortium for Political and Social Research.

Chapter 3

Lane, J. & Fox, K. A. (2013). Fear of property, violent, and gang crime: Examining the shadow of sexual assault thesis among male and female offenders. *Criminal Justice and Behavior, 40*(5), 472–496.

Morgan, K. O., Morgan, S., & Boba, R. (2010). *Crime: State rankings 2010.* Washington, DC: CQ Press.

Reaves, B. A. (2013). *Felony defendants in large urban counties, 2009—Statistical tables.* Washington, DC: U.S. Department of Justice, Bureau of Justice Statistics.

Steffensmeier, D., Zhong, H., Ackerman, J., Schwartz, J., & Agha, S. (2006). Gender gap trends for violent crimes, 1980 to 2003: A UCR–NCVS comparison. *Feminist Criminology, 1*(1), 72–98.

Truman, J., Langton, L., & Planty, M. (2013). *Criminal victiminzation, 2012* (Publication No. NCJ 243389). Washington, DC: Bureau of Justice Statistics.

Chapter 4

Morgan, K. O., Morgan, S., & Boba, R. (2010). *Crime: State rankings 2010.* Washington, DC: CQ Press.

Piquero, A. R., Sullivan, C. J., & Farrington, D. P. (2010). Assessing differences between short-term, high-rate offenders and long-term, low-rate offenders. *Criminal Justice and Behavior, 37*(12), 1309–1329.

Salkind, N. J. (2011). *Statistics for people who (think they) hate statistics* (4th ed.). Thousand Oaks, CA: Sage.

Snell, T. L. (2014). *Capital punishment, 2012—Statistical tables* (BJS Publication No. NCJ 245789). Washington, DC: U.S. Department of Justice.

Sorensen, J., & Cunningham, M. D. (2010). Conviction offense and prison violence: A comparative study of murderers and other offenders. *Crime & Delinquency, 56*(1), 103–125.

Truman, J., Langton, L., & Planty, M. (2013). *Criminal victimization, 2012* (BJS Publication No. NCJ 243389). Washington, DC: U.S. Department of Justice.

Chapter 5

Copes, H., Kovandzic, T. V., Miller, J. M., & Williamson, L. (2014). The lost cause? Examining the Southern culture of honor through defensive gun use. *Crime & Delinquency, 60*(3), 356–378.

Perry, S. W., & Banks, D. (2011). *Prosecutors in state courts, 2007—Statistical tables* (Publication No. NCJ 234211). Washington, DC: Bureau of Justice Statistics.

Pogarsky, G., & Piquero, A. R. (2003). Can punishment encourage offending? Investigating the "resetting" effect. *Journal of Research in Crime and Delinquency, 40*(1), 95–12.

Chapter 6

Klinger, D. A. (1995). Policing spousal assault. *Journal of Research in Crime and Delinquency, 32*(2), 308–324.

Paoline, E. A., III, Lambert, E. G., & Hogan, N. L. (2006). A calm and happy keeper of the keys: The impact of ACA views, relations with coworkers, and policy views on the job stress and job satisfaction of correctional staff. *The Prison Journal, 86*(2), 182–205.

Reaves, B. A. (2013). *Felony defendants in large urban counties, 2009—Statistical tables.* Washington, DC: U.S. Department of Justice, Bureau of Justice Statistics.

Chapter 7

Bouffard, L. A. (2010). Period effects in the impact of Vietnam-era military service on crime over the life course. *Crime & Delinquency*. Prepublished September 8, 2010. Doi:10.1177/0011128710372455

Kane, R. J., & Cronin, S. W. (2010). Associations between order maintenance policing and violent crime: Considering the mediating effects of residential con-

text. *Crime & Delinquency*. Prepublished May 28, 2009. Doi:10.1177/0011128709336940

Morris, R. G., & Worrall, J. L. (2010). Prison architecture and inmate misconduct: A multilevel assessment. *Crime & Delinquency*. Prepublished May 28, 2009. do:10.1177/0011128709336940

Chapter 8

Bureau of Justice Statistics. (n.d.). *Census of jail inmates: Individual-level data, 2005* [computer file]. Ann Arbor, MI: Inter-University Consortium for Political and Social Research. Doi:10.3886/ICPSR20367.v1

Deslauriers-Varin, N., Beauregard, E., & Wong, J. (2011). Changing their mind about confessing to police: The role of contextual factors in crime confession. *Police Quarterly, 14*(5), 5–24.

Martin, K. R., & Garcia, L. (2011). Unintended pregnancy and intimate partner violence before and during pregnancy among Latina women in Los Angeles, California. *Journal of Interpersonal Violence, 26*(6), 1157–1175.

Saum, C. A., Hiller, M. L., & Nolan, B. A. (2013). Predictors of completion of a driving under the influence (DUI)

court for repeat offenders. *Criminal Justice Review, 38*(2), 207–225.

U.S. Department of Health and Human Services, Centers for Disease Control and Prevention, National Center for Injury Prevention and Control, & United States Consumer Product Safety Commission. (n.d.). *Firearm Injury Surveillance Study, 1993–2010* [computer file]. ICPSR33861-v1. Atlanta, GA: U.S. Department of Health and Human Services, Centers for Disease Control and Prevention, National Center for Injury Prevention and Control [producer]; Ann Arbor MI: Inter-University Consortium for Political and Social Research [distributor].

Chapter 10

Gibson, C. L., Walker, S., Jennings, W. G., & Miller, J. M. (2010). The impact of traffic stops on calling the police for help. *Criminal Justice Policy Review, 21*(2), 139–159.

Jordan, K. L., & Freiburger, T. L. (2010). Examining the impact of race and ethnicity on the sentencing of juveniles in the adult court. *Criminal Justice Policy Review, 21*(2), 185–201.

Chapter 11

Barnoski, R. (2005). *Sex offender sentencing in Washington State: Recidivism rates.* Olympia, WA: Washington State Institute for Public Policy.

Bureau of Justice Statistics. (1998). *Juvenile Defendants in Criminal Court, 1998* [data file]. Washington, DC: U.S. Department of Justice.

Corsaro, N., Brunson, R. K., & McGarrell, E. F. (2013). Problem-oriented policing and open-air drug markets: Examining the Rockford pulling levers

deterrence strategy. *Crime & Delinquency, 59*(7), 1085–1107.

Ostermann, M., & Matejkowski, J. (2014). Estimating the impact of mental illness on costs of crimes: A matched samples comparison. *Criminal Justice and Behavior, 41*(1), 20–40.

Wright, K. A., Pratt, T. C., & DeLisi, M. (2008). Examining offending specialization in a sample of male multiple homicide offenders. *Homicide Studies, 12*(4), 381–398.

Chapter 12

Bureau of Justice Statistics. (2006). *State court processing statistics, 1990–2006: Felony defendants in large urban counties.* Ann Arbor, MI: Inter-University Consortium for Political and Social Research.

Duff, J. C. (2010). Report of the director of the Administrative Office of the United States Courts. Retrieved from www.uscourts.gov/uscourts/Statistics/WiretapReports/2009/2009Wiretaptext.pdf

Franklin, T. W., & Fearn, N. E. (2010). Sentencing Asian offenders in state courts: The influence of a prevalent stereotype. *Crime & Delinquency. OnLineFirst.*

Tang, C. M., Nunez, N., & Bourgeois, M. (2009). Effects of trial venue and pretrial bias on the evaluation of juvenile defendants. *Criminal Justice Review, 34*(2), 210–225.

Chapter 13

Henson, B., Reyns, B. W., Klahm, C. F., IV, & Frank, J. (2010). Do good recruits make good cops? Problems predicting and measuring academy and street-level success. *Police Quarterly, 13*(1), 5–26.

Morgan, K. O., Morgan, S., & Boba, R. (2010). *Crime: State rankings 2010.* Washington, DC: CQ Press.

Reisig, M. D., Pratt, T. C., & Holtfreter, K. (2009). Perceived risk of Internet theft victimization: Examining the effects of social vulnerability and financial impulsivity. *Criminal Justice and Behavior, 36*(4), 369–384.

Chapter 14

Henson, B., Reyns, B. W., Klahm, C. F., IV, & Frank, J. (2010). Do good recruits make good cops? Problems predicting and measuring academy and street-level success. *Police Quarterly, 13*(1), 5–26.

Mears, D. P., Mancini, C., & Stewart, E. A. (2009). Whites' concern about crime: The effects of interracial contact. *Journal of Research in Crime and Delinquency, 46*(4), 524–552.

Petkovesek, M. A., & Boutwell, B. B. (2014). Childhood intelligence and the emergence of low self-control. *Criminal Justice and Behavior.* Prepublished online. Doi:10.1177/0093854814537812

Wright, K. A., Pratt, T. C., & DeLisi, M. (2008). Examining offending specialization in a sample of male multiple homicide offenders. *Homicide Studies, 12*(4), 381–398.

Index

Figures and tables are indicated by *f* or *t* following the page number.

Proportionate reduction in error (PRE), 219

Proportions (*p*)

overview, 34–35

confidence intervals, 180–183

defined, 34

formula for, 34

hypothesis testing with two population proportions, 251–255, 252*f*

probability compared, 122

Pulling levers approach, 3–4, 10, 250–251

Punishment, effects of, 108–110

p value, 221

Qualitative variables. *See* Categorical levels of measurement

Quantitative variables. *See* Continuous levels of measurement

Racial/ethnicity issues

conducted energy device use, 16

gun ownership and, 18

Hispanics who called police, 46, 46*f*

Hispanic victims, number of, 36*t*

mean age of arrest and ethnicity, 242

non-Hispanics who called police, 48*f*, 66, 67*f*

sentencing and race, 271

stopped drivers, 42*f*

unintended pregnancy and intimate partner violence, 172–173

waived juveniles and sentencing, 205

White's with Black friends and concern about crime, 5, 336–337

Racialization of violent crime, 5

Range (*R*), 98–99*t*, 98–100

Rates, 37–38, 37–38*t*, 55–58, 58*f*

Ratio variables, 24–25, 26*t*

r coefficient

coefficient of determination and, 309–310

defined, 297

formula for, 302

magnitude of, 309–310

sampling distribution for, 298, 298*f*

sign of, 309–310

strong versus weak values of, 299

See also Pearson's correlation

Recidivism, 251–255, 270–271, 270*f*

Regression analysis

overview, 322

alternatives, 339–342

bivariate regression, 322–331, 323*f*, 323*t*, 328*f*

defined, 322

multiple regression, 331–333

in SPSS, 334–335*f*, 334–338

Repeated-measures designs, 235, 246

Repetition for learning, 13, 189

Replication, importance of, 9

Reporting of crime, 7, 43, 44*f*

Representativeness, importance of, 8

Research hypotheses, 193–198, 195*f*, 197*t*, 199*t*

Research types, 9–11

Residual, 324

Restricted multiplication rule for independent events, 130–131

Rockford Police Department (RPD), 3–4, 10, 250–251

Rotating panel designs, 7

Row proportions and percentages, 39–40

Rule of the complement, 95, 122

Salkind, N. J., 83

Sample distributions, 149–153, 150–151*f*, 152–153*t*, 153–154*f*

Samples, 8–9, 149

Sample size

chi-square and, 217

confidence intervals and, 172

expected frequencies adding up to sum of, 214

importance of, 150

indicating, 34

sampling distributions and, 156–157

Sampling distributions

overview, 153–157, 155–158*f*

chi-square and, 207

defined, 149, 234

r coefficient, 298, 298*f*

slope coefficients, 327, 328*f*

standard error, 240–241, 245, 248

Sampling error

overview, 152–153, 153–154*f*, 153*t*

defined, 152, 163, 192

true difference compared, 192–193

SAS, 12

.sav file extensions, 54

Scatterplots, 323, 323*f*

Science, defined, 8, 9

Scientific method, 8–9

Security level of prisons, 42*f*, 43

Self-control, 4, 9–10, 332–333

Self-defense, gun use and, 17, 106

⊛SAGE research**methods**

The essential online tool for researchers from the world's leading methods publisher

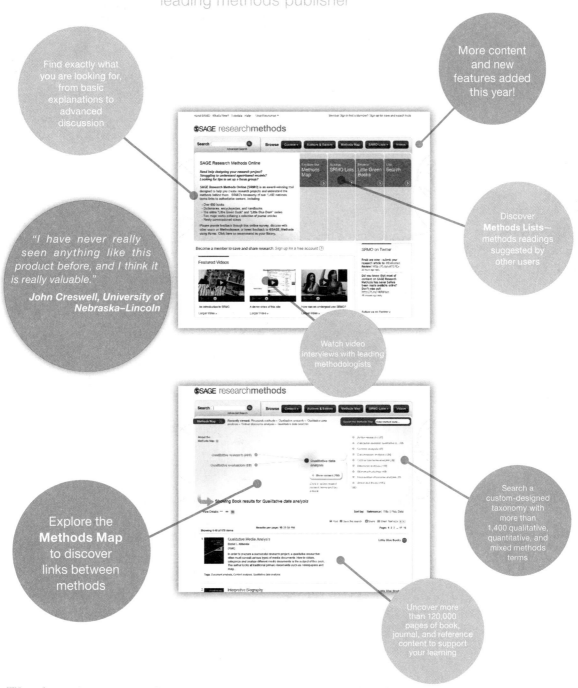

Find exactly what you are looking for, from basic explanations to advanced discussion

More content and new features added this year!

"I have never really seen anything like this product before, and I think it is really valuable."

John Creswell, University of Nebraska–Lincoln

Discover **Methods Lists**—methods readings suggested by other users

Watch video interviews with leading methodologists

Explore the **Methods Map** to discover links between methods

Search a custom-designed taxonomy with more than 1,400 qualitative, quantitative, and mixed methods terms

Uncover more than 120,000 pages of book, journal, and reference content to support your learning

Find out more at
www.sageresearchmethods.com